SIXTH EDITION

THEATER
The Lively Art

Edwin Wilson

The City University of New York, Emeritus

Alvin Goldfarb

Western Illinois University

Mc
Graw
Hill

Boston   Burr Ridge, IL   Dubuque, IA   Madison, WI   New York   San Francisco   St. Louis
Bangkok   Bogotá   Caracas   Kuala Lumpur   Lisbon   London   Madrid   Mexico City
Milan   Montreal   New Delhi   Santiago   Seoul   Singapore   Sydney   Taipei   Toronto

To Our Wives, Catherine Wilson and Elaine Goldfarb

The McGraw·Hill Companies

 **Higher Education**

Published by McGraw-Hill, an imprint of The McGraw-Hill Companies, Inc., 1221 Avenue of the Americas, New York, NY 10020. Copyright © 2008, 2005, 2002, 1999, 1996, 1991 by Edwin Wilson and Alvin Goldfarb. All rights reserved. No part of this publication may be reproduced or distributed in any form or by any means, or stored in a database or retrieval system, without the prior written consent of The McGraw-Hill Companies, Inc., including, but not limited to, in any network or other electronic storage or transmission, or broadcast for distance learning.

This book is printed on acid-free paper.

2 3 4 5 6 7 8 9 0 DOC/DOC 0 9 8 7

ISBN-13: 978-0-07-351411-6
MHID: 0-07-351411-X

Editor in Chief: *Emily Barrosse*
Publisher: *Lisa Moore*
Sponsoring Editor: *Chris Freitag*
Marketing Manager: *Pamela Cooper*
Developmental Editor: *Caroline Ryan*
Project Manager: *Christina Gimlin*
Manuscript Editor: *Susan Gamer*

Art Director: *Jeanne Schreiber*
Design Manager: *Marianna Kinigakis*
Art Editor: *Ayelet Arbel*
Photo Research: *Inge King*
Production Supervisor: *Randy Hurst*
Composition: *10/12 Sabon by Prographics*
Printing: *45# Pub Matte Plus, R. R. Donnelley Crawfordsville*

Front cover: In a scene from "The Color Purple," based upon the novel by Alice Walker and the Warner Bros./Amblin Entertainment motion picture, from left: Francesca Harper, Jamal Story, Stephanie Guiland-Brown and Elisabeth Withers-Mendes. Directed by Gary Griffin; choreographed by Donald Byrd; Associate Director: Nona Lloyd; book by Marsha Norman; scenic design by John Lee Beatty; lighting design by Brian MacDevitt; costume design by Paul Tazewell. Photo: Sarah Krulwich/The New York Times. *Back cover:* Richard Griffiths (Hector) in "The History Boys" by Alan Bennett; directed by Nicholas Hytner; Lyttleton Theatre/National Theatre. Photo: © Donald Cooper/Photo*stage*, England.

Library of Congress Cataloging-in-Publication Data
Wilson, Edwin.
   Theater: the lively art / Edwin Wilson, Alvin Goldfarb.
      p.   cm.
   Includes bibliographical references and index.
   ISBN 978-0-07-351411-6 (pbk.: alk. paper)
      0-07-351411-X (pbk.: alk. paper)
   1. Theater. 2. Theater—History. I. Goldfarb, Alvin. II. Title.
PN2037.W57 2008
792—dc22
                                           2006046878

The Internet addresses listed in the text were accurate at the time of publication. The inclusion of a Web site does not indicate an endorsement by the authors or McGraw-Hill, and McGraw-Hill does not guarantee the accuracy of the information presented at these sites.

www.mhhe.com

Brief Contents

Contents

PART 2

Creating Theater

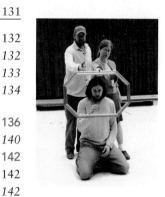

CHAPTER 9

Theater Spaces

CHAPTER 10

Designers: Scenery and Costumes

CHAPTER 11

Designers: Lighting and Sound

CHAPTER 12

Profile of a Production

PART 3

Theater Tradition and Theater Today

CHAPTER 13

Greek and Roman Theaters

CHAPTER 14

Asian and Medieval Theaters

CHAPTER 15

Renaissance Theaters

CHAPTER 16

Theaters from the Restoration through Romanticism 313

CHAPTER 17

Early Modern Theater Movements   343

CHAPTER 18

Twentieth-Century Theatrical Diversity   367

CHAPTER 19

Contemporary Trends

Preface

Theater is not only an art form, it is one of the performing arts. As such its quality is elusive. Theater exists only at the moment when a performance occurs, and to study it in a book or classroom is to be one step removed from that immediate experience. This fact is uppermost in the minds of those who teach theater in a classroom setting. At the same time, it is also known that an introduction to theater course can immeasurably enhance an audience's comprehension of theater.

The experience of seeing theater can be many times more meaningful if audience members understand a number of things: the component parts of theater; the various creative artists and technicians who make it happen; the tradition and historical background from which theater springs; and the genre or movement of which a particular play is a part. It is our hope that *Theater: The Lively Art* will provide the background to make this possible and that it will encourage and inspire students to become lifelong audience members if not actual participants in theater.

In its sixth edition, *Theater: The Lively Art* remains a comprehensive introductory theater text that incorporates a number of elements in one volume: an introduction to the audience's experience of theater, an investigation of the elements of theater, and a study of the important developments in the history of theater.

Several things set *Theater: The Lively Art* apart from other introductory texts. A particularly important element is our emphasis on the audience. All students reading the book are potential theatergoers, not just in their college years but throughout their lives. We have therefore attempted to make *Theater: The Lively Art* an ideal one-volume text to prepare students as future audience members. It will give them a grasp of how theater functions, of how it should be viewed and judged, and of the tradition behind any performance they may attend.

In addition to serving as an ideal text for nonmajors, *Theater: The Lively Art* will also prepare students who wish to continue studies in theater, as majors, as minors or as students from other disciplines who take advanced courses. It provides a foundation for further studies in every aspect of theater: acting, directing, design, dramatic literature, history, theory, and criticism.

ORGANIZATION

The sixth edition introduces a new organization by including a brand new Part One, *The Theater in Today's World*. This new part opens the book by discussing the unique nature of theater as an art form, and by highlighting the multicultural nature of the theater that today's students will experience. Right from the start, students are given the groundwork for understanding the many influences on theater, how theater surrounds us in everyday life, and the wide diversity of the theater today. This new part will give students a good foundation for studying the elements of theater, in Part Two.

In Part Two, *Creating Theater,* we introduce students to the people who make theater possible, to the elements of theater, and to significant concepts of theater.

- First, we explore the role of the *audience.* Not only do audiences form a vital link in any theater event, but it is the first role with which students are likely to identify.
- We then examine *acting,* including various acting techniques and methods of training performers. Next, we look at the work of the *playwright,* or the person or group creating a

script, particularly in the creation of dramatic structure and dramatic characters. To help students understand the latter, we continue with dramatic genres and investigate point of view in a text as expressed in *tragedy, comedy,* and so forth. Then we study the important role of *director.*

- Next, we study *design* and *technical production,* including the nuts-and-bolts aspects of *scenery, costumes, lighting,* and *sound.*

At the end of Part Two, we profile the professional theater production of *Great Expectations,* staged at the Mill Mountain Theater in Roanoke, Virginia. This unique chapter offers students an insider's view of how the elements of theater come together, from costume and set design to closing curtain.

In Part Three, *Theater Tradition and Theater Today,* we begin a survey of theater history with Greek theater and continue to the present. This look at the history of theater is not intended to be a substitute for advanced courses on theater history. At the same time, we believe that we have covered every important movement, every key figure, and every relevant aspect of the development of theater.

The final three chapters (Chapters 17, 18, and 19) are devoted to theater of the past hundred years. The forces that began a century ago—in realism and departures from realism, in acting techniques, in the emergence of the director, in scene and lighting design—defined the theater as it exists today.

TEXT FEATURES

Getting Started in Theater

In boxes throughout Part Two, autobiographical accounts from playwrights, performers, directors, designers, and others explain how various individuals became attracted to theater, received their training, and were given their first opportunities to work in theater. Students should find these first-hand accounts not only informative but insightful, providing them with a genuine sense of what involvement in theater means.

Play Synopses

Summaries of plays, collected in an appendix at the end of the book, provide the necessary context for discussion of both the elements and the history of theater in Parts Two and Three. Eleven important plays, ranging from Greek to modern and including representative works by Asian, African American, and women playwrights, are included. The summaries are comprehensive accounts of the action of these plays. Discussion questions for each of the play synopses are included on the Web site for the text, which is discussed in detail later in the preface.

Making Connections

This feature in Parts One, Two and Three examines the close relationship between theater and other forms of popular entertainment through the ages, from the mimes and jugglers of ancient Rome to the circuses and vaudeville of the nineteenth century to the rock concerts and theme parks of today.

Living Histories

Appearing throughout Part Three, every period includes a narrative of an actual event, taking the readers back in time so they have a sense of being in the audience at a performance of, say, *Antigone* in Athens in 441 B.C.E., or at the premiere of *Hamlet* at the Globe Theatre in London.

Timelines

For each period and country addressed in Part Three, timelines outline landmark events and accomplishments, in the social and political arenas on one side and significant theater events on the other. Within the chapters in Part Three, each section contains background information on the political, scientific, and cultural milieu in which theater developments unfold.

Writing Style

A sense of immediacy and personalization has been a goal in our writing style. We have attempted to write *Theater: The Lively Art* in the most readable language possible. To this end, we have dispensed with dry, pedantic language, and wherever possible we have avoided "laundry lists" of names, dates, and titles. The book contains a wealth of information, but we hope it is presented in a manner that makes it vivid and alive.

NEW TO THIS EDITION

Part One

A brand new Part One is included in the sixth edition. "The Theater in Today's World" examines the multicultural and diverse nature of theater, right from the start. By grouping these three chapters into this newly formed part, we begin our study of theater by examining the many crosscurrents which make up the theater today's students will experience. The new Part One includes the following chapters:

- Chapter 1, Experiencing Theater Today, is fundamentally the same as in previous editions. This chapter asks the question, "Why go to the theater?" and highlights how theater is unique from other art forms.
- Chapter 2, Theater in Everyday Life, is a new chapter, and discusses how theater permeates our lives. Students will gain an understanding of how theatrical elements are all around them, from television to rock concerts to sporting events.
- Chapter 3, Today's Diverse Theater, is a new chapter. This chapter discusses how national borders in theater have become blurred, much the same way globalization has affected the non-theater world around us. This chapter illustrates the impact of our multicultural society on theater. The chapter includes coverage of Multiethnic Theaters, African American Theater, Asian American Theater, Latino/Latina Theater, Native American Theater, Feminist Theater, Gay and Lesbian Theater, and Political Theater.

Chapter 12: Profile of a Production

Always a popular feature, this chapter in the sixth edition profiles a new production of *Great Expectations,* a musical adaptation of Charles Dickens' novel, written by Edwin Wilson. Through a photo essay, students will follow the show, staged at the Mill Mountain Theater, from its inception to the final production. This chapter is an excellent demonstration of how the elements studied in Part Two can come together with exciting results. It provides students with a look into the making of a performance through costume and set sketches to set design and rehearsal photographs.

Production Photos

Once again, almost all of the color and black and white production photographs are new. These include new photos from recent performances of *Jersey Boys, The Color Purple, Spamalot, The Pajama Game,* and *The Odd Couple.* Also, many global theater productions have been included in this edition, such as Zulu *Macbeth* and Japan's *Ataka.* The illustrations we've chosen—both photographs and line drawings—do not exist in isolation but instead help to explain and enhance the material in the text. Moreover, the photographs have been selected to be dynamic and "dramatic" in and of themselves.

SUPPORT FOR INSTRUCTORS

Please note: the supplements listed here may accompany your text. Please contact your local McGraw-Hill representative for details concerning policies, prices, and availability. If you are not sure who your representative is, you can find him or her by using the Rep Locator at www.mhhe.com.

Instructor's Manual and Testing Program

McGraw-Hill offers an Instructor's Manual and Testing Program to all instructors who adopt *Theater: The Lively Art* for their course. The Instructor's Manual is downloadable from the password-protected section of the Online Learning Center to accompany this text (see below). Each chapter of the Instructor's Manual includes:

- Full set of test questions
- Overview and outline of each text chapter
- List of significant names and terms found in the chapter
- Questions for student essays or discussions
- Suggestions for demonstrations and exercises for class involvement
- Play recommendations for the chapter

Computerized Testing Program

Also on the Instructor's side of the Online Learning Center, a computerized Testing Program is available. This testing engine enables instructors to generate quizzes and tests in an easy-to-use and customizable way.

Online Learning Center with Video Clips of Plays

www.mhhe.com/livelyart6

The Online Learning Center is an Internet-based resource for students and faculty. Instructor's Resources are password-protected and offer complete text of the Instructor's Manual, the Computerized Testing Program, a correlation guide for the *Anthology of Living Theater,* and a link to our customizable database of plays. Now, the OLC also offers video clips of live play performances and interviews with actors, directors and other theater personnel. These video clips are organized by chapter and include quizzes after each one, to assess student understanding.

Additionally, the Online Learning Center offers chapter-by-chapter quizzes for testing students. These brief quizzes are different from those offered in the Instructors' Manual and generate instant grades; the results can be e-mailed directly to the instructor with the click of a button. This special quizzing feature is a valuable tool for the instructor who requires a quick way to check reading comprehension and basic understanding without using valuable class time. To receive your password for the site, contact your local sales representative or e-mail us at *theater@mcgraw-hill.com.*

Online Course Support

The online content of *Theater: The Lively Art* is supported by WebCT, eCollege.com, and Blackboard. To find out more, contact your local McGraw-Hill representative or visit www.mhhe.com/solutions.

As an adopter, you may also be eligible to use our PageOut Service to get your course up and running online in a matter of hours—at no cost to you and without knowing HTML! To find out more contact your local McGraw-Hill representative or visit www.pageout.net.

STUDENT RESOURCES

Online Learning Center with Video Clips of Plays

www.mhhe.com/livelyart6

The Online Learning Center has become even more robust with this edition, now showcasing video clips of live play performances. Quizzes accompany each video clip. The OLC boasts a wide variety of resources keyed directly to this edition.

- **Video clips** (discussed above) from live theater performances and interviews with professionals in the field give students a visual resource for many of the concepts discussed in the text. The video clips are organized by chapter, and are followed by short quizzes to help students assess their understanding.
- An Interactive **Timeline of Theater History** highlights important people, events, and movements, from the origins of theater to the present.
- *The Theatergoer's Guide* is an excellent introduction to the art of attending and critiquing a play. This Guide will assist students in everything from making theater reservations

and knowing when to applaud to evaluating a performance and doing research on the Internet.

- **Glossary Terms**
- **Weblinks** to Theater Research
- **Homework Quizzes** that can be e-mailed directly to instructors

ACKNOWLEDGMENTS

There is a long list of colleagues and others who have helped to make this book possible and to whom we are deeply grateful. We thank Professor J. Thomas Rimer and Professor James V. Hatch for providing valuable material on Asian theater and African American theater respectively. In addition, we are particularly grateful to Sam Lieter of Brooklyn College CUNY for reviewing and assisting in the revisions of the Asian sections. For material on Native American theater, we are deeply indebted to Ann Haugo of Illinois State University.

Special thanks go to Scott Walters, who developed the Instructor's Manual, Testing Program, and content on the Online Learning Center. We thank our indexer, Nancy Ball.

At Western Illinois University, we'd like to thank theater graduate assistant Stephen Harrick for providing research assistance. A further expression of thanks is due to everyone at the Mill Mountain Theater Company in Roanoke, Virginia, who helped to make Chapter 12 possible.

Reviewers

Many instructors have given us comments, suggestions and feedback over the first five editions of this text. For their assistance in the development of the sixth edition, we would like to thank the following reviewers:

Barbara Burgess-Lefebvre, *West Virginia Wesleyan College*

Brook Davis, *Wake Forest University*

Pamela Fields, *Scottsdale Community College*

Matthew Gitkin, *University of Miami, Coral Gables*

Daniel Inouye, *Baylor University*

Douglas Rosentrater, *Bucks County Community College*

Terry D. Smith, *University of South Carolina*

Two absolutely irreplaceable people have been with us from the beginning: Susan Gamer is our copyeditor extraordinaire, and Inge King is simply the finest, most talented, and most astute photography editor in the business. Finally, we would like to thank our hardworking and supportive team at McGraw-Hill. First, our development editor, Caroline Ryan, and our sponsoring editor, Chris Freitag. We extend our appreciation as well to our production manager, Christina Gimlin; our designer, Marianna Kinigakis, and our production supervisor, Tandra Jorgensen.

THEATER
The Lively Art

Theater in Today's World

Today's theater encompasses several worlds; it cuts across many art forms, many cultural phenomena, many nations, many personal preferences and identities. A director who embodies much of this is Robert Wilson, who draws from the visual arts as well as the performing arts, and from diverse cultures, for his theater pieces. In addition, Wilson directs in many parts of the world. The scene here is from *I La Galigo*, a music theater work based on an Indonesian creation myth. *I La Galigo* was presented at the Lincoln Center Festival.
(© Stephanie Berger)

Experiencing Theater Today

◄ **THEATER TODAY:**

ECLECTIC AND EXCITING

YokastaS Redux *is a theater piece by
Richard Schechner and Saviana Stanescu,
directed by Schechner, which presents
Jocasta, the mother of Oedipus, at four
stages in her life. A reworking of the
Greek myth, it concentrates on Jocasta
in a way none of the original Greek
tragedies did. In the scene here, from a
production at La Mama Etc. in New
York City, Daphne Gaines plays one of
the four Jocasta figures. (© Ryan Jensen)*

5

Why do we go to the theater? In a world that is filled with an immense number of opportunities for entertainment, including television, film, DVDs, Internet sites, digital games, amusement parks, and sporting events, why do audiences continue to seek out live theater productions in cities across the globe? Why do young audience members attend experimental performances in tiny spaces retrofitted to function as theaters?

In this chapter, we will try to discover why people go to the theater today, especially when there are so many other forms of entertainment competing for our time and financial resources. We will also try to discover the unique characteristics of theater that make it the *lively art*.

THE TERM *THEATER*

However, before answering these questions, we should speak briefly about the word *theater* itself. To begin with, there is the way the word is spelled. The British, and many people in the United States and Canada, spell it *theatre*. There is no right or wrong about this; how the word is spelled is a matter of personal choice, and we have chosen the less formal spelling *theater*. Then there is the word's meaning—or rather its meanings, since there are several. *Theater* denotes, first of all, a building in which theatrical performances take place, and in this sense the term refers to a physical space. But the word also refers to an art form, and to a discipline. In the same way that we speak of other art forms—opera, dance, and music—we speak of theater: *theater* encompasses the history, practices, and institutions of the art form.

WHY DO WE GO TO THE THEATER?

The Unique Quality of Theater

To return to our earlier question—why we go to the theater and study theater—the most immediate reason has to do with the word *live*. We call theater the *lively art* not only because it is exciting, suspenseful, and amusing but also because it is alive in a way that makes it different from every other form of dramatic presentation.

The special nature of theater becomes more apparent when we contrast the experience of seeing a drama in a theater with seeing a drama on film or television. In many ways the dramas presented are alike. Both offer a story told in dramatic form—an enactment of scenes by performers who speak and act as if they are the people they represent—and film and television can give us many of the same feelings and experiences that we have when watching a theater performance. One can learn a great deal about theater from watching a play on film or television, and the accessibility of film and television means that they have a crucial role in our overall exposure to the depiction of dramatic events and dramatic characters.

Nevertheless, there is a fundamental difference, and we become aware of that difference when we contrast theater with movies. This contrast does not have to do with technical matters, such as the way films can show outdoor shots made from helicopters, cut instantaneously from one scene to another, or create interplanetary wars or cataclysmic events by using special effects. The most significant difference between films and theater is the *relationship between the performer and the audience.* The experience of being in the presence of the performer is more important to theater than anything else. No matter how closely a film follows the story of a play, no matter how involved we are with the people on the screen, we are always in the presence of an *image,* never a person.

We all know the difference between an image of someone and the flesh-and-blood reality. How often we rehearse a speech we plan to make to someone we love or fear. We run through the scene in our mind, picturing ourselves talking to the other person—declaring our love, asking for help, asking for a raise. But when we meet face-to-face, it is not the same. We freeze and find ourselves unable to speak; or perhaps our words gush forth incoherently. Seldom does the encounter take place as we planned.

Like films, television seems very close to theater; sometimes it seems even closer than film. Television programs sometimes begin with words such as "This program comes to you live from Burbank, California." But the word *live* must be qualified. Before television, *live* in the entertainment world meant "in person": not only was the event taking place at that moment; it was taking place in the physical *presence* of the spectators. Usually, the term *live television* still means that an event is taking place at this moment, but "live" television does *not* take place in the presence of the viewer. In fact, it is generally far removed from the television audience, possibly half a world away. In television, like film, we see an image—in the case of TV, on a small screen—and we are free to look or not to look, or even to leave the room.

The fascination of being in the presence of a person is difficult to explain but not difficult to verify, as the popularity of rock stars attests. No matter how often fans have seen a favorite star in the movies or heard a rock singer on tape, CD, television, or a computer screen, they will go to any lengths to see her or him in person. In the same way, at one time or another each of us has braved bad weather and shoving crowds to see celebrities at a parade or a political rally. The same pull of personal contact draws us to the theater.

At the heart of the theater experience, therefore, is the performer-audience relationship—the immediate, personal exchange whose chemistry and magic give theater its special quality. During a stage performance the actresses and actors can hear laughter, can sense silence, and can feel tension in the audience. In short, the audience can affect, and in subtle ways change, the performance.

At the same time, members of the audience watch the performers closely, consciously or unconsciously asking themselves questions: Are the performers talented? Have they learned their parts well? Are they convincing in their roles? Will they do something surprising? Will they make a mistake? At each moment, in every stage performance, the audience is looking for answers to questions like these. The performers are alive—and so is the very air itself—with the electricity of expectation. It is for this reason, as well as the reasons mentioned above, that we speak of theater as the lively art.

A Historical Reason to Attend Theater

There is a second reason to attend and study theater: history. Theater is the foundation of all drama: in films, on television, on computer screens, in theme parks, and in fact in every medium. The ancient Greeks, 2,500 years ago, established the categories of tragedy and comedy that are still used today. They also developed dramatic structure, acting, and theater architecture. Roman domestic comedies are the prototype of every situation comedy we see in the movies or on television.

In other words, though we may not be aware of it, each time we see a performance we are taking part in theater history. When audiences watch a performance of a Shakespearean play in an outdoor theater—for example, at the Shakespeare festival in Ashland, Oregon; or at the Old Globe in San Diego, California—they are not only watching a play by a dramatist who lived 400 years ago but are also sharing in an environment, a configuration of audience and stage space, that goes back much farther, to the ancient Greeks.

TAKING PART IN THEATER HISTORY
When we attend a theater performance, each one of us is participating in theater history: seeing either a new play or a revival of an older one. A good example is the audience shown here at a production of Shakespeare's King Lear *at a 1,200-seat Elizabethan theater, the Allen Pavilion at the Oregon Shakespeare Festival. These spectators are part of a tradition that dates back to England 400 years ago. Farther back, attendance at outdoor theater events began in Greece in the fifth century* B.C.E. *(© T. Charles Erickson)*

When an audience is in a theater with a picture-frame stage, seeing a drama by the French playwright Molière, the spectators are not only partaking of a theatrical tradition that traces its roots to seventeenth-century France. They are also partaking of a tradition that goes back to Italian commedia dell'arte, which came to prominence a century earlier. And the theater space goes back to the proscenium stage, which originated during the Italian Renaissance in the early seventeenth century.

Similarly, at a college production of Bertolt Brecht's *The Good Person of Setzuan,* the audience members are not only seeing a play by one of the most innovative playwrights of the twentieth century; they are seeing a play that was strongly influenced by techniques of ancient Asian theater.

Theater and the Human Condition

There is a third reason to attend and study theater. Throughout its history theater has had a twofold appeal. One attraction is the sheer excitement or amusement of a theater event. The other is the unique ability of theater to incorporate in dramatic material profound, provocative, timeless observations about the human condition. Ideas, moral dilemmas, probing insights—these have long found vivid expression in exceptional plays and exceptional performances. Moreover, in theater these performances are live, not reproduced on a film or television screen.

In Greek and Shakespearean tragedy, and in the works of modern playwrights like Henrik Ibsen, Anton Chekhov, Eugene O'Neill, Tennessee Williams, Arthur Miller, Lorraine Hansberry, and August Wilson, we encounter questions and issues that strike at the very heart of human existence. In the comedies of the French playwright Molière we see personal foibles exposed as they have rarely been before or since.

Finally, theater also differs in significant ways from the live performances of entertainers such as rock stars. Rock musicians make no pretense of offering the same kind of experience as a production by a theater company. A drama or a piece of performance art has a structure—a beginning, middle, and end—a purpose, a cast of characters, a completeness that a concert by a rock artist would never aspire to.

In other words, theater is an art form with its own characteristics: its own quality, coherence, and integrity.

THEATER AS AN ART FORM

To understand theater as an art form, it is useful to look first at art in general.

What Is Art?

As has often been observed, art is a mirror or reflection of life: an extension or a projection of how we live, think, and feel. Art reveals to us what people treasure and admire, and what they fear most deeply. Art is not only something we find desirable and enjoyable; it seems to be an absolute necessity for human survival.

There are feelings, emotions, and ideas that cannot be expressed in any way other than through art. The beauty of a face or a haunting landscape may be impossible to convey in words, but it can be revealed in a painting; a complex personality can be captured in a novel or a play in a way that reveals the person's innermost soul; joy or anguish can often be communicated most directly and completely through music, poetry, or drama. Without these modes of expression—that is, without art—human beings would be as impoverished and as helpless as they would be if they tried to live without language.

Characteristics of Art. Art can be divided into three categories: *literary, visual,* and *performing.* The literary arts include novels, short stories, and poetry. The visual arts include painting, sculpture, architecture, and photography. The ***performing arts*** are theater, dance, opera, and music. (Film, another art form, partakes of both the visual and the performing arts.)

One characteristic of all art—visual, literary, or performing—is that it is selective. As the three categories suggest, different art forms focus on certain elements and eliminate others. The visual arts, for example, deal solely with sight and touch—what we can see and feel—and they exclude sound. When we visit an art gallery, there is a hush in the air because the concentration is purely on what the eye observes. Moreover, in the visual arts, a composition is frozen and constant. We value the visual arts partly because they capture subjects—faces, landscapes, a series of colors or shapes—and hold them fast in a painting or a sculpture. We can look at a statue of a Roman soldier from 2,000 years ago, or a Madonna and Child painted 500 years ago, and see exactly the same artifact that its first viewers observed.

Music, to take another example, concentrates on sound. Although we may watch a violinist playing with a symphony orchestra or observe a soprano singing at a recital, the essence of music is sound. We prove this whenever we close our eyes at a concert, and whenever we listen to recorded music. In both cases, the emphasis is totally on sound. By concentrating on sound, we block out distractions and give our full attention to the music itself. This kind of selectivity is one quality that makes any art form effective.

Another characteristic of art is its relationship to time or space, and thus a second way to differentiate the arts is in temporal and spatial terms. The visual arts exist in space, which is their primary mode of existence. They occupy a canvas, for instance, or—in the case of architecture—a building. By contrast, music

THE PERFORMING ARTS

Like theater, opera, and music, dance is one of the performing arts, which share a number of characteristics. For example, all these arts move through time, they require interpreters as well as creators, and must be seen live by an audience. In this photo we see the Kremlin Ballet performing Swan Lake *in Skopje, Macedonia.* (Chris Pizzello/AP Images)

moves through time. It does not occupy space; musicians performing a symphony exist in space, of course, but the music they perform does not. The music is an unfolding series of sounds, and the duration of the notes and the pauses between notes create a rhythm that is an essential part of music. This, in turn, becomes a time continuum as we move from one note to the next.

Unlike painting and sculpture on the one hand or music on the other, theater, dance, and opera occupy both time and space. Let's now consider the special characteristics of the performing arts.

Characteristics of the Performing Arts.   The performing arts, of which music, theater, and dance are a part, have several characteristics in common. One is the movement through time described above. Another is that they require interpreters as well as creators. A playwright writes a play, but actors and actresses perform it; a composer writes a piece of music that singers and instrumentalists will perform; a choreographer develops a ballet that dancers will interpret.

Another quality shared by the performing arts is that they require an audience. A performance can be recorded on film or tape, but the event itself must be "live," that is, it must occur in one place at one time with both performers and audience present. If a theater performance is recorded on film or tape without the presence of an audience, it becomes a movie or a television show rather than a theater experience. To put this distinction another way, when an audience watches a film in a movie theater, there are no performers onstage; there are only images on a screen. Hence there is no interaction between performers and audience. Such interaction is absolutely essential to the performing arts. In Chapter 4, we will talk more about the special nature of "live" performance and the crucial role of the audience.

In addition to the general qualities we have been discussing, each art form has unique qualities and principles that set it apart from other art forms and help us to understand it better. When we know how shapes and designs relate to overall composition, for instance, and how colors contrast with one another and complement one another, we are in a better position to judge and understand painting. In the same way, we can appreciate theater much more if we understand how it is created and what elements it consists of. We'll now consider theater as an art form, and the creation and elements of theater will be the focus of Part Two of this book.

The Art of Theater

Elements of Theater.   When we begin to examine theater as an art form, we discover that there are certain elements common to all theater. These elements are present whenever a theater event takes place; without them, an event ceases to be theater and becomes a different art form and a different experience.

Audience.   Although this may not be readily apparent, a necessary element for theater is the audience. In fact, the essence of theater is the interaction between performer and audience. A theater, dance, or musical event is not complete—one could almost say it does not occur—unless there are people to see and hear it. When we read a play in book form, or listen to recorded music, what we experience is similar to looking at a painting or reading a poem: it is a private event, not a public one, and the live performance is re-created and imagined rather than experienced firsthand.

Later, we will explain this in more detail, but now we can note simply that in the performing arts a performance occurs when the event takes place, not before and not after. All the performing arts, including theater, are like an electrical connection: the connection is not made until positive and negative wires touch and complete the circuit. Performers are half of that connection, and audiences are the other half.

One audience member who is not essential to the theater experience, but who can enhance it for other audience members, is the critic. He or she can provide criteria by which audiences can judge productions and can offer helpful information about the playwright, the play, theater history, and other important subjects. The critic's contributions make attendance at the theater more meaningful, and often more enjoyable.

Performers. Another absolutely essential element for theater is performance: people onstage presenting characters in dramatic action.

Acting is at the heart of all theater. One person stands in front of other people and begins to portray a character—to speak and move in ways that convey an image of the character. At this point the magic of theater has begun: the transformation through which an audience accepts, for a time, that a performer is actually someone else. The character portrayed can be a historical figure, an imaginary figure, or even a self-presentation; still, everyone accepts the notion that it is the character, not the actor or actress, who is speaking.

Acting is a demanding profession. In addition to native talent—the poise and authority needed to appear onstage before others, and the innate ability to create a character convincingly—acting requires considerable craft and skill. Performers must learn to use both voice and body with flexibility and control; they must be able, for example, to make themselves heard in a large theater even when speaking in a whisper. (This takes extensive physical and vocal training, which we will discuss in more detail in Chapter 5.) Performers must also be able to create believability, or the emotional truth of the characters they portray; that is, the audience must be convinced that the actor or actress is thinking and feeling what the character would think and feel. (This, too, is a difficult task requiring a special kind of training—which we will also discuss in Chapter 5.)

Text or Script.   Another element essential to theater is the *script* or *text* that is performed. In its written form, it most commonly takes the form of a *script*. The person who creates the text is usually the playwright. He or she transforms the raw material—the incident, the biographical event, the myth—into a drama that features characters talking and interacting with one another. Making this transformation is not easy. It requires intimate knowledge of stage practices, of how to breathe life into characters, of how to build action so that it will hold the interest of the audience and arouse anticipation for what is coming next. In other words, the playwright must create characters and develop a dramatic structure. The term *text* is used to discuss any type of theatrical activity presented on stage, for example, all forms of pop entertainment, as well as performances created by performers or directors. Frequently, the term text is all-inclusive, and is sometimes used in place of script. A specific example of a non-literary, theatrical text would be an improvisitory presentation created by actors on a street, in a remodeled school, or in a theater.

Along with structure, a text must have a focus and a point of view. Who and what is the text about? Are we supposed to regard the characters and the events as sad or funny? The person or persons who create the text have the power as well as the responsibility to direct our attention toward certain characters and away from others. We will discover more about how these tasks are accomplished when we look at the nature of a dramatic text in Chapters 6 and 7.

Director.   An additional key element of a theater production is the work of the *director:* the person who rehearses the performers and coordinates their actions to make certain that they interpret the text appropriately, intelligently, and excitingly. As we will see in Chapter 8, the separate role of the director became prominent for the first time in modern theater, but many of the functions of the director have always been present.

Theater Space.   Another necessary element of theater is the *space* in which performers and audiences come together. It is essential to have a stage, or some equivalent area, where actors and actresses can perform. It is also essential to have a place for audience members to sit or stand. We will discover that there have been several basic configurations of stage spaces and audience seating. Whatever the configuration, however, a stage and a space for the audience must be a part of it. Also, there must be a place for the actors and actresses to change costumes, as well as a way for them to enter and exit from the stage.

Design Elements.   Closely related to the physical stage is another important element: the design aspects of a production. Design includes visual aspects—costumes, lighting, and some form of scenic background—and a nonvisual aspect, sound.

A play can be produced on a bare stage with minimal lighting, and with the performers wearing everyday street clothes. Even in these conditions, however, some attention must be paid to visual elements; there must, for instance, be sufficient illumination for us to see the performers, and clothes worn onstage will take on a special meaning even if they are quite ordinary.

Usually, visual elements are prominent in theater productions. Costumes, especially, have been a hallmark of theater from the beginning; and scenery has sometimes become more prominent than the performers. In certain arrangements, visual aspects come to the forefront; in others—such as the arena stage, where the audience surrounds the action—elaborate scenery is impractical or even impossible.

The visual aspects of theater are particularly interesting to trace through history because their place in theater production has shifted markedly from time to time. For example, stage lighting changed dramatically when the electric light-bulb came into use at the end of the nineteenth century.

As we noted above, a design element that is not visual is sound. This, too, is a modern element that has come into its own with modern technology. Of course, there were always sound effects, such as thunder and wind created by offstage machines; and there was frequently music, especially during certain periods, when every intermission was accompanied by orchestral performances. In modern times, though, with electronic inventions, there are far more elaborate sound effects; and frequently there are also microphones, sometimes in the general stage area and sometimes actually worn by the performers.

To sum up, the following are the major elements of theater:

Audience
Performers
Text, with its structure, characters, and point of view
Director
Theater space
Design aspects: scenery, costume, lighting, and sound

Theater as a Collaborative Art. It is important to stress that theater is a collaborative art. For a theater event to take place, its various elements must be brought together and coordinated.

The director must stage the play written by the playwright and must share with the playwright an understanding of structure, theme, and style. At the same time, the director must work closely with performers in rehearsing the play, and with the designers of scenery, lights, costumes, and sound, to bring the production to fruition. During performances many elements must be coordinated: the work of actors and actresses along with technical aspects—scene changes, lighting shifts, and sound cues. The people working on these elements are joined, in turn, by a number of collaborators: stage manager, stage carpenters, makeup experts, those who make costumes, and computer lighting experts. In an ensemble piece, where the play is actually composed by a group of actors working with a director, collaboration is more important than ever.

THEATER AS A COLLABORATIVE ART
Like many of the performing arts, theater is a collaborative art in which playwrights, performers, directors, and designers must work together. In the scene here, the director Oskar Eustis is rehearsing actors for a production of Shakespeare's Henry V *at the Trinity Repertory Theatre in Providence, Rhode Island. (© T. Charles Erickson)*

Another essential component in this collaborative enterprise is the business and administrative side of a production or theater organization. This includes producers and managers, and their staffs—the people who organize and administer press and public relations, advertising, scheduling, fund-raising, and all the details of keeping the theater running smoothly, including ticket sales, ticket taking, and ushering.

Ultimately, the many elements integrated in a production—text, direction, design, and acting, assisted by the technical side and the business side—must be presented to an audience. At that point occurs the final collaboration in any theater enterprise: the performance itself before spectators.

We will understand both the collaborative process and the individual elements of theater when we examine these elements in detail in Chapters 4 through 11. Then, in Chapter 12, we will see how these elements are brought together.

But before we turn to those elements and how theater is created, we need to discuss more specifically how theater is the foundation for many other contemporary popular entertainments and dramatic arts. We need to discover how theatrical traditions affect film, television, digital media, and even rock and roll and sporting events.

SUMMARY

The theater experience has been created many thousands of times over the centuries and continues to be created every day throughout the world. A great variety of theater experiences can be found in the United States today.

To have a full and rewarding appreciation of theater, it is important to understand that theater is an art form, and that theater has a long and fascinating history.

Art forms can be categorized as literary, visual, and performing; theater is one of the performing arts. All art is selective, and selectivity is one way of distinguishing one art form from another. Art forms may also be distinguished in terms of time and space: the visual arts exist primarily in space; music exists in time rather than space; and theater (along with dance and opera) exists in both time and space.

Important characteristics of the performing arts include the need for interpreters and the need for an audience.

Understanding theater involves understanding its history, its elements, and how it is created.

The major elements of theater are audience, performers, text, director, theater space, and design elements. Because these elements must be coordinated, theater is a collaborative art.

KEY TERMS

Director The person who rehearses and coordinates performers to ensure that they interpret the text appropriately.

Performing arts Theater, dance, opera, and music. Film also partakes of the performing arts.

Text Also, **script.** Story, incident, or event put into theatrical form.

Theater space The place where performers and audiences come together.

THEATER ON THE WEB

For more research and to learn more about the topics in this chapter, please visit the Online Learning Center at **www.mhhe.com/livelyart6**.

CHAPTER 2

Theater in Everyday Life

◄ **THEATER ACROSS TODAY'S
CULTURE**

The musical The Color Purple *is adapted
from a novel by Alice Walker about the
African American experience. Many
different cultures, not only African
American but Hispanic, Asian, and
Native American, have a place in today's
diverse theater in the United States.
Shown here is LaChanze, who plays the
character Celie, in a scene from* The
Color Purple *at the Alliance Theater,
Atlanta, where the production orginated.*
(© Joan Marcus)

HOW THEATER PERMEATES OUR LIVES

Most of us would be surprised at the extent to which theater permeates and informs every aspect of our lives. Think of how often we use theater as a metaphor to describe an activity in daily life. We say that someone is melodramatic or highly theatrical or acts like a prima donna. When we don't believe children, we say that they are play-acting. We refer to the battleground on which a war is fought as its theater. As we will note in Chapter 5, acting is part of our everyday lives. We describe the role-playing we do in our professional and personal spheres as if we were performers on the stage of life. Children and adults imitate behaviors that they admire, in the same way as actors and actresses mimic behavior.

As we go through our university careers, we play many roles, such as student, friend, romantic partner, organization member, and student government leader.

Clearly, theater is an activity that we use to describe how we live. And theatricality is all around us in many of the popular forms that engage us. The relationship between theater, film, and television, for example, is quite apparent.

THEATER AND TELEVISION

On television, we can see a wide range of dramatic offerings. Daytime soap operas present a variety of domestic crises in family and other relationships. These daytime dramas use many theatrical devices to ensure our continued viewing. A suspenseful moment concludes each segment; heightened music and emotions capture our attention. Recognizable character types, such as young lovers, difficult parents, doctors, lawyers, and criminals, inhabit the world of the soap operas, such as the long-running *General Hospital*. There are also popular stars who have significant audience followings and intensely loyal fans, such as Susan Lucci. The Daytime Emmy Awards recognize the popularity of soap operas and their stars.

Nighttime situation comedies depict young as well as middle-age characters in farcical and humorous encounters. These comic television shows have, throughout the history of the medium, focused on domestic situations, language filled with sexual double meaning, physical humor, and recognizable situations. Classic situation comedies, such as *I Love Lucy, Leave It to Beaver, The Dick Van Dyke Show, The Mary Tyler Moore Show, Seinfield, Will and Grace, Friends,* and *Everyone Loves Raymond* all reflect comic traditions, techniques, characters, and structures developed earlier in theater. These series also reflect the importance of the popular comic stars who capture audiences' attention through their great verbal and physical skills.

Hospital and police shows, as well as earlier popular westerns, present the thrills and suspense of traditional melodrama. The stereotypical characters, including the heroes and villains; the focus on the spectacular and the grotesque; and the neat and happy resolutions are all related, as we shall see, to nineteenth-century melodrama. The popularity of the television series *CSI* and *Law and*

Order is related to their use of traditional characteristics of the suspenseful melodramas of earlier eras.

Popular television variety shows throughout the medium's history, such as *Ed Sullivan, Saturday Night Live,* and *Mad TV,* have all been influenced by earlier popular theatrical forms that we will discuss later in our text, such as touring farce performers, minstrelsy, burlesque, and vaudeville. The long-running format of *Saturday Night Live,* which combines take-offs of serious films or literature, satire of political figures, exaggerated fictional characters, and popular musical acts, is an exact replica of vaudeville, a popular theater form of the early twentieth century.

On television, even news documentaries are framed in dramatic terms: a car crash in which a prom queen dies; a spy caught because of an e-mail message; a high government official or corporate officer accused of sexual harassment. Extremely popular reality shows are also staged like theatrical events. Many of the shows focus on highly dramatic situations and turn the real-life individuals into theatrical characters. On shows such as *Survivor* and *American Idol* participants and stars are portrayed as heroes and villains. Many reality shows, such as *The Bachelor* and *The Nanny,* focus on romantic or domestic situations. And we all know that the reality shows are theatrically manipulated to create a sense of dramatic tension, ongoing suspense, and heightened conflict among the participants.

THEATER AND FILM

Even more clearly, film has been greatly influenced by theater. The movies provide dramatic material of many kinds: science fiction; romantic and domestic comedies; action-packed stories of intrigue; historical epics; and even film versions of classical plays, such as Shakespeare's *Hamlet, Othello,* and *Romeo and Juliet.* And we should note that there is a combination of film and video when we watch movies at home on a DVD or VCR player.

Theatrical *genres* and specific plays have been appropriated by film. Recent successful film musicals, such as *Chicago, Rent,* and *The Producers* are movie versions of hugely successful stage musicals. As mentioned earlier, classical and contemporary plays are frequently adapted into movies.

In addition, most film genres borrow from past theatrical traditions. For example, popular cinematic melodramas, such as the 2005 version of *King Kong* (which some critics describe as a three-act film, clearly referring to the stage), the *Lord of the Rings* trilogy, and the *Harry Potter* films, reflect the characteristics of the theatrical genre and earlier theatrical innovations. We shall see that the intense interest in creating awe-inspiring special effects was as prevalent in nineteenth-century theater as it is in twenty-first-century film.

Just as we are intrigued by the lives of film stars, earlier theatrical audiences were often obsessed with theatrical stars. There are many earlier theatrical parallels to the great personalities who dominate film today. Stars such as Tom Cruise, Nicholas Cage, Brad Pitt, Angelina Jolie, Jamie Foxx, and Julia Roberts continue the tradition of the theatrical idols of earlier eras.

Making Connections

Film and the Other Mass Media

FILM AND THEATER
Theater and film have had a close relationship. Theater artists have worked in both media. In addition, film artists have appeared in theater presentations more and more frequently. A good example is Hugh Jackman, who made a reputation in such films as the X-Men *series, and also was successful in the theater in such musicals as* Oklahoma! *and* The Boy from Oz, *seen here.* (Left, Sara Krulwich/The New York Times; right, Photofest/© Twentieth Century Fox. All rights reserved.)

In the twentieth century, theater saw the development of competitors for audiences. The popularity of film, radio, and television affected theater. The relationship between film and theater is clearly apparent. Throughout the twentieth century, theater artists were captured by the allure of film, which can provide greater financial success and international popularity.

The first motion picture camera was invented in Thomas Edison's laboratory in 1888. In 1895, two French brothers, Auguste and Louis Lumière, developed the art of projecting film onto a larger screen. In the first decade of the twentieth century, films began to tell complete stories and were mass-presented. In the second decade of the century, full-length films were popularized and silent film stars, such as Charlie Chaplin, Buster Keaton, and Lillan Gish, were world-renowned. In addition, great film directors, such as D. W. Griffith, Sergei Eisenstein, and Carl Dreyer, revolutionized the art of filmmaking.

With the advent of sound in 1927 and the development of color technology in the 1930s, film became even more competitive with theatrical art, stealing artists and audience members. In the last half of the twentieth century, film technology became still more sophisticated, with the development of wide screens, special effects, digital sound, and a host of other innovations.

Radio and television also became the home of dramatic entertainments. Radio developed at the turn of the twentieth century; by the 1920s, commercial broadcasts and networks were established. In the United States in the 1930s, radio soap operas, dramas, and comedies became popular escapes from the depression. One of the most famous radio dramatizations was Orson Welles's *War of the Worlds,* which, when it was broadcast in 1938, fooled many listeners into believing that Earth had been attacked by aliens from outer space. (Welles and his actors were all theater personalities.) Radio presented these forms of dramatic entertainments throughout the 1940s.

Television surpassed radio in the 1950s and became the popular competitor of both film and theater. Although the roots of television can be traced back to developments in the 1920s, and early television broadcasting began in the 1930s, television became a mass entertainment in the early 1950s. Like film, television became more popular with innovations such as color and the recently introduced high-definition digital television (HDTV). In all countries, television has attracted theater and film artists, again because of the promise of financial reward and international recognition.

The relationship between theater and all these media is quite clear. Theater artists frequently are lured away to perform in these media. Film, radio, and television often adapt dramatic materials into films. Think about all the adaptations of Shakespeare's works into movies. There have been many filmed versions of *Hamlet* and *Romeo and Juliet,* for example. Some of these versions use the original texts; some, such as *Romeo Must Die* (2000), use the plotline as the basis of a new contemporary entertainment.

Yet in recent years, there has also been a new phenomenon: the return of theater artists from these electronic media to the live art. Recent productions in London and New York starred well-known film actors who had begun their careers as stage performers. Kevin Spacey, Matthew Broderick (in the musical version of *The Producers* and in the recent revival of *The Odd Couple*), Liam Neeson, Judi Dench, Julia Roberts, and Hugh Jackman are just a few of the actors who have crossed from film and television back to theater. Some critics suggest that actors return to the stage because of theater's unique quality: the intersection of live performers with the live audience.

THEATER AND FILM
Ever since film began, it has been closely allied to theater, using the same stories and the same characters, and developing narrative in a similar way. For example, the action adventure film King Kong *can be considered a three-act film, analogous to a three-act play. One difference, of course, is the elaborate scenic effects used in today's films; these are impossible to duplicate in the theater. Seen here is the actress Naomi Watts as Ann Darrow in* King Kong, *directed by Peter Jackson.* (© Pierre Vinet/Universal Pictures/ZUMA/Corbis)

In addition, since the inception of commercial film, there has been a great deal of crossover by theater and film artists. As we shall see, many film stars began their careers in theater. For that matter, Hollywood frequently raided the New York theater for actors, directors, and writers during the 1930s, 1940s, and 1950s. Many current film and television stars began their careers in theater and return to it on occasion; one example is Denzel Washington, who starred in a New York production of Shakespeare's *Julius Caesar* in 2005. And many renowned contemporary playwrights, such as Sam Shepard and David Mamet, write for film. (Shepard is also a successful film actor.) Tony Kushner, the Pulitzer Prize–winning author of *Angels in America,* was the screenwriter for Steven Spielberg's film *Munich* (2005).

In recent years, many movie and television stars, whose entire careers have been in these media, have performed onstage as an artistic challenge. For example, in New York in 2006, a revival of *Three Days of Rain* by the acclaimed playwright Richard Greenberg was an immediate box-office blockbuster. What attracted audiences was the production's star, Julia Roberts.

And just as film stars are admired for their wealth and status, while at the same time their personal lives are viewed suspiciously—for example, consider the furor over the romantic intrigue involving Jennifer Aniston, Brad Pitt, and Angelina Jolie—so, too, were theatrical stars from the earliest times on. This obsession with the lives of stars is reflected today in the popularity of such tabloids and magazines as *Star, National Enquirer,* and *People;* and in just the same way, there were earlier theatrical publications that reported about the lives of stage personalities.

THEATER AND ROCK AND ROLL

When we turn from electronic media to live performance, we see that theater has pervaded and influenced a popular musical form with which we are all familiar: rock and roll. Throughout its history, rock has appropriated theatrical elements. In addition, when rock stars have come under attack for their controversial subject matter or performance styles, many have used theatrical comparisons to defend their work. When Madonna undertook the controversial tour that was documented in the film *Truth or Dare,* she justified the performance as follows:

> My show is not a conventional rock show, but a theatrical presentation of my music. And like theater, it asks questions, provokes thought, and takes you on an emotional journey—portraying good and bad, light and dark, joy and sorrow; redemption and salvation.[1]

Like Madonna, numerous rock stars have created theatrical characters for their performances. Beginning with Little Richard and Elvis Presley in the 1950s, and continuing with the Beatles in the 1960s, through punk rock, glam rock, rap, hip-hop, and other forms, musical performers have used costumes, props, and makeup to create theatrical characterizations. The actual performers were

---

[1]From the documentary film *Truth or Dare,* directed by Alex Keshishian, Miramax Films, 1991.

often less recognizable than their stage personae.

The connection between rock performance and theater is also illustrated by the many rock stars who have acted, including: Elvis Presley, the Beatles, Madonna, Mark Wahlberg, Ice T., Tupac Shakur, Eminem, Jack Black, Beyoncé, André Benjamin from OutKast, Ludacris, LL Cool J, Queen Latifah, and 50 Cent, to name just a few. Sean ("Puff Daddy") Combs appeared in 2004 in a Broadway production of *A Raisin in the Sun*. The hip-hop and rap star Mos Def has also been a successful actor, having performed on television as a teenager and starred on Broadway in the Pulitzer Prize–winning play *Top Dog/Underdog* and in films such as *The Italian Job* (2003) and *16 Blocks* (2006). Def has compared his careers in acting and music, stating: "It takes a lot less time to get recognized as a musician than an actor. When you're a musician, you're always the star. When you're an actor, you're part of a cast of many."[2]

THEATRICALITY IN THE POPULAR ARTS
Good examples of the crossover of theatrical elements between popular art and traditional theater are the elaborate presentations by a number of rock groups, which feature elaborate costumes, stunning lighting and sound, and full-scale scenic effects. A case in point is Beyoncé, seen here performing at the 2004 Verizon Ladies First concert at the Arrowhead Pond of Anaheim, California. (Chris Pizzello/AP Images)

The popularity of music videos on MTV and VH1 also reflects the integration of theatrical elements into rock and roll. These videos turn many songs into visual, dramatic narratives. Current rock concerts are also highly theatrical events, using live performers, lights, sound, and properties in ways that are like multimedia presentations. For example, the popular group U2 used all these elements in a concert tour, "Elevation," performing in front of a heart-shaped set, with a "runway" stage that allowed the lead singer to be almost completely surrounded by the audience. The pop stars Justin Timberlake and Christina Aguilera have also staged their concerts like theater performances, with spectacular lighting effects and dance routines. Even classic rock groups, such as the Rolling Stones, have added highly visual theatrical elements to their touring shows to appeal to more contemporary fans.

For that matter, recent acoustic tours by some well-known rock stars are a reaction against these intensely theatricalized concerts and reflect a desire to return the focus to the live performer. We shall see that some contemporary theatrical theorists and experimental artists also argue for diminishing spectacular scenery and using fewer special effects, to reestablish the primacy of live performance.

In the past few years, there has also been a new phenomenon in musical theater: the use of rock as the score for musicals. The most popular example of such

[2]Carla Ray, "Mos Def Heads to Broadway," *Billboard*, Vol. 2, August 2002.

A POPULAR MUSICAL FORM: THE "JUKEBOX MUSICAL"
American musicals are based on all kinds of sources: novels, straight plays, and films, as well as biographies and history. A popular source in recent years has been popular songs: songs written by one person or group, and songs made popular by a single singer or a group. Mamma Mia!— featuring the songs of ABBA—is a good example. A more recent example is Jersey Boys, seen here, a musical based on songs made popular by Frankie Valli and the Four Seasons. The performers, from the left, are: J. Robert Spencer as Nick Massi; Christian Hoff as Tommy DeVito; John Lloyd Young as Frankie Valli; and Daniel Reichard as Bob Gaudio. (Sara Krulwich/The New York Times)

a musical is *Mamma Mia* (1999), using the songs of a group from the 1980s, ABBA. Other examples include *Lennon* (2005); *All Shook Up* (2005), using Elvis Presley's hits; *Good Vibrations* (2004), using songs by the Beach Boys; and *Jersey Boys* (2004), tracing the career of a pop group of the 1960s, the Four Seasons. In Savannah, Georgia, the musical revue *Jukebox Journey* has run for over 1,000 performances at the Savannah Theatre, which is on a site where there has been a playhouse since 1818.

THEATRICALITY IN AMUSEMENT PARKS, MUSEUMS, LAS VEGAS, AND SPORTING EVENTS

Rock illustrates that we have come to expect theatrical elements as part of our popular entertainments and that theater is around us in many unexpected venues. Amusement parks like Disney World, Sea World, and Universal Studios incorporate theatrical material; most, for example, present staged productions based on films, which attract huge audiences. The rides at these amusement parks also

LAVISH STAGE SHOWS IN CASINOS AND THEME PARKS

One type of show that is highly theatrical in nature is the spectacle, such as those presented by the Cirque du Soleil. For its presentation in Las Vegas, Cirque du Soleil developed an extravaganza, a large part of which takes place underwater, in a huge tank that can be raised and lowered to stage level. Shown here, in the Duo Trapeze act from the show "O," are performers on horses coming out of the water and acrobats on a trapeze. (Photo: Véronique Vial. Costumes: Dominique Lemieux/© Cirque du Soleil)

incorporate theatricality by placing the participant in a theatrical environment and a dramatic situation. Rides such as *ET, Raiders of the Lost Ark,* and *Twilight Zone: Tower of Terror,* allow the rider to be an actor in a dramatic plotline often based on films, in a space that functions as a kind of stage setting.

We can also see theater around us in many other everyday activities. Many restaurants, such as the Rainforest Cafes, have theatricalized environments. Shopping centers and specialty stores, such as Niketown and American Girl,

Making Connections

The Digital Arts

THEATER AND DIGITAL MEDIA

A question that confronts theater is its relationship with the popular digital media. Will theater lose audience members to interactive video or to live Web broadcasts? How will theater incorporate these new electronic arts? Here we see Jada Pinkett Smith playing the video game "Enter the Matrix," at a party to celebrate its release in 2003, at Warner Bros. lot in Burbank, California. (Chris Pizzello/AP Images)

Once again, in the twenty-first century, theater finds itself in competition with other popular forms of entertainment. With the development of computer technology and various forms of digital entertainment, some cultural analysts wonder whether audiences will ever leave their homes to go and watch live performers.

The Internet has revolutionized audiences' access to music (resulting, for example, in the legal battles over Napster), to video, and to live events. Do audiences really need to go to the theater when they can view people living their daily lives, in real time, on computer screens?

And what about the live-action games that are available? Will audiences leave their homes when they can create their own dramatic scenarios and play those dramatizations out on their computers or on large-screen monitors?

And will DVD at home lead audiences to forsake film houses and theaters? Through DVD, the audience member can even alter the experience, view multiple endings, learn more about the artistic process, and take greater control of the material being viewed.

Yet theater continues to thrive, and audience members do leave their homes. They seek out the live experience. Audiences want to be in the presence of live actors and in the community of other theatergoers. As the critic Michael Feingold of the *Village Voice* aptly reassures and warns the theater world:

> The theater has a future, in our geography as well as in our souls. . . . Millions of desk-locked, glazed-eyed Web workers will be flooding the streets, desperate for un-plugged, un-downloaded human experience. We had better be ready for them. We had better know our history, our mission, our tradition, our means for reaching audiences, and our justification for addressing them (June 7–13, 2000).

What is also likely is that theater will, as always, find ways to appropriate elements from these digital media as it constructs a living art for the new century and for new audiences.

LAS VEGAS AS THEATRICAL ENVIRONMENT
Almost the entire central part of Las Vegas, Nevada, is a gigantic stage set. Everything from the pyramids to the Eiffel Tower and New York City is reproduced there. Seen here is a re-creation of the Grand Canal in Venice to house shops at the Venetian Hotel Las Vegas. (© Andreas Stertzing/VISUM/The Image Works)

contain spaces for performances that highlight specific holiday seasons or product lines.[3]

Museums have recently adopted some of these theatrical techniques to attract audiences. For example, the new Abraham Lincoln Presidential Library and Museum in Springfield, Illinois, includes stage presentations about this famous president as well as about how historians and archivists work. The museum also contains many exhibits that function like stage settings, including a reproduction of the log cabin in which Lincoln originally lived.

In cities such as Orlando, Florida, dinner theaters present theatrical entertainments based on Roman gladiators, medieval knights, and gangsters of the 1930s.

---

[3]We would like to thank Chris Jones, chief theater critic of the *Chicago Tribune*, who presented some of these concepts in a talk at Western Illinois University on April 17, 2006.

Medieval Nights is an extremely popular dinner theater entertainment in Orlando, New Jersey, and Chicago. Las Vegas is a highly theatricalized environment. Its hotels—such as New York, New York; the Bellagio; Luxor; and Mandelay Bay—are constructed almost like huge theatrical sets. Lavish stage shows, such as *Mystere* and *O* by Cirque du Soleil, the Celine Dion extravaganza, and Elton John's stage show, use all the elements of theater to entertain audiences. Possibly the most spectacular is *KA,* a $165 million production of the Cirque du Soleil, staged at the MGM Grand by the avant-garde Canadian director Robert LePage. In addition, many performance artists and Broadway productions have set up resident companies in Las Vegas, including Blue Man Group, *The Phantom of the Opera,* and *Spamalot.* These theater productions are even modified to meet the time limitations of the traditional Las Vegas stage show.

Contemporary sporting events also integrate significant theatrical elements. Sports arenas, as we will note later, function much like theater spaces. The introduction of sports teams before the start of competitions is often highly staged, with spectacular sound, lighting, and visual effects. Halftime shows, particularly at championship games such as the Super Bowl, are often huge stage spectacles with musicians, dancers, and special effects. The controversy over the performance by Janet Jackson and Justin Timberlake during the Super Bowl of 2004, when Jackson exposed one of her breasts on television, reflects the centrality of the halftime show. In addition, the theatricality of the commercials during the Super Bowl is sometimes as highly discussed as the game itself.

THEATER AND DIGITAL MEDIA

At the start of the twenty-first century, digital media are omnipresent; and the immensely popular interactive computer, Internet, and video games are also clearly influenced by theater. Whether they are games we play on our computers or on playstations or x-boxes, such as *Dragon Quest VIII* or *Final Fantasy VII,* these digital entertainments usually present a theatrical plotline in which we engage. Many of these story lines are based on popular melodramatic premises taken from films, comic books, and other entertainments. Some are based on historic events, such as actual wars and battles; others are fictional tales. Their goal is to make us feel as if we are actors within the universe of the game. The desire to create realistic special effects graphics continues a tradition that began with nineteenth-century stage melodrama, continued into film and television, and now is an engaging element of these digital games.

There are also interactive theatrical role-playing websites on the Internet. These websites all allow the participant to feel as if she or he is an actor in a theatricalized fantasy world. Even websites that are supposedly realistic chat rooms allow us to play roles as if we are actors in a performance for an unseen audience.

While there is an abundance of dramatic materials available in movie houses, on television, on videos and DVDs, in amusement parks, at sporting events, in video games, and on the Internet, theater itself is also a highly diverse and eclectic art form that attracts a wide spectrum of audience members and artists. This diversity, which reflects the multiculturalism of our global society, will be reviewed briefly in Chapter 3 and then surveyed even more fully in Part Three.

SUMMARY

We can see the impact of theater all around us today. Theater exists in many aspects of our everyday lives and has influenced many of our popular entertainments.

Theater permeates our everyday lives as we and those with whom we interact play roles. We play such roles at work, at home, and with those we know and love.

Theater has greatly influenced television and film. We can see the impact of theater in the content of television shows and movies.

Our interest in media stars' performances and lives parallels the way audiences throughout the history of theater have engaged with actors and actresses.

Rock and roll performances emphasize stage spectacle, lighting, and sound effects.

We can also see theatrical influences in our visits to amusement parks and museums.

When we visit dinner theaters throughout the country, and when we visit Las Vegas, we recognize the pervasiveness of theatrical elements.

KEY TERM

Genres Categories of artworks, based on style, form, or subject matter.

THEATER ON THE WEB

For more research and to learn more about the topics in this chapter, please visit the Online Learning Center at **www.mhhe.com/livelyart6.**

CHAPTER 3

Today's Diverse Theater

◀ TODAY'S DIVERSE THEATER

Patrick Tshanini reenacts a part from The Zulu Macbeth *outside Shakespeare's Globe Theatre, with St. Paul's Cathedral in the background. The cast of the Umabatha Company, made up of Zulu from South Africa, mainly from Johannesburg and Durban, toured England and other countries with their performance of* Macbeth. *(© Adrian Dennis/epa/Corbis)*

CROSS-CULTURAL TRENDS

Thomas Friedman, in his acclaimed book *The World Is Flat,* analyzes how globalization has affected business and industry in our contemporary society. One can no longer tell whether a product is made by a company of a specific country, because most major corporations are multinational. The automobile industry clearly reflects the trend toward industrial globalization, as does the personal computer industry. A car created today by a Japanese, Korean, Chinese, or German manufacturer may be assembled in the United States. A PC may be assembled in the United States, but the manufacturer's twenty-four-hour help desk may be located in India.

The same is true in today's theater. Many diverse groups influence one another to create the contemporary theatrical landscape. Theater artists cross national boundaries to stage their works with artists of other countries. Popular works tour the world and cross-pollinate other theatrical ventures.

Casts and production companies are made up of individuals of various nationalities and ethnicities. A classic American musical staged in London with British performers—such as a recent revival of *Oklahoma!*—may be remounted in New York City by the original English director and producer along with the American choreographer, but with American actors. An Israeli director may cast Israeli and Palestinian performers in a Shakespearean drama.

Experimental artists appropriate the styles and techniques of traditional theaters from around the world. Artists mix and match all sorts of styles, historic antecedents, materials, and techniques. An experimental theater director in Minneapolis may apply traditional Chinese techniques from Beijing opera in a daring adaptation of a realistic drama from the late nineteenth century by the Norwegian playwright Ibsen, *White Boned Demon.* The director may then restage this work at an experimental noncommercial theater space in New York City and then again direct it with college students at a university in Illinois.

DIVERSITY IN AMERICAN THEATER

The diversity of contemporary theater in the United States is striking. There are artists who reflect the multicultural landscape of American society and focus on significant concerns and issues of many historically underrepresented groups.

Clearly, there is an impressive variety of theatrical events in contemporary American theater. Audiences today can see revivals of the best theater from the past: Greek, Elizabethan, French, and Spanish. They can see theater from Asia, Africa, and Latin America; new plays; and avant-garde and experimental works. There are productions in translation of the best new plays from other countries. Audiences can see multicultural theater—African American, Asian American, Hispanic, Native American. They can also see political theater, and theater reflecting the viewpoint of a number of minorities and special groups such as feminist theater and gay and lesbian theater. What's more, these productions can be seen in a wide variety of theater environments.

MIXING PAST AND PRESENT

In today's theater, artists mix and match all sorts of styles, historical antecedents, and genders. A good example is the hip-hop play The Seven *based on Aeschylus's* Seven against Thebes. *Mixing classical sources with pop culture,* The Seven *tells the story of Oedipus and his two sons Polynices and Eteocles in the language of rap, doo-wop, funk, and other contemporary idioms. Shown here is the cast in a production at the New York Theater Workshop.* (Sara Krulwich/The New York Times)

One hallmark of contemporary theater is that all these strands exist simultaneously. As all this suggests, our contemporary theater is complex. If theater mirrors the society in which it is produced, it is not surprising that ours is fragmented, reflecting the complexity of today's life.

One way to understand the rich assortment of theatrical organizations and theatrical venues that make up the mosaic of contemporary theater is to look at one locality as a microcosm of theater across the United States. The city we have chosen is Chicago. In many ways what is happening in Chicago mirrors what is happening elsewhere, in the diverse types of theater on display, as well as in the variety of theater spaces where theater is being offered.

To begin with, there are traditional Broadway-style commercial theaters, including the Ford Center, the Oriental, the Cadillac Palace, and the LaSalle Bank (formerly the Shubert). Not only do they offer touring Broadway shows; these theaters in recent years have been the tryout house for such musicals as *The Producers, Spamalot,* and *The Pirate Queen.*

When we move to the not-for-profit world, Chicago has a number of resident professional theaters. The largest, the Goodman, is a flagship regional theater that has launched several plays by August Wilson as well as other important new works. Following closely behind the Goodman is Steppenwolf, founded in 1976. Steppenwolf's original company included many actors who became stars, including John Malkovich (1953–), Gary Sinise (1955–), and Laurie Metcalf (1955–), and it evolved into a leading established regional theater.

Steppenwolf is known as an *off-Loop theater*, meaning that it is outside the downtown commercial section of Chicago. (The equivalent in New York City is off-Broadway and off-off-Broadway, which have been sites of significant noncommercial theater activity. We discuss them more fully later in our text.)

Other major off-Loop theaters in Chicago include Wisdom Bridge (where Robert Falls, currently artistic director of the Goodman, began his directing

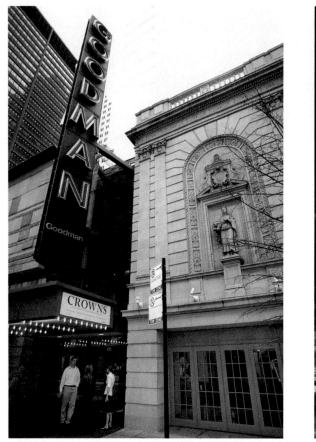 

CHICAGO: A VITAL THEATER CENTER
There are active theater centers throughout the United States, with a healthy mix of commercial and not-for-profit theaters, as well as large and small theaters. A good example is Chicago, which has large commercial venues; large not-for-profit theaters, such as the Goodman, shown here, and others like Steppenwolf; a Shakespeare theater; and many small theaters, known as off-Loop theaters. A prominent director in Chicago has been Mary Zimmerman, whose production of Pericles *by Aeschylus at the Goodman Theatre is also shown here. (M. Spencer Green/AP Images) (Liz Lauren/Goodman Theatre)*

career), the Organic, the Body Politic, St. Nicholas, and Victory Gardens. These theaters also introduced successful actors and many significant playwrights. Lookingglass Theatre, founded in Chicago in 1988, has received praise for its productions of literary adaptations that use intriguing staging devices.

Chicago also has the Chicago Shakespeare Theater, one of many Shakespeare theaters and festivals around the country. All in all, there are over 150 Shakespeare festivals in the United States, with more than thirty located in California alone. Year after year, Shakespeare remains the most frequently produced playwright in America.

Chicago has multicultural theater companies that perform works for and by African Americans, Mexican Americans, and other ethnic groups. Chicago also has many smaller companies that parallel the noncommercial off-off-Broadway theaters of New York City. (The off-Loop theaters mentioned earlier began as such smaller ventures and then evolved into more successful established companies that have sometimes transferred shows to commercial New York theaters.)

Along with the many professional theaters in Chicago, there are excellent college and university theaters—such as DePaul, and Northwestern in Evanston, Illinois—which produce high-quality work. This multiplicity of activity, at so many levels, can be found in cities large and small in almost all fifty states as well as in Canada and throughout the world.

TRADITIONAL AND AVANT-GARDE THEATER

Two broad strains in our diverse contemporary theater are the *traditional* and the *avant-garde*. Traditional plays more or less follow the pattern of plays from the past in structure, theme, and approach. Traditional theater practice presents works in an understandable, logical, recognizable style. Traditional theater remains vibrant, and the vast majority of theatergoers attend, and prefer, traditional plays and productions.

At the same time, experimental and avant-garde artists have challenged preconceived ideas about theater and presented a number of arresting alternatives to establishment drama. Theater that breaks away from the mainstream was part of the landscape for most of the twentieth century and is continuing in the twenty-first. This type of theater has frequently appealed to a small audience, often young people who question prevalent traditional theatrical practices.

There are, of course, many theater artists who work in both traditional and experimental styles. We will discuss renowned theater artists whose work reflects both these trends—traditional and experimental—in Chapters 17, 18, and 19 of our text.

MULTIETHNIC THEATERS

Before we discuss specific multiethnic points of view in theater, we should make one point. Although many theater artists do want to write from a specific ethnic

TRADITIONAL AND AVANT-GARDE THEATER
Theater today is eclectic and widely diversified. Periods, styles, theatrical purposes, and approaches are often mixed, or coexist side by side. Shown here is a scene from a production by a well-known avant-garde theater group: Richard Foreman's Ontological-Hysteric Theater. The production, called Zomboid! (Film/Performance Project No. 1), has Foreman's signature mixture of many theatrical elements and styles, including a combination of theater and film. From left, the actors are: Caitlin McDonough Thayer, Temple Crocker, Stephanie Silver, and Katherine Brook. (Sara Krulwich/The New York Times)

or gender point of view, there are others who happen to be members of an ethnic group, or who espouse feminism or a political outlook, but who do not want to be identified solely, or even primarily, on that basis—or on the basis of their gender. For instance, there are playwrights who happen to be Latin American or African American but want to be known simply as playwrights, without any ethnic identification. In the same way, there are people who are gay or lesbian, or who are strong feminists, but who want to be known chiefly, or even exclusively, as dramatists, not as gay dramatists, lesbian dramatists, or feminist dramatists.

It is also true that theater companies, producers, or playwrights who are identified with an ethnic or gender group may well include in their presentations characters belonging to those groups, and wish to see them treated with understanding and insight, but who include them as part of a larger picture.

Having noted some of the variations that occur within ethnic and minority playwriting and production, let us briefly highlight some of the multicultural theater movements that we will survey more fully in Chapters 17, 18, and 19.

African American Theater

African American theater—also referred to as *black theater*—is a prime example of a theater that reflects the diversity of American culture and the contributions of a particular group to the culture. African American theater is theater written by and for black Americans or performed by black Americans. It partakes of two important traditions. One is the western theater tradition, in which actors like Paul Robeson (1898–1976) and writers like Lorraine Hansberry (1930–1965) have been significant. The other is a tradition that traces its origin to theater in Africa and the Caribbean. Contemporary African American theater focuses on the continued struggle for equality and social justice in the United States as well as on racism throughout American history. As we will see, there have been and are African American artists who work in a variety of theatrical styles, including traditional drama, musicals, and experimental performance art.

LATINO-LATINA THEATER
Among the important theaters that represent the wide diversity of theater in the United States is Latino-Latina theater. Shown here is a scene from Electricidad, *based on Sophocles's* Electra. *In this scene, Abula, on the right (Ivonne Coll), begs her granddaughter Electricidad (Cecilia Suarez) to let her father go. This production at the Goodman Theatre in Chicago was directed by Henry Godinez.* (Michael Brosilow)

Asian American Theater

For most of the nineteenth century and the first half of the twentieth century, Asians appeared in dramatic offerings strictly as stereotypes. With the coming of cultural and ethnic awareness in the 1960s and 1970s, this situation began to change. As we will see in Chapter 19, there have been a significant number of theater companies, individual playwrights, and experimental artists who have focused on issues confronting Asian Americans as they dealt with American society during the last four decades.

Latino and Latina Theater

Latinos and Latinas are the fastest-growing ethnic population in the United States and come from many different nations. Contemporary Latino-Latina theater in the United States—also referred to as Hispanic theater—can be divided into at least three major groups: Chicano theater, Cuban American theater, and Puerto Rican or Nuyorican theater. There are also Latino and Latina theater artists who dramatize the concerns of Colombians, Salvadorans, Argentineans, and many other populations. The complexity and diversity of Latino-Latina theater will be examined more fully in Chapter 18.

Native American Theater

Strictly speaking, there was no Native American theater tradition; rather, there were spiritual and social traditions that had theatrical elements. These were found primarily in ancient rituals and communal celebrations, which were often infused with cosmic significance. Also, in these traditions, unlike traditional western theater, there was no audience as such: those observing were considered participants just as much as the principal performers. Many of these ceremonies and the like were outlawed by the American government in the nineteenth century. Thus the rituals and ceremonies, which had strong theatrical components—not to mention significant spiritual and cultural value—were forced to go "underground" if they continued at all.

The American Indian Religious Freedom Act of 1972 made it legal once again for certain ceremonies, such as the sun dance, to resume. An increased awareness of these rituals and celebrations contributed to the emergence of the vibrant Native American theater that we will survey later, in Part Three.

Feminist Theater

Feminist theater focuses on issues relevant to women as they struggle to deal with male-dominated societies. Worldwide, many female playwrights and theater artists question traditional gender roles and the place of women in society. Some of these playwrights argue for equality within the status quo; others argue that we should recognize the uniqueness of womanhood and that a complete social change is needed.

In the 1970s and 1980s, as the feminist movement gained international attention, there were a number of successful female playwrights in the United States, as in many other countries. Feminist theater companies, during the same time period, forced audiences to reexamine their own gender biases and those of their society. Some scholars estimate that more than 100 feminist companies have been founded in the United States. Clearly, feminist theater has roots in the past, since there were significant female playwrights at least as early as the Middle Ages. When we survey theater history, in Part Three, we will highlight the accomplishments of these female theater artists.

Gay and Lesbian Theater

Lesbian theater groups can be part of feminist theater, but gay and lesbian theater is also a distinct movement. A number of plays and performers introduced homosexual and lesbian themes into theater before the 1960s. For example, in the nineteenth century and the early twentieth century there was a considerable amount of cross-dressing in performances: men often appeared in drag and women in men's clothing, raising questions about sexual and gender roles.

With the rise of the gay rights movement in the 1960s, there was an explosion of plays and theater companies that focused on issues related to sexual orientation and the status of gays and lesbians in the contemporary world. As we will see, though a number of these theater groups have not survived, individual performers and playwrights in gay and lesbian theater remain very much in the spotlight.

Political Theater

Many of the plays as well as the artists among the multiethnic groups—African American, Latino and Latina, Asian American, and others—have a political as well as an aesthetic purpose. They speak up for the rights and recognition of their particular ethnic group. The same could be said of feminist theater and of gay and lesbian theater: the playwrights who focus on these concerns are often passionate about a specific political position, and that is clearly reflected in their work.

There are also other theaters and artists who are part of majority society and who believe that art must have a social conscience and must be used to change

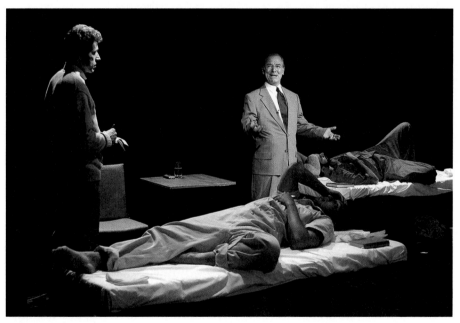

POLITICAL THEATER
A popular form that has emerged in the past half century is political theater based on facts. This includes documentary theater taken from court trials, congressional hearings, and interviews. Shown here is a rehearsal of Guantanamo: Honor Bound to Defend Freedom, *a moving drama, compiled from captives' letters and public testimony from their families, attorneys, and public officials. It was originally created by the Tricycle Theatre in London and focuses on five British detainees imprisoned at the U.S. detention camp in Cuba. In this scene from the production staged in New York at the 45 Bleecker Street Theater, the actors are, from left, Joris Stuyck, Aasif Mandvi, Robert Langdon (standing) as Defense Secretary Donald Rumsfeld, and Waleed Zuaiter. (© Richard Termine)*

social conditions. For example, in a reaction to the Bush administration and many of its policies, especially the war in Iraq, there was an outpouring of plays that were largely political. One example is *Embedded* by the well-known film actor Tim Robbins, which is about control of the media in Iraq. Another example of recent political theater is *Exonerated*, which uses actual transcripts of people who had been sentenced to death row but were later proved to be innocent and employs rotating stars to read these transcripts.

DIVERSITY AND MULTICULTURALISM

The two words that best characterize today's theater are *diversity* and *multiculturalism:* diversity because the types of theater available to audiences are so wide-ranging and because the audiences themselves are so diverse; and multiculturalism because contemporary theater embraces such a wide variety of social groups and concerns. When we explore contemporary theater history at the end of Part Three, it will become even clearer how diverse and multicultural the theatrical landscape remains in the twenty-first century.

In Part One we have looked at theater in its broader aspects. In Chapter 1 we observed the significance of theater, its component parts, and theater as an art form. In Chapter 2 we examined theater in the context of today's culture: the way it relates to other art forms and to everyday life. In Chapter 3 we discussed the diversity of theater today and the many forms it takes, as well as the multicultural and multiethnic aspects of theater. In Part Two we will examine theater itself and the many elements that come together to create a theater event: acting, directing, the text, the design elements, and one often overlooked element, with which we begin, the audience.

SUMMARY

Two terms that describe our theater today are *diverse* and *multicultural.* We can see the impact of our multicultural society on today's theater.

Contemporary theater reflects cross-cultural influences. Many productions are created by multinational theater companies. Many productions in the United States and western Europe reflect the influence of traditional theaters from other parts of the world.

Contemporary theater also reflects our diverse society. There are theaters that focus on the issues of many underrepresented groups, including African Americans, Latinos and Latinas, Asian Americans, gays and lesbians, and women.

Contemporary theater is also frequently experimental and avant-garde in nature, though most audiences continue to attend traditional dramatic offerings.

There are also many artists who believe that the purpose of theater is political and that theater should encourage societal change.

KEY TERMS

Avant-garde theater Experimental theater that breaks away from the traditional mainstream.

Off-Loop theater In Chicago, theater that is presented outside the city's downtown commercial section.

Traditional theater Theater that presents works in an understandable, logical, recognizable style.

THEATER ON THE WEB

For more research and to learn more about the topics in this chapter, please visit the Online Learning Center at **www.mhhe.com/livelyart6.**

Creating Theater

PART 2

OUTLINE

A theater production is most often created by a director taking a text—either a new play or one from the past—and working with actors and designers to develop a stage piece. At times directors work without a text, or combine a text with other elements. Such a director is Lee Breuer, whose production of *Red Beads* is shown here. Presented by Mabou Mines, the production featured animated design and puppetry by Basil Twist. The red in the photo is billowing silk, like parachute fabric, manipulated by black-clad puppeteers, one of whom can be seen in the lower right corner of the photograph. Meanwhile a figure, right, hovers over the scene from on high. This production was at Skirball Center for the Performing Arts, in New York City, September 2005.
(© Beatriz Schiller)

CHAPTER 4

Audiences and Critics

◀ **THE AUDIENCE PLAYS AN ESSENTIAL ROLE**

The audience and the performers are the two basic elements in any theater experience. The presence of the audience sets theater apart from other forms of entertainment such as film or television. Shown here is the audience gathered outside the Majestic Theater for a performance of The Phantom of the Opera. *(© Geraint Lewis)*

47

THE THEATER AUDIENCE

If you asked someone to list the essential components of a theater experience, the chances are the person might say the actors, the script, and the stage; he or she might also mention the scenery and costumes. If you pressed for further elements, however, the list would still probably not include a crucial ingredient—the audience.

This is understandable—particularly today, when film and television are so pervasive. In these two media, which are so much like theater in many ways, the "product," as it is sometimes called, stands alone as a finished production. When you watch a film at home on a DVD, it has been completed and is in its absolutely final form. The same is true of a film in a movie theater; when released it might be shown in 1,000 theaters simultaneously across the United States, and it will be exactly the same in each location, night after night. The audience watches but plays no part in what appears on the screen.

Theater is different. It is not different just because film or television is flexible and has a wider range of visual effects, though that is the case. In film, computer-generated effects can take us to the land of the dinosaurs in the past or to some interplanetary war in the future; and helicopter shots can let us climb Mount Everest or swoop into the Grand Canyon.

Clearly, this is one difference between theater and film, but there is another. Even when the story and the characters presented in the two are identical—in a film and stage presentation of Shakespeare's *Romeo and Juliet,* for instance—there is a less obvious but equally important difference: the fact that each theater performance is unique and occurs in the presence of an *audience*. The ramifications of the audience are far-reaching. To begin with, the performers have no opportunity to play a scene over or to correct mistakes. Most people are aware that in creating a film most scenes are filmed a number of times. These repetitions are called "takes," and there may be four, five, or even twenty takes before the director feels that a scene is "right." Moreover, once scenes are filmed, the director decides in the editing room where each scene begins and ends and how scenes are joined together.

In theater, there is no repeating and no editing. The performers onstage move through a production from beginning to end, and if there is a mishap—if an actor forgets a line, or an unexpected noise occurs offstage—the performers must recover and carry on. The result of all this is that each theater event is live, immediate, and unique.

The dynamics and the excitement of being in the presence of a living person are as old as time and have not changed despite the many technological advances of recent years. People still wait for hours or stand in the rain to see a rock star or a hip-hop performer in person, although the same performer is readily available on a CD, video, or DVD. The same is true of film personalities and charismatic political figures—people eagerly throng to see someone "in person." This same chemistry is possible at every stage performance when the actors and actresses and the members of the audience are in the same place at the same time.

There is another aspect in which the audience plays a significant part: the effect the audience has on performers. The drama critic Walter Kerr (1913–1996) explained the special relationship between audience and performers at a theater event:

> It doesn't just mean that we are in the personal presence of performers. It means that they are in our presence, conscious of us, speaking to us, working for and with us until a circuit that is not mechanical becomes established between us, a circuit that is fluid, unpredictable, ever-changing in its impulses, crackling, intimate. Our presence, the way we respond, flows back to the performer and alters what he does, to some degree and sometimes astonishingly so, every single night. We are contenders, making the play and the evening and the emotion together. We are playmates, building a structure.[1]

In other words, the audience has an enormous effect on actors and actresses. They are buoyed up by a responsive audience and discouraged by an unresponsive one. Sometimes, if an audience is not reacting, they might try harder than ever to make contact. This is the case not only with comedy, where laughter is a clear gauge of the audience's response, but also with serious drama. Performers know whether or not spectators are caught up in the action. When audience members are involved in a serious play, they become very quiet; you can sense their fierce concentration. When an audience is not engaged there may be noticeable coughing or rustling of programs. Reacting to this, actors and actresses will change their performances in subtle but very real ways.

---

[1]Source: Walter Kerr, "We Call It 'Live' Theater, but Is It?" *The New York Times,* January 2, 1972. Copyright 1972 by The New York Times Company. Reprinted by permission.

How the Audience Participates

At the heart of the theater experience, then, is the performer-audience relationship: the immediate, personal exchange; the chemistry and magic that give theater its special quality. We might ask how the audience becomes involved in a theater event, aside from sending the performers such obvious signals as laughter, silence, and palpable tension. The answer lies in the power of the imagination.

Audience members do not participate physically in a theater performance, the way they would if they were riding a bicycle, working at a computer, or singing in a chorus. Rather, they participate *vicariously*, through the mind and the heart. The astonishing thing is how powerful these aspects of the human psyche are. Through our imagination, we come to believe in the reality of what we see onstage and to identify with the characters. We feel deep sympathy for those we sense are being treated unjustly, and we suffer with them; we feel hatred for those we consider mean or despicable; we laugh at those we consider foolish.

The events onstage become so real that we often forget who we are and where we are and enter the imaginary world we see before us. We can be transported to a foreign country, to another century, to an imaginary place—or to the kitchen of people who might be our own neighbors. Some situations in theater are so vivid and so engrossing that we cry real tears, even though a part of us knows that the events onstage are not actually happening and that the people are only actors and actresses. This experience comes about because of a phenomenon that the English poet and critic Samuel Taylor Coleridge (1772–1834) called *willing suspension of disbelief*. In other words, we want so much to believe in the reality of what is happening onstage that we willingly put aside all literal and practical considerations in order to enter into the world of the drama.

Another factor that allows us to enter into an imaginative world—even though we are aware that it is separate from everyday reality—is referred to as *aesthetic distance*. Aesthetic distance is a requirement of virtually all involvement with the arts. It means that the viewer, spectator, or audience member must be in some sense separated from the performance or object—and must be aware that it is a work of art—in order to experience its aesthetic qualities. Paradoxically, once the proper distance is established, the observer can enter into the experience fully and completely.

Throughout theater history, the power of the audience's mental and emotional participation has manifested itself in both positive and negative ways. Negatively, it has taken the form of censorship—which indicates that those in authority fear the effect theater can have on audiences. The Greeks of ancient Athens considered certain subjects unfit for drama and banned them. In fourth-century Rome, in the early days of Christianity, the church had a great deal to do with stopping theatrical activity. In 1642, the Puritans closed all the theaters in England. In modern times, there have been many examples of censorship, especially in places like China and various totalitarian countries, where only drama that has been approved of by the political authorities can be presented.

Positively, the power of audience participation can be seen in many ways. To take just one example, many political groups and other groups use theater as a means of educating people or furthering a cause. In recent times, we have seen theater representing various groups: feminist theater, gay theater, and radical political theater, for instance. The people who present such productions feel that the imaginative and symbolic power of theater will affect their audiences.

In sum, the ability of the audience to enter into the world presented onstage is one reason why it is always a key factor in any theater event.

Diversity of Audiences

Makeup of Audiences: Past and Present.   As we trace the history of theater, one thing we will note is that the makeup of audiences has varied from time to time and from place to place. In ancient Greece, for example, a large percentage of an entire city, such as Athens or Epidaurus, would attend the theater. The same was true of medieval theater in western Europe and England. When we come to Restoration theater in England during the late seventeenth century, however, we find that the audience was often rarefied, consisting primarily of the upper classes. This affected the kind of writing and acting seen onstage; as a result, Restoration plays still remain less accessible to the general population. In Europe in the nineteenth century, theater once again came to be a form of art popular with a wide range of people. In various Asian countries, as well, theater in some eras was only for an elite audience or for the upper classes; but at other times it included audiences from the general population.

In today's theater there is a great diversity in both the size and the makeup of those who are present at a theater event. As to size, in a small, intimate theater, there may be no more than 100 or 200 people attending. On the other hand, at a large city auditorium, there may be 2,000 or 3,000 people, or even more, watching a large-scale musical. This factor will make a difference, both to audience members and to performers. In an intimate space there is more awareness, on the part of everyone, of the interaction between actors and spectators. In a large amphitheater, a different, less personal relationship exists. In a theater somewhere in between—a house that seats 800 or 900 people—the relationship will be a mixture of the two. (We will consider the actor-audience relationship in the context of theater spaces in more detail in Chapter 9.)

Aside from the question of size, today there is often a wide variety in the makeup of theater audiences. Some audiences are homogeneous: the audience members come mostly from similar backgrounds and experience. A good example would be a college or university theater production in which the audience consists primarily of students, faculty members, and their friends. Another example would be a performance presented to a group of senior citizens in a retirement village. Other audiences are heterogeneous, such as the spectators at free performances of Shakespeare in an outdoor amphitheater in a city park. Here you would find people of many ethnic and social backgrounds and of all ages. A third audience mix would be found at a Broadway theater or in a similar theater in

PHYSICAL THEATER HELPS SHAPE THE EXPERIENCE
The size, shape, and configuration of a theater affect the audience's experience. The theater may be small and intimate; it may be indoors or outdoors; it may be large and expansive: all these factors will have an impact on the experience of attending the performance, even though we usually think that the only important aspect is what occurs onstage. Here the informal, outdoors setting for a production of Greenshow *at the Utah Shakespearean Festival establishes a mood and atmosphere far different from what would be experienced at a formal, indoor theater, especially if it had elegant furnishings and a traditional appearance.* (© Utah Shakespearean Festival. Photo by Karl Hugh.)

any large city. The members of the audience would be mostly middle-class and upper-class but might include children, students, or foreign visitors. Even among traditional audience groups such as these, however, the chemistry of the audience will change from night to night for no apparent reason. At a comedy, for instance, on some nights the audience will laugh at everything; on other nights, audience members may enjoy the show just as much, but they will barely chuckle and seem never to indulge in a hearty laugh.

Where We See Theater. In addition to diversity in the makeup of audiences and in their reactions, there are various places where theater can be seen. One place is a Broadway theater or its counterpart in other parts of the country. This is usually a large, formal theater, frequently with a picture-frame stage. Another category is resident professional theater. Such a theater is generally smaller than a Broadway-type space and is a not-for-profit operation. Resident professional theaters are found in cities throughout the United States and Canada. A third category consists of small theaters—usually under 250 seats—as well as theaters created from other spaces such as lofts, warehouses, and former churches. Still another group of theaters can be found on the campuses of colleges and universities. Intended for the productions of theater and drama departments, they range from small to somewhat larger theaters, and from formal arrangements to experimental spaces. Along with those listed above are stages reserved for children's theater or theater for youth, focusing on productions for and about young people.

Audiences Today: Multicultural and Diverse. Along with the variety of spaces and audiences described above, there is a further factor that has affected the makeup of contemporary audiences. As discussed in Part One, increasingly, people in the United States are becoming aware of the multiracial and multicultural aspects of our society. In the late nineteenth century and the early twentieth century, the United States was known as a "melting pot," a term implying that the aim of many foreign-born people who came here was to become assimilated and integrated into the prevailing white, male, European culture. (Women during this era had to fight for very basic rights, such as voting.) In recent decades, however, many people in our society have come to believe that such a homogeneous culture has many biases; as a result, they urge us to recognize, maintain, and celebrate our differences. This trend toward diversity has been reflected in theater; many organizations have emerged that present productions by and for groups with special interests. They represent a number of political, ethnic, gender, sexual-orientation, and racial entities. These theater groups, which will be discussed in detail in Chapters 18 and 19, include the following:

African American

Asian American

Latino and Latina

Native American (American Indian)

Feminist

Gay and lesbian

In brief, the role of the audience is crucial to a theater event, because of the importance of the performer-audience relationship. The audience completes a sort of electrical circuit that provides the immediacy and excitement of the live theater performance. In addition, the makeup of the audience is a key factor, and one that audience members themselves should be aware of. When you are attending a performance the following are questions for you, as an individual audience member, to consider. Is the audience a homogeneous group—similar in background and attitude—or a diverse one? Do you, as a member of the audience, relate to other audience members or not? Is the event being presented primarily by and for a particular group—cultural, social, gender, or political? If so, are you a member of the group, or outside it? During the performance, is the audience involved in the production or not? If it is a serious event, is the audience concentrating and empathizing? If the event is comic, is the audience caught up in the amusement and laughter?

THE THEATER CRITIC

A person who can be considered a special type of audience member is the critic. A simple definition of a *critic* is someone who observes theater and then analyzes and comments on it. In a sense the critic stands between the theater event and the audience, serving in ideal circumstances as a knowledgeable and highly sensitive audience member. At the same time, most theatergoers are amateur critics. When a person says about a performance, "It started off great, but it fizzled," or "The star was terrific, just like someone in real life," or "The woman was OK, but the man overacted," he or she is making a critical judgment. The difference between a critic and an ordinary spectator is that the critic presumably is better informed about the event and has developed a set of standards by which to judge it.

The reason audiences can learn from critics is not only that critics impart information and judgments but also, as suggested above, that the critic shares with audience members the point of view of the spectator. Unlike those who create theater—writers, performers, designers—critics sit out front and watch a performance just as other members of the audience do. By understanding how the critic goes about his or her task, audience members can increase their knowledge of how theater works and make their own theater experiences more meaningful.

What Is Criticism?

The popular image of the theater critic is a caustic writer who makes sharp, rapier-like thrusts at performers and playwrights. Some epithets of critics have become legendary. John Mason Brown (1900–1969) described an actress's performance in a production of Shakespeare's *Antony and Cleopatra* by saying, "Tallulah Bankhead barged down the Nile last night as Cleopatra and sank." When Katharine Hepburn (1907–2003), who was a stage actress before she went into films, appeared in the play *The Lake,* the critic Dorothy Parker (1893–1967) wrote that Hepburn "runs the gamut of emotions from A to B." Before he became a playwright, George Bernard Shaw was a critic, and he had harsh things to say about a number of people, including Shakespeare: "With the single exception of Homer, there is no eminent writer, not even Sir Walter Scott, whom I can despise so entirely as I despise Shakespeare when I measure my mind against his."

But criticism is much more than this sort of thing. The word *criticize* has at least two meanings. Perhaps the most familiar meaning is "to find fault," and that is what we see in the comments above. But *criticize* also means "to understand and appraise," and this meaning is much more important for a theater critic.

Critics and Reviewers

In theater, a distinction is often made between the critic and the reviewer. A *reviewer* usually works for a newspaper, a magazine, or a television station and reports on what has occurred at a theater event. He or she will explain briefly what the theater event is about, describing its plot and stating whether it is a musical, a comedy, or a serious play. The reviewer will generally add an opinion on whether or not the event was done well and is worth seeing. In most instances, the reviewer is restricted by time or space. A reviewer on a television news program, for instance, will have only a minute or two on the air to describe a play and offer a reaction. A newspaper reviewer, similarly, is restricted by space and by the need to submit his or her article quickly to meet a deadline.

Many reviewers have limited experience and training in their specialty. They may have taken college courses in theater and the other arts, but frequently they come from other positions in television or print journalism, such as general or investigative reporting. Once they are assigned to theater, however, conscientious reviewers should make it their job to become as knowledgeable as possible. This type of review is important to the general audience, which turns to reviewers for information about arts events and guidance in deciding whether or not to attend, especially when an event is expensive.

In contrast to a reviewer, a *critic* goes into greater detail in describing and analyzing theater events, and has the time and space to do so. Critics generally publish their analyses in magazines and scholarly journals. At times they go beyond articles and essays to write books about playwrights, plays, or theatrical movements. Critics also attempt to put a playwright or a group of plays into the larger context of theater history and into the broad framework of the arts and society.

Ideally, a critic should have a thorough grounding in the history of theater, in the elements that make up theater, and in the nature of acting and production. He or she should be able to analyze a script for structure and meaning, should understand various styles of acting, and should be aware of the visual aesthetics of theater. The critic should then use this knowledge to discuss—both for audiences and for the theater community—just what is right and wrong about a production.

Mel Gussow: Critic

Mel Gussow was a critic and theater writer for the New York Times *and a recipient of the George Jean Nathan Award in dramatic criticism. He published books on his interviews with the playwrights Samuel Beckett, Harold Pinter, and Tom Stoppard. In the spring of 2000, he received numerous awards for his book* Edward Albee: A Singular Journey. *Mel Gussow died in 2005.*

I have been with the *New York Times* serving as theater critic and writer about theater since 1969, but my interest in theater began when I was still in school. It came into particular focus while I was undertaking graduate studies.

While studying at Columbia University's Graduate School of Journalism, I spent my evenings in the theater. It was the 1955–1956 season, an astonishingly diverse year, with *My Fair Lady, A View from the Bridge, The Diary of Anne Frank, The Most Happy Fella,* Jason Robards in *The Iceman Cometh,* Orson Welles in *King Lear* (he was in a wheelchair at the performance I attended), and, most important of all, the Broadway premiere of *Waiting for Godot.*

I saw everything on Broadway and many plays off-Broadway, which had become a burgeoning theatrical movement, led by the New York Shakespeare Festival, the Phoenix Theater, and David Ross's productions of Chekhov. More than anything else, that season encouraged my enthusiasm for theater—for the idea of becoming a drama critic. Earlier, at Middlebury College, I had reviewed plays for the student newspaper and had taken courses in playwriting, theater history, and Shakespeare. But that year was at the core of my theatrical education.

My professional critical life did not actually begin until the early 1960s at *Newsweek* magazine, where I wrote feature stories about the arts, movie reviews, and occasional reviews of off-Broadway shows. When T. H. Wenning, the magazine's distinguished theater critic, suddenly became ill and incapacitated soon after the Broadway opening of Edward Albee's *Who's Afraid of Virginia Woolf?* I acted as that magazine's critic. I began my regular theater reviewing at the top, with the Albee play, and then during the rest of the season covered plays and musicals across the board, from Harold Pinter one-acts to *Beyond the Fringe.* Since this was the time before bylines in news magazines, few people knew that I was a critic. But I knew I was a critic.

Generally speaking, the critic's audience is more specialized and demanding than the reviewer's audience. The critic's readers or viewers have a right to expect informed judgments and helpful background information.

Preparing for Criticism

How do critics and reviewers prepare for their work? We said above that, ideally, a critic should have a complete and thorough knowledge of all aspects of theater. A reviewer's knowledge is not expected to be as extensive as that of a critic, but it should be as comprehensive as possible.

Reviewers or critics have individual preferences with regard to reading a play before seeing a performance. Because acting and directorial interpretation are crucial in a theater experience, some prefer to see a performance without specific preparation. Others, especially when they are seeing a classic such as a Shakespearean play, prefer to refresh their memory of the text by reading the play beforehand.

Criteria for Criticism

It has been suggested that there are three questions the critic should ask in assessing a theater event: (Incidentally, these are also questions audience members can ask.)

1. What is the playwright or production attempting to do?
2. How well has it been done?
3. Is it worth doing?

In looking at these three questions, it must be remembered that in theater both the play and the production are under consideration. Critics, therefore, must make it clear whether they are assessing a script, a production, or both.

Question 1: What Is Being Attempted?   In answering the first question, the critic must explain exactly what is being attempted, both by the playwright and by the director. Sometimes this is clear—in a comedy or farce, for example—but sometimes it is not.

A playwright, for instance, may be attempting to use satire to criticize excessive behavior, but this might not be obvious from what the audience sees onstage. Perhaps a playwright is parodying the work of another writer—that is, deliberately imitating and making fun of the other writer. If the audience understands this, it will make the play clearer.

Regarding the work of the director, the critic again must determine what is being attempted. Is the director trying to present a play exactly as the playwright intended, or is he or she trying something different? An *auteur director* (discussed in Chapter 8) usually attempts to present his or her own version of a dramatic work, not necessarily that of the playwright. The critic should make this clear to the reader, to help audiences understand what is happening onstage.

Question 2: How Well Has the Attempt Succeeded?   In answering the second question, the critic makes a personal evaluation. How well has the playwright realized his or her goals, and how well have the performers and the director brought the play to life? Generally a reviewer or critic makes personal evaluations in arriving at a conclusion and does not take into account the reactions of the audience. At times, however, the reviewer might comment on the response of the audience, especially if audience members reacted favorably to a play that the reviewer did not regard as well written or well acted.

Question 3: Was the Attempt Worth Making?   In answering the third question, the critic evaluates the overall undertaking. Is this kind of play or production valid? Does it fulfill a legitimate purpose? Is it meaningful or significant? Is the play or production itself a worthwhile undertaking?

A critic should clearly state the context in which he or she is making this value judgment. It may be in terms of other plays in the same historical period; it may be in terms of great plays from all periods; it may be in terms of plays of the same genre, such as tragedies, comedies, or melodramas; or it may be in terms of the arts generally, setting this work in the context of other performing arts and

Making Connections

Different Critics, Different Views

Nathan Lane and Matthew Broderick in The Odd Couple. (© Sara Krulwich/The New York Times)

It is important for playgoers to remember that critics often have divergent views about the same production. An example is found in two quite different judgments of a revival of Neil Simon's *The Odd Couple.* This play, first produced on Broadway in 1965 and later successful as a film and a television series, deals with two apartment mates who are totally different. Felix is fastidious and Oscar is sloppy and always unkempt. In short, they are about as dissimilar as two people can be, and their dissimilarity is the source of much of the comedy. A revival on Broadway in 2005 starred Nathan Lane and Matthew Broderick, two actors who had paired well in the musical of *The Producers.* As seen in the two commentaries below, Clive Barnes, writing in the *New York Post,* gave the production a rave review, praising the play and the actors very highly. Michael Feingold of the *Village Voice,* on the other hand, had many reservations about both the play and the performances. Feingold questioned how these two actors ever got together, and he questioned some of the acting, especially that of Broderick.

Clive Barnes, *New York Post*

Steal tickets if you can—the chemistry's still there. Burdened by nearly impossible expectations, Nathan Lane and Matthew Broderick proved the right couple for Neil Simon's "The Odd Couple," which opened last night at the Brooks Atkinson Theatre. Wearing the albatrosses around their necks as jauntily as neckties, Broadway's highest-paid double act performed impeccably in roles that bear the burden of theatrical legend. What with Art Carney and Walter Matthau in the original 1965 stage production; Jack Lemmon and Matthau in the 1968 movie; Tony Randall and Jack Klugman, long on television, then (briefly) on stage—Simon's yin-and-yang pairing of neatnik with slobnik is rich with glory. When the impossibly prissy Felix Ungar (Broderick) is thrown out by his wife and comes to live with his best buddy, a divorced sportswriter, Oscar Madison (Lane), it's soon apparent that here is a twain that can never meet. It's going to be a bumpy journey—and a hilarious play.

Simon has been called, often disparagingly, the king of the one-liners, but here, as when Oscar describes Felix as a man "who wears a seat-belt at a drive-in movie," they add something to the character and action. The play's construction is as calculated as archicture. From its smoky beginning at Oscar's apartment to the intervention of the crazy Pigeon sisters living upstairs and on to the climactic poker party, Simon doesn't put a building brick wrong.

Director Joe Mantello (Mike Nichols did the honors back in '65) is attentive to the play's every twist and nuance. He acutely accents the possibilities for visual humor, deftly caught by John Lee Beatty's period-perfect settings and the costumes by Ann Roth. The casting is superb (at these prices, it should be) and the visuals, delicious. Not only are Broderick and Lane highly physical performers—throw them a ball and they'll trip with it—but Mantello wrests humor from the sheer contrast in height between Lane and the towering Brad Garrett (making his Broadway debut, after TV's "Everybody Loves Raymond," as Murray the cop) and the avian movements of the chirping Pigeon sisters.

Along with the admirably deliberate Garrett, Oscar's poker buddies include the seasoned and fussy Lee Wilkof, a continuously but nicely harassed Rob Bartlett and a properly distressed Peter Frechette. As that very British brace of Pigeons, Gwendolyn (Olivia d'Arbo) and Cecily (Jessica Stone) exude a nice blend of scattiness, sexiness and sweetness. Of course, it's Oscar and Felix audiences have come to see, and they will not be disappointed. Lane, with his rolypoly body, Gothic-arched eyebrows and gravelly voice that travels the five boroughs, makes a perfect Oscar—explosively short-fused, quietly sentimental, with the manners and body language of a lovable lout. As in "The Producers," but with a quite different dynamic, Broderick's wimpily hypochondriac and terminally prim Felix makes the perfect foil: a Laurel to Lane's Hardy.

Hardy laurels all round.

Michael Feingold, *Village Voice*
Unlike the bulk of Neil Simon's work, *The Odd Couple* is very nearly a play for about two-thirds of its length. It has characters who are, with one exception, close to three-dimensional human existence; it has a believable situation from which understandable conflicts arise; and only a small percentage of its dialogue sounds as if the characters kept a resident gag writer on the premises. Later Simon plays would pursue all of *The Odd Couple*'s weaknesses, instead of its strengths, with dismaying success, and they would lack, to boot, the mythic image at its core which is the real secret of this comedy's strength: two hopelessly incompatible people who are, nonetheless, friends for life and inextricably bound together. Messy, heedless Oscar and fastidious, overcautious Felix are an iconic pair, classic enough in their mismatch to rank with the great comic teams. The only hard part is figuring out how they got to be friends: . . . Fifteen minutes of Felix's obsessive-compulsive fussing with clean ashtrays and room deodorizer could permanently destroy any poker party, and it's hard to imagine his even being willing to sit down in the chaos of debris and dirty laundry that Oscar's apartment has become after six wifeless months.

Joe Mantello's heavily anticipated (and already sold out) new production shows both *The Odd Couple*'s strengths and its weaknesses. Salted with plot twists that still twist and jokes that still tickle, the comedy wends its way through enough laughs to make a pleasant evening, and Nathan Lane, while giving Oscar dimension and pathos, mines quite a few more. Lee Wilkof and Peter Frechette, unsurprisingly, give him effective help as two of his four cronies. (Wilkof's slouch as he reluctantly crosses to answer the door is the evening's best sight gag.) Matthew Broderick, conversely, is almost too perfectly cast as Felix: Playing to the character's inhibitions, he creates a figure who's beyond odd—far too weird to be imaginable at this poker party. This tends to loosen the play's grounding in humanity and pull it toward the more fantastical kind of vaudeville sketch comedy, in which the characters' distance from reality is underscored. Along with some supporting performances that lack the depth provided by Wilkof and Frechette, the eerie figure that Broderick cuts thins the play's overall effect, moving it away from its roots in human nature and towards its flickering end in TV sitcom. Art Carney, creating the role in 1965, was of course escaping not only from the two-dimensional world of sitcom but from a loutish role (Norton on *The Honeymooners*) far closer to Oscar than to Felix; the audience that came in with TV expectations had the extra pleasure of watching him invent a character wholly unlike what they "knew" him to be. It's Broderick's ill luck to have played fussy and repressed roles before, but the repertory company that would allow him to break out of his familiar persona and play Oscar instead hasn't yet been created, and isn't likely to turn up on Broadway any decade soon.

even the visual arts. The important thing is not simply to evaluate but also to explain the basis for judgment.

Theater encompasses a broad range of activities, from low farce to high tragedy, and so value is not merely a question of depth or profundity but often a question of comparing the goal with the achievement. If the purpose of a play is clearly understood to be entertainment, for example, then the question becomes how well this intention is carried out in the production. On the other hand, a play can be pretentious, claiming to have depth when it actually does not, and a critic should point that out.

It is important to remember, with regard to evaluative criticism, that reactions to theater—as to all art—are highly subjective. In theater, unlike geometry or physics, there is no right or wrong answer. Nor are there absolutes in theater, like the mathematical fact that 8 times 9 equals 72. Sincere, intelligent people often disagree on whether or not a play is profound, moving, or skillfully written. There are principles of dramatic structure, as we will discover in Chapter 6, and there are aesthetic criteria that we can apply to scenery and costumes. However, the ultimate test is whether or not one is affected by a performance, and whether one thinks a play is exceptional or merely routine—and this is up to the individual spectator.

At the same time, there is no doubt that critics can be helpful in answering such questions. Critics can provide valuable information and incisive opinions that help us arrive at our own independent judgment. Perhaps one way to view critics is to say that while we should not slavishly follow their ideas, we should at the same time learn from them everything we can.

Descriptive versus Prescriptive Criticism

Historically critics have generally taken one of two different approaches. The first approach, which can be called *descriptive criticism,* is an attempt to describe as clearly and accurately as possible what is happening in a performance. The second approach can be called *prescriptive criticism,* meaning that the critic not only describes what has been done but offers advice and sometimes even insists on what should be done.

Two theater critics from ancient times established these different approaches. In the fourth century B.C.E., the Greek philosopher Aristotle undertook to analyze the tragedies of playwrights like Aeschylus, Sophocles, and Euripides. Aristotle was also a scientist, and his method was chiefly to describe tragedy: to break it down into its component parts and to note how it worked and what effect it had on spectators.

On the other hand, in the first century B.C.E. the Roman writer Horace attempted not just to describe theater but to prescribe what it should be. In other words, he wanted to establish rules. He said, for example, that tragedy and comedy should never be mixed in the same play and that dramatic poetry should instruct as well as please the audience.

Since the time of Aristotle and Horace, critics have tended to fall into one category or the other: either analyzing and describing, or setting down rules. The prescriptive approach, it should be noted, entails the danger of becoming overly rigid and moralistic in judging what theater should be, and of excluding drama that audiences find both meaningful and pleasurable.

Having looked at the audience and the critic, we turn next, in Chapter 5, to the people who bring a play to life—the performers.

SUMMARY

The presence of an audience is an essential element in a live theater performance. Just as no two performances of the same production are ever exactly alike, no two audiences are identical. Each audience is composed of a different mix of people, with varied ages, educational backgrounds, and occupations. Among the diverse groups toward which productions are aimed and whose members constitute specific audience groups are African Americans, Asian Americans, Latinos and Latinas, Native Americans, feminists, gays and lesbians, and other political and experimental groups. Also, the particular response of each audience affects the acting of the performers.

A special member of the audience is the critic or reviewer, who is assumed to be a knowledgeable observer of the theater event. A reviewer is usually a reporter for a newspaper, magazine, or television station. After viewing a theater event, the reviewer describes it and gives his or her own opinion as to whether it was well done and is worth seeing.

A critic, usually writing for a magazine or scholarly journal, describes and analyzes a theater event in greater detail than the reviewer does. The critic should have a solid education in theater history, dramatic literature, and theatrical production so that he or she can offer readers an informed judgment along with useful background information.

Theater criticism may be either descriptive, explaining what actually happens onstage; or prescriptive, offering advice and prescribing what should take place.

KEY TERMS

Aesthetic distance Physical or psychological separation or detachment of audience from dramatic action, usually considered necessary for artistic illusion.

Auteur director A director who believes that his or her role is to be the author of a production. An auteur director's point of view dominates that of the playwright, and the director may make textual changes and modifications.

Descriptive criticism Criticism that attempts to describe as clearly and accurately as possible what is happening in a performance.

Prescriptive criticism Criticism that offers advice and sometimes suggests rules for what should be done in theater.

THEATER ON THE WEB

For more research and to learn more about the topics in this chapter, please visit the Online Learning Center at **www.mhhe.com/livelyart6**.

Acting for the Stage

◀ **THE ART OF ACTING**

Acting is a demanding profession, requiring extensive training in vocal work, physical movement, character development, and many other skills. Along with the craft are certain indefinable qualities such as being able to connect with the audience and project the personality and complexity of the character being portrayed. Seen here are Tom Nelis as Oberon and Christina Rouner as Titania in A Midsummer Night's Dream, *by William Shakespeare, directed by Kim Rubinstein at the Long Wharf Theatre. The set and costume designs were by G. W. Mercier, and the lighting design was by Joel Moritz.*
(© T. Charles Erickson)

63

The two most essential elements in a theatrical event are the audience and the performers. Having looked at the audience in Chapter 4, we turn in this chapter to the other part of the actor-audience relationship—the performers. Acting is almost as old as the human race. From the earliest days of civilization, people have mimicked other people and have told stories, imitating the voices and gestures of the characters in those stories. There have also been rituals and ceremonies in which the celebrants wore costumes and performed assigned roles—one example is a priest in a church service.

Today, in schools, on street corners, and at parties we often see people performing or imitating others in some way. When telling a story, a person often adopts the voices and attitudes of the characters; some people seem to be particularly adept at doing this and are referred to as "natural" actors or actresses. The desire to imitate others, or to take on the personality of an imaginary character, seems irresistible; and the pleasure we take in watching others do this is universal. In this process of enactment and impersonation is the origin of stage acting. A closely connected type of "acting" in daily life is role-playing. The current term *role model* refers to a person whose life, or "role," serves as a model or guide for others to emulate or imitate.

In theater, this practice of imitation becomes conscious and deliberate. *Acting* can be defined as assuming a role onstage; to put it another way, acting is impersonating a character in a dramatic presentation before an audience. Actors and actresses develop their craft and then carefully rehearse a play in order to bring the text to life. In the process, they speak words and perform actions that give flesh and blood to the characters on the page.

A HISTORICAL PERSPECTIVE: DEMANDS OF CLASSICAL ACTING

Before the twentieth century, the challenges facing performers were dictated by the very specific demands of the type of theater in which performers appeared. Both classic Greek theater and traditional Asian theater stressed formal movement and stylized gestures similar to classical ballet. The chorus in Greek drama both sang and danced its odes, and Asian theater has always had a significant component of singing and dancing. In addition, Greek performers wore masks and Asian performers often wore richly textured makeup.

In western theater, from the time of the Renaissance through the nineteenth century, actions onstage were not intended to replicate the movements or gestures of everyday life. For example, performers would often speak not to the character they were addressing but directly to the audience.

In England during the eighteenth and nineteenth centuries, acting alternated between exaggerated and more natural styles. Throughout this period, every generation or so an actor or actress would emerge who was praised for performing in a less grandiose, more down-to-earth way. But exaggerated or not, performance before the twentieth century was more formal and stylized than the acting we are accustomed to onstage, and especially in films and on television.

No one would expect an actress or actor today to perform a classical play in the manner in which it was originally presented; such a performance would seem ludicrous. Besides, we do not know exactly how classical acting looked or sounded. At the same time, it should be clear that any performer today who is appearing in a play from the past must develop a special set of skills and be able to respond successfully to a number of challenges.

As an example, let us consider an actor undertaking the role of Hamlet. He must convince the audience that he is experiencing numerous and often contradictory emotions: that he is aware of lies and treachery taking place around him; that he is saddened by the recent death of his father and the hasty marriage of his mother to his uncle; that he believes his uncle has murdered his father; that he wants to murder his uncle but cannot bring himself to do so; that he berates himself for not being more decisive; that he loves Ophelia but is repelled by the web of circumstances in which he is caught and of which she is an unwitting part.

For an actor, one aspect of conveying these emotions lies in developing the inner feelings that Hamlet has from moment to moment. How does it feel to have such conflicting emotions about your mother or about your duty? An actor playing Hamlet must answer such questions; he must understand in his own innermost depths what Hamlet's emotions are like and then communicate them to the audience.

At the same time, the actor must have a sense of the physical and vocal qualities that a man like Hamlet would have. How would Hamlet walk? How would he handle a sword? How would he greet a friend like Horatio? What movements and gestures would he use? How would he speak? What vocal range and speech patterns would he use?

Along with these personal characteristics, moreover, the actor playing Hamlet must be able to speak Shakespeare's lines distinctly and intelligently. This is particularly true of Hamlet's soliloquies—the speeches he delivers while alone onstage. Because much of the language of Shakespeare's plays is poetry, and because there are many extended phrases that must be spoken without interruption, the speeches call for tremendous breath control. To achieve beauty of sound, the performer must, in addition, have a resonant voice; and to achieve clarity, he must have an accurate understanding of the words.

In portraying Hamlet, an actor must also have athletic ability and control of his body. If the stage setting has ramps and platforms, he must be able to navigate them with ease; and since he must engage in a sword fight with Laertes in a scene near the end of the play, he must have mastered many of the techniques of fencing.

Similarly, an actress playing Ophelia must have a wide range of accomplishments. She must be able to portray the interior emotions of the character convincingly, speak clearly and intelligently, move with poise and authority, and interact with the other performers. In addition, the role calls for the actress to sing and to play a scene in which she must convince us that Ophelia has lost her sanity, although of course the actress herself is perfectly sane.

We should note that in addition to roles like Ophelia or Juliet in Shakespeare, an actress—like an actor—might be called on to perform many different kinds of roles, using a variety of techniques and approaches. For instance, she will

DEMANDS OF CLASSICAL ACTING
Classical acting—that is, acting in traditional or classical plays from the past—makes a number of demands on the performer. It calls for expert control of the body, for such activities as fencing, and for excellent vocal control in order to speak verse eloquently and project the voice. It also calls for an intelligent understanding of the text and the character, as well as a grasp of history. Seen here is David Oyelowo playing the title role in a production of Henry VI *by the Royal Shakespeare Company in England. (Manuel Harlan/© The Governors of the Royal Shakespeare Company)*

probably be called on to play characters in modern realistic plays: Nina in Chekhov's *The Sea Gull,* for example, or Laura in Tennessee Williams's *The Glass Menagerie,* or the young woman leaving prison in Marsha Norman's *Getting Out.* She will also be asked to undertake roles in the classics: female characters in Shakespeare, Antigone or Electra in Sophocles, or one of the ingenues in a play by Molière. If she wants to appear in musical theater, she will have to master singing and dancing as well as acting. And there are also experimental and avant-garde theater events, which often call for special skills such as mime and acrobatics.

THREE CHALLENGES OF ACTING

Throughout theater history it can be said that three main challenges have faced an actor or actress:

1. To acquire the many skills—both physical and vocal—that stage performances demand; in other words, to master the craft of acting
2. To make characters believable
3. To integrate these two, that is, to combine skills with credibility

To understand the first two aspects of acting, we will examine them separately. We begin with the craft of acting—specific techniques required in performance—and then turn to the believability of characters.

James Earl Jones: Performer

James Earl Jones is one of the most prominent American actors of the last half century. He has played leading roles year after year onstage and in films, appearing in productions from the play The Great White Hope *to the film series* Star Wars.

My whole career, starting off-off-Broadway in the late 1950s, has grown in small, incremental steps. I can remember the summer of 1960, when I did my first work for the New York Shakespeare Festival. Alan Schneider was going to direct *Measure for Measure* in the park, and when I went backstage after seeing another play he had directed, I approached him and said, "Mr. Schneider, I'm an actor, and in reading the plays you'll be directing this summer for Joe Papp, I noticed there's a character called Abhorson in *Measure for Measure.* It appears that he wears a mask. It shouldn't matter whether he's Caucasian, African, or Asian skin color. I want to play that character." He said, "OK, OK"—without reading me. One doesn't think of Alan Schneider being intimidated at all, but he later told me, "You were pretty large. I saw you, and you meant it." . . .

I also had the chance to do a Shakespeare Festival play with Mitchell Ryan. Mitchell was going to play Leontes, the king in The

Winter's Tale, and I could play his majordomo, Camillo. It was not a great role, but it meant working with Mitchell and playing a mature, responsible, stable, human Shakespearean character. In the back of my mind, I was working towards a shot at playing Othello someday. . . . The next season, I was asked to play Othello to Mitchell Ryan's Iago. That casting, I think, is the best choice ever made, in terms of an American production of the play—to have Othello and Iago the same age, the same size, the same temperament, the same zodiac sign even. . . .

Those were wonderful years off-Broadway. The spring after I played my first roles at the Shakespeare Festival, I was in the United States premiere of Jean Genet's *The Blacks,* which ran for several seasons. That company included many of the African American actors you know of now—Roscoe Lee Browne, Cicely Tyson, Godfrey Cambridge, Louis Gossett. . . .

My father gave me a sense of the reality of the business. . . . I geared my standard of living to the real income. I didn't live in plush or drive plush. In my early days, the best domicile I had was a cold-water flat in that hub between Little Italy and Chinatown. It cost nineteen dollars a

month. . . . I did not raise my standard of living until *The Great White Hope* in 1968. . . . Not-for-profit theater is like subsistence farming. You're not there to make a killing. You're there hopefully to have a good, a fruitful, a productive season. . . .

Coming right off the service in the American Theatre Wing, I knew physical training. At the Wing it was called body movement . . . and we did a lot of fencing. That training continued through all the years at the Shakespeare Festival. . . . My voice is both a gift and something I worked for. The genetic gift was a vocal timbre that has to do with resonating cavities, size of body, and so on, and I inherited that from my father, who is six feet four. . . . I've concluded, by the way, that speech is not natural to human beings. Sound is, music perhaps . . . but speech is an intellectual exercise that's acquired. I had no trouble speaking *Fences* because August Wilson is a great poet. I'm from the south, and he was writing his characters from the south, so a lot of things fell right into place.

Source: *Actors' Lives: On and Off the American Stage* by Holly Hill, copyright 1993 by Holly Hill. By permission of Theatre Communications Group.

Mastering the Craft of Acting

Many techniques of acting are the equivalent of technical skills required in the other performing arts, such as learning the movements of ballet and developing the physical agility to carry them out, or mastering a musical instrument and learning to play it successfully in public.

The Performer's Body.   Traditional theater makes strong demands on the performer's body. In Shakespeare, for instance, performers must frequently run up and down steps or ramps, confront other characters in sword fights, and enact prolonged death scenes. Anyone who has seen an impressive sword fight onstage senses how difficult it must be. A duel, in which the combatants strike quickly at one another—clashing swords continually without hitting each other—resembles a ballet in its precision and grace, and it entails a great deal of physical exertion.

Adept physical movement is also required in modern realistic acting. For example, an activity in a modern play analogous to a sword fight would be a headlong fall down a flight of stairs or two people engaged in a knife fight, like the one in Arthur Miller's *A View from the Bridge*.

PHYSICAL DEMANDS OF PERFORMING
Acting requires physical as well as emotional and vocal resources. This is especially true in performing the classics, which require physical agility and extensive vocal ability; and in performing musicals, which call for dancing, singing, and other special skills. Here we see two experts practicing hand-to-hand combat. On the left is the fight teacher Corinna May, and on the right is the fight master Tony Simotes of Shakespeare and Company. (© Richard Feldman/Shakespeare and Company, Lenox, Massachusetts)

Warm-Up Exercises for Body and Voice

To give an indication of the types of exercises performers must undertake during their years of training—and during their careers as professionals—it is interesting to look at some samples of warm-up exercises. The exercises here are designed to relax the body and the voice.

The following are typical warm-up exercises for body movement:

1. Lie on your back; beginning with the feet, tense and relax each part of the body—knees, thighs, abdomen, chest, neck—moving up to the face. Note the difference in the relaxation of various muscles and of the body generally after the exercise is completed.

2. Stand with feet parallel, approximately as far apart as the width of the shoulders. Lift one foot off the ground and loosen all the joints in the foot, ankle, and knee. Repeat with the other foot off the ground. Put the feet down and move to the hip, spine, arms, neck, etc., loosening all joints.

3. Stand with feet parallel. Allow all tension to drain out of the body through the feet. In the process, bend the knees, straighten the pelvis, and release the lower back.

4. Begin walking in a circle; walk on the outside of the feet, then on the inside, then on the toes, and then on the heels. Notice what this does to the rest of the body. Try changing other parts of the body in a similar fashion and observe the effect on feelings and reactions.

5. Imagine the body filled with either helium or lead. Notice the effect of each of these sensations, both while standing in place and while walking. Do the same with one body part at a time—each arm, each leg, the head, etc.

The following *vocal exercises* free the throat and vocal cords:

1. Standing, begin a lazy, unhurried stretch. Reach with your arms to the ceiling, meanwhile lengthening and widening the whole of your back. Yawn as you take in a deep breath and hum on an exhalation. Release your torso so that it rests down toward your legs. Yawn on another deep breath and hum on an exhalation. On an inhalation, roll up the spine until you are standing with your arms at your sides. Look at something on the ceiling and then at something on the floor; then let your head return to a balance point, so that the neck and shoulder muscles are relaxed.

2. Put your hands on your ribs, take a deep breath, and hum a short tune. Repeat several times. Hum an *m* or *n* up and down the scale. Drop your arms; lift the shoulders an inch and drop them, releasing all tension.

3. Take a deep breath and with the palm of your hand push gently down on your stomach as you exhale. Do this several times. Exhale on sighs and then on vowels.

The Performer's Voice.   Another key requirement for performers is to make certain that the lines they speak are heard clearly by the audience. To be heard throughout a theater seating a thousand people, a performer must *project*—throw his or her voice into the audience so that it penetrates to the uttermost reaches of the theater. In modern realistic plays this task is made more difficult by the necessity of maintaining believability. For example, in real life the words of a man and a woman involved in a love scene would be barely audible even to people only a few feet away; in a theater, however, every word of such a scene must be heard by the entire audience. A performer needs to strike a balance, therefore, between credibility and the necessity of being heard.

In western theater before the modern period, from the fifth century B.C.E. in Greece to the middle of the nineteenth century, vocal demands on actors and actresses were even greater than they are today. The language of plays was most often poetry; and poetry—with its demanding rhythms, sustained phrases, and exacting meters—required intensive training in order for the performer to speak the lines intelligently and distinctly. There were problems of projection, too. A Greek amphitheater was an acoustical marvel, but it seated as many as 15,000 spectators in the open air, and throwing the voice to every part of the theater was no small task.

In Elizabethan England, Christopher Marlowe, a contemporary of Shakespeare, wrote superb blank verse that made severe demands on performers' vocal abilities. One example is found in Marlowe's *Doctor Faustus.* Here is a speech by Faustus to Helen of Troy, who has been called back from the dead to be with him:

> O' thou art fairer than the evening's air
>
> Clad in the beauty of a thousand stars;
>
> Brighter art thou than flaming Jupiter
>
> When he appear'd to hapless Semele;
>
> More lovely than the monarch of the sky
>
> In wanton Arethusa's azured arms;
>
> And none but thou shalt be my paramour!

These seven lines of verse are a single sentence and, spoken properly, will be delivered as one overall unit, with the meaning carried from one line to the next. How many of us could manage that? A fine classical actor can speak the entire passage as a whole, giving it the necessary resonance and inflection as well. Beyond that, he can stand onstage for 2 or 3 hours delivering such lines.

Today, because of microphones and sound amplification, we have increasingly lost our appreciation of the power of the human voice. But in the past, public speakers from Cicero to Abraham Lincoln stirred men and women with their oratory; and throughout its history, the stage has provided a natural platform for stirring speeches. Beginning with the Greeks and continuing through the Elizabethans, the French and Spanish theaters of the seventeenth century, and other European theaters at the close of the nineteenth century, playwrights wrote magnificent lines that performers, having honed their vocal skills to a fine point, delivered with zest. Any performer today who intends to act in a revival of a traditional play must learn to speak and project stage verse, which requires much the same kind of vocal power and breath control as opera.

In order to develop projection and balance it with credibility, a performer must train and rehearse extensively. For example, an actor or actress might use breathing exercises, controlling the breath from the diaphragm rather than the throat so that vocal reproduction will have power and can be sustained. Many of these exercises are similar to those used by opera singers. Also, head, neck, and shoulder exercises can be used to relax the muscles in those areas, thus freeing the throat for ease of projection.

Centering. As a part of body and voice training, many acting teachers emphasize *centering*. This is a way of pulling everything together and allowing the performer to eliminate any blocks that impede either the body or the voice. Centering involves locating the place—roughly in the middle of the torso—where all the lines of force of the body come together. It is the "point of convergence of the muscular, emotional and intellectual impulses within our bodies."[1] When performers are able to "center" themselves, they achieve a balance, a freedom, and a flexibility they could rarely find otherwise.

VOICE PROJECTION
Among the skills that actors and actresses must develop is using the voice to project it to the far reaches of an auditorium, to modulate it, to articulate poetry properly, and in some cases to master accents. Shown here is Jude Law playing the title character in Doctor Faustus *at the Young Vic Theatre in London. Marlowe's play makes both physical and vocal demands on the performer, with extended, intricate poetry that must be spoken clearly and forcefully. (© Donald Cooper/Photostage, England)*

All this should make it clear that to master the many techniques required to play a variety of roles and to be at ease onstage—moving and speaking with authority, purpose, and conviction—performers must undergo arduous training and be genuinely dedicated to their profession.

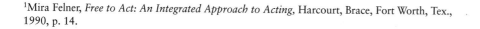

[1]Mira Felner, *Free to Act: An Integrated Approach to Acting,* Harcourt, Brace, Fort Worth, Tex., 1990, p. 14.

PORTRAYING A BELIEVABLE CHARACTER
Since the advent of realistic theater, at the end of the nineteenth century, a primary challenge for performers is making the characters they portray convincing and credible. Many techniques and exercises have been developed for this, but it also calls for total sincerity on the part of the performer. Shown here are Bill Irwin as George and Kathleen Turner as Martha in Edward Albee's Who's Afraid of Virginia Woolf? *(Sara Krulwich/The New York Times)*

Making Characters Believable

Along with developing the craft of acting, a performer's second major task is credibility. If the audience is to believe in the characters that appear onstage, performers must be convincing.

The Development of Realistic Acting. From the mid-seventeenth century on, serious attempts were made to define the craft or technique of credible, natural acting. Such an approach became more important than ever at the end of the nineteenth century, when drama began to depict characters and situations close to everyday life. Three playwrights—Henrik Ibsen of Norway, August Strindberg of Sweden, and Anton Chekhov of Russia—perfected a type of drama that came to be known as *realism*. This drama was called realistic because it closely resembled what people could identify with and verify from their own experience. In performing plays by these dramatists, not only the spirit of the individual dramatic characters but also the details of their behavior had to conform to what people saw of life around them. This placed great demands on actors and actresses to avoid any hint of fakery or superficiality.

The Stanislavski System: A Technique for Realistic Acting. Before the realistic drama of the late 1800s, individual actresses and actors, through their own talent and genius, had achieved believability onstage, but no one had developed a system whereby it could be taught to others and passed on to future generations. The person who eventually did this most successfully was the Russian actor and director Konstantin Stanislavski.

A cofounder of the Moscow Art Theater in Russia and the director of Anton Chekhov's most important plays, Stanislavski was also an actor. By closely observing the work of great performers of his day, and by drawing on his own acting experience, Stanislavski identified and described what these gifted performers did naturally and intuitively. From his observations he compiled and then codified a series of principles and techniques.

We might assume that believable acting is simply a matter of being natural; but Stanislavski discovered first of all that acting realistically onstage is extremely artificial and difficult. He wrote:

All of our acts, even the simplest, which are so familiar to us in everyday life, become strained when we appear behind the footlights before a public of a thousand people. That is why it is necessary to correct ourselves and learn again how to walk, sit, or lie down. It is essential to reeducate ourselves to look and see, on the stage, to listen and to hear.[2]

To achieve this "reeducation," Stanislavski said, "the actor must first of all believe in everything that takes place onstage, and most of all, he must believe what he himself is doing. And one can only believe in the truth." To give substance to his ideas, Stanislavski developed a series of exercises and techniques for the performer that had the following broad aims:

1. To make the outward behavior of the performer—gestures, voice, and rhythm of movements—natural and convincing.
2. To have the actor or actress convey the goals and objectives—the inner needs—of a character. Even if all the visible manifestations of a character are mastered, a performance will appear superficial and mechanical without a deep sense of conviction and belief.
3. To make the life of the character onstage not only dynamic but continuous. Some performers tend to emphasize only the high points of a part; in between, the life of the character stops. In real life, however, people do not stop living.
4. To develop a strong sense of ensemble playing with other performers in a scene.

Let us now look in some detail at Stanislavski's techniques.

Relaxation. When he observed the great actors and actresses of his day, Stanislavski noticed how fluid and lifelike their movements were. They seemed to be in a state of complete freedom and relaxation, letting the behavior of the character come through effortlessly. He concluded that unwanted tension has to be eliminated and that the performer must at all times attain a state of physical and vocal relaxation.

Concentration and observation. Stanislavski also discovered that gifted performers always appeared fully concentrated on some object, person, or event while onstage. Stanislavski referred to the extent or range of concentration as a *circle of attention.* This circle of attention can be compared to a circle of light on a darkened stage. The performer should begin with the idea that it is a small, tight circle including only himself or herself and perhaps one other person or one piece of furniture. When the performer has established a strong circle of attention, he or she can enlarge the circle outward to include the entire stage area. In this way performers will stop worrying about the audience and lose their self-consciousness.

---

[2]Constantin Stanislavski, *An Actor Prepares,* Theater Arts, New York, 1948, p. 73.

**THE IMPORTANCE OF SPECIFICS
IN CREATING A CHARACTER**

*One of the techniques for acting emphasized by
Stanislavski is concentrating on specific actions and
details. An example, in a performance of Shakespeare's*
Macbeth, *is having Lady Macbeth (Seana McKenna)
attempt to burn an incriminating document. The
production was at the Stratford Festival in Stratford,
Ontario. (Cylla von Tiedemann)*

Importance of specifics. One of Stanislavski's techniques was an emphasis on concrete details. A performer should never try to act in general, he said, and should never try to convey a feeling such as fear or love in some vague, amorphous way. In life, Stanislavski said, we express emotions in terms of specifics: an anxious woman twists a handkerchief, an angry boy throws a rock at a trash can, a nervous businessman jangles his keys. Performers must find similar concrete activities. Stanislavski points out how Shakespeare has Lady Macbeth in her sleepwalking scene—at the height of her guilt and emotional upheaval—try to rub blood off her hands.

The performer must also conceive of the situation in which a character exists—what Stanislavski referred to as the *given circumstances*—in terms of specifics. In what kind of space does an event take place: formal, informal, public, domestic? How does it feel? What is the temperature? The lighting? What has gone on just before? What is expected in the moments ahead? Again, these questions must be answered in concrete terms.

Inner truth. An innovative aspect of Stanislavski's work has to do with inner truth, which deals with the internal or subjective world of characters—that is, their thoughts and emotions. The early phases of Stanislavski's research took place while he was also directing the major dramas of Anton Chekhov. Plays like *The Sea Gull* and *The Cherry Orchard* have less to do with external action or what the characters say than with what the characters are feeling and thinking but often do not verbalize. It becomes apparent that Stanislavski's approach would be very beneficial in realizing the inner life of such characters.

Stanislavski had several ideas about how to achieve a sense of inner truth, one being the **magic if.** *If* is a word that can transform our thoughts; through it we can imagine ourselves in virtually any situation. "*If* I suddenly became wealthy . . ." "*If* I were vacationing on a Caribbean island . . ." "*If* I had great talent . . ." "*If* that person who insulted me comes near me again . . ." The word *if* becomes a powerful lever for the mind; it can lift us out of ourselves and give us a sense of absolute certainty about imaginary circumstances.

Action onstage: What? Why? How? Another important principle of Stanislavski's system is that all action onstage must have a purpose. This means that

ENSEMBLE PLAYING

Experienced performers are aware of the importance of playing together: listening carefully to one another, sensing each other's actions and moods, and responding alertly. Ensemble playing is especially important in plays where interaction between characters is a crucial ingredient. In the scene here, from the play Twelve Angry Men, *we see a number of characters interacting in a jury room.* (Sara Krulwich/The New York Times)

the performer's attention must always be focused on a series of physical actions (also called *psychophysical actions*), linked together by the circumstances of the play. Stanislavski determined these actions by asking three essential questions: What? Why? How? An action is performed, such as opening a letter (the *what*). The letter is opened because someone has said that it contains extremely damaging information about the character (the *why*). The letter is opened anxiously, fearfully (the *how*), because of the calamitous effect it might have on the character.

Through line of a role. According to Stanislavski, in order to develop continuity in a part, the actor or actress should find the *superobjective* of a character. What is it, above all else, that the character wants during the course of the play? What is the character's driving force? If a goal can be established toward which the character strives, it will give the performer an overall objective. From this objective can be developed a *through line* that can be grasped, as a skier on a ski lift grabs a towline and is carried to the top. Another term for through line is *spine*.

To help develop the through line, Stanislavski urged performers to divide scenes into units (sometimes called *beats*). In each unit there is an objective, and the intermediate objectives running through a play lead ultimately to the overall objective.

Ensemble playing. Except in one-person shows, performers do not act alone; they interact with other people. Stanislavski was aware that many performers tend to "stop acting," or lose their concentration, when they are not the main characters in a scene or when someone else is talking. This tendency destroys the through line and causes the performer to move into and out of a role. That, in turn, weakens *ensemble playing*—the playing together of all the performers.

Stanislavski and Psychophysical Action.

Stanislavski began to develop his technique in the early twentieth century, and at first he emphasized the inner aspects of training: for example, various ways of getting in touch with the performer's unconscious. Beginning around 1917, however, he began to look more and more at purposeful action, or what he called *psychophysical action*. A student at one of his lectures that year took note of the change: "Whereas action previously had been taught as the expression of a previously-established 'emotional state,' it is now action itself which predominates and is the key to the psychological."[3] Rather than seeing emotions as leading to action, Stanislavski came to believe that it was the other way around: purposeful action undertaken to fulfill a character's goals was the most direct route to the emotions.

Modern Approaches to Realistic Acting.

In the second half of the twentieth century, there were three broad approaches to actors' training in the United States. Two of these derived from the methods of Stanislavski.

In the 1930s and 1940s a number of performers and directors in the United States became greatly interested in the ideas of Stanislavski. One of these, Lee Strasberg, a founder of the Actors Studio in New York City, focused on the inner aspects of Stanislavskian theory. Strasberg emphasized a technique called *emotional recall*, a tool intended to help performers achieve a sense of emotional truth onstage. It consists of remembering a past experience in the performer's life that is similar to one in a play. By recalling sensory impressions of an experience in the past (such as what a room looked like, and the temperature and any prevalent odors in the room), emotions associated with that experience are aroused and can be used as the basis of feelings called for in a role in a play.

Though the teachings of Strasberg and his followers were successful with certain performers, other acting teachers, such as Stella Adler (1902–1992), Sanford Meisner (1905–1997), and Uta Hagen (1919–2004), felt that Strasberg emphasized the inner aspects of acting to the exclusion of everything else. Following the lead of Stanislavski in his later approach with psychophysical action, they bal-

---

[3]Jean Benedetti, *Stanislavski,* Routledge, New York, 1988, p. 217.

REQUIREMENTS FOR SPECIAL FORMS OF THEATER

Musical theater like classical or avant-garde theater, makes its own demands. Musical performers often must be able to sing and dance, as well as to play convincing characters. In the production of Stephen Sondheim's Sweeney Todd *shown here, the director John Doyle asked his performers to play musical instruments as well as enact assigned roles.* (Sara Krulwich/The New York Times)

anced the emphasis on inner resources with the inclusion of given circumstances and purposeful action.

A third approach was really an update of older methods that stressed classical training. The idea was that the methods of American disciples of Stanislavski might work well for realistic drama, but not so well for the works of writers such as Shakespeare and Molière. Thus, institutions like the Juilliard School in New York City included a strong curriculum of classical training in vocal techniques and body movement, as well as special techniques such as fencing.

Ideally, given the diversity of today's theater, many feel that the best modern training for actors should be well-rounded and include aspects of various approaches.

Additional Training Techniques. An approach to actors' training, as well as to directing, that is gaining acceptance and wider use in our contemporary theater is known as "viewpoints" theory. Based on ideas from the avant-garde choreographer Merce Cunningham (1919–) and the experimental director Jerzy Grotowski, viewpoints theory was originally incorporated into performance training at the Experimental Theatre Wing of NYU/Tisch School of the Arts. It combines elements of dance and stage movement with concepts of time and space. Initially viewpoints theory had six components: space, time, shape, movement, story, and emotion. The director Anne Bogart (1951–), one of the chief proponents of this theory has further broken the element of time into four segments and space into

Making Connections

Acting

Edie Falco in 'Night, Mother.
(Sara Krulwich/The New York Times)

Edie Falco and James Gandolfini in The Sopranos. (Photofest)

Many performers have been successful in theater as well as film and television. They include such well-known actresses and actors as Meryl Streep, Al Pacino, Glenn Close,

Kevin Spacey, Sarah Jessica Parker, Matthew Broderick, and Calista Flockhart. Meryl Streep is an excellent example of a stage performer who has had a remarkable film and television career. Streep was trained at the Yale School of Drama and came to the attention of New York theater audiences for her work at Joseph Papp's off-Broadway Public Theater. Her film work includes memorable roles in *The Deer Hunter* (1978), *Kramer vs. Kramer* (1979), *Sophie's Choice* (1982), *Out of Africa* (1985), *Music of the Heart* (1999), *The Hours* (2002), *Adaptation* (2002), and *The Devil Wears Prada* (2006). Streep has received thirteen Oscar nominations for her film work and in 1978 won an Emmy award for her performance in the television miniseries *Holocaust*. In the summer of 2001, she performed again on stage in the Public Theatre's Central Park production of *The Seagull*. In 2006, she appeared in Central Park in *Mother Courage*. In 2003, she appeared in the critically acclaimed HBO television adaptation of *Angels in America,* directed by Mike Nichols, who has also worked in theater, film, and TV.

Edie Falco has also worked in various theatrical media. Falco is the Emmy Award–winning actress on the

acclaimed HBO series *The Sopranos*. Her other television credits include *Oz* and *Homicide: Life on the Streets*. Falco has also appeared in films, including *The Addiction* (1995), *Cop Land* (1997), and *Sunshine State* (2002). She was praised for her performance off-off-Broadway in *Side Man* in 1996 and then later in its Broadway and London productions. In 2004 she appeared on Broadway in *'Night, Mother*.

What are the similarities and differences between performing on a stage in front of an audience and acting before a camera for film or television? Among the similarities are the fact that in both fields the performer must create a character, usually someone unlike himself or herself. The performer in both cases must memorize lines, perfect movements, develop the personality of the character, and interact with other performers. The research and preparation for these tasks are quite similar for stage, film, and television.

But there are significant differences. In movies and television, short scenes are filmed, often not in the sequence in which they will ultimately appear. Several scenes, for instance, might take place in a town square; one will come at the beginning, one at the end, and two in between. These scenes would all be filmed at one time. In this case, the mood and circumstances at the beginning and end would be different, but the performer would have to move from one to the other with little transition or preparation.

Also, in film or television, a scene may be shot over and over until the director is satisfied with the results. For that matter, the film director exerts great control over the film performance. How the director frames the actor or chooses the shot (for example, a close-up or long shot), determines how the audience views the performer. How a scene is edited can also influence how the audience perceives the performance. The film director Alfred Hitchcock (1899–1980) claimed that he, not his actors, created their performances.

In contrast to this, the performer onstage must go straight through the play from start to finish with no interruptions, except possibly an intermission. Stage actors must also develop the ability to project their voices throughout the theater. The stage performers in a realistic play must be able, for example, to convince the audience that they are speaking quietly but yet project so that even those seated in the back row of the auditorium can hear. Also, the stage actor must be able to create a physical performance that

can be seen by all the audience members; this requires that even the slightest gesture must be somewhat heightened.

In addition, performers onstage are playing before an audience, so that, in a sense, they are being tested every moment. Moreover, the audience throughout a performance is sending signals to the actors, some silent and some in the form of laughter or exclamations. The presence of the audience, therefore, is a constant challenge and reinforcement.

five segments. Viewpoints theory provides a new vocabulary for certain elements that have always been significant in performance and directing: spatial relationships onstage, movement, the notion of time, and so forth.

In modern training of actors and actresses, teachers borrow from other disciplines. A good example is Asian theater. Stylization and symbolism characterize the acting of the classical theaters of India, China, and Japan. To achieve the absolute control, the concentration, and the mastery of the body and nerves necessary to carry out the stylized movements, performers in the various classical Asian theaters train for years under the supervision of master teachers. Every movement of these performers is prescribed and carefully controlled, combining elements of formal ballet, pantomime, and sign language. Each gesture tells a story and means something quite specific—a true symbolism of physical movement.

One Asian discipline, not from theater but from martial arts, which modern acting teachers have found helpful is tai chi chuan, commonly called *tai chi*. Unlike some martial arts, tai chi is not aggressive: it is a graceful, gentle exercise regimen performed widely by men, women, and children in China. It has spread to other countries, where it is sometimes practiced in conjunction with meditation or body awareness. The movements of tai chi are stylized and often seem to be carried out in slow motion. Among other things, tai chi requires concentration and control, both valuable qualities for a performer.

Another field to which people involved in training actors and actresses have turned is the circus. Juggling, for instance, teaches both coordination and concentration. Acrobatics make the body limber, and other activities call for teamwork of a very high order.

Training for Special Forms of Theater. Certain types of theater and theater events require special discipline or training. For example, musical theater obviously requires talent in singing and dancing. Coordination is also important in musical theater: the members of a chorus must frequently sing and dance in unison.

Pantomime is another demanding category of performance: without words or props, a performer must indicate everything by physical suggestion, convincingly lifting an imaginary box or walking against an imaginary wind.

Various forms of modern avant-garde and experimental theater also require special techniques. A good example is Eugène Ionesco's play *Rhinoceros.* During the course of this play, one of the two chief characters turns into a rhinoceros. The actor playing this part does not actually put on horns or a leathery hide. Rather, he must physically transform himself by means of his posture, voice, and general demeanor. In another avant-garde play, Samuel Beckett's *Happy Days,* an actress is buried onstage in a mound of earth up to her waist in the first act, and up to her neck in the second. She must carry on her performance through the entire play while virtually immobile. In some types of avant-garde theater, the performers become acrobats, make human pyramids, or are used like pieces of furniture.

In the theaters of Robert Wilson and of Mabou Mines and similar groups, story, character, and text are minimized or even eliminated. The stress, rather than being on a narrative or on exploring recognizable characters, is on the visual and ritualistic aspects of theater, like a series of tableaux or a moving collage. Stage movement in this approach to theater is often closely related to dance; thus the performers must have the same discipline, training, and control as dancers. In Wilson's work, performers are frequently called on either to move constantly or to remain perfectly still. In *A Letter to Queen Victoria,* two performers turn continuously in circles like dervishes for long periods of time—perhaps 30 or 40 minutes. In other works by Wilson, performers must remain frozen like statues.

Synthesis and Integration

The demands made on performers by experimental and avant-garde theaters are only the most recent example of the rigorous, intensive training that acting generally requires. The goal of all this training—both internal and external—is to create for the performer an instrument that is flexible, resourceful, and disciplined.

When a performer is approaching a role in a play, the first task is to read and analyze the script. The actress or actor must discover the superobjective of the character she or he is playing and put together not only the spine of the role but the many smaller moments, each with its own objective and given circumstances.

The next challenge is to begin specific work on the role. In taking this step, some performers begin with the *outer* aspects of the character—with a walk, or a posture, or a peculiar vocal delivery. They get a sense of how the character looks in terms of makeup and other characteristics, such as a mustache or hairstyle. They consider the clothes the character wears and any idiosyncrasies of speech or movement, such as a limp or a swagger. Only then will they move on to the inner aspects of the character: how the character feels; how the character reacts to people and events; what disturbs the character's emotional equilibrium; what fears, hopes, and dreams the character has.

Other performers, by contrast, begin with the *internal* aspects: with the feelings and emotions of the character. These performers delve deeply into the psyche of the character to try to understand and duplicate what the character feels inside. Only after doing this will they go on to develop the outer characteristics. Still other performers work on both aspects—inner and outer—simultaneously.

What is important to remember is that whatever the starting point, the end result must be a synthesis of these two aspects. The various aspects of the craft of acting must be blended into a seamless whole; the inner emotions and feelings and the outer physical and vocal characteristics become one. Only then will the character be forcefully and convincingly portrayed. This process is termed *integration*.

Finally, we must realize that although a competent, well-trained performer may become a successful actress or actor, another ingredient is required in order to electrify an audience as truly memorable stage artists do. This results from intangibles—qualities that cannot be taught in acting schools—which distinguish an acceptable, accomplished actor or actress from one who ignites the stage. *Presence, charisma, personality, star quality:* these are among the terms used to describe a performer who communicates directly and kinetically with the audience. Whatever term one uses, the electricity and excitement of theater are enhanced immeasurably by performers who possess this indefinable attribute.

JUDGING PERFORMANCES

As observers, we study the techniques and problems of acting so that we will be able to understand and judge the performances we see. If a performer is unconvincing in a part, we know that he or she has not mastered a technique for truthful acting, such as the system developed by Stanislavski and his successors. We recognize that a performer who moves awkwardly or cannot be heard clearly has not been properly trained in body movement or vocal projection. We learn to notice how well performers play together: whether they listen to one another and respond appropriately. We also observe how well performers establish and maintain contact with the audience.

Before leaving the subject of the performer, we should note that actors and actresses have always held a fascination for audiences. In some cases this is because they portray larger-than-life characters; it can also result from the exceptional talent they bring to their performances. Also, of course, some performers have personal charisma or appeal. Theater audiences have often responded to stars onstage in the same way that people tend to respond to a rock star or a film star. There is something in these personalities that audiences find immensely attractive or intriguing. Moreover, the personal lives of actors are often of great interest to the public, and some people find it difficult to separate a stage character from the offstage woman or man.

In Chapter 6, we turn to the way a script is created—the script being the blueprint for a production.

SUMMARY

All human beings engage in certain forms of acting; imitation and role-playing are excellent examples of acting in everyday life. Acting onstage, however, differs from acting in everyday life. Historically, stage performances have required exceptional physical and vocal skills: moving with agility and grace, to engage in such things as sword fights and death scenes; dealing with poetic devices (meter, imagery, alliteration, etc.); and projecting the voice to the farthest reaches of the theater space.

From the end of the nineteenth century to the present day, many plays have been written in a very realistic, lifelike style. The characters in these plays resemble ordinary people in their dialogue, behavior, etc. Presenting them requires that performers make the characters they portray believable and convincing.

A Russian director, Konstantin Stanislavski, developed a system or method of acting to enable performers to believe in the "truth" of what they say and do and to project this to the audience.

Modern approaches to realistic acting by such teachers as Lee Strasberg, Stella Adler, Sanford Meisner, and Uta Hagen have built on and departed from aspects of Stanislavski's theories.

Exercises and tasks have been developed to train performers. These include numerous physical and vocal exercises and techniques taken from other disciplines such as tai chi and the circus. Centering is often emphasized as part of body and voice training. Avant-garde theater and certain other types of theater make additional demands on the performer with regard to voice and body training.

Audience members should familiarize themselves with the problems and techniques of acting in order to judge performances properly.

KEY TERMS

Emotional recall Stanislavski's exercise that helps the performer present realistic emotions. The performer feels a character's emotion by thinking of an event in his or her own life that led to a similar emotion.

Ensemble playing Acting that stresses the total artistic unity of a group performance rather than individual performances.

Magic if Stanislavski's acting exercise that requires the performer to ask, "How would I react if I were in this character's position?"

Realism Broadly, an attempt to present onstage people and events corresponding to those in everyday life.

For more research and to learn more about the topics in this chapter, please visit the Online Learning Center at **www.mhhe.com/livelyart6.**

CHAPTER 6

The Playwright: Creating the Text

◀ **THE PLAYWRIGHT AND THE THEATER**

In most cases, the ideas for a play—the story, characters, language, plot development, and themes—originate with the playwright. The playwright, in turn, must work with many others— performers, a director, designers, technicians—in order to bring the play to life. Shown here is the late August Wilson, the African American playwright who undertook the task of dramatizing the African American experience through each decade of the twentieth century. Many people consider Wilson the outstanding American playwright of the late twentieth century. He is seen here at the Yale Repertory Theatre in New Haven, Connecticut. (Sara Krulwich/The New York Times)

A theater production is a collaboration, not only between the audience and the performers but among a whole range of people who work together to make it happen. In the balance of Part Two of this volume, we look at these various elements and components: acting, directing, design, and so forth. All of these are essential, but like any enterprise, a theater production must begin somewhere, and in most cases that starting point is the script, also referred to as the text. The script provides the road map for a production in somewhat the same way that an architect's blueprint provides guidelines for constructing a building. For nearly 2,500 years the script or text was understood to be the domain of the dramatist or playwright. He or she chose the story to be told, selected the dramatic episodes, including the order in which they were to unfold, and wrote the dialogue for the characters to speak.

THE PLAYWRIGHT'S ROLE

We should note at this point that some contemporary commentators have questioned what they refer to as the "centrality" of the playwright and the play. These critics point out that there have been companies whose performers or directors, sometimes with the assistance of audiences, improvise presentations: they create a presentation while actually performing it. There have also been times when texts were developed by performers or by a director who assembled material from various sources. Some theorists argue, therefore, that an "authorless" theater exists: theater in which performers create their own works, sometimes using a traditional text only as a jumping-off point. An example of this concept of authorless theater might be performance art (which is discussed in Chapter 19); some contemporary performance artists create pieces in which they narrate details from their own lives.

Theorists who question the centrality of the text also argue that the playwright's importance has been overstated—that a play is simply a suggestion or starting point and that the artists who create a stage presentation are its true "authors." In addition, they hold that each audience member may create his or her own "reading" of a production; in this sense, the spectator is the "author," and any discussion of a play's theme or meaning is inappropriate.

While certain analysts have adopted this concept, many others continue to take a more traditional approach. Also, the argument seems to be in some instances a question of semantics. If a theater piece is created by a group of performers or by a director, then these people are in effect operating as playwrights. The playwright's function has not been eliminated; it is simply being carried out by someone else.

This consideration does not answer the question of the playwright's centrality, of course, but our purpose in this book is not to try to settle such arguments. Although many contemporary theories challenge us to rethink the place of the playwright in theater, the fact remains that throughout the history of both western and eastern theater the significant role of the playwright has been widely accepted. Whether it is a dramatist like Sophocles, Shakespeare, or Ibsen in the west, or Chikamatsu—an eighteenth-century Japanese dramatist—in the east, both their own contemporaries and later generations have seen their dramatic

Suzan-Lori Parks: Playwright

A recipient of a MacArthur Foundation "genius" award in 2001, Ms. Parks is the author of more than fifteen plays, including The America Play, Venus, In the Blood, *and* Topdog/Underdog, *which won the Pulitzer Prize for drama in 2002.*

. . . Some people start from a love for theatre and go on from there. But I was a short-story writer in a class with James Baldwin when I was a student at Mount Holyoke College. He was teaching creative writing at Hampshire College and I took a class with him. We had to read our stories out loud for the class and I loved reading aloud. So he said, "You should try playwriting," and I said, "I'll try it." That's how I got into it. So the love of theatre and interest in theatre came after, came through the writing. . . .

The first real time I spent in the theatre at Mount Holyoke was when I went up there in March [1997] to direct *Devotees in the Garden of Love* [1991]. I studied some theatre at Hampshire College because you could take courses there. I remember I read *For Colored Girls* and directed it in college—but not in the theatre. We just brought some people together and put on a show. . . . I remember a teacher of mine in the English Department at Mount Holyoke. I was walking down the hall one day and she saw me coming and ran in her office and came back out with a book and kind of held it out like I was a train and she had the mailbag and I just took it and kept walking, and I got to the end of the hall and it was *Funnyhouse of a Negro* [by Adrienne Kennedy]. So I read it and reread it and reread it and reread it. It also had a hand in shaping what I do. . . .

I graduated in '85 and went to London for a year and studied acting because I thought I was going to be a writer. . . . I said if I'm going to do this playwriting thing which I enjoy, I should study acting. I didn't want to study writing because I didn't think it was going to help me.

Source: Suzan-Lori Parks from *Playwright's Voice* by David Savran, Copyright 1999. By permission of Theatre Communications Group.

texts as foundations on which productions are based, and it is this aspect of theater which we discuss in Chapters 6 and 7.

CREATING THE TEXT: THE TASKS INVOLVED

The playwright, or whoever creates a dramatic text, has a number of questions to answer and many choices to make, involving at least six aspects of a drama:

1. Selecting the specific subject of the play
2. Determining focus and emphasis
3. Establishing purpose
4. Developing dramatic structure
5. Creating dramatic characters
6. Establishing point of view

In this chapter, we will examine the first five of these aspects. In Chapter 7, we will look at point of view.

SUBJECT

The subject matter of drama is always human beings. In theater, unlike certain other art forms—music, for instance, or abstract painting—people are invariably at the center. At the same time, a play cannot simply be about "human beings" or "people" in general, or even about "people's concerns," and the first task of the person or persons creating a dramatic text is therefore to decide what aspect of human existence to write about.

Will the drama be based on history—for example, an episode or incident from the Civil War, from World War II, or from the war in Iraq? Or will it be based on biography—on the life of Abraham Lincoln, Eleanor Roosevelt, or Martin Luther King Jr.? Another possibility is the dramatization of someone's personal life: confronting some problem of growing up, or facing a personal crisis as an adult. A different possibility would be an imaginary story, resembling everyday life or based on a fantasy or nightmare.

FOCUS AND EMPHASIS

Along with selecting a subject to be dramatized, the dramatist must decide whom and what to focus on. For example, the same playwright can emphasize a particular character trait in one play and a very different trait in another play. This is what the Norwegian playwright Henrik Ibsen often did. In his *Brand*, the leading character is a stark, uncompromising religious man who will sacrifice everything—family, friends, love—for his principles. On the other hand, in Ibsen's *Peer Gynt*, the central character is just the opposite: a man with no principles who is always compromising, always running away.

In determining focus, a playwright may need to decide how to interpret the characters and events of an existing story; in doing this, the playwright may even change the order of events. A good example is the way three tragic dramatists of ancient Greece dealt with the myth of Electra. This myth concerns Electra's revenge on her mother, Clytemnestra, who has murdered Electra's father, Agamemnon, and then married a lover, Aegisthus. In wreaking revenge on Clytemnestra, Electra enlists the help of her brother, Orestes, who has just returned from exile. In *The Libation Bearers* (458 B.C.E.) by Aeschylus, and also in *Electra* (c. 412 B.C.E.) by Euripides, Electra and Orestes first murder Clytemnestra's lover, Aegisthus, and then murder Clytemnestra herself—their mother. This puts emphasis on the horror and aberration of killing one's own mother. But Sophocles saw the story differently. He wanted to emphasize

EMPHASIS AND POINT OF VIEW

Henrik Ibsen makes it clear that his play Peer Gynt *is about the title character, who is in virtually every scene. The play itself—which is serious but has numerous comic and tragicomic episodes—ranges over many years and many locations. The character of Peer is always compromising, always running away, and Ibsen shows the consequences of that. Here, Uwe Bohm as Peer, and Judith Stobenreuter as Anitra, are riding on a pig, in the Berliner Ensemble production of* Peer Gynt *at the Lyceum Theatre during the Edinburgh Festival. (© Geraint Lewis)*

that Electra and Orestes are acting honorably and obeying an order from the gods. He therefore needed to play down the murder of the mother, and so in his version of *Electra* (c. 410 B.C.E.) he reversed the order of the murders: Clytemnestra is killed first, and then the action builds to the righteous murder of Aegisthus.

By means of focus, then, whoever creates a text lets us know whom the play is about—the main character or characters—and how we are to view the characters: whether we are to look at them favorably or unfavorably.

DRAMATIC PURPOSE

Another challenge in creating a script or text is to determine the purpose of a play. A purpose may be casual or unconscious, or conscious and deliberate, but every theater event is intended in one way or another to serve some purpose.

Throughout theater history, plays have been written to serve different purposes: to entertain, to probe the human condition, to provide an escape, to impart information. Various types of contemporary theater are frequently presented for a specific purpose: these include feminist theater, Latino or Latina theater, and African American theater. In theater of this kind, those who create the event are addressing the concerns of a particular constituency.

There is a long tradition of theater as a source of entertainment—similar to modern situation comedies on television and comic films that offer us pleasure and an escape from the cares of everyday life. The comedies of the Roman playwrights Plautus and Terence, written 2,000 years ago, were designed for this sort of entertainment. In the United States, for many years Broadway provided comedies that were written purely for fun.

There have been times when plays were intended primarily to teach. In the medieval period, prior to the late fifteenth century, very few people could read or write. In order to teach people about the Bible, the church encouraged plays that presented religious stories and precepts. Today, political dramatists often write plays specifically to put forward their own opinions and ideas.

At times, the purpose of drama has been to raise philosophical questions or to probe timeless themes, such as why the innocent suffer or why there is so much hatred and violence in the world.

Sometimes a play is intended simply to thrill or frighten us. A horror story or a melodrama is not supposed to make us think or meditate; it is intended to draw us into the action so that we will experience the same fears and apprehensions as the characters.

At times a play serves more than one purpose. Satirical comedies may be intended not only to make us laugh, but also to take stabs at hypocrites or charlatans. The works of the French playwright Molière are frequently of this kind: comical, but also revealing human folly. His *Tartuffe,* for instance—about a man who moves into a household falsely posing as a pious cleric—is an indictment of hypocrisy but is also amusing.

Whatever their approach, those creating a text should make the purpose of a theater event clear. Sometimes a playwright may begin working without an exact

Making Connections

Writers

The playwright David Mamet. (© Gerry Goodstein)

How do we compare writing for the stage and writing for films or television? Obviously, many writers engage in both, moving from theater to films or television and back again. Some writers, however, seem to have a natural affinity for one field or the other. There are playwrights who have never attempted to write screenplays and never want to. By the same token, there are people who write for films or television who have never been interested in writing plays or musicals for the stage.

David Mamet is a good example of a writer who frequently moves back and forth between theater and film. Others who write primarily for theater at times write films as well; they include Neil Simon, John Guare, and Marcia Norman. Many playwrights write almost exclusively for theater; they include Edward Albee, Paula Vogel, Terence McNally, A. R. Gurney, Tina Howe, and Lanford Wilson.

Whatever path a writer takes, he or she must meet the requirements we discuss in this chapter: decide on the subject, develop a plot, create the characters, compose the dialogue, and undertake all other necessary steps in creating a completed script. In undertaking these tasks, the writer for film or television must follow a path similar to that of the playwright for the stage, but there are important differences. The requirements of film, for instance, are not the same as those for the stage. Many scenes in film are action scenes: shots from a helicopter, shots of car crashes, a villain stalking his prey. Such scenes may be described by the writer, but their realization is mostly in the hands of the director and cinematographer. They contain almost no dialogue. As a rule, whatever the story line, there is far less dialogue in a film than in a play.

Because of the nature of theater, as opposed to film or television, the role of the writer is different in other ways. The Dramatists Guild contract, under which most dramas are produced, states unequivocally that no dialogue in a production may be deleted or changed without the permission of the author. By contrast, in films and television two things happen. First, there are often a number of writers on a script. There may be two, three, or more. This means that no one writer has the authority to maintain his or her vision over the material. Second, the writer is unable to prevent changes in the script made by directors, producers, performers, or other writers. Thus in films and television, as compared with theater, the writer has less control over what happens to his or her words.

Another crossover area for dramatic writers would be opera and musical theater, where the playwright would provide the libretto, and perhaps the lyrics as well. When working on an opera or musical piece, the dramatist must collaborate with a composer as well as with a director and others.

purpose—the purpose may emerge only as the script goes through several revisions. Before a play goes into production, however, the playwright should know where it is headed. Once the purpose is clear, the director, performers, and designers join the playwright in working to achieve it.

After subject, focus, and purpose have been decided, two crucial steps in developing a play are creating dramatic structure and creating dramatic characters.

Before we discuss these in detail, however, a word about the writing process is in order. In choosing a subject, developing a structure, or creating characters, the person or persons creating the script will often work intuitively, sometimes even subconsciously. When the imagination of the playwright, for instance, is captured by a certain episode or attracted to certain characters, he or she begins to create a drama. Usually a play evolves, rather than being put together in a mechanical fashion.

In past eras, the type of structure used and the characters chosen by a playwright were in some measure the traditionally accepted practices of a given period and society. Playwrights in ancient Greece, for example, based both their plots and their characters on well-known myths. In modern times, however, playwrights often begin without a clear plan and only later discover the type of structure and the nature of the characters they have chosen to create.

STRUCTURE IN DRAMA

Though it may not be readily apparent, every work of art has some type of structure. When does the action of a play begin? How are the scenes put together? How does the action unfold? What is the high point of the action? Questions like these are related to dramatic structure, but we should note that structure is significant in all art.

In a sense, the structure of a play is analogous to that of a building. In designing a building, an architect plans a skeleton or substructure that will provide inner strength; the architect determines the depth of the foundation, the weight of the support beams, and the stress on the side walls. Similarly, a playwright develops a dramatic structure. The playwright introduces various stresses and strains in the form of conflicts; sets boundaries and outer limits, such as how many characters participate, how long the action lasts, and where it takes place; and calculates dynamics—when tension increases and slackens. Some feminist critics argue that the playwright's gender might also influence structure and that feminist dramas are less linear and less traditional in building dramatic tension.

Buildings vary enormously in size and shape: they can be as diverse as a skyscraper, a cathedral, and a cottage. Engineering requirements vary according to the needs of individual structures: a gymnasium roof must span a vast open area, and this calls for a construction different from that of a sixty-story skyscraper.

Plays, too, vary; they can be tightly or loosely constructed, for instance. The important point is that each play, like each piece of architecture, should have its own internal laws and its own framework, which give it shape, strength, and meaning. Without structure, a building will collapse, and a play will fall apart.

Naturally, structure is manifested differently in theater and architecture. A play is not a building; it unfolds through time, developing like a living organism. As we experience this development, we become aware of a play's structure because we sense its underlying pattern and rhythm. The repeated impulses of two characters in conflict, the quickening pace and mounting tension of a heated argument—these elements insinuate themselves into our subconscious like a drumbeat. Moment by moment we see what is happening onstage; but below the surface we sense the structure, the framework of the dramatic action.

Essentials of Dramatic Structure

There are several essentials of dramatic structure. First, the story on which a drama is based must be turned into a plot. Second, the plot involves action. Third, the plot includes conflict. Fourth, there are strongly opposed forces. Fifth, a reasonable balance is struck between the opposed forces.

Plot. Our first essential of dramatic structure, *plot,* is the arrangement of events or the selection and order of scenes in a play. The term *plot* can mean a secret scheme or plan. The word is also used to describe the sequence of scenes or events in a novel, but we are speaking here specifically of plot in drama.

A dramatic plot is usually based on a story. Stories are as old as the human race, and today stories form much of the substance of our daily conversation, of newspapers and television, of novels and films. Every medium presents a story in a different form. In theater, the story must be presented by living actors and actresses on a stage in a limited period of time, and this requires selectivity. Thus the plot of a play differs from a story. A *story* is a full account of an event or series of events, usually in chronological order; a *plot* is a selection and arrangement of scenes from a story for presentation onstage. The plot is what actually happens onstage, not what is talked about.

For example, the story of Abraham Lincoln begins with his birth in a log cabin and continues to the day he is shot at Ford's Theater in Washington. In developing a plot for a play about Lincoln, however, the playwright must make choices. Will the play include scenes in Springfield, Illinois, where Lincoln served as a lawyer and held his famous debates with Stephen A. Douglas? Or will the entire play take place in Washington after Lincoln has become president? Will there be scenes with Lincoln's wife, Mary Todd; or will all the scenes involve government and military officials? Decisions like these must be made even when a play is based on a fictional story: the plot must be more restricted and structured than the story itself.

Action. A second essential of dramatic structure is *action.* If we were to construct a "grammar of theater," the subject would always be human beings—dramatic characters who represent human concerns. In linguistic grammar, every

subject needs a verb; similarly, in the grammar of theater, dramatic characters need a verb—some form of action that defines them. The word *drama* actually derives from a Greek root, the verb *dran*, meaning "to do" or "to act." At its heart, theater involves action.

Conflict.   A third essential of dramatic structure is **conflict,** the collision or opposition of persons or forces in a drama that gives rise to dramatic action. We can perhaps best understand dramatic conflict in terms of everyday experience. People often define themselves by the way they respond to challenges, such as marriage, a job, sudden good fortune, or a serious illness. If they cannot face up to a challenge, that tells us one thing; if they meet it with dignity, even though defeated, that tells us another; if they triumph, that tells us something else. We come to know our family, our friends, and our enemies by being with them over a period of time. We see how they respond to us and to other people, and how they meet crises in their own lives and in ours.

In life, this process can take years—in fact, it continues to unfold for as long as we know a person—but in theater we have only a few hours. The playwright, therefore, must devise means by which characters will face challenges and be tested in a short time. The American playwright Arthur Miller called one of his plays *The Crucible* (1953). Literally, a crucible is a vessel in which metal is tested by being exposed to extreme heat. Figuratively, a crucible has come to stand for any severe

STRONGLY OPPOSED FORCES
In developing a dramatic structure, a playwright sets powerful forces and characters against one another to provide conflict and dramatic confrontations. A good example is the opposition between a husband (here played by Ian Mckellen) and his wife (Helen Mirren) in Strindberg's Dance of Death. *(Sara Krulwich/The New York Times)*

test of human worth and endurance—a trial by fire. Every play provides a crucible of a sort: a test devised by the playwright to show how the characters behave under stress. Such a test, and the characters' reaction to it, is one way that the meaning of a play is brought out.

Opposed Forces. A fourth essential of dramatic structure, closely related to conflict, is strongly *opposed forces*. By this we mean that the people in conflict in a play are fiercely determined to achieve their goals; moreover, they are powerful adversaries for one another. The conflicting characters have clear, strong goals or objectives; that is, they have goals they want desperately to achieve, and they will go to any length to achieve them. For example, Macbeth, in the play by Shakespeare, wants to become king; Jean, the servant in August Strindberg's *Miss Julie*, wants to achieve independence; Blanche DuBois, in Tennessee Williams's *A Streetcar Named Desire,* wants to find a haven in the home of her sister. In fighting for their goals, two or more characters find themselves in opposition; and the strength of both sides must be formidable.

A perfect example of two characters bound to clash is found in *A Streetcar Named Desire*. Blanche DuBois is a faded southern belle trying desperately to hold onto her gentility; the crude, aggressive Stanley Kowalski is the chief threat to her stability and her survival. On his side, Stanley, who is insecure about his lack of education and refinement, is provoked almost to the breaking point by Blanche and her superior airs.

One device often used by dramatists to establish friction or tension between forces is restricting the characters to members of a single family. Relatives have built-in rivalries and affinities: parents versus children, sisters versus brothers. As members of the same family, moreover, they have no avenue of escape.

Mythology, on which so much drama is based, abounds with familial relationships. Shakespeare also frequently set members of one family against each other: Hamlet opposes his mother; King Lear is opposed by his daughters. In modern drama, virtually every writer of note has dealt with close family situations. The American dramatist Eugene O'Neill wrote what many consider his finest play, *Long Day's Journey into Night,* about the four members of his own family.

In plays not directly involving families, the characters are usually still in close proximity. They are fighting for the same turf, the same throne, the same woman or man.

Balance of Forces. A fifth essential of dramatic structure is some sort of *balance* between the opposed forces: that is, the people or forces in conflict must be evenly matched. In almost every case, one side eventually wins, but before this final outcome the opposing forces must be roughly equal in strength and determination.

In most sporting events, there are rules ensuring that the contest will be as equal as possible without coming to a draw, and this notion is equally important in theater. In sports, fans want their team to win, but they would prefer a close, exciting contest to a one-sided runaway. The struggle, as much as the outcome, is a source of pleasure; and so rules are set up, with handicaps or other devices for equalizing forces. In basketball or football, when one team scores, the other team gets the ball so that it will have a chance to even the score. In theater, too, a hard-fought and relatively equal contest is usually set up between opposing forces: the vulnerable, artistic Blanche, for example, faces the brutish Stanley.

Creating a Dramatic Structure

A dramatic structure begins with the all-important opening scene.

Opening Scene. The first scene of a drama starts the action and sets the tone and style for everything that follows. It tells us whether we are going to see a serious or a comic play, and whether the play will deal with affairs of everyday life or with fantasy. The opening scene also sets the action in motion, giving the characters a shove and hurtling them toward their destination.

Providing the characters with a problem or establishing an imbalance of forces compels the characters to respond. Generally, the problem or imbalance has occurred just before the play begins, or it arises immediately after the play opens. In *King Oedipus,* for example, a plague has struck the city just before the opening of the play. In *Hamlet,* "something is rotten in the state of Denmark" before the play opens; and early in the play the ghost of Hamlet's father appears to tell Hamlet that he must seek revenge. At the beginning of *Romeo and Juliet,* the Capulets and the Montagues are at one another's throats in a street fight.

As these examples suggest, in the opening scene the characters are thrust into a situation that provides the starting point for the play.

Obstacles and Complications. Having confronted the initial challenge of the play, the characters then move through a series of steps alternating between achievement and defeat, between hope and despair. The moment they accomplish one goal, something cuts across the play; a new hurdle or challenge is thrown up that they must overcome. These hurdles blocking a character's path—or outside forces that are introduced at an inopportune moment—are known as *obstacles* and *complications.*

Shakespeare's *Hamlet* provides numerous examples of obstacles and complications. Hamlet, suspecting that his uncle, Claudius, has killed his father, seeks revenge; but Claudius, as king, controls the army and other instruments of power. Thus the authority of the throne is one obstacle standing in Hamlet's way.

August Wilson: Playwright

August Wilson, in recent decades, was the best-known African American playwright. He won Pulitzer Prizes for Fences *in 1987 and* The Piano Lesson *in 1990. His other well-known works include* Ma Rainey's Black Bottom, Joe Turner's Come and Gone, Two Trains Running, Seven Guitars, Jitney, Gem of the Ocean, *and* Radio Golf. *Wilson died in 2005.*

What were your early experiences in theatre? I was a participant in the Black Power movement in the early sixties and I wrote poetry and short fiction. I was interested in art and literature and I felt that I could alter the relationship between blacks and society through the arts. There was an explosion of black theatre in the late sixties—theatre was a way of politicizing the community and raising the consciousness of the people. So with my friend, Rob Penny, I started the Black Horizons Theatre of Pittsburgh in 1968.

I knew nothing about theatre. I had never seen a play before. I started directing but I didn't have any idea how to do this stuff, although I did find great information in the library. We started doing Baraka's plays and virtually anything else out there. I remember the *Drama Review* printed a black issue, somewhere around '69, and we did every play in the book. I tried to write a play but it was disastrous. I couldn't write dialogue. Doing community theatre was very difficult—rehearsing two hours a night after people got off work, not knowing if the actors were going to show up. In '71, because of having to rely so much on other people, I said "I don't need this," and I concentrated on writing poetry and short stories.

Then in 1976 a friend of mine from Pittsburgh, Claude Purdy, was living in L.A. He came back to Pittsburgh and came to a reading of a series of poems I'd written about a character, Black Bart, a kind of Western satire. He said, "You should turn this into a play." He kept after me and eventually I sat down and wrote a play and gave it to him. He went to St. Paul to direct a show and said, "Why don't you come out and rewrite the play?" He sent me a ticket and I thought, "A free trip to St. Paul, what the hell?" So I went out and did a quick rewrite of the play. That was in November '77. In January '78, the Inner City Theatre in Los Angeles did a staged reading of it.

Source: August Wilson from *In Their Own Words: Contemporary American Playwrights* by David Savran, copyright 1988 David Savran. By permission of Theatre Communications Group.

When Hamlet stages the "play within a play," Claudius's reaction confirms his guilt, and Hamlet's path to revenge seems clear. But when Hamlet first tries to kill Claudius, he discovers him at prayer. A complication has been introduced: if Claudius dies while praying, he may go to heaven rather than to hell, and so Hamlet does not kill him.

Later, Hamlet is in his mother's bedroom when he hears a noise behind a curtain. Surely Claudius is lurking there, and Hamlet can kill him instantly. But when Hamlet thrusts his sword through the curtain, he finds that he has killed Polonius, who is the father of Ophelia, the young woman Hamlet is supposed to marry. This is another complication: the murder of Polonius gives Claudius a pretext for sending Hamlet to England with Rosencrantz and Guildenstern, who carry a letter instructing the king of England to put Hamlet to death.

Hamlet gets out of this trap and returns to Denmark. Now, at last, it seems that he can carry out his revenge. But he discovers that Ophelia has killed herself while he was away; and her brother, Laertes, is seeking revenge on Hamlet. This is still another complication: Hamlet is prevented from killing Claudius because he must also deal with Laertes. In the end, Hamlet does carry out his mission—but only after many interruptions.

Crises and Climaxes.   As a result of conflicts, obstacles, and complications, dramatic characters become involved in a series of *crises.* Some crises are less complicated than those in *Hamlet,* some even more complicated. A play builds from one crisis to another; when the first crisis is resolved, the action leads to a second crisis, and so on. The final and most significant crisis is referred to as the *climax.* Sometimes there is a minor climax earlier in a play and a major climax near the conclusion. In the final climax, the issues of the play are resolved—either happily or tragically, depending on the genre.

Two Basic Structures: Climactic and Episodic

Over the long history of western theater, playwrights have usually adopted one or the other of two basic dramatic structures: *climactic,* or *intensive,* **structure;** and *episodic,* or *extensive,* **structure.** In certain periods, playwrights have combined the two. There are other forms of structure, which we will discuss, but let us consider climactic and episodic structure first.

Climactic Plot Construction.   A dramatic form first used in Greece in the fifth century B.C.E. reemerged, somewhat altered, in France in the seventeenth century;

OBSTACLES AND COMPLICATIONS
In developing a dramatic plot, the playwright often incorporates obstacles and complications that impede the movement of the main characters in their attempt to reach their goals. Obstacles and complications also add interest, suspense, and complexity to the dramatic action. A good example of a play with many obstacles and complications is Shakespeare's Romeo and Juliet. *In this scene we see Tiffany Scott (left) as Juliet and Paul Hurley as Romeo in a production at the Utah Shakespearean Festival.* (© Utah Shakespearean Festival. Photo by Karl Hugh.)

in the late nineteenth century and the twentieth century, this same form was adopted in Norway, Sweden, France, and (somewhat later) the United States. This we call *climactic* or *intensive.* We use these terms because in this kind of dramatic construction, all aspects of a play—duration, locale, action, and number of characters—are severely restricted; this results in a contained, or intense, structure, in which little time passes until the climax occurs.

   A good example of climactic structure is found in *'Night, Mother,* by the modern American playwright Marsha Norman. The play takes place in one space, the kitchen and living room of a home; it involves only two people, a mother and daughter; and it occurs over a brief period, 1½ hours. Also, it has a single action: the daughter is determined to commit suicide and the mother to prevent her.

CLIMACTIC STRUCTURE

In climactic structure, everything is restricted: the action occurs in a brief time, in limited locations, and with very few characters involved. Climactic structure was first developed in western theater by the Greek dramatists of the fifth century B.C.E. in Athens. For example, Sophocles's play Oedipus the King *involves only a few characters and occurs over a short time in one place: the front of the palace of Oedipus. Shown here, in a production by the Hartford Stage Company, are Reg Flowers as Oedipus and Stephanie Berry as Jocasta—the mother of Oedipus, whom he unknowingly takes as his wife.* (© Jennifer W. Lester)

Climactic plots have several distinctive characteristics, which we'll consider one by one.

The Plot Begins Late in the Story. The first hallmark of climactic drama is that the plot begins quite late in the story, at a point where the story has reached a climax. It focuses on a moment when everything comes to a head, lives fall apart, fate closes in, and there is a final showdown between characters. Because the plot deals with a culmination of events, climactic form is sometimes called *crisis drama,* or *drama of catastrophe.*

King Oedipus by Sophocles offers a good example. When Oedipus is born, it is predicted that he will kill his father and marry his mother; and so his parents, the king and queen of Thebes, order that he be left in the wilderness to die. He is saved, however, and taken to another country where he is raised by another king and queen as their own son. As he grows up, he hears the prophecy about himself; and, assuming that his adoptive parents are his real ones, he leaves home. He goes to Thebes, where he does kill his natural father and marry his mother, not knowing who they are. He becomes king of Thebes; and when a plague strikes the kingdom, he sets out to find the person who has murdered the former king— not knowing that he himself is the murderer. All this happens *before* the play begins. The drama itself focuses on the single day when the full story emerges.

Whether it is *King Oedipus,* or Ibsen's *A Doll's House,* or Tennessee Williams's *Cat on a Hot Tin Roof,* any play in climactic form concentrates on the final hours of a long sequence of events. Because so much has happened before the play begins, details about the past must be provided during the course of the play. In drama, the term for this information is *exposition.*

The effect of beginning the action near the climax of events is to give a play a very sharp focus and a strong sense of immediacy. In climactic form, everything is concentrated on the showdown, the payoff, the final confrontation.

Scenes, Locales, and Characters Are Restricted. Climactic structure is restricted not only in time but also in other ways. For example, it has a limited number of long scenes or acts. Critics in the Renaissance said that a play must have five acts. For much of the nineteenth and twentieth centuries, three acts were standard. Today, the norm is two acts, though the long one-act play, performed without intermission, is also common.

Limited scenes in a play usually entail a restricted locale. All the action in *King Oedipus* takes place in front of the royal palace. *No Exit,* a climactic play by the French writer Jean-Paul Sartre, confines its three characters to one room from which, as the title suggests, there is no escape. Writers like Ibsen and Strindberg also frequently confined their plays to one room, and contemporary plays provide numerous instances of this device.

Climactic dramatic structure also has a limited number of characters. Aside from the chorus, Greek drama generally has four or five principal characters. *King Oedipus* has four: Oedipus, Jocasta, Creon, and Teiresias. French neoclassical drama and many modern plays have the same number of principal characters: four or five.

Construction Is Tight.   Construction is tight in a climactic play: events are arranged in an orderly, compact way, with no loose ends. It is like a chain linked by cause and effect. As in a detective story, A leads to B, B to C, which causes D, leading in turn to E, and so on. This chain of events is unbreakable: once the action begins, there is no stopping it.

The French playwright Jean Anouilh (1910–1987), in his *Antigone* (1943), compares tragedy to the workings of a machine.

> The spring is wound up tight. It will uncoil itself. That is what is so convenient in tragedy. The least little turn of the wrist will do the job. . . . The rest is automatic. You don't need to lift a finger. The machine is in perfect order; it has been oiled ever since time began and it runs without friction.[1]

This applies to every play in climactic form. The aim is always to make events so inevitable that there is no escape—at least, not until the very last moment, when a ***deus ex machina*** may intervene to untangle the knot. *Deus ex machina* is Latin for "god from a machine" and comes from ancient Greece and Rome, when a mechanical contraption on the roof of the stage house was used to bring the gods onstage to resolve the action at the end of a play. The term *deus ex machina* has come to stand for any plot contrivance used to resolve a play at the end.

Episodic Plot Construction.   When we turn from climactic structure to episodic structure, we find a very clear contrast in almost every respect.

Episodic structure emerged during the Renaissance in England—Shakespeare's plays offer a prime example—and in Spain, in the plays of Lope de Vega and his contemporaries. Later, episodic form was adopted by the German playwrights Goethe and Schiller during the romantic period, in the late eighteenth century and the early nineteenth century. It was also used in the late nineteenth century by the Norwegian playwright Henrik Ibsen and in the twentieth century by the German playwright Bertolt Brecht. The following are the characteristics of episodic structure.

---

[1]Jean Anouilh, *Antigone,* Lewis Galantière (trans. and adaptor), Random House, New York, 1946, p. 36. Copyright 1946 by Random House.

People, Places, and Events Proliferate. A typical episodic play covers an extended period of time, sometimes many years, and ranges over a number of locations. In one play, we can go anywhere: to a small antechamber, a large banquet hall, the open countryside, a mountaintop.

Short scenes, some only a half-page or so in print, alternate with longer scenes. The large number of characters and scenes in three plays will serve to indicate the expansive nature of episodic drama: Shakespeare's *Antony and Cleopatra* has thirty-four characters and more than forty scenes; his *Julius Caesar* has thirty-four characters and eighteen scenes; *The Sheep Well* by his Spanish contemporary Lope de Vega has twenty-six characters and seventeen scenes.

There May Be a Parallel Plot or a Subplot. One technique of episodic drama is the *parallel plot*, or **subplot.** In Shakespeare's *King Lear,* for example, Lear has three daughters, two evil and one good. The two evil daughters have convinced their father that they are good and that their sister is wicked. In the subplot—a counterpart of the main plot—the Earl of Gloucester has two sons, one loyal and one disloyal; and the disloyal one has deceived his father into thinking that he is the loyal one. Both old men have misjudged their children's true worth, and in the end each is punished for his mistake: Lear is bereft of his kingdom and his sanity; Gloucester loses his eyes. The Gloucester plot, with complications and developments of its own, parallels and reinforces the Lear plot.

Contrast and Juxtaposition Are Used. Another technique of episodic drama is juxtaposition or contrast. Rather than moving in linear fashion, the action alternates between different kinds of elements.

For one thing, as we have noted, short scenes alternate with longer scenes. *King Lear* begins with a short scene between Kent and Gloucester, goes next to a long scene in which Lear divides his kingdom, then returns to a brief scene in which Edmund declares his intention to deceive his father.

Also, public scenes alternate with private scenes. Shakespeare's *Romeo and Juliet* opens with a public scene: a street fight between the Capulet family and the Montague family. This is followed by a private scene between Paris and Juliet's father, Lord Capulet; next comes another private scene, between Romeo and Benvolio; then there is still another private scene, between Lady Capulet and Juliet's nurse. Then comes a public street scene, followed by a public scene at a masked ball.

In addition, comic scenes often alternate with serious scenes. In *Macbeth,* just after Macbeth has murdered King Duncan, there is a knock on the door of the castle. This is one of the most serious moments in the play, but the man who goes to open the door is a comic character, a drunken porter, whose speech is a humorous interlude in the grim business of the drama. In *Hamlet,* a gravedigger and his assistant are preparing a grave for Ophelia when Hamlet comes onto the scene. The gravediggers are joking about death; but for Hamlet, who soon learns that the grave is Ophelia's, it is a somber moment.

The Overall Effect Is Cumulative. Unlike climactic drama, episodic plays do not necessarily have a close cause-and-effect development, with each action following logically and inevitably from what precedes it. Rather, episodic drama creates an impression of events piling up: a tidal wave of circumstances and emotions sweeping over the characters. Rarely is a character's fate determined by a single letter, a single incident, or a single piece of new knowledge. Time and again, Hamlet has proof that Claudius has killed his father; but it is a whole onrush of events—not a single piece of hard evidence—that eventually leads him to kill Claudius.

Combinations of Climactic and Episodic Construction. There is no rule requiring a play to be exclusively episodic or exclusively climactic; these forms are not watertight compartments. It is true that during certain periods one form or the other has been predominant. And it is not easy to mix the two, because each has its own laws and its own inner logic. In various periods, however, they have been successfully integrated.

For example, climactic and episodic construction are combined in the comedies of late-seventeenth-century England—the Restoration period. In the late nineteenth century, the Russian dramatist Anton Chekhov combined elements of both forms, and in the twentieth century the two forms were frequently integrated.

Other Dramatic Structures

During the twentieth century, new types of dramatic structure appeared. In some cases, such as ritual structure, the form amounted to adaptation of an ancient

*One device used in episodic
drama is the juxtaposition
and alternation of serious
and comic scenes.
Shakespeare often
incorporates this technique
in his plays. A good
example is the grave-
digging scene in* Hamlet,
*in which a comic episode
is surrounded by quite
serious scenes. Shown here
is Simon Russell Beale as
Hamlet (right) with Denis
Quilley as the Grave
Digger holding a skull, in
a production at the Royal
National Theatre in
London.* (© Donald
Cooper/Photo*stage,*
England)

structure for modern use. We will now look briefly at these variations in dramatic structure, returning to many of them in Part Three, when we study the historical periods in which they first appeared.

Ritual as Structure.   Just as acting is a part of everyday life so is ritual, though we are generally unaware of it. Basically, *ritual* is a repetition or reenactment of some proceeding or transaction that has acquired special meaning. It may be a simple ritual like singing the national anthem before a ball game or a deeply religious ritual like the Catholic mass. We all develop ritualistic patterns of behavior in our personal lives, such as following the same routine when we get up in the morning or taking a day off on Sunday. As we shall see, some historians have theorized that theater grew out of rituals and ritualistic enactments of ancient peoples.

In contemporary theater, some avant-garde groups have made a conscious attempt to return theater to ritual and to focus on ritualistic, repetitive actions which are not necessarily realistic but symbolic.

Patterns as Structure.   Related to ritual are *patterns* of events. In Samuel Beckett's *Waiting for Godot*, the characters have no personal history, and the play does not build to a climax in the ordinary way. But if Beckett has abandoned many techniques of traditional structure, he has replaced them with something else—a repeated sequence of events containing its own order and logic. The play has two acts, and in each act a series of incidents is duplicated. There are differences between the two acts, but the identical sequences of events achieve a pattern that takes on a ritualistic quality.

Comparing Climactic and Episodic Form

CLIMACTIC

1. Plot begins late in the story, toward the very end or climax.
2. Covers a short space of time, perhaps a few hours or at most a few days.
3. Contains a few solid, extended scenes, such as three acts with each act comprising one long scene.
4. Occurs in a restricted locale, such as one room or one house.
5. Number of characters is severely limited—usually no more than six or eight.
6. Plot is linear and moves in a single line with few subplots or counterplots.
7. Line of action proceeds in a cause-and-effect chain. The characters and events are closely linked in a sequence of logical, almost inevitable development.

EPISODIC

1. Plot begins relatively early in the story and moves through a series of episodes.
2. Covers a longer period of time: weeks, months, and sometimes many years.
3. Has many short, fragmented scenes; sometimes alternates of short and long scenes.
4. May range over an entire city or even several countries.
5. Has a profusion of characters, sometimes several dozen.
6. Is frequently marked by several threads of action, such as two parallel plots, or scenes of comic relief in a serious play.
7. Scenes are juxtaposed to one another. An event may result from several causes, or from no apparent cause, but arises in a network or web of circumstances.

The table above outlines the chief characteristics of climactic and episodic forms and illustrates the differences between them. It is clear that the climactic and episodic forms differ from each other in their fundamental approaches. One emphasizes constriction and compression on all fronts; the other takes a far broader view and aims at a cumulative effect, piling up people, places, and events.

Serial Structure.   Another kind of structure is a *series* of acts or episodes—individual theater events—offered as a single presentation. In this case, individual segments are strung together like charms on a bracelet or beads on a necklace. Sometimes a central theme or common thread holds the various parts together; sometimes there is little or no connection between the parts.

One example of serial structure is the musical revue, which has a series of short scenes, songs, and dance numbers. An evening of one-act plays is another example.

Avant-Garde and Experimental Structures.   In the second half of the twentieth century, several groups in Europe and the United States experimented with ritual as a dramatic form. These groups included the Polish Laboratory Theatre, the Living Theatre, the Performance Group, and the Wooster Group. Such groups questioned long-held beliefs about traditional theater and dramatic structure, and one purpose of their experiments was to return to the ritualistic, religious roots of theater.

From their experiments, these groups developed several significant departures from traditional theater practice. Among them were (1) interest in *ritual* and *ceremony;* (2) emphasis on *nonverbal theater,* that is, theater stressing gestures, body movements, and wordless sounds rather than logical or intelligible language; (3) reliance on *improvisation,* or scenarios developed by performers and directors; (4) stress on the physical *environment* of theater, including a restructuring of the spatial relationship between performers and audience; and (5) stress on each audience member's developing his or her own interpretation of the work being presented.

We should note that there were many historical forerunners of these avant-garde techniques, which we shall review when we discuss modern theater.

Segments and Tableaux as Structure.   Robert Wilson and Richard Foreman, who will be discussed in Chapter 19, organize their avant-garde productions into units analogous to the frames of film and television, or to the still-life tableaux of painting or the moving tableaux of dance. Frequently, directors like Foreman and Wilson will use rapid movements—as in silent films—or slow motion. At times, several actions will occur simultaneously. All of these, however, relate both to an image and to a tableaux or frame.

CREATING DRAMATIC CHARACTERS

Along with creating dramatic structure, another major challenge for the person or persons developing a script is creating the characters who will carry out the action. In drama, as opposed to a novel or a short story, everything must be transformed into conversation between characters—called *dialogue*—or into action. Literature can rely on passages describing what the characters are thinking and how they react to each other; in theater, however, everything must be enacted by the characters.

Though they often seem like real people, dramatic characters are actually created in the imagination of a playwright. By carefully emphasizing certain features of a character's personality and eliminating others, the dramatist can show us in two hours the entire history of a person whom we might need a lifetime to know in the real world. In *A Streetcar Named Desire,* for example, we come to know Blanche DuBois, in all her emotional complexity, better than we know people we see every day. As we become intimately acquainted with Blanche, the dramatist reveals to us not only her biography but her mind and soul.

In deciding what to emphasize about a character and how to present the character, a playwright has wide latitude. A stage character can be drawn with a few quick strokes, as a caricaturist sketches a political figure; can be given the surface detail and reality of a photograph; or can be fleshed out with the more interpretive, fully rounded quality of an oil portrait.

Types of Dramatic Characters

Extraordinary Characters.   Heroes and heroines of most important dramatic works before the modern period are *extraordinary* in some way—that is, "larger than life." Historically, major characters have been kings, queens, generals, members of the nobility, or other figures clearly marked as holding a special place in society.

In addition to filling prestigious roles, extraordinary characters generally represent some extreme of human behavior—men and women at their worst or best. Lady Macbeth is not only a noblewoman; she is one of the most ambitious women ever depicted. In virtually every instance, extraordinary characters are men and women at the breaking point, at the outer limits of human capability and endurance.

For example, the young Greek heroine Antigone and the medieval religious figure Joan of Arc are the epitome of the independent, courageous female, willing to stand up to male authority with strength and dignity. Two heroes from ancient Greece, Prometheus and Oedipus, are men willing to face the worst the gods can throw at them and accept the consequences. Among those qualifying as human beings at their worst is the Greek heroine Medea, who murders her own children.

Comic characters can also be extremes. For instance, the chief character in *Volpone,* by Shakespeare's contemporary, the English comic dramatist Ben Jonson, is an avaricious miser who gets people to present him with expensive gifts because they mistakenly think he will remember them in his will.

EXTRAORDINARY CHARACTERS
The heroes and heroines of drama of the past—classical tragedies and historical plays—were usually kings, queens, members of the nobility, and military leaders: in other words, figures who by their very positions were exceptional. They may have been evil characters, or noble ones, but they stood above the crowd, both because of their position in society and because of their characteristics. A good example is the title character in Shakespeare's King Lear, *played here by Christopher Plummer in a production at Lincoln Center. Vain, arrogant, egotistical, imperious, and later humbled, but also a king, Lear is clearly larger than life.* (© Joan Marcus)

Kings, queens, and other extraordinary figures have continued to be treated in drama of the last hundred years; but beginning in the eighteenth century, ordinary people took over more and more from royalty and the nobility as the heroes and heroines of drama—a reflection of what was occurring in real life as monarchies became less powerful and democracy took hold. Nevertheless, the leading figures of drama continued to be exceptional men and women at their best and worst. The heroine of August Strindberg's *Miss Julie* is a neurotic, obsessive woman at the end of her rope. In *Mother Courage* by Bertolt Brecht, we see a woman who will sacrifice almost anything to survive; she even loses a son by haggling over the price of his release from detention. *The Emperor Jones*, by Eugene O'Neill, shows the downfall of a powerful black man who has made himself the ruler of a Caribbean island.

Representative or Quintessential Characters. Though many characters of modern drama are extraordinary, a new type of main character has emerged—one who is three-dimensional and highly individual, but at the same time ordinary. He or she stands apart not by being exceptional, but by being typical of a large, important sector of the population. Rather than being "worst," "best," or some other extreme, such characters are notable because they embody the characteristics of an entire group. We can call these characters *representative* or *quintessential.*

REPRESENTATIVE OR QUINTESSENTIAL CHARACTERS
In much of modern realistic theater, the main characters are distinguished not by being extraordinary or larger than life, but by being "representative" of a whole group or type. In the play A Doll's House *by Henrik Ibsen, Nora and her husband, Torvald, are such characters. The two are played here by Janet McTeer and Owen Teale, in a production on Broadway.* (© Joan Marcus)

A good example of a representative character is Nora Helmer, the heroine of Henrik Ibsen's *A Doll's House*. Though Nora secretly forged a signature to get money that saved the life of her husband when he was very ill, he regards her as spoiled and flighty. All her life, in fact—first by her father and now by her husband—she has been treated as a doll or a plaything, never as a mature, responsible woman. In the last act of the play, Nora rebels: she makes a declaration of independence to her husband, slams the door on him, and walks out. It has been said that Nora's slamming of the door marked the beginning not only of modern drama but of the emancipation of modern women. Nora's demand that she be treated as an equal has made her typical of all housewives who refuse to be regarded as pets. *A Doll's House* was written in 1879, but today—well over a century later—Nora still symbolizes the often inferior position of women.

Another example of a representative character is Willy Loman, in Arthur Miller's *Death of a Salesman*. Willy stands for all salesmen, traveling on "a smile and a shoeshine." He has accepted a false dream: the idea that he can be successful and rich by putting up a good front and being "well liked."

Nora Helmer and Willy Loman are both examples of characters who stand apart from the crowd, not by standing above it but by embodying the attributes of a certain type of ordinary person.

Stock Characters. Many characters in drama are not "complete," not "three-dimensional." Rather, they symbolize and throw into bold relief a particular type of person to the exclusion of virtually everything else. They are called *stock characters,* and although they can be found in almost all kinds of drama, they appear particularly in comedy and melodrama.

Among the most famous examples of stock characters are those in *commedia dell'arte,* a form of comic improvisational theater that flourished in Italy from the late sixteenth century to the eighteenth century. In commedia dell'arte, there were no scripts; there was only an outline of the action, and the performers supplied the words. There was a set group of stereotypical characters, each one invariably wearing the same costume and displaying the same personality traits. The bragging soldier, called Capitano, always boasted of his courage in a series of fictitious military victories. Pantalone, an elderly merchant, spoke in clichés and chased young women; and a pompous character, Dottore, spouted Latin phrases to impress others with his learning. Among the servant characters, Harlequin was the most popular; both cunning and stupid, he was at the heart of every plot complication.

The familiar figures in situation comedies on television are good examples of stock characters in our own day. The conceited high school boy, the prejudiced

A DOMINANT TRAIT

A favorite character of many comic writers through the ages has been one with a clear, strong trait that overrides all others: jealousy, avarice, miserliness, pomposity, and so forth. A good example is Mrs. Malaprop in The Rivals *by Richard Brinsley Sheridan. Mrs. Malaprop invariably uses long words in the wrong way, making her an immensely comic figure. Here, she is played by Mary Louise Wilson in a production at the Huntington Theatre. (© T. Charles Erickson)*

father, the harried mother, the dumb blond waitress, the efficient career person, the tough private detective—we can see such stereotypical characters every day on television. We recognize their familiar traits, and their attitudes and actions are always predictable.

Characters with a Dominant Trait.   Closely related to stock characters are characters with a ***dominant trait,*** or *humor.* One aspect of such a character dominates, making for an unbalanced, often comic, personality. Ben Jonson titled two of his plays *Every Man in His Humour* (1616) and *Every Man Out of His Humour* (1616); and he usually named his characters for their single trait or humor. In his play *The Alchemist* (1610), the characters have names like Subtle, Face, Dapper, Surly, Wholesome, and Dame Pliant.

Playwrights of the English Restoration also gave characters names that described their personalities. In *The Way of the World,* by William Congreve, one character is called Fainall, meaning "feign all"—that is, he constantly pretends. Other characters are Petulant, Sir Wilful Witwoud, Waitwell, and Lady Wishfort, the last being a contraction of "wish for it." Molière frequently emphasized the dominant trait of the main character in his titles: *The Miser, The Misanthrope, The Would-Be Gentleman* (1670), *The Imaginary Invalid.*

NONHUMAN CHARACTERS

Sometimes characters are nonhuman, though even they usually have human characteristics. This is a tradition that goes back to the comedies of Aristophanes in Greece during the fifth century B.C.E. *A modern example is found in the play* Seascape *by Edward Albee, in which two characters are lizards (who also happen to be quite human). Shown here as the lizards are Annalee Jeffries and David Patrick Kelly in a production at the Hartford Stage Company. (© T. Charles Erickson)*

Minor Characters.   Characters who play a small part in the overall action are called *minor characters.* Usually, they appear briefly and serve chiefly to further the story or to support more important characters.

Narrator or Chorus.   Generally, a *narrator* speaks directly to the audience, frequently commenting on the action. The narrator may or may not have a dramatic persona in the same sense as the other characters. In Tennessee Williams's *The Glass Menagerie,* the narrator is also a character in the play; in Thornton Wilder's *Our Town,* the narrator becomes several characters during the course of the action. Greek drama used a *chorus* that commented, in song and dance, on the action of the main plot and reacted to it.

Nonhuman Characters.   In many primitive cultures, performers portrayed birds and animals, and this practice has continued to the present. Aristophanes, the Greek comic playwright, used a chorus to play the title parts in his plays *The Birds* (414 B.C.E.) and *The Frogs* (405 B.C.E.). In the modern era, the absurdist playwright Eugène Ionesco has people turn into animals in *Rhinoceros* (1959).

The contemporary American playwright Edward Albee has performers play lizards in *Seascape* (1974).

Occasionally, playwrights use other kinds of nonhuman roles. For example, as we shall see, medieval dramatists who wrote morality plays created characters representing ideas or concepts.

While authors may create nonhuman characters, however, we should note that their focus is always on drawing parallels with the human experience.

Juxtaposition of Characters

In creating characters, a playwright can use them in combinations that will bring out certain qualities.

One such combination consists of a *protagonist* and an *antagonist.* These terms come from Greek theater. A *protagonist* is the leading character in a play, the chief or outstanding figure in the action. An *antagonist* is the character who opposes the protagonist. In Shakespeare's *Othello,* for example, the protagonist is Othello and the antagonist is Iago, his chief opponent. Through the interaction and conflict between protagonist and antagonist, the individual qualities of both characters emerge.

Another way to contrast characters is to set them side by side rather than in opposition. Frequently, a dramatist will introduce secondary characters to serve as *foils* or *counterparts* to the main characters. In *Hedda Gabler,* by Henrik Ibsen, the main character, Hedda, is destructive and willful, bent on having her own way. Mrs. Elvsted, another character in the play, is Hedda's opposite in almost every regard.

In this chapter, we have examined the work of the person or persons creating a dramatic text. We have looked at the development of subject, focus, and purpose and the creation of dramatic structure and dramatic characters. In Chapter 7 we turn to another aspect of the script: point of view as it manifests itself in dramatic genres.

SUMMARY

The person or persons creating a dramatic text have a number of tasks and responsibilities: to develop the subject, focus, and purpose of the text. Beyond that, those creating a text must develop a dramatic structure and dramatic characters.

Like an architect planning a building, those who create a text must develop a structure for a play. Essentials of dramatic structure include plot, conflict, strongly opposed forces, and a reasonable balance between those forces. Working with these essentials, the playwright creates the structure. An opening scene starts the action and sets the tone and style. Then the characters, motivated by objectives or goals, encounter a series of obstacles and complications. The result is a succession of crises leading to the most important crisis, the climax.

In the past, playwrights generally used either climactic or episodic structure. In climactic form, all aspects of a play—such as action, duration, and number of characters and locales—are restricted; in episodic form, these aspects are all expanded. At certain times in theater history, climactic and episodic form have been combined.

A playwright or the equivalent must also create characters, using dialogue and action. Playwrights of the past usually presented extraordinary, "larger than life" characters. A modern dramatist is less likely to present elevated characters such as kings and queens, but present-day playwrights still often give us exceptional characters—people at their best or their worst. Today's playwrights might also choose to present ordinary but representative characters, typical of a large portion of the population. A playwright may also use stock characters, easily recognizable stereotypes.

The playwright or whoever creates a text juxtaposes characters to highlight their individual traits—for example, opposing the main character or protagonist with an antagonist or a contrasting character.

KEY TERMS

Action According to the Greek philosopher Aristotle, a sequence of events linked by cause and effect, with a beginning, middle, and end. Said by Aristotle to be the best way to unify a play. More generally, the central, unifying conflict and movement through a drama.

Antagonist Opponent of the protagonist in a drama.

Chorus In ancient Greek drama, a group of performers who sang and danced, sometimes participating in the action but usually simply commenting on it. In modern times, performers in a musical play who sing and dance as a group.

Climactic structure Also referred to as *intensive structure*. Dramatic structure in which there are few scenes, a short time passes, there are few locales, and the action begins chronologically close to the climax.

Climax Often defined as the high point in the action or the final and most significant crisis in the action.

Commedia dell'arte (koh-MAY-dee-ah dehl-AHR-teh) Form of comic theater, originating in sixteenth-century Italy, in which dialogue was improvised around a

loose scenario calling for a set of stock characters.

Complication Introduction, in a play, of a new force that creates a new balance of power and entails a delay in reaching the climax.

Conflict Tension between two or more characters that leads to crisis or a climax; a fundamental struggle or imbalance—involving ideologies, actions, personalities, etc.—underlying a play.

Crisis Point within a play when the action reaches an important confrontation or takes a critical turn. In the tradition of the well-made play, a drama includes a series of crises that lead to the final crisis, known as the climax.

Deus ex machina (DEH-oos eks MAH-kih-nah) Literally, "god from a machine," a resolution device in classic Greek drama; hence, intervention of supernatural forces—usually at the last moment—to save the action from its logical conclusion. In modern drama, an arbitrary and coincidental solution.

Dialogue Conversation between characters in a play.

Dominant trait Found in certain theatrical characters: one paramount trait or tendency that overshadows all others and appears to control the conduct of the character. Examples could include greed, jealousy, anger, and self-importance.

Episodic structure Also referred to as *extensive structure*. Dramatic structure in which there are many scenes, taking place over a considerable period of time in a number of locations. Many episodic plays also use such devices as subplots.

Exposition Imparting of information necessary for an understanding of the story but not covered by the action onstage; events or knowledge from the past, or occurring outside the play, which must be introduced for the audience to understand the characters or plot.

Minor characters In a drama, those characters who have small, secondary, or supporting roles. These could include soldiers and servants.

Obstacle That which delays or prevents the achieving of a goal by a character. An obstacle creates complication and conflict.

Plot As distinct from story, the patterned arrangement in a drama of events and characters, with incidents selected and arranged for maximum dramatic impact. Also, in Elizabethan theaters, an outline of the play that was posted backstage for the actors.

Protagonist Principal character in a play, the one whom the drama is about.

Representative characters Characters in a play who embody characteristics that represent an entire group.

Ritual Specifically ordered ceremonial event, often religious.

Stock character Character who has one outstanding trait of human behavior to the exclusion of virtually all other attributes. These characters often seem like stereotypes and are most often used in comedy and melodrama.

Subplot Secondary plot that reinforces or runs parallel to the major plot in an episodic play.

THEATER ON THE WEB

For more research and to learn more about the topics in this chapter, please visit the Online Learning Center at **www.mhhe.com/livelyart6**.

CHAPTER 7

Tragedy or Comedy? Dramatic Genres

◄ **COMEDY OR TRAGEDY?**

Drama is often put into categories: tragedy, comedy, tragicomedy, melodrama, and so forth. Sometimes these categories overlap, but ever since the ancient Greeks separated tragedy and comedy and provided a mask for each, the practice of dividing drama into various types or genres has proved helpful to practitioners and audiences alike. A drama that fulfills the requirements of tragedy is Shakespeare's Othello. *The production shown here was directed by Joe Dowling at the Guthrie Theatre, and features Lester Purry (Othello) and Cheyenne Casebier (Desdemona). (© T. Charles Erickson)*

113

Before we look at viewpoint in dramatic writing, we should note that not only do those who create theater adopt different points of view toward events and toward life in general; all of us do. Depending on our perspective, we can see the same subject as funny or sad, take it seriously or laugh at it, make it an object of pity or of ridicule. Just why we look at events from different points of view is difficult to say, but there is no question that we do. The English author Horace Walpole (1717–1797) wrote: "This world is a comedy to those that think, a tragedy to those that feel."

In theater, this question of viewpoint—looking at people or events from a particular perspective—becomes crucial. Viewpoint is not taken for granted, as it is in everyday life; rather, it is a conscious act on the part of whoever creates the text. To take an example, in most cases death is considered a somber matter; but in his play *Arsenic and Old Lace* (1941), the dramatist Joseph Kesselring (1902–1967) makes it clear that we are to regard death as comic. Kesselring presents two elderly women who kill no fewer than twelve old men by serving them arsenic in glasses of wine. But because the dramatist makes a joke of the way the women prepare the poison and because he removes from the play any feeling that the deaths are to be taken seriously, he engenders in the audience the notion that it is all in fun.

WHAT IS GENRE?

In theater, viewpoint is incorporated in what is known as *genre*—a French word meaning "category" or "type." Before examining genre, we should note that often a play does not fit neatly into a single category. Those who create a text do not write categories or types of plays; they write individual, unique works—and preoccupation with genre may distract us from the individuality of a play or a production. Still, if we keep these reservations in mind, we will find that it is helpful to understand the traditional genres into which western dramatic literature has fallen.

The oldest and best-known genres in theater are *tragedy* and *comedy*. The Greeks, who first made a clear distinction between the two approaches, created a mask for tragedy and a mask for comedy, and these masks have become a symbol for theater. Before we look specifically at tragedy and comedy, we should note that point of view in drama is strongly influenced by the way a society regards human life.

TRAGEDY

Tragedy is serious drama involving important personages caught in calamitous circumstances; it evokes in the audience fear and apprehension for the characters who are suffering, and admiration for the courage they display. Many people consider tragedy the loftiest and most profound form of theater—in fact, one of the most meaningful forms of expression in any of the arts. Why is this so? For one thing, tragedy probes very basic questions about human existence. Why are people sometimes extremely cruel? Why is the world so unjust? Why are men and women called on to endure suffering? What are the limits of human suffering and endurance? In the midst of cruelty and despair, what are the possibilities of human achievement? To what heights of courage, strength, generosity, and integrity can human beings rise?

Tragedy assumes that the universe is indifferent to human concerns, and often cruel or malevolent. Sometimes the innocent suffer while the evil prosper. Some human beings are capable of despicable deeds; others confront and overcome adversity, attaining a nobility that places them, in the words of the psalmist in the Bible, "a little lower than the angels."

Conditions for Tragedy: Theater and Society

When we study theater history, we recognize that theater, like any art form, does not occur in a vacuum. It is created by artists who live in a given culture at a given time. They are shaped by their culture, even though they may question it or rebel against it.

For example, in western civilization, the eighteenth century was known as the age of enlightenment and the nineteenth century as the century of progress. Over the course of these two centuries, there were political revolutions in France and America, the industrial revolution, and many scientific advances. As a result, the eighteenth and nineteenth centuries were optimistic periods, when it was felt that our worst problems—poverty, disease, injustice—could be solved. This point of view is hardly conducive to tragedy.

By contrast, other periods of western civilization were characterized by a point of view receptive to tragedy. The outlook of these societies created what might be called the *conditions* or *climate* for tragedy. In general, there seem to be two such conditions—which at first appear mutually contradictory but are actually two sides of the same coin. One side of this tragic coin is the idea that human beings are capable of extraordinary accomplishments; the other is the idea that the world is potentially cruel and unjust. Both conditions are evidently necessary; for example, the eighteenth and nineteenth centuries in Europe reflected the concept of humanity as capable of vast accomplishments, but not the concept of the world as cruel and unjust.

Two periods in which both ideas were prominent, and which did prove conducive to tragedy, were the golden age of Greece in the fifth century B.C.E. and the Renaissance (the fourteenth through seventeenth centuries) in Europe. In both eras, human beings were exalted above all else; the gods and nature were given much less prominence. A look at the history of the two periods shows that the horizons of human achievement were considered unlimited. In the fifth century B.C.E., Greece was truly enjoying its golden age, in commerce, politics, science, and art: Pythagoras had recently formulated his theories of mathematics; Socrates was holding his philosophical discourses; and the Parthenon was being built atop the Acropolis in Athens. Nothing seemed impossible in the way of architecture, mathematics, trade, or philosophy. The same was true in Europe and England during the Renaissance. Columbus had reached the new world in 1492; the

A CLIMATE FOR TRAGEDY

Two historical periods particularly suited for the creation of dramatic tragedies were ancient Greece and the Renaissance. Shown here in a production of a play from the Greek period is the British actress Vanessa Redgrave portraying the title character in Euripides's Hecuba *at the Brooklyn Academy of Music. (© Richard Termine)*

possibilities for trade and exploration appeared infinite; science and the arts were on the threshold of a new day.

In both periods, celebration of the individual was apparent in all the arts, including drama. The Greek dramatist Sophocles exclaimed:

> Numberless are the wonders of the world.
> but none
> More wonderful than man.

And in the Renaissance, Shakespeare has Hamlet say:

> What a piece of work is man! How noble in reason! How infinite in faculty!
> In form, in moving, how express and admirable! In action how like an angel!
> In apprehension how like a god!

The credo of both ages was expressed by Protagoras, a Greek philosopher of the fifth century B.C.E.:

> Man is the measure of all things.

But both periods also reflect the other side of the tragic coin. Along with exalted humanism, there was a simultaneous awareness of what life can do to men and women: an unflinching admission that life can be, and in fact frequently is, cruel, unjust, and even meaningless. Shakespeare, writing in 1606, put it this way in *King Lear:*

> As flies to wanton boys, are we to the gods;
> They kill us for their sport.

In *Macbeth,* he expressed it in these words:

> Out, out brief candle!
> Life's but a walking shadow, a poor player
> That struts and frets his hour upon the stage
> And then is heard no more; it is a tale
> Told by an idiot, full of sound and fury,
> Signifying nothing.

The Greek golden age and the Renaissance, then, encompassed both attitudes toward existence: the greatness of human beings on the one hand, and the cruelty of life on the other. These two sides of the tragic coin are the indispensable conditions for the creation of tragedy.

We must note, however, that—important as it is—the outlook of a society serves only as a background in creating theater. The foreground is the highly personal point of view of the individual artist. This is proved by the fact that playwrights within the same era vary greatly. At the same time that Euripides was writing tragedies in ancient Greece, Aristophanes was writing satirical farces. In France in the seventeenth century, Molière was writing comedies while Jean Racine was writing tragedies. In the modern period particularly, drama expresses a multiplicity of individual viewpoints.

THE TRAGIC HERO
In classic or traditional tragedy, the hero or heroine is caught in circumstances from which there is no escape and which lead inevitably to a fateful end. A good example is the title character in Shakespeare's Hamlet. *Shown here is Simon Russell Beale as* Hamlet *in a production at London's Royal National Theatre. (© Donald Cooper/Photostage.)*

Traditional Tragedy

Tragedy can be divided into two basic kinds: traditional and modern. Let's begin by looking at traditional tragedy. We have noted that Greece in the fifth century B.C.E. and certain European countries in the Renaissance were conducive to tragedy. What characteristics do the traditional tragedies of these periods have in common?

Tragic Heroes and Heroines.   Generally, the hero or heroine of a traditional tragedy is an extraordinary person: a king, a queen, a general, a member of the nobility—in other words, a person of stature. Because these heroes and heroines are important, they stand not only as individuals but as symbols of an entire culture or society. Also, the central figure of a traditional tragedy is caught in a set of tragic circumstances. In traditional tragedy, the universe seems to trap the hero or heroine in a fateful web.

Tragic Irretrievability.   The tragic situation becomes irretrievable: there is no turning back, no way out. Tragic heroes and heroines suffer a cumulative series of reversals. The figures of traditional tragedy find themselves in situations from which there is no honorable avenue of escape; they must go forward to meet their tragic fate.

MODERN TRAGEDY

A number of plays by serious playwrights of the past 145 years can be classified as contemporary or modern tragedies. Though they do not have certain elements of traditional tragedy—such as poetry or characters from the nobility—they deal with similar themes in a profound way. A good example is Miss Julie *by Strindberg, in which a neurotic young woman from a well-to-do family is locked in a struggle of love and hate with a servant, Jean. In the production shown here, by the Two River Theatre Company, Heather Lea Anderson plays Julie and Ed Onipede Blunt portrays Jean. (© T. Charles Erickson)*

Acceptance of Responsibility. A tragic hero or heroine accepts responsibility for his or her actions and also shows a willingness to suffer and an immense capacity for suffering. In many traditional tragedies, the hero or heroine recognizes the flaw or fault of character that leads to the tragic downfall.

Tragic Verse. The language of traditional tragedy is *verse*. Because it deals with lofty and profound ideas, tragedy soars to the heights and descends to the depths of human experience; and many people feel that such thoughts and emotions can be best expressed in poetry.

The Effect of Tragedy. When the elements of traditional tragedy are combined, they appear to produce two contradictory reactions simultaneously. One reaction is pessimistic: the heroes or heroines are "damned if they do and damned if they don't," and the world is a cruel, uncompromising place. And yet, in even the bleakest tragedy, there is affirmation. One source of this positive reaction is the drama itself. Traditional tragic playwrights, although telling us that the world is in chaos, at the same time strike a note of affirmation by the very act of creating such carefully shaped and brilliant works of art.

When we come to the theaters of fifth-century Greece (in Chapter 13), the English Renaissance (in Chapter 15), and neoclassical France (also in Chapter 15), we will look at specific examples of traditional tragedy and their unique characteristics.

Modern Tragedy

Tragedies of the modern period—that is, beginning in the late nineteenth century—do not have queens or kings as central figures, and they are written in prose rather than poetry. For these reasons, as well as more philosophical reasons, there are those who argue that modern tragedies are not true tragedies.

On the other side, those who argue in favor of modern tragedy point out that modern dramatists probe the same depths and ask the same questions as their predecessors: Why do men and women suffer? Why is there violence and injustice in the world? And perhaps most fundamental of all: What is the meaning of life? When we turn to theater of the late nineteenth century and the twentieth century, we will examine specific examples of plays that have been called "modern tragedies."

COMEDY

Comedy is humorous drama whose characters, actions, and events are intended to provoke amusement and laughter. People who create comedy are not necessarily frivolous or unconcerned with important matters; they may be extremely serious in their own way. Consider three comic dramatists from different periods —Aristophanes in classical Greece, Molière in seventeenth-century France, and George Bernard Shaw in modern Britain. All three cared passionately about human affairs and human problems. But they—and others like them—took a comic view of life; they saw the world differently from someone whose outlook is somber; they made their points with a smile, an arched eyebrow, a deep laugh. As they observed human follies and excesses, they developed a keen sense of the ridiculous, showing us things that make us laugh.

Laughter is one of the most elusive of human reactions; no one—from philosophers to psychoanalysts—has provided a fully satisfactory explanation of why we laugh. Most people do agree, however, that laughter is quintessentially human. Other creatures express pain and sorrow—emotions we associate with tragedy—but apparently only human beings laugh.

It should also be noted that there are many kinds of laughter, ranging all the way from mild amusement at a witty saying or a humorous situation to a belly laugh at wild physical comedy, to cruel derisive laughter at someone who is different. (An example of derisive laughter would be a group of children mocking a newcomer to their school or neighborhood who seems "different"—perhaps a child with a physical disability or a speech impediment.) Theater, which reflects society, includes a similar range of comedy, from light comedies to outrageous farces.

Characteristics of Comedy

If we cannot fully explain comedy, we can at least understand some of the principles that make it possible.

Suspension of Natural Laws.   One feature of most comedy is a temporary suspension of the natural laws of probability and logic. Actions in a comic play do not have the same consequences as actions in real life.

In comedy, when a haughty man walking down a street steps on a child's skateboard and goes sprawling on the sidewalk, we do not fear for his safety or wonder if he has been hurt. In comedy, the focus is on the man's being tripped up

SUSPENSION OF NATURAL LAWS IN COMEDY

One of the devices that make comedy possible and that add greatly to the pleasure of comedy is the suspension of natural laws. We are prepared to laugh at things in a stage comedy that we would never laugh at in real life. Also, events and characters can be juxtaposed in a way they never could in the everyday world. The characters and events in Shakespeare's The Comedy of Errors *are an example. In the scene shown here, we see two characters from the play, Angelo and Antipholus, played by Brian Baumgartner and Judson Pearce Morgan, in a production at the Guthrie Theater in Minneapolis. Note the exaggeration in the costume at the left, and in the gestures of both characters. (©Michal Daniel)*

and getting his comeuppance. We have in some sense suspended our belief in injury. In burlesque, a comic character can be hit on the backside with a fierce thwack, and we laugh, because we know that only his or her pride is hurt. In fact, at one point in stage history a special stick, made of two flat wooden slats fastened closely together, was developed to make the sound of hitting even more fearsome: when this stick hit someone, the two slats would slap together, making the whack much louder. The device was known as a ***slapstick,*** and its name came to describe all kinds of raucous, knockabout comedy.

Prime examples of the suspension of natural laws in comedy are silent movies and film cartoons. In animated cartoons, characters are hurled through the air like missiles, shot full of holes, and flattened on the sidewalk after falling from buildings; but they always get up, with little more than a shake of the head. The audience has no thought of real injury, of cuts or bruises, because the real-life chain of cause and effect does not apply.

Under such conditions, murder itself can be viewed as comic. The American playwright Arthur Kopit (1937–   ) titled one of his plays *Oh, Dad, Poor Dad, Mama's Hung You in the Closet and I'm Feeling So Sad* (1960). In Kopit's play, as in *Arsenic and Old Lace,* the serious aspects of murder have been eliminated. We do not dwell on the fact that people are being killed, and we have none of the feelings we would usually have for victims; as a result, we are free to enjoy the irony and incongruity of the situation.

Contrast between Individuals and the Social Order. Comedy develops when two elements—a basic assumption about society and the events of the play—cut against each other like the blades of a pair of scissors. In most instances, comic writers accept the notion of a clear social and moral order in their society; it is not the social order that is at fault when something goes wrong but the defiance of that order by individuals. Human excess, fraud, hypocrisy, and folly are laughed at against a background of normality and moderation. This view, we should note, is in contrast to the view of many serious plays, particularly tragedies, which assume that society itself is upside down, or that, in Hamlet's words, "the time is out of joint."

In Molière's comedy *Tartuffe,* for example, the chief character is a charlatan and hypocrite who pretends to be pious and holy, going so far as to wear clerical garb. He lives in the house of Orgon, a foolish man who trusts him implicitly. The truth is that Tartuffe is trying to acquire Orgon's wife as well as his money; but Orgon, blind to Tartuffe's real nature, is completely taken in by him. The audience and Orgon's family are aware of what is going on; they can see how ludicrous these two characters are, and in the end both Tartuffe's hypocrisy and Orgon's gullibility are exposed. But it is the individual—not religion or marriage —that is ridiculed. What Molière criticizes is the *abuse* of religion and marriage.

Many modern comedies reverse the scissors blades; their basic assumption is that the world is not orderly but absurd or ridiculous. Society, rather than providing a moral or social framework, offers only chaos. Against this background, ordinary people are set at odds with the world around them, and the comedy results from thrusting normal people into an abnormal world. This condition—a normal person in an upside-down world—is found especially in tragicomedy and theater of the absurd, both of which will be discussed later in this chapter.

The Comic Premise. Suspension of natural laws (together with the scissors effect of setting a ridiculous person in a normal world or vice versa) makes possible the development of a comic premise. A *comic premise* is an idea or concept that turns the accepted notion of things upside down. This idea becomes the basis of a play: it provides thematic and structural unity and serves as a springboard for comic dialogue, comic characters, and comic situations.

The Greek satiric dramatist Aristophanes was a master at developing a comic premise. In *The Clouds* (423 B.C.E.), Aristophanes pictures the philosopher Socrates as a man who can think only when perched in a basket suspended in midair. In *The Birds,* two ordinary men persuade a chorus of birds to build a city between heaven and earth. The birds comply, calling the place Cloudcuckoo Land, and the two men sprout wings to join them. In *Lysistrata,* Aristophanes has the women of Greece go on a sex strike; they will not make love to their husbands until the husbands stop fighting a prolonged war and sign a peace treaty with their opponents.

The comic premise—along with the suspension of natural laws—leads to exaggeration and incongruity in several areas of comedy: verbal humor, characterization, and comic situations. These will be explored in detail when we discuss individual comedies in Part Three.

Forms of Comedy

Depending on the dramatist's intent and comic techniques, comedy takes various forms, including farce, burlesque, satire, domestic comedy, comedy of manners, and comedy of ideas.

Farce. *Farce* thrives on all forms of exaggeration—broad physical humor, plot complications, stereotyped characters. It has no intellectual pretensions but aims simply at entertainment and laughter. One hallmark of farce is excessive plot

THE FUN OF FARCE

In farce everything is in fun, and events do not have the serious consequences they do in real life. Exaggeration—in language, in characters, in plot developments—is one of the main ingredients of farce. Shown here is a scene from a classic modern farce about backstage life in the theater, Noises Off! *by Michael Frayn. The production at the Royal National Theatre in London features Arden Gillett (left) as Garry Lejeune and Jeff Rawle as Frederick Fellowes. (© Donald Cooper/Photostage)*

complications, and its humor usually results from ridiculous situations as well as pratfalls and horseplay. It relies less on verbal wit than the more intellectual forms of comedy do, though puns are used frequently in farce.

In modern times, the Marx brothers' films of the 1930s are examples of farce, as are the films of the actor Jim Carrey (1962–   ), such as *Liar, Liar; Me, Myself, and Irene; Bruce Almighty;* and *Fun with Dick and Jane.* Mistaken identity, chase scenes, mock violence, rapid movement, and accelerating pace—as in a slapstick scene in a hotel room or a restaurant—are typical of farce. In bedroom farce, marriage and sex are objects of fun; in other types of farce, medicine, law, and business can serve as the butt of jokes.

Burlesque. *Burlesque* also relies on knockabout physical humor, gross exaggerations, and occasional vulgarity. Historically, burlesque was a ludicrous imitation of other forms of drama or of individual plays. The *Austin Powers* and *Scary Movie* films are contemporary examples. In the United States, the term *burlesque* came to describe a type of variety show featuring low comedy skits and attractive women.

Satire. *Satire* uses wit—especially sophisticated language—irony, and exaggeration to expose or attack evil and foolishness. Satire can attack one specific figure, or it can be more inclusive, as in Molière's *Tartuffe,* which ridicules religious hypocrisy generally.

Domestic Comedy. *Domestic comedy* usually deals with family situations and is found most frequently today in television situation comedies—sitcoms—that feature members of a family or neighborhood friends caught up in a series of complicated but amusing situations. Television shows like *Everybody Loves Raymond, Will and Grace, Two and a Half Men,* and *Desperate Housewives* would be good examples. This form of comedy was once a staple of theater and can still be found onstage in plays by writers like Neil Simon (1927–   ).

Comedy of Manners. Concerned with pointing up the foibles and peculiarities of the upper class, *comedy of manners* uses verbal wit to depict the charm of its characters and expose their social pretensions. Rather than relying on horseplay, it stresses witty phrases and clever barbs. In England, a line of comedies of manners runs from William Wycherley, William Congreve, and Oliver Goldsmith in the seventeenth and eighteenth centuries to Oscar Wilde (1854–1900) in the nineteenth century and Noël Coward (1899–1973) in the twentieth.

Comedy of Ideas.   Many plays of the British writer George Bernard Shaw could be put under a special heading: *comedy of ideas*. In plays like *Arms and the Man* (1894), Shaw used comic techniques to debate intellectual propositions such as the nature of war, cowardice, and romance.

Clearly, comedy comes in many forms, from the most basic type, designed only to provide a laugh, to the more intellectual type, designed to make us think while we are being entertained. In between are many combinations of these two types. Underlying them all, though, is an emphasis on humor. Whatever its form, comedy focuses on the follies and foolishness of men and women, sometimes with a rueful shrug, sometimes with a wry smile, and sometimes with an uproarious laugh.

TYPES OF COMEDY

Comedy takes a number of forms, depending on whether the emphasis is on verbal wit, plot complications, or the characters' eccentricities, as well as on the degree of fantasy and exaggeration, and the emphasis on high comedy or low comedy. Shown here is an example of comedy of manners, which emphasizes verbal wit and the characters' eccentricities. The play is Oscar Wilde's The Importance of Being Earnest *in a production at the Ahmanson Theatre in Los Angeles, directed by Peter Hall. Left to right are Robert Petkoff as Algernon Moncrieff, Lynn Redgrave as Lady Bracknell, and Charlotte Parry as Cecily Cardew. (© Craig Schwartz)*

HEROIC DRAMA

We have begun with the two fundamental genres: tragedy and comedy. However, other genres have also been important in theater history, including heroic drama, melodrama, domestic drama, and tragicomedy.

The term *heroic drama* refers to serious drama that has heroic or noble characters and certain other traits of classic tragedy—such as dialogue in verse, elevated language, or extreme situations—but differs from tragedy in important respects. One way is in having a happy ending; another is in assuming a basically optimistic worldview, even when the ending is sad.

If heroic drama has a happy ending, the chief characters go through many trials and tribulations but finally emerge victorious. We agonize with the hero or heroine, but we are aware all the time that the play will end well. Several Greek plays that are ordinarily classified as tragedies are actually closer to what we are calling heroic drama. In Sophocles's *Electra*, for instance, Electra suffers grievously, but at the end of the play she and her brother Orestes triumph. In the late seventeenth century in England, a form of drama called heroic drama or

HEROIC DRAMA

Though it has many of the characteristics of tragedy, heroic drama differs in usually having a happy ending, or an ending in which the dead hero or heroine is exalted in some way. A drama of the late nineteenth century that has many elements of tragedy, including dialogue in verse, is Cyrano de Bergerac. *The title character dies at the end, but he feels triumphant. Shown here in the role of Cyrano is Geraint Wyn Davies at the Shakespeare Theatre in Washington, D.C. (© Richard Termine)*

heroic tragedy was precisely the type of which we are speaking—a serious play with a happy ending for the hero or heroine. Although many Asian dramas—from India, China, and Japan—resist the usual classifications and involve much dance and music, they often bear a close resemblance to heroic drama. Frequently, for example, a hero goes through a series of dangerous adventures, emerging victorious at the end. The vast majority of Asian dramas end happily.

A second type of heroic drama involves the death of the hero or heroine, but neither the events along the way nor the conclusion can be thought of as tragic. *Cyrano de Bergerac,* written in 1897 by Edmond Rostand, is a good example. The title character, Cyrano, dies at the end, but only after his love for Roxanne, hidden for 15 years, has been revealed. He dies a happy man, declaring his opposition to oppression and secure in the knowledge that he did not love in vain. *Saint Joan* (1923), by George Bernard Shaw, is another example: Joan is burned at the stake, but her death is actually a form of triumph; moreover, Shaw provides an epilogue in which Joan reappears after her death.

In the history of theater, heroic drama occupies a large and important niche, cutting across Asian and western civilization, and across periods from the Greek golden age to the present.

MELODRAMA

The term *melodrama* means "song drama" or "music drama." Though it originally comes from the Greek, it usually refers to a theatrical form made popular by the French at the end of the eighteenth century and the beginning of the nineteenth. "Music" here refers to the background music that accompanied these plays, similar to the music played along with silent films and to background music in sound films.

In early melodrama, a premium was put on surface effects, especially those creating suspense, fear, nostalgia, and other strong emotions in the audience. The heroes and heroines of melodrama were clearly delineated and stood in sharp contrast to the villains; the audience sympathized with the good characters and despised the bad ones. Melodrama had easily recognizable stock characters: the threatened young woman, the sidekick (a comic foil to the hero), and the calculating villain. The highly moral tone of traditional melodrama meant that the conflict between good and evil was clearly and firmly established, and virtue was always victorious. In order to keep the audience's interest, melodrama—both past and present—has a suspenseful plot, with a climax at the end of each act. Today, melodramas on television, such as adventure stories, detective stories, and cop shows, have a climax—a car crash, a sudden confrontation, a discovery of important evidence—just before each commercial break.

Most types of nineteenth-century melodrama have modern equivalents. Domestic melodrama has a counterpart in television soap opera. Frontier melodrama has become the western. Crime melodrama is now the popular mystery or detective show. Nautical melodrama, which dealt with sailors and pirates, was the forerunner of the swashbuckler or underwater film. Equestrian melodrama, which featured horses performing spectacular tricks, was the ancestor of various television and film melodramas starring animals.

DOMESTIC OR BOURGEOIS DRAMA

In the eighteenth and nineteenth centuries, there was a marked rise in the importance of ordinary men and women. With the industrial revolution and the expansion of trade, the merchant class came very much to the forefront and began to replace kings, queens, and the nobility—dukes and duchesses, earls and countesses—as both social and political leaders. With the emergence of this new class of ordinary citizens, there was a call for drama dealing not with royal families but with people from everyday life. As a result, drama began to change.

In England in 1731, George Lillo (1691–1739) wrote *The London Merchant*, about a merchant's apprentice who is led astray by a prostitute and betrays his good-hearted employer. This play, like others that came after it, overstated the case for simple working-class virtues; but it dealt with recognizable people from the daily life of Britain, and audiences welcomed it.

From these beginnings, *bourgeois* or *domestic drama* developed throughout the balance of the eighteenth century and the whole of the nineteenth, until it achieved a place of prominence in the works of Ibsen, Strindberg, and later writers such as Arthur Miller, Tennessee Williams, Lorraine Hansberry, and August Wilson. Problems of society, struggles within a family, dashed hopes, and renewed determination are characteristic of domestic drama. *Domestic* means "related to the household or the family," and most of the plays in this category deal with people from everyday life—usually the members of a family—in their own homes.

In the last 150 years, domestic drama has replaced both classical tragedy, as written by the Greeks and the Elizabethans, and heroic drama as the predominant type of serious drama. Domestic drama that is serious but has a happy ending has replaced heroic drama; and domestic drama with an unhappy ending that is sufficiently penetrating or profound has become a modern form of tragedy.

TRAGICOMEDY

Drama has often combined serious and comic material in the same play, and at times in the past there have been dramas classified as tragicomedies. It was in the twentieth century, however, that the genre of tragicomedy came to the forefront. What exactly is *tragicomedy?*

Traditionally, comedy has been set in opposition to tragedy or serious drama: serious drama is sad, comedy is funny; serious drama makes people cry, comedy makes them laugh; serious drama arouses anger, comedy brings a smile. The two, however, are not always as clearly separated as this polarity suggests. For instance, a great deal of serious drama has comic elements. Shakespeare included comic characters in several of his serious plays: the drunken porter in *Macbeth,* the grave-digger in *Hamlet,* and Falstaff in *Henry IV, Part 1* are examples. One of the best-known of all medieval plays, *The Second Shepherds' Play,* concerns the visit of the shepherds to the manger of the newborn Christ child. While they are spending the night in a field, Mak, a comic character, steals a sheep and takes it to his house; he and his wife put it into a crib, pretending that it is their baby (a parody of Christ in the manger). When the shepherds discover what Mak has done, they toss him in a blanket, and after this horseplay the serious part of the story resumes.

Such alternation of serious and comic elements is a practice of long standing, but *tragicomedy* does not refer to plays that simply shift from serious to comic and back again. In tragicomedy, the point of view is itself mixed; the overall or prevailing attitude is a *synthesis,* or fusion, of the serious and the comic. One eye looks through a comic lens and the other through a serious lens; and the two points of view are so intermingled as to become one—like a food that tastes sweet and sour at the same time.

Shakespearean Tragicomedy

In addition to his basically serious plays and his basically comic plays, Shakespeare wrote others, such as *Measure for Measure* (1604) and *All's Well That Ends Well* (1602), which seem to be a combination of tragedy and comedy. Because they do not fit neatly into one category or the other, these plays have been dubbed *problem plays.* The "problem," however, arises largely because of a difficulty in accepting the tragicomic point of view, for these plays have many attributes of a fusion of tragic and comic. In *Measure for Measure,* for instance, Angelo—a puritanical, austere man—condemns young Claudio to death for having made his fiancée pregnant. When Claudio's sister, Isabella, comes to plead for her brother, Angelo is overcome by passion and tries to make Isabella his mistress. Angelo's sentencing of Claudio is serious, but the bitter irony that arises when Angelo himself is guilty of even worse "sins of the flesh" is comic. The result is a situation that is simultaneously tragic and comic.

Modern Tragicomedy

In the modern period—during the last hundred years or so—tragicomedy has become a predominant form. A statement made by the Danish philosopher Søren Kierkegaard (1813–1855) as early as 1842 can serve to set the tone for the tragicomic attitude: "Existence itself, the act of existence, is a striving and is both pathetic and comic in the same degree."

The plays of Anton Chekhov, written at the end of the nineteenth century, reflect this spirit. Chekhov called two of his major plays comedies; but Stanislavski, who directed them, called them tragedies—a confusion arising from Chekhov's mixture of the serious and the comic. One illustration of Chekhov's approach is found in a scene at the end of the third act of his play *Uncle Vanya*, first produced in 1899. Vanya and his niece, Sonya, have worked and sacrificed for years to keep an estate going in order to support her father, a professor. At the worst possible moment, just when Vanya and Sonya have both been rebuffed by people they love, the professor announces that he wants to sell the estate, leaving Vanya and Sonya with nothing. A few moments later Vanya comes in to shoot the professor. He waves his gun in the air like a madman and shoots twice, but he misses both times and then collapses on the floor. In this scene, Vanya and Sonya are condemned to a lifetime of drudgery and despair—a grim fate—but Vanya's behavior with the gun (it is doubtful that he honestly means to kill the professor) is wildly comic.

After World War II, a new type of drama emerged called ***theater of the absurd,*** and many absurdist plays can be considered tragicomedy. They probe deeply into human problems and cast a dark eye on the world; yet they are also imbued with a comic spirit—among other traditional manifestations of humor, they include juggling, acrobatics, clowning, and verbal nonsense. Three important absurdist playwrights are Eugène Ionesco, Samuel Beckett, and Harold Pinter. (Beckett's play *Waiting for Godot* will be discussed in detail in Chapter 18.) Pinter has called his plays *comedies of menace,* suggesting their juxtaposition of the serious and the comic. His characters are often pursued and persecuted by unknown people and forces, but the action also has a comic component.

In tragicomedy, a smile is frequently cynical, a chuckle may be tinged with a threat, and a laugh is sometimes bitter. In the past, the attitude that produced such combinations was the exception rather than the rule, but in our day it seems far more prevalent—and relevant. As a result, tragicomedy has taken its place as a major genre alongside more traditional approaches.

In this chapter we have examined the point of view—tragic, comic, tragicomic—that informs the theater experience. In chapter 8 we turn to the director and the producer.

SUMMARY

An essential element of theater is a dramatic text or script created by a playwright, or by someone else functioning as a playwright.

An important aspect of a dramatic text is the point of view, which determines *genre*—a French term for "type" or "category." The two oldest and best-known theatrical genres are tragedy and comedy.

Particular societies as well as individual playwrights are often predisposed to a tragic point of view. For example, two historical periods conducive to tragedy were the fifth century B.C.E. in Greece and the period from the late sixteenth century to the early seventeenth century in the European Renaissance.

Comedy may take a variety of forms, including farce, burlesque, satire, domestic comedy, comedy of manners, and comedy of ideas.

Although tragedy and comedy are the two fundamental genres, there are other important genres, including heroic drama, melodrama, domestic or bourgeois drama, and tragicomedy.

KEY TERMS

Bourgeois or domestic drama Drama dealing with problems—particularly family problems—of middle- and lower-class characters. There are serious and comic domestic dramas.

Burlesque Satire of a serious form of literature.

Comedy In general, a play that is light in tone, in concerned with issues that are not serious, has a happy ending, and is designed to amuse.

Comedy of manners Form of comic drama that became popular in seventeenth-century France and the English Restoration, emphasizing a cultivated or sophisticated atmosphere and witty dialogue.

Comic premise Idea or concept in a comedy that turns the accepted notion of things upside down.

Farce Dramatic genre usually regarded as a subclass of comedy, with emphasis on plot complications and with few or no intellectual pretensions.

Genre Category or type of play.

Heroic drama Serious but basically optimistic drama, written in verse or elevated prose, with noble or heroic characters in extreme situations or unusual adventures.

Melodrama Dramatic form made popular in the nineteenth century that emphasized action and spectacular effects and also used music; it had stock characters and clearly defined villains and heroes.

Satire Dramatic form using techniques of comedy—such as wit, irony, and exaggeration—to attack and expose folly and vice.

Slapstick Type of comedy or comic business that relies on ridiculous physical activity—often violent in nature—for its humor.

Theater of the absurd Plays expressing the dramatist's sense of the absurdity and futility of existence.

Tragedy Dramatic form involving serious actions of universal significance and with important moral and philosophical implications, usually with an unhappy ending.

Tragicomedy During the Renaissance, a play having tragic themes and noble characters but a happy ending; today, a play in which serious and comic elements are integrated.

For more research and to learn more about the topics in this chapter, please visit the Online Learning Center at **www.mhhe.com/livelyart6.**

CHAPTER 8

The Director and the Producer

◀ **THE DIRECTOR AND THE PRODUCER**

The director coordinates the activities of performers and designers in bringing the playwright's script to life. He or she confers with the dramatist, studies the script, chooses and rehearses the actors, and guides the work of the designers. Seen here, in a rehearsal of Silk *at the Goodman Theater in Chicago, is the director Mary Zimmerman with two cast members: Christopher Donahue (as the Narrator) and Ryan Artzberger (as Herve Joncour). (Michael Brosilow)*

THE DIRECTOR

In preparing a production, the person most closely associated with the performers is the director, who not only guides the performers but coordinates the entire artistic side of the production. More than any other person, the director is responsible for the overall style, pace, and visual appearance of a production. The entire process requires organizational skills as well as aesthetic sensibility—qualities the director must have in abundance. In modern theater the director is indispensable, but this role was not always so comprehensive.

Evolution of the Director

It is sometimes argued that the theater director did not exist before 1874, when George II, duke of Saxe-Meiningen, determined to make the productions of his court theater in Germany as effective as possible. He supervised every element, paid great attention to details, and strove for historical accuracy in order to create an integrated whole. It is true that beginning with Saxe-Meiningen, the director emerged as a full-fledged, indispensable member of the theatrical team, taking a place alongside the playwright, the performers, and the designers. Though the title may have been new, however, the function of the director has always been present in one way or another.

We know, for example, that the Greek playwright Aeschylus directed his own plays and that the chorus in a Greek play rehearsed under the supervision of a leader for many weeks before a performance. At various times in theater history, the leading performer or playwright of a company served as a director, though without the name. Molière, for instance, not only was the playwright and the chief actor of his company but functioned as its director also. We know from Molière's short play *The Impromptu of Versailles* that he had definite ideas about how actors and actresses should perform; no doubt the same advice he offered in that play was frequently given to his performers in rehearsal. When Hamlet gives instructions and advice to the players who are about to perform the "play within the play," we could say that he is functioning as a director of this visiting theatrical troupe. In fact, in England after the time of Shakespeare, from the seventeenth century through the nineteenth, there was a long line of performer-managers who gave strong leadership to their theater companies and performed many of the functions of the director, although they still were not called by that name.

The actual term *director* came into common usage at the end of the nineteenth century. It is perhaps significant that the emergence of the director as a separate creative functionary coincides with important social changes that began to take place during the nineteenth century. First, with Sigmund Freud, Charles Darwin, and Karl Marx there came a shift in established social, religious, and political concepts. Second, there was a marked increase in communication. With the advent of the telegraph, the telephone, photography, motion pictures, and eventually television and the Internet, various cultures that had remained remote from or even unknown to one another suddenly became linked. The effect of these two changes was to alter the monolithic, ordered view of the world that individual societies had maintained. There is a close relationship between theater and society: when a society has an ordered, unified view of the world, its drama reflects this; and when a society views the world as a changing, heterogeneous, global culture, its drama will reflect that outlook.

Before the changes of the late nineteenth century and the early twentieth century, consistency of style in theater was easier to achieve. Within a given society, writers, performers, and audiences stood on common ground. For example, the comedies of the English playwrights William Wycherley and William Congreve, written at the end of the seventeenth century, were aimed at an elite, upper-class audience that relished gossip, acid remarks, and well-turned phrases. The society's code of behavior was well understood by performers and audiences alike. Questions of style in a production hardly arose, because a common approach to style was already present in the very fabric of society. The way a man took a pinch of snuff, or a nobleman flirted with a maid, or a lady flung open her fan was so clearly delineated in daily behavior that performers had only to refine and perfect these actions for the stage.

In such a society, the task of the manager or leader of a theatrical company was not really to impose a style on a production but simply to prevent the performers from overacting, to see that they spoke their lines properly, and to ensure that the cast worked together as a unit. Today, however, because style, unity, and a cohesive view of society are so elusive, the director's task is more important. The director must draw disparate elements together to create a unified whole.

Today's directors get their training in a variety of ways. Many of them begin as actors and actresses and find that they have a talent for working with other people and for coordinating the work of designers as well as performers. Others train in the many academic institutions that have specific programs for directors. These institutions include large universities that offer theater as part of a liberal arts program, as well as conservatories and other specialized schools.

The Auteur Director

An important development during the twentieth century was the emergence of the *auteur director.*

Auteur is a French word meaning "author." Just after World War II, French film critics began using this term to refer to certain cinema directors, who, they said, were really the authors of the films they made. In these films, point of view —and the implementation of a point of view—came almost entirely from the director rather than from a writer. Since then, the term *auteur* has also been applied to a type of stage director.

Once the director came to the forefront as a full-fledged member of the creative theatrical team, most directors worked closely with a text. Almost from the start, however, there was a breed of director who took a different approach. Interestingly enough, one of the first and most important of these began his work with Stanislavski and then went out on his own: this was Vsevolod Meyerhold in the early twentieth century. Meyerhold, a Russian like Stanislavski, developed a type of theater in which he controlled all the elements. He would rewrite or eliminate text in order to

THE AUTEUR DIRECTOR

There is a twentieth-century tradition of directors who have imposed their own vision and ideas on a theatrical production. Sometimes they take an older text and place it in a different time period; sometimes they create a new theater piece out of older plays; sometimes they add other elements to a drama, such as acrobatics, film, and dance. Here we see the auteur director Ariane Mnouchkine rehearsing The Flood Drummers *at the Théâtre du Soleil in Paris. (© Martine Franck/Magnum Photos)*

present his own vision of the material, but the text was only one of many elements that he used for his own purposes. Performers, too, were subject to his overall ideas; often, for example, they were called on to perform like circus acrobats or robots. The finished product was frequently exciting and almost always innovative, but it represented Meyerhold's point of view, strongly imposed on all the elements, not that of a writer or anyone else.

Many avant-garde directors of the twentieth century followed in Meyerhold's footsteps. They could also be classified as auteur directors because they did not see themselves as serving the purposes of a text; rather, they demanded that the text serve their purposes. For some of them—such as the director Robert Wilson, who produced visual tableaux and called for ritualistic, repetitive movements by his performers—the text is only fragmentary and is one of the least important elements. Auteur directors do not hesitate to alter texts drastically; to combine texts from different sources; to introduce other elements such as film, video, dance, and the visual arts; or to rearrange times and places in which the action of a dramatic piece occurs. In such cases, the director is actually serving not only as director but also as author; and it is the director's vision that controls what the audience sees onstage.

The Director at Work

In this chapter, however, we will focus on the more traditional director rather than the auteur director. A traditional director begins with a close examination of the text. This is true whether the play is from the past—a work by Shakespeare or Molière, for instance—or is a new work that has not been produced before.

The director must first of all understand dramatic purpose and dramatic structure (covered in Chapters 6 and 7). What is the playwright's intention: to entertain, to educate, or to arouse strong feelings in the audience? What is the playwright's point of view toward the characters and events of the play: does he or she see them as tragic or comic? How has the playwright developed the action in the play: in other words, how is the play constructed? Such considerations are crucial because the director is the one person who must have an overall grasp of the text, in order to guide the performers in making it come alive. If an actor or actress has a question about a character or about the meaning of a scene, the director must be able to provide an answer.

In preparing a production, one of the director's first steps is to discover the *spine* of the play. The American director and critic Harold Clurman says in his book *On Directing* that a director's first task is to find in the text the general action that "motivates the play." The director must determine the "fundamental

drama or conflict" of which "the script's plot and people are the instruments."[1] Clurman calls this fundamental action or conflict the "spine;" it could also be called the *main action* of the play.

As they seek an approach to a text—a way to translate it from page to stage —directors sometimes develop a *directorial concept*. The directorial concept is an overall image or metaphor of a play. For example, a director might develop a concept of Shakespeare's *Macbeth* in terms of "blind ambition." In their insatiable desire for power, both Macbeth and Lady Macbeth are blind to the immorality, the dangers, and the consequences of their actions. Following this notion, the concept of blindness—of what people can and cannot see—would permeate the play.

At the same time that the director becomes thoroughly familiar with all aspects of the text, he or she begins casting the play. The term ***casting*** comes from sculpture—from casting a mold. In theater, it refers to finding an actor or actress for each role. In the past—in Shakespeare's day, for example—a company of performers worked together regularly, and it was understood who would play the hero, who the clown, who the young female lead, and so forth. In modern times, when very few theaters have a repertory company of regular performers, directors hold ***auditions*** at which actors and actresses try out for various roles. Sometimes performers will be interviewed, and sometimes they will be asked to read

THE DIRECTOR AT WORK
The modern director works closely with the playwright on a new script or develops an understanding and interpretation of a well-known script, casts and rehearses the play, and works closely with the designers and others to bring the play to fruition. The auteur director creates his own theater piece. He or she determines the text of the work. Shown here is the auteur director Peter Brook with actors in the Mahabharata in Paris, August 1987. (© Julio Donoso/Corbis Sygma)

---

[1] Harold Clurman, *On Directing*, Macmillan, New York, 1992, p. 27.

Richard Foreman: Director, Playwright, and Designer

Richard Foreman, a director-designer-playwright, founded the Ontological-Hysteric Theatre in New York City in 1968. He has also coproduced his work with the New York Shakespeare Festival and the Wooster Group. Foreman has directed for the Hartford Stage Company and the New York Shakespeare Festival.

How does a young man born in Staten Island, removed to Scarsdale, who goes to Brown and Yale in the 1950s, and then goes to New York to write Broadway comedies, become a unique revolutionary artist in the theatre? For some reason, from the time that I was very young, I had an attraction for the strangest material. I read *The Skin of Our Teeth* for the first time at about twelve and thought, "It's like a dream, it's so weird, it's wonderful." I remember seeing Elia Kazan's production of *Camino Real,* which I dragged my Scarsdale parents to, and they said, "What's this all about?"

I have always gravitated to things that try to talk to some more spiritually oriented level, rather than realistic discussions and manipulations of the real, practical, empirical world in which we live.

Then the big revelation was discovering Brecht—and especially his saying that you could have a theater that was not based on empathy. For some reason, even at an early age what I hated in the theatre was a kind of asking for love that I saw manifested on the stage, getting a unified reaction from everybody in the audience. Brecht said it didn't have to be like that, and until I was in my middle twenties, he was the beginning, middle, and end of everything for me. That only changed when I came to New York and encountered the beginnings of the underground film movement, and that reoriented me, because up to that point I had thought of America as being rather unsophisticated, naive and simplistic as compared with the complexities and aggressiveness of European art and thought. Then in America, in the middle 1960s, I discovered people my age were making their own movies, operating on a level that was akin to poetry rather than storytelling. And I thought, "Aha! Why can't the techniques of poetry that operate in film, operate in theatre?" I came to terms with trying to make an American kind of art that exploited and put onstage everything that up till then I had wanted to reject about myself. I gravitated to theatre even though I was opened up by filmmakers.

Source: Richard Foreman, from *The Director's Voice: Twenty-One Interviews* by Arthur Bartow, copyright 1988 by Arthur Bartow. By permission of Theatre Communications Group.

scenes from the play being produced or from another play. Sometimes, too, a director is already familiar with the work of a performer, having seen or worked with the person before. From a combination of auditions and previous knowledge, the director casts the play, deciding which actor or actress will play each of the parts.

While the director is preparing the script and choosing the performers, he or she is also working closely with the scene, costume, lighting, and sound designers to develop the visual and aural aspects of the production. This is the point at which questions of style and genre become important. The director and the designers must work closely together to be certain that the acting style will be reinforced by the visual elements, and vice versa. Performers who will be speaking high-flown language, as in an Elizabethan play, would seem out of place in a setting that

looked like a suburban backyard. In the same way, if a play
is set in a modern living room,
one would not want the performers to act as if they were
the chorus in a Greek tragedy.
The director also makes certain that the physical appearance of the production is itself
consistent and unified.

A few weeks before the
play is to be performed for the
public, the director begins rehearsals. This is the period
when he or she works most
intensively with the performers. The director explains the
text—not only the meaning of
the play but the style in which
it will be presented—and then
begins to work with the actors
and actresses. At first they may
read through the text while
simply sitting around a table;
next they "get the play on its
feet," beginning to sketch in
the details of the setting and
the characters' interaction.

DIRECTORIAL CONCEPT

*At times, directors create an overall image or metaphor for interpreting a play. This serves
to illuminate the text and give unity and cohesion to the production. Frequently the director
develops an approach that throws new light on the text, or reminds us of past approaches
to a play. An artistic director who has done this in recent years at the reconstructed
Shakespeare's Globe Theater in London is Mark Rylance. For a production of Shakespeare's*
Richard III, *Rylance decided to have an all-female cast, which is a reversal of the practice in
Elizabethan times of having all male casts. Seen here in the production, directed by Barry
Kyle, are Kathryn Hunter on the left as the title character, and Amanda Harris as the Duke
of Buckingham. (© Donald Cooper/Photostage)*

Initially, the performers work with the text still in their hands. Gradually,
they memorize their lines and flesh out their characters. Each performer begins to
discover emotional depths in his or her character and becomes aware of the dynamics of scenes where the character confronts others. In the beginning, individual scenes are prepared separately; later, a whole act is put together. After that,
the entire play is rehearsed so that the performers get a sense of its overall shape.

In preparing the action onstage, the director keeps in mind what the production will look like to the audience. In a sense, the director is the eye of the audience
—a person who sits out front and sees the performance before the public does. To
ensure a smooth, clear flow of stage action, the director develops the blocking
with the performers. **Blocking** means the arrangement and movements of performers
ers relative to each other as well as to furniture and to the places where they enter
and leave the stage. If two performers are playing a scene together, they must both
be seen clearly by the audience, and they must be in positions that allow them to
play the scene to maximum effect. The director also coordinates stage business. In
contrast to blocking, which has to do with movements and physical arrangements
onstage, *business* is the term for activities of performers such as opening an um-
brella, writing a letter at a desk, arranging pillows on a sofa, and the like.

In all this, the director is aware of the **stage picture** or *visual composition,* that is, how the entire scene onstage will appear to the audience. Is the placement of performers balanced? Is it aesthetically pleasing? One goal of the director is to make the visual images onstage striking and effective. Also, the director underscores the meaning of specific scenes through visual composition. The spatial relationships of performers convey information about characters. For example, important characters are frequently placed on a level above other characters—on a platform, say, or a flight of stairs.

Another spatial device is to place an important character alone in one area of the stage while grouping other characters in another area; this draws the spectator's eye to the character standing alone. In addition, if two characters are opposed to each other they should be placed in positions of physical confrontation on the stage. Visual composition is more crucial in plays with large casts, such as Shakespearean productions, than in plays with only two or three characters.

The director gives shape and structure to a play in two dimensions: in *space,* as was just described, and in *time.* Since a production occurs through time, it is important for the director to see that the *movement,* the *pace,* and the *rhythm* of the play are appropriate. If the play moves too quickly, if we miss words and do not understand what is going on, it is the director's fault. The director must determine whether there is too little or too much time between speeches or whether a performer moves too slowly or too quickly across the stage. The director must attempt to control the pace and rhythm within a scene—the dynamics and the manner in which the actors and actresses move from moment to moment—and the rhythm between scenes.

GUIDING THE PERFORMERS' MOVEMENTS
In a musical, the person who directs the dancers is the choreographer. But there is also other movement, which is the responsibility of the director. Shown here is George C. Wolfe, on the left, the artistic director of the Public Theater in New York City, directing Queen Esther and other members of the cast in a rehearsal of the musical Harlem Song. *(Tyler Hicks/The New York Times)*

The director must see to it that the movement from moment to moment and scene to scene has enough thrust and drive to maintain our interest. Nothing interrupts the flow, the rhythm, the focus of a production more than action that is sporadic or too slow. However, variety is also important. If a play moves ahead at only one pace, the audience will become fatigued simply by the monotony of that pace.

Before rehearsals, the director has met with the scene, costume, lighting, and sound designers to develop the approach to the play in each of these areas. While rehearsals with the performers are proceeding, other activities that will eventually be under the director's control are also going forward: the people building the scenery and costumes and the technicians preparing the lights and sound are doing their work.

Just before the play is to be shown to the public, these elements are brought together, under the supervision of the director, in a *technical rehearsal.* At this point, production elements are integrated for the first time in a *run-through:* the performers wear their costumes to get accustomed to them, and the lighting and sound "cues" are set with the performers onstage. Scene changes are rehearsed and coordinated. Following this comes the *dress rehearsal,* when the play is performed as it will be for the public. This is when last-minute problems are discovered and dealt with.

Then the play is performed for the first time before audiences. These first performances, often called *previews,* are dress rehearsals for an invited audience. We have seen in Chapter 4 how vital the audience is to a production. In previews, the audience's reaction first becomes part of the production process. The response from the audience lets the director and performers know whether a comedy is as funny as they thought, or whether a serious play holds people's attention. The audience lets everyone know which scenes are successful and which are not, so that adjustments can be made if there are problems.

The Director's Collaborators

In addition to working closely with performers, the director, the designers, and the playwright, the director has other collaborators who are essential to a production. In musical theater, these others would include the composer, lyricist, choreographer, and music director. In a nonmusical play, various technicians and artists may be indispensable to the director. For example, a fencing or fight consultant may be needed for a classic play, such as a play by Shakespeare. If a play calls for regional accents—as in a Tennessee Williams play set in the south—a vocal coach would be helpful.

Another important member of the production team is the ***stage manager,*** the person who coordinates all the rehearsals and the actual running of a performance. The stage manager calls rehearsals; lets the performers know their rehearsal schedule; makes all important announcements concerning technical rehearsals and other events involving performers; coordinates all the elements of light, sound, and scene changes during the technical rehearsals and previews; and is in charge of all the same elements, as well as the entrances and exits of performers, during each performance. Clearly, the stage manager is an essential member of any production team: he or she has the immense responsibility of seeing to it that a performance comes off satisfactorily.

In Europe, there is a long-standing practice of having a ***dramaturg***—a literary manager or dramatic adviser—collaborate with the director. In the United States, the role of the dramaturg or literary manager is relatively new; but in recent years many regional professional groups and nonprofit theaters have engaged full-time dramaturgs. In a number of the directorial decisions outlined above, a dramaturg can be extremely helpful. Among the duties frequently undertaken by the dramaturg are discovering and reading new plays, working with playwrights to develop new scripts, identifying overlooked plays from the past, preparing information on the history of classical works, researching past productions and criticism, and writing program articles. The dramaturg can also aid the director in making decisions regarding style, approach, and concept.

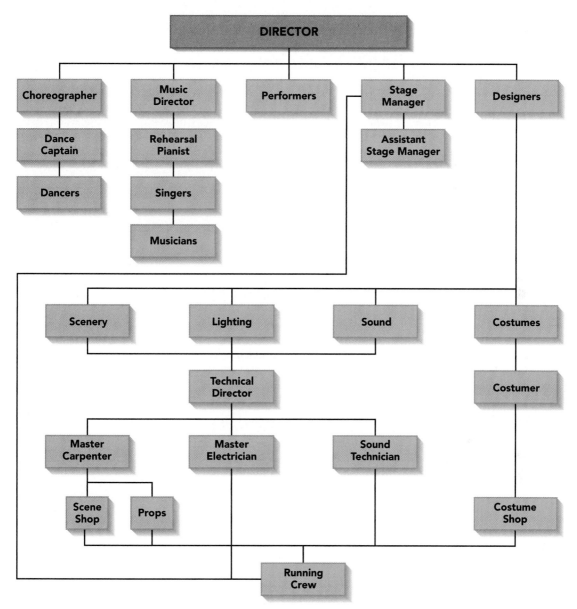

DUTIES OF A DIRECTOR IN A THEATER PRODUCTION

Once a director has decided on a script (and worked with the playwright, if it is a new play), he or she must organize the entire artistic side of the production. This chart indicates the many people the director must work with and the many elements that must be coordinated.

Emily Mann: Playwright-Director

Emily Mann is currently artistic director of the McCarter Theatre in New Jersey. She has also directed at the Guthrie Theater, the Brooklyn Academy of Music, and the Actors Theater of Louisville. She received Obie awards in 1981 for distinguished playwriting and directing for her play Still Life. *Her play* Execution of Justice *won a Drama Desk Award in 1986. In 1994, she adapted and directed* Having Our Say. *She also directed the Broadway production of the Pulitzer Prize–winning play* Anna in the Tropics *in 2003.*

How did you get interested in theatre?   I was in high school, at the University of Chicago Laboratory School, in 1966 and things in my neighborhood were heating up. The Hyde Park area was a seat of political ferment: the Weathermen and SDS, the Panthers ten blocks away. Elijah Muhammad lived three doors down, drugs were coming in, people were getting heavily politicized. When we arrived in 1966 the neighborhood was integrated and absolutely for integration. By '68, with Black Power, the separatist movement had taken hold and there was a lot of heartbreak for everyone.

I was always interested in music, writing, art, and literature, and the theatre became a place where these came together in a very exciting way. You worked in a collaborative fashion and made something beautiful, something positive or critical—but still in a positive way—to say to a community. It felt much better to me than being one in a mass of people marching—not that I didn't march, but I have always distrusted crowds. I don't like that anonymity, being part of a group that can get whipped up. I'm sure it's all my training about Nazi Germany. This rather brilliant guy at the Laboratory high school, Robert Keil, took a lot of emotionally churned up, smart, excited and excitable young people and turned all that energy into an artistic endeavor, making theatre.

I hadn't really had much interest in theatre before that. I remember my first Broadway show was *Fiorello!* about the mayor of New York. We were invited to go because my father, who's a historian, had just written the biography of LaGuardia. I was very excited—I was seven, I think—and I got to go backstage and meet Tom Bosley. But theatre never occurred to me as something you actually did, as a serious person in the world.

Source: Emily Mann from *In Their Own Words: Contemporary American Playwrights* by David Savran, copyright 1988 David Savran. By permission of Theater Communications Group.

THE PRODUCER OR MANAGER

Audiences frequently confuse directors with producers, perhaps because both the director and the producer function behind the scenes. Actually, the *producer,* or *manager,* is the director's counterpart in the business and management side of a theater production. Here, too, coordination of elements is crucial, and the producer or manager is the person chiefly responsible. As the term itself suggests, the producer is a key figure in a production.

Producers in Commercial Theater

In commercial theater, a producer has many responsibilities. In general, the producer oversees the entire business side of a production, including publicity. His or her duties include the following:

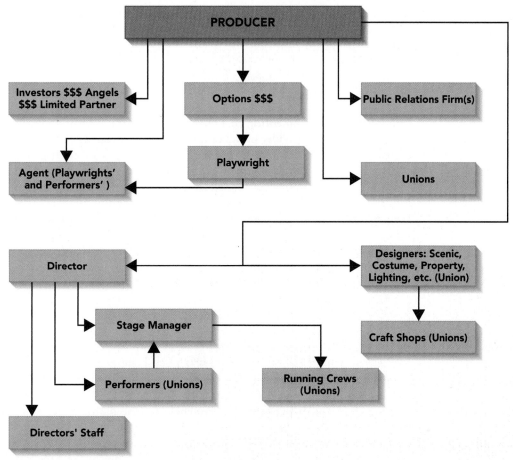

RESPONSIBILITIES OF THE COMMERCIAL THEATER PRODUCER

When a commerical theater production is mounted, the person responsible for organizing the full range of nonartistic activities is the producer. This chart, which shows the producer at the top, indicates the people the producer must deal with and the numerous elements he or she must coordinate.

1. Raising money to finance the production
2. Securing rights to the script
3. Dealing with the agents for the playwright, director, and performers
4. Hiring the director, performers, designers, and stage crews
5. Dealing with theatrical unions
6. Renting the theater space
7. Supervising the work of those running the theater: in the box office, auditorium, and business office
8. Supervising the advertising
9. Overseeing the budget and the week-to-week financial management of the production

If a production is to succeed, the producer must have the artistic sensibility to choose the right text and hire the right director. Aside from raising capital and having the final say in hiring and firing, the producer oversees all financial and business operations in a production.

Noncommercial Theaters

Administrative Organization of a Nonprofit Theater. Most nonprofit theaters —including those in smaller urban centers as well as large noncommercial theaters in major cities like New York, Chicago, and Los Angeles—are organized with a board of directors, an artistic director, and an executive or managing director.

The board is responsible for selecting both the artistic and the managing directors. The board is also responsible for overseeing the financial affairs of the theater, for fund-raising, for long-range planning, and the like. To carry out some of these tasks, the board frequently delegates authority to an executive committee.

The *artistic director* is responsible for all creative and artistic activities. He or she selects the plays that will constitute the season and chooses directors, designers, and other creative personnel. Frequently the artistic director also directs one or more plays during the season.

Responsibilities of the Noncommercial Producer or Manager. The managing director in a noncommercial theater is, in many respects, the counterpart of a producer in commercial theater. In both a commercial production and the running of a nonprofit theater organization, the tasks of the person in charge of administration are many and complex.

The producer or manager is responsible for the maintenance of the theater building, as well as for the budget, making certain that the production stays within established limits. The budget includes salaries for the director, designers, performers, and stage crews, and expenditures for scenery, costumes, and music. Again, an artistic element enters the picture; some artistic decisions—such as whether a costume needs to be replaced or scenery needs to be altered—affect costs. The producer or manager must work very closely with the director and the designers in balancing artistic and financial needs.

The producer or manager is also responsible for publicity. The audience would never get to the theater if it did not know when and where a play was being presented. A host of other tasks come under the supervision of the producer or manager: tickets must be ordered, the box office must be maintained, and plans must be made ahead of time for how tickets are to be sold. The securing of ushers, the printing of programs, and the maintenance of the auditorium—usually called the *front of the house*—are also the responsibility of the producer or manager.

Once again, plans must be made well in advance. In many theater organizations, an entire season—the plays that will be produced, the personnel who will be in charge, and the supplies that will be required—is planned a year ahead of time. Coordination and cooperation are as important in this area as they are for the production onstage. (For the organization of a nonprofit theater company, see the chart on the next page.)

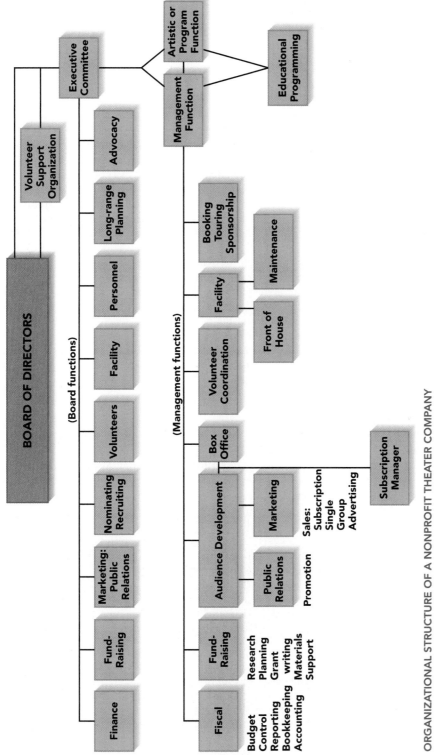

ORGANIZATIONAL STRUCTURE OF A NONPROFIT THEATER COMPANY

A nonprofit theater is a complex institution with many facets. This chart shows the various activities that must be organized for the successful management of such a theater.

In Chapter 9 we will turn our attention to the places where audiences interact with performers and where directors stage their productions, as we examine the variety of theater spaces available to contemporary audiences.

SUMMARY

The special function of the director emerged during modern times, when the great diversity of styles in modern theater and the international nature of theater required someone to provide an overall vision for a production and to coordinate all the elements. The director begins by analyzing the text, whether it is a classic or a new play. The director discovers the meaning and the intention of the playwright in order to translate these into stage terms. To do this organically and effectively, the director frequently develops a concept, an overall image or point of view, that will guide and inform the work of everyone connected with the production. An auteur director usually substitutes his or her own vision for that of the playwright, choosing texts to be used and rearranging time periods and other elements.

The director works with the actors and actresses, supervising rehearsals and guiding their performances. The director has many other duties as well. He or she casts the play, selecting an actor or actress for each role. Also, the director works closely with scene, costume, lighting, and sound designers, coordinating the visual elements of the production. The overall artistic quality of the production—its style, pace, and visual appearance—is also the responsibility of the director.

The director may have many collaborators, such as a choreographer, a stage manager, and a dramaturg. Behind the scenes, the producer or manager works to coordinate the business and management elements.

KEY TERMS

Artistic director Person responsible for all creative and artistic activities for resident and repertory companies.

Auditions Tryouts held for performers who want to be considered for roles in a production.

Auteur director A director who believes that his or her role is to be the author of a production. An auteur director's point of view dominates that of the playwright, and the director may make textual changes and modifications.

Blocking Pattern and arrangement of performers' movements onstage with respect to each other and to the stage space, usually set by the director.

Casting Assigning roles to performers in a production; this is usually done by the director.

Director In American usage, the person responsible for the overall unity of a production and for coordinating the work of contributing artists. The American director is the equivalent of the British producer and the French *metteur-en-scène*.

Dramaturg Literary manager or dramatic adviser of a theater company.

Dress rehearsal Rehearsal in which a play is performed as it will be for the public, including all the scenery, costumes, and technical effects.

Front of the house All of the nonproduction elements of the theater space that relate to the audience's experience, including the auditorium, lobby, and box office.

Pace Rate at which a performance is played; also, to play a scene or an entire event to determine its proper speed.

Producer In American usage, the person responsible for the business side of a production, including raising the necessary money. (In British usage, a producer is the equivalent of an American director.)

Run-through Rehearsal in which the cast goes through the entire text of the play in the order that it will be performed.

Spine In the Stanislavski method, a character's dominant desire or motivation; usually thought of as an action and expressed as a verb.

Stage manager Person who coordinates all the rehearsals for the director and runs the actual show during its performances.

Stage picture Visual composition: how an entire scene onstage will appear to the audience.

Technical rehearsal Rehearsal at which all the design and technical elements are brought together.

THEATER ON THE WEB

For more research and to learn more about the topics in this chapter, please visit the Online Learning Center at **www.mhhe.com/livelyart6.**

CHAPTER 9

Theater Spaces

◀ **WHERE THEATER TAKES PLACE**

Western theater began in ancient Greece. To present their plays, the Greeks created amphitheaters by placing seats on a hillside surrounding a circle and a stage space at the base of the hill. Through the years, performance spaces have been developed in many sizes and shapes: large and small, indoors and outdoors, and with important variations in the physical relationship of the stage to the spectators. The ancient Greek theater seen here is at Epidauros. (© Jose Fuste Raga/Corbis)

A theater event occurs in a place where the audience and performers come together. Since theater is a live experience, the physical environment where it happens becomes an essential ingredient.

In addition to a stage—the area where the actors and actresses perform—and an adjoining space where the spectators sit or stand, a theater space also includes a place adjacent to the stage where performers can change costumes and from which they can make entrances and exits. For the audience, provision is made for a lobby and other public spaces.

A theater space can be indoors or outdoors, permanent or temporary, large or small. However, it is interesting to note that throughout theater history four fundamental stage arrangements have been predominant. Each has its own advantages and disadvantages, each is suited to certain types of plays and certain types of productions, and each provides the audience with a somewhat different experience.

The four basic arrangements are: (1) the proscenium, or picture-frame, stage; (2) the thrust stage with three-quarters seating; (3) the arena, or circle, stage; and (4) created and found stage spaces. We will learn their features and characteristics as we look at each more closely, beginning with the proscenium stage. (There are also spaces that combine characteristics of these four types.)

PROSCENIUM OR PICTURE-FRAME STAGE: HISTORY AND CHARACTERISTICS

For many people, the most familiar type of stage is the *proscenium,* or *picture-frame,* stage. In this arrangement, the audience faces in one direction, as in a movie theater, and the action onstage is seen through a frame of some kind.

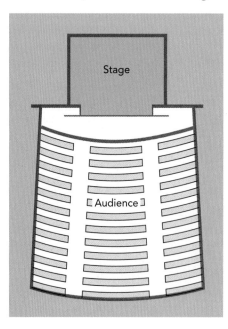

PROSCENIUM THEATER
The audience faces in one direction, toward an enclosed stage encased by a picture-frame opening. Scene changes and performers' entrances and exits are made behind the proscenium opening, out of sight of the audience.

The term *proscenium* comes from the *proscenium arch,* the frame that separates the stage from the auditorium and forms an outline for the stage. This frame was first introduced in Italy during the Renaissance in the early seventeenth century. Although in the past it was an actual arch, today it is usually a rectangle. Before the 1950s, there was usually a curtain just behind the proscenium opening; when the curtain rose, it revealed the "picture." Another term for this type of stage is *fourth wall,* from the idea of the proscenium opening as an invisible or transparent wall through which the audience looks at the other three walls of a room.

The auditorium itself is slanted downward from the back of the auditorium to the stage. (In theater usage, the slant

THE MODERN PROSCENIUM-STAGE THEATER

In this cutaway drawing we see the audience seating at the left, all facing in the one direction toward the stage. Behind the orchestra pit in the center is the apron on the stage; and then the proscenium frame, behind which are the flats and other scenic elements and —at the far right—a cyclorama. Overhead, scenery can be raised into the fly loft above the stage area.

of an auditorium or stage floor is called a *rake.*) The stage itself is raised several feet above the auditorium floor, to increase visibility.

The main floor where the audience sits is called the *orchestra.* (This is the modern usage of the term *orchestra;* in ancient Greek theater, the orchestra was the circular acting area at the base of a hillside amphitheater.) There is usually a balcony (sometimes there are two balconies), protruding about halfway over the main floor, to provide additional seating. In certain theaters, as well as in similar concert halls and opera houses, there are horseshoe-shaped tiers or boxes ringing the auditorium for several floors above the orchestra.

Beginning in the late seventeenth century, the proscenium theater was adopted in virtually every European country. The popularity of this type of stage spread throughout the United States in the nineteenth century and the early twentieth.

The stage area of all these proscenium theaters was usually deep, allowing for elaborate scenery and scene shifts; and there was a tall *fly loft* above the stage to hold scenery. The loft had to be more than twice as high as the proscenium opening so that scenery could be concealed when it was raised, or *flown,* above the stage. Scenery was usually hung by ropes or cables on a series of parallel pipes,

THE PROSCENIUM STAGE

In a proscenium theater, the audience faces in one direction—toward the stage—and the stage itself is enclosed in a giant picture frame through which scenery and action are viewed. This arrangement is perfect for the box set as well as for spectacular scenic effects. Seen here is a typical proscenium space, the Broadhurst Theater in New York. (© Peter Aaron/Esto)

one behind the other, running from side to side across the stage. With this arrangement, many pieces of scenery could be raised and lowered. Ingenious mechanisms for raising and lowering scenery were developed during the Italian Renaissance, when the proscenium stage was being refined.

Throughout the seventeenth and eighteenth centuries, there were times when everyone—audiences, scene designers, and technicians—seemed so carried away with spectacle that it was emphasized above everything else, sometimes even above the text and the acting. In Paris, for example, there was a theater called the *Salle des Machines*—"Hall of Machines"—its name indicating that visual effects were its chief attraction. At times there was nothing onstage but visual display: cloud machines brought angels or deities from up high; rocks opened to reveal wood nymphs; a banquet hall was changed to a forest; smoke, fire, twinkling lights, and every imaginable effect appeared as if by magic. Later, such heavy concentration on spectacle went out of favor for many years; but fascination with this type of theater returned in the latter part of the twentieth century and in the early twenty-first century, in Broadway musicals such as *The Phantom of the Opera, The Producers, Hairspray, Wicked,* and *The Color Purple.* The proscenium stage is ideal for such spectacles because the machinery and the workings of the scene changes can be concealed behind the proscenium opening.

In addition to providing an opportunity for spectacle, the proscenium stage offers other advantages. Realistic settings—a living room, an office, a kitchen—are particularly effective in a proscenium theater. The illusion of a genuine, complete room can be created more easily with a proscenium stage than with any other kind. Also, the strong central focus provided by the frame rivets the atten-

THE PROSCENIUM: IDEAL FOR SPECTACLE

One advantage of a proscenium theater is that it allows elaborate scenery and effects to be created behind the proscenium opening. Machinery for changing scenery can be hidden, and impressive visual pictures can appear as if by magic. Here is a scene from the musical Hairspray, *which features the kinds of elaborate set changes and scenic effects associated with large-scale musical productions.* (© Paul Kolnik)

tion of the audience. There are times, too, when the audience wants the detachment—the distancing—that a proscenium provides.

There are also disadvantages, however. As we have seen, the proscenium stage creates a temptation to get carried away with visual pyrotechnics. In addition, a proscenium stage tends to be remote and formal. Some spectators prefer the intimacy and informality—the experience of being close to the action—found in the thrust and arena theaters.

THRUST STAGE: HISTORY AND CHARACTERISTICS

In one form or another, the *thrust stage* has been the most widely used of all theater spaces. In the basic thrust arrangement, the audience sits on three sides, or in a semicircle, enclosing a stage that projects into the center. At the back of the playing area is some form of stage house providing for the performers' entrances and exits, and for scene changes. The thrust stage offers a sense of intimacy, giving the "wraparound" audience a feeling of surrounding the action. At the

same time, the rear wall of the thrust stage—the facade of the stage house—provides a focused background for the action in the playing area.

The thrust stage was developed by the Greeks for their tragedies and comedies. Before they had formal theaters, the Greeks had areas for religious ceremonies and tribal rituals. It is believed that these areas sometimes took the form of a circle in a field, with an altar at the center. In forming their theaters, the Greeks modified this arrangement by placing the circle, which they called the *orchestra,* at the base of a curving hillside. The slope of the hill formed a natural amphitheater for the spectators, and the level circle at the foot formed the stage. At the back of the circle, facing the hillside, there was a stage house which had formal doors for the performers' entrances and exits, that created a background for the action, and provided a place for changing costumes. The stage house and the audience seat-

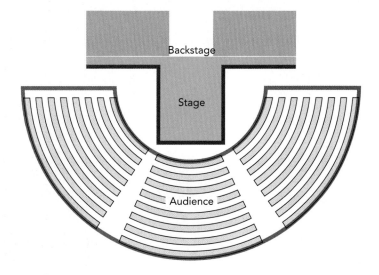

THRUST STAGE WITH
THREE-QUARTERS
SEATING
*The stage is surrounded on
three sides by the audience.
Sometimes seating is a
semicircle. Entrances and
exits are made from the
sides and backstage.
Spectators surround the
action, but scene changes
and other stage effects are
still possible.*

ing in Greek theaters began as wooden structures in the fifth century B.C.E., but during the next two centuries they came to be made of stone. The largest Greek theaters seated 15,000 or more spectators. This design was duplicated all over Greece, particularly in the years following the conquests of Alexander the Great during the early fourth century B.C.E. Remnants of these theaters remain today throughout that part of the world, in such places as Epidaurus, Priene, Ephesus, Delphi, and Corinth.

The Romans adapted the Greek form, making it a complete structure and developing a theater that was not strictly a thrust but a forerunner of the proscenium. Instead of using the natural amphitheater of a hillside, they created a freestanding stone structure in which the stage house was joined to the seating area and the orchestra was a semicircle. In front of the stage house, which was decorated with arches and statues, they erected a long platform stage where most of the action occurred.

In the medieval period, formal theater, which had disappeared for several hundred years, was revived. Short religious plays in Latin began to be presented in churches and cathedrals in England and parts of continental Europe. Around 1300 C.E., religious plays written in the common language were presented outdoors. One popular space for these outdoor performances was another form of the thrust, known as a *platform stage.* A simple platform was set on wooden supports called *trestles* (hence, this arrangement is sometimes also called a *trestle stage*), with a curtain at the back that the performers used for entrances and costume changes. The area underneath the stage was closed off and provided a space from which devils and other characters could appear, sometimes in a cloud of smoke. In some places the platform was mounted on wheels (a *wagon stage*) and moved from place to place through a town. The audience stood on three sides of the platform, making it an improvised thrust stage. This type of performance space was widely used between the thirteenth and fifteenth centuries in England

THE RESTORED SHAKESPEARE'S GLOBE THEATRE

On the South Bank of the Thames River in London, a theater has been constructed quite near the site of the original Globe, built in 1599. It was for this theater that Shakespeare and several of his contemporaries wrote their most masterful dramas. The reconstruction has attempted to duplicate the original dimensions, use the same materials, and in general create for audiences an experience similar to the one for audiences in Shakespeare's time. Shown here is an audience attending a production at the reconstructed Globe. (© Andrea Pistolesi/Image Bank/Getty)

and various parts of continental Europe. (We will discuss more fully debates surrounding pageant wagon staging in Chapter 14.)

In the sixteenth century, just before Shakespeare began writing for the theater, a particular type of thrust stage took shape in England. A platform stage was set up at one end of the open inner courtyard of an inn. Such a courtyard was surrounded on four sides by the interior walls of the inn, three or four stories high. The rooms facing the courtyard served as boxes for some of the spectators; on the ground level, other spectators stood on three sides of the stage. The fourth side of the courtyard, behind the platform, served as the stage house. Interestingly, an almost identical theater took shape in Spain at the same time. Spanish inns were called *corrales,* and this name was given to the courtyard theaters that developed there.

Formal English theaters of Shakespeare's day, such as the Globe and the Fortune, were similar to the inn theaters: some of the spectators stood in an open area around a platform stage while others sat in three levels of closed galleries at the

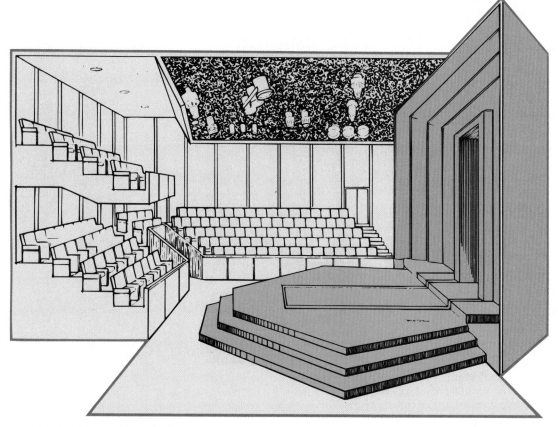

A MODERN THRUST-STAGE THEATER
This cutaway drawing of a thrust stage shows how the playing area juts into the audience, which surrounds the stage on three sides. This configuration affords intimacy, but at the back (shown here at the right) is an area that furnishes a natural backdrop for the action.

back and sides. A roof covered part of the stage; at the back, some form of raised area served for balcony scenes, such as the one in *Romeo and Juliet.* On each side at the rear were doors used for entrances and exits. (In the spring of 1997, a reproduction of the Globe Theater was opened on the South Bank of the Thames River in London, only a short distance from the site of the original Globe. Built to the same dimensions as the original and using authentic materials, it re-creates the feeling of the thrust theater used in Shakespeare's day.)

English theaters like the Globe and the Fortune were a fascinating combination of diverse elements: they were both indoors and outdoors, and some spectators stood while others sat; also, the audience was made up of almost all levels of society. The physical environment must have been stimulating, since performers standing at the front of the thrust stage were in the center of a hemisphere of spectators—on three sides around them as well as above and below. Although such a theater held 2,000 spectators or more, no one in the audience was more

THE JAPANESE NŌ STAGE

An ancient Asian form of the thrust stage is the nō stage in Japan. It is a platform stage with the audience sitting on one side and in front. Originally it was an outdoor theater with a covered stage. In modern times, the entire theater is enclosed, as if the outdoor space had been moved indoors, but the theater itself remains. Seen here is a production of the nō play Ataka *at the National Nō Theatre in Tokyo, Japan. (© Toshiro Morita/HAGA/The Image Works)*

than 60 feet or so from the stage, and most people were much closer. Being in the midst of so many people, enclosed on all sides, but with the open sky above, must have instilled a feeling of great communion among the spectators and the performers. (A drawing of a typical Elizabethan theater can be found in Chapter 15.)

Shortly after Shakespeare's day, in the latter part of the seventeenth century, two things occurred, not only in England and Spain but throughout Europe: theater moved completely indoors, and the stage began a slow but steady retreat behind a frame—the proscenium opening—which enclosed the stage action. For the next two centuries the thrust theater was in eclipse, and it was not to reappear until around 1900, when a few theaters in England began using a version of the thrust stage to produce Shakespeare.

The return of the thrust stage in Great Britain and the United States during the past hundred years has resulted from a growing realization that certain plays—not only works of Shakespeare but those of his fellow Elizabethans and the playwrights of the Spanish golden age—can be done best on a stage similar to the one for which they were written. In the United States and Canada, the thrust stage was not revived until after World War II; since then, however, a number of fine thrust-stage theaters have been built, including the Tyrone Guthrie in Minneapolis; the Shakespeare Theater in Stratford, Ontario; the Mark Taper Forum in Los Angeles; and the Long Wharf in New Haven.

The basic stage of traditional Chinese and Japanese drama (including nō theater in Japan) is a form of thrust stage: a raised, open platform, frequently covered by a roof, with the audience sitting on two or three sides around the stage. Entrances and exits are made from doors or ramps at the rear of the stage.

The obvious advantages of the thrust stage—the intimacy of the three-quarters seating, the close audience-performer relationship, and the fact that so many of the world's great dramatic works were written for it—give it a significant place in theater.

ARENA STAGE: HISTORY AND CHARACTERISTICS

The *arena stage,* also called *circle theater* or *theater-in-the-round,* has a playing space in the center of a square or circle, with seats for spectators surrounding it. This arrangement is similar to that in sports arenas that feature boxing or basketball. The stage may be raised a few feet off the main floor, with seats rising from the floor level; or it may be on the floor itself, with seats raised on levels around it. When the seating is close to the stage, there is usually some kind of demarcation indicating the boundaries of the playing area.

One advantage of the arena theater is that it offers the most intimacy, particularly in comparison with the picture-frame stage. With the performers in the center, even in a large theater, the audience can be closer to the action because seating is on all four sides instead of only one side. If the same number of people attend a performance in an arena theater and a picture-frame theater, at least half of those in the arena theater will be nearer the stage. Moreover, in an arena theater there is no frame or barrier to separate the performers from the audience.

An arena arrangement also allows for the unconscious communion that is created when people form a circle. The configuration of a circle seems to come naturally to human beings: we embrace with encircling arms, form circles to play children's games, and make human enclosures around fires and altars. An unusual event will automatically draw people into a circle to watch; during a street fight, for instance, notice how the onlookers form a circle, to take a close look without getting so near that they would become involved. In view of this universal instinct to form circles, it is not surprising that virtually all primitive forms of theater were "in the round."

There is also a practical, economic advantage to the arena stage: any large room can be converted into this arrangement. You simply designate a playing space, arrange rows of seats around the sides, and hang lights on pipes above,

A CONTEMPORARY ARENA THEATER
Arena theaters attempt to capture the intimacy and immediacy of primitive theater. They use only the barest essentials of stage scenery but the full resources of contemporary stage lighting. Seen here is the arena stage space at A Contemporary Theatre in Seattle, Washington. (Steve Keating for Callison Architecture, Courtesy of A Contemporary Theatre, Seattle)

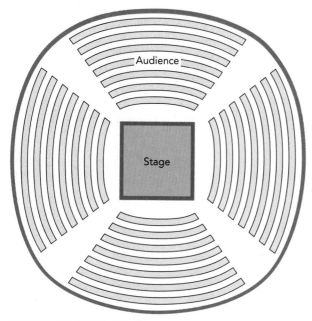

PLAN OF AN ARENA STAGE

The audience sits on four sides or in a circle surrounding the stage. Entrances and exits are made through the aisles or through tunnels underneath the aisles. A feeling of intimacy is achieved because the audience is close to the action and encloses it.

and you have a theater. Elaborate scenery is unnecessary; in fact, it is impossible because it would block the view of large parts of the audience. A few pieces of furniture, with perhaps a lamp or sign hung from the ceiling, are all you need to indicate where a scene takes place. Many low-budget groups have found that they can build a workable and even attractive theater-in-the-round when a picture-frame theater would be out of the question.

These two factors—intimacy and economy—no doubt explain why the arena theater is one of the oldest stage spaces. As we have mentioned, ceremonies in ancient Greece were held in a circular space, which was the forerunner of the Greek thrust stage. From as far back as we have records, we know that religious observances and tribal rituals in all parts of the world have been held in some form of circle theater. One example is the war dance of the Apache; another is the festival plays of Tibet, which portray the struggle of Buddhism to supplant an earlier religion. In the medieval period, several of the religious plays in England and France were performed in arena-

A CONTEMPORARY ARENA THEATER

Arena theaters attempt to capture the intimacy and immediacy of primitive theater. They use only the barest essentials of stage scenery but the full resources of contemporary stage lighting.

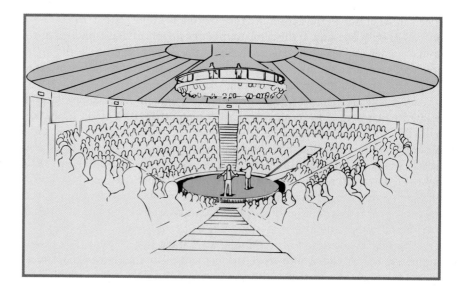

type spaces. In the modern period in the United States, there was a proliferation of arena stages after World War II.

In spite of its long history and its recent resurgence, however, the arena stage has often been eclipsed by other forms. One reason is that its design, while allowing for intimacy, also dictates a certain austerity: elaborate scenery, for example, is impossible because it would block the view of many spectators. Also, performers must make all their entrances and exits along aisles that run through the audience, and so they can sometimes be seen before and after they are supposed to appear onstage.

These problems may explain why some of the circle theaters which opened in the United States 30 or 40 years ago have since closed. A number survive, however, and continue to do well, one of the best-known being the Arena Stage in Washington, D.C. In addition, throughout the country there are a number of tent theaters in arena form, where concerts and revivals of musicals are given.

Before we leave the three major types of theater arrangements—proscenium, thrust, and arena—we should point out that with each of them, there is customarily space just outside the main seating and stage areas where the audience assembles and tickets are sold and taken. Also, backstage or offstage, there must be dressing rooms for performers and facilities for the stage manager, the stage crews, and anyone else concerned with mounting and running a show. (**Running** is the term used to describe the unfolding of a performance. When actors, actresses, and stage crew move through a performance, they are said to be *running the show*.)

CREATED OR FOUND SPACES

A fourth type of stage is called *created* or *found space*. This term means that a theater is set up in a space not ordinarily used for performance. All early theaters probably began in some type of created or found space. Tribal ceremonies, for example, were performed in outdoor spaces such as a circle with an altar at the center. In the Middle Ages, theater performances were originally held in churches or cathedrals. When these performances became longer and more secular in nature, they were presented outside; but even then, there were no permanent theaters—only temporary stages erected in the "found" space of town squares.

In recent years, there has been renewed interest in the concept of theater performed in unusual places: street corners, public parks, and the like. This is meant partly to bring theater closer to people, and partly to put theater into a new and different context so that people will think about its purpose and impact. Nontheater spaces are often of special interest to experimental, avant-garde, or political theater practitioners. In the 1960s, the Polish director Jerzy Grotowski made novel use of space an important part of his productions, rearranging an open area in different configurations for different plays. In his production of a play about Doctor Faustus, for example, Faustus gives a banquet; for this, Grotowski filled the open theater space with two long tables at which audience

Making Connections

Popular Performance Spaces

Many spaces used for live popular entertainments are reminiscent of theater environments. Arenas used for sports, circuses, and rock concerts are configured much like the theatrical spaces discussed in this chapter. Madison Square Garden in New York, Soldier Field in Chicago, and the Rose Bowl in Pasadena, California, are all large spaces that primarily house sporting events but are also used for rock concerts and other popular spectacles.

Madison Square Garden, for example, has housed the Ringling Brothers and Barnum and Bailey Circus, an extravagant staging of *The Wizard of Oz*, Frank Sinatra, Barbara Streisand, Bruce Springsteen, the Grammys, and the VH1 Awards, to name just a few events. This means that an arena like the Garden is often equipped with the most innovative technology for lighting, stage, and sound effects.

Spectacular performance spaces for magicians, circuses, and concerts are also found in all of the extravagant hotels in Las Vegas. There is live entertainment presented in spaces at fairgrounds and amuse-

A SPORTS SPECTACLE

An event such as a game in a basketball arena has a number of similarities to a theatrical event: a focus of attention like a stage; an audience surrounding it; a common bond between spectators and athletes, who bear resemblances to performers in the theater. The arena shown here is the Superdome in New Orleans, Louisiana. (Andy Lyons/Getty Images)

ment parks as well. To explore the variety of popular spaces and entertainments in the United States you might want to visit the website *www.amusementbusiness.com.*

These spaces for popular performance are most often configured in the round, with spectators surrounding the events. (Some are configured three-quarter-round.) The reason is to maximize the number of audience members as well as to create an electrifying, interactive environment. With these configurations, the spectators are also able to watch and possibly influence each other's reactions.

Such popular performance spaces are usually extremely large, much larger than environments created exclusively for theater. For example, the Rose Bowl accommodates 92,542 for football games. Even a comparatively small collegiate athletics facility, Western Hall on the campus of Western Illinois University, can accommodate approximately 5,100 spectators.

The relationship between spaces for popular entertainment and theatrical environments is complex. In later chapters, we will see that often in theater history, spaces were used for popular arts and for theatrical performances. Modern theater artists have experimented with staging dramatic performances within spaces created for circuses and concerts.

For that matter, the performance qualities of sports, the circus, and rock concerts underscore their shared heritage with the theatrical arts. It is not surprising, then, that their spaces for performance are also similar.

members sat, as if they were guests at a dinner party, while the actors and actresses performed on the tabletops. For another play, which took place in a mental hospital, the action was set inside a simulated hospital ward, with the performers on beds and the spectators moving around the beds.

One manifestation of found or created space has been *street theater,* which takes place—as the name suggests—in the streets. One purpose of street theater is to bring performances to neighborhoods, especially in inner cities, where people do not normally attend traditional theater. Street theater can also serve a political purpose: it is sometimes used to make a moral or political point, by people who feel that being in the streets will bring their message home to audiences more forcefully.

By now, every conceivable type of space has been used for theater: lofts, warehouses, fire stations, basements, churches, breweries, gymnasiums, jails, parks, subway stations. Of course, such sites present problems for any kind of long-range theater. They are, obviously, impermanent, and matters such as how to handle tickets raise difficult questions. Also, there is usually only a minimum of scenery, and the accommodations for spectators can be less than ideal. Nevertheless, created and found spaces have been important at various times in theater history and take their place as one of the four major theater arrangements or environments.

MULTIFOCUS ENVIRONMENTS

An approach that sometimes accompanies unusual theater arrangements is **multifocus theater.** Put simply, this means that there is more than one playing area (such as the four corners of a room), and that something is going on simultaneously in several areas. Multifocus theater is somewhat like a three-ring circus, where we see an activity in each ring and must either concentrate on one ring or divide our attention.

CREATED OR FOUND THEATER SPACE

Frequently in modern theater, directors or groups have worked in nontraditional spaces: either putting a theater production in a space ordinarily used for another purpose or creating a space in an empty area. A good example was Deborah Warner's The Angel Project, which was staged at different locations throughout New York City. The one shown here was an installation in an empty office in a high-rise building. The audience traveled from place to place to experience the event in a series of spaces. (© Stephanie Berger)

There are several theories behind the idea of multifocus theater. One theory is that a multifocus event is more like everyday life; if you stand on a street corner, for instance, there is activity all around you—in the four directions of the streets and in the buildings above—not just in one spot. You select which area you will observe, or perhaps you watch several areas at once. The argument is that you should have the same choice in theater.

In a multifocus production, no single space or activity is supposed to be more important than any other. Each spectator either takes in and synthesizes several impressions at once or selects one impression as most arresting and concentrates on that. There is no such thing as the "best seat in the house"; all seats are equally good, because the activity in all parts of the theater is equally important. Sometimes multifocus theater is joined with *multimedia theater*—a presentation using some combination of acting, film, dance, music, slides, video, and light shows.

ALL-PURPOSE AND EXPERIMENTAL SPACES

Because of the interest in a variety of spaces in modern theater productions, and to meet the requirements of different kinds of productions, a number of theater

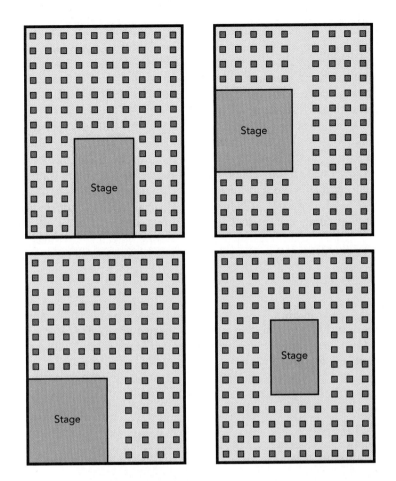

THE MULTIPURPOSE OR "BLACK BOX" THEATER
A popular type of modern theater is the multipurpose space, sometimes called a "black box." It consists of an open space with perhaps a pipe grid on the ceiling from which lighting and sound instruments can be suspended. A stage platform can be positioned at any place in the space, and movable chairs for spectators can be placed around the playing area. The diagram at the left suggests some of the possibilities of stage arrangements in a multipurpose theater.

complexes—including many college theater departments—have built spaces that can be adapted to an almost infinite range of configurations. These spaces are sometimes referred to as **black boxes.** Seats, lights, platforms, levels—every aspect is flexible and movable. In this kind of space, designers can create a proscenium, a thrust, an arena, or some combination of these. Moreover, the designers can also create corner stages, island stages, and multifocus arrangements with playing areas in several parts of the studio or another flexible space.

Open studios and similar adaptable, experimental spaces are especially important for avant-garde theater troupes, college theater organizations, and groups engaged in workshop productions of new works, whether by individual playwrights, performance artists, or collectives.

In conclusion, we should note that simply assigning a theater to a category does not adequately describe the environment; we must also take into account a number of other variables in theater architecture. Two theaters may be of the same type but still be quite different in location, size, ornateness, and atmosphere; for instance, one may be indoors and the other outdoors.

We should also note that questions of appropriateness and aesthetic distance arise. By *appropriateness,* we mean the relationship of a stage space to a play or production. With regard to environment, **aesthetic distance** denotes the appropriate amount of spatial separation between performers and audience. For example, the theater space for a large-scale spectacular musical should be different from that for a small-scale intimate drama.

In discussing theater spaces, another thing to remember is that the modern period is unique in having so many forms available simultaneously. Audiences in the United States today can enjoy theater in a multitude of settings. Not only do we have examples of all four major types of theater spaces; there is great variety within each of those types. There are thrust stages outdoors, such as the Shakespeare Festival theater in New York's Central Park and other similar outdoor theaters; and there are small indoor thrust stages in cities all across the country, as well as larger ones such as the Guthrie Theater in Minneapolis and the Mark Taper Forum in Los Angeles. The same variety is seen in arena and proscenium theaters.

In Chapters 10 and 11 we will turn to aspects of theater closely associated with theater space: the visual elements—scenery, costumes, and lighting—that become a part of the space, and the sound that fills it.

SUMMARY

An indispensable element of all theatrical productions is the physical space in which the performance occurs. A theater space must include a place for the spectators to sit or stand. Theater spaces may be indoors or outdoors, and of any size or shape, but four basic arrangements have prevailed throughout theater history.

Probably the best-known arrangement is the proscenium-arch or picture-frame stage. First introduced in Europe during the Italian Renaissance, it grew in popularity throughout Europe and the United States, and it is still frequently used. The action takes place behind the proscenium arch, which can also be used to conceal elaborate machinery for creating realistic or spectacular scenic effects.

In the earliest western theaters, the most popular arrangement was the thrust stage with three-quarters seating, developed by the ancient Greeks and adapted by the Romans. Variations of the thrust stage were also used in English courtyard theaters and Spanish corrales, and for traditional Chinese and Japanese drama.

Another basic arrangement of theater space is the arena stage, or theater-in-the-round. Arena staging brings more of the audience closer to the stage than is possible with a proscenium or thrust arrangement; thus one of the advantages of the arena stage is a sense of intimacy between audience and performers.

The fourth type of theater arrangement is created or found space: performances that take place not in a permanent theater but in a park, a church, a garage, or some other place that does not usually serve as a theater.

All four types of theater spaces are used in the United States today, as are many variations, including the multifocus space and the flexible experimental theater.

KEY TERMS

Aesthetic distance Physical or psychological separation or detachment of audience from dramatic action, usually considered necessary for artistic illusion.

Arena stage Stage entirely surrounded by the audience; also known as theater-in-the-round.

Black box A theater space that is open, flexible, and adaptable, usually without fixed seating or a permanent stage area. It is economical and particularly well suited to experimental work.

Corral Theater of the Spanish golden age, usually located in the courtyard of a series of adjoining buildings.

Created or found space Space not originally intended for theater use which is converted for productions. Avant-garde artists often produce in found spaces.

Fly loft Space above the stage where scenery may be lifted out of sight by means of ropes and pulleys.

Fourth-wall convention Pretense that in a proscenium-arch theater the audience is looking into a room through an invisible fourth wall.

Multifocus theater Theater in which something is going on simultaneously in several playing areas.

Multimedia theater Use of electronic media—such as slides, film, and videotape—in live theatrical presentations.

Orchestra Ground-floor seating in an auditorium; also, a circular playing space in ancient Greek theaters.

Platform stage Elevated stage with no proscenium.

Proscenium (pro-SEEN-ee-um) Arch or frame surrounding the stage opening in a box or picture stage.

Rake An upward slope of the stage floor away from the audience; also, to position scenery on a slant or at an angle other than parallel or perpendicular to the curtain line.

Run Operation of a show; also, the length of time a production is performed.

Thrust stage Theater space in which the audience sits on three sides of the stage.

Wagon stage Low platform mounted on wheels or casters by means of which scenery is moved on- and offstage.

THEATER ON THE WEB

For more research and to learn more about the topics in this chapter, please visit the Online Learning Center at **www.mhhe.com/livelyart6**.

CHAPTER 10

Designers: Scenery and Costumes

◀ **THE VISUAL ELEMENTS: SCENERY AND COSTUMES**

Designers—especially scene and costume designers—determine the look of a production. Scenery and costumes emphasize whether a production is realistic or nonrealistic and whether it is modern or historical; and they add color and visual excitement. Shown here is the visual realization of a musical, Monty Python's Spamalot, *with Simon Russell Beale and Lauren Kennedy. The scenic and costume design was by Tim Hatley.* (© Joan Marcus)

As spectators sit in a theater, watching what unfolds before them, they naturally focus most keenly on the performers. But audiences also notice the visual images created by scenery, costumes, and lighting—and they may also hear music underscoring the action, and sound effects such as rain, thunder, or traffic. These visual and aural elements, which add a significant ingredient to the total mixture of theater, are created and organized by designers.

The *scene designer* is responsible for the stage set, which can run the gamut from a bare stage furnished only with stools or orange crates to the most elaborate large-scale production. No matter how simple, however, every set has a design. Even the absence of scenery constitutes a stage set and can benefit from the ideas of a scene designer. The *costume designer* is responsible for selecting, and in many cases creating, the outfits and accessories worn by performers.

Designers must deal with practical as well as aesthetic considerations. A scene designer must know in which direction a door should open onstage, how high each riser should be on a flight of stairs, what materials work best in building scenery, and what kinds of paint to use for painting it. A costume designer must know how much material it takes to make a certain kind of dress and how to "build" clothes so that performers can wear them with confidence and have freedom of movement.

In this chapter, we will deal with scene and costume design. Chapter 11 will take up lighting and sound design.

SCENE DESIGN

The Scene Designer's Objectives

In preparing scenery for a stage production, a scene designer has the following objectives:

1. Help set the tone and style of the production
2. Establish the locale and period in which the play takes place
3. Develop a design concept consistent with the director's concept
4. Provide a central image or metaphor, where appropriate
5. Ensure that scenery is coordinated with other production elements
6. Solve practical design problems

Establishing Tone and Style.   A stage setting can help establish the mood, style, and meaning of a play. In the arts, *style* refers to the *manner* in which a work is done: how scenery looks, how a playwright uses language or exaggerates dramatic elements, how performers portray characters. (A realistic acting style, for example, resembles the way people behave in everyday life; in contrast, the lofty quality of traditional tragedy calls for formal, larger-than-life movements and gestures.)

A slapstick farce might call for a design style involving comic, exaggerated scenery, like a cartoon; and perhaps for outrageous colors, such as bright reds and oranges. Such scenery would match the acting, which would also be exagger-

Robin Wagner: Scene Designer

Robin Wagner has been designing sets in New York for more than two decades. His work includes the Broadway shows A Chorus Line; 42nd Street; The Great White Hope; Kiss Me, Kate; Saturday Night Fever; Crazy for You; Angels in America; *and* The Producers. *He was recently inducted into the Theatre Hall of Fame.*

Robin, tell us about how you began your career. I'm from San Francisco originally. I had a regular high school education and then two years of art school at the California School of Fine Arts. Aside from little projects in high school, I didn't have any particular theater instruction. I'd never really given much thought to what goes on behind the scenes—as far as I was concerned, theater was just a group of actors who showed up onstage and put on a play. In fact, I was out of high school and an art student before I was exposed to theater. And then when I took a closer look, I discovered that the accumulation of all the work that goes on behind the scenes was even more interesting to me than what was going on in the performance. I realized that it requires so many people to produce a play that I knew there was room for me.

I worked at a number of so-called weekend theaters in San Francisco—the equivalent of off-off-Broadway in New York—where there was no pay but plenty of variety. I started painting scenery and working backstage, but I also had a little design experience. I was fortunate in starting in a city like San Francisco, where at that time there were very few professional designers. Even though I was only an art student just out of high school, I got experience designing that I would never have had if I had had any competition. I first came to New York in 1958, when the Actor's Workshop production of *Waiting for Godot* that I designed was selected to go to the World's Fair in Brussels. My first real training was in New York, working for three years as an assistant to Oliver Smith, who designed *Hello, Dolly* and *110 in the Shade*. After I worked around the country at a number of regional theaters, I returned to New York and worked off-Broadway until I was asked to design *Hair*. It was 1968, and *Hair* was a breakthrough musical—it had a completely different kind of sound.

ated, with lots of physical comedy—people tripping over carpets, opening the wrong doors, and so forth. A satire would call for a comment in the design, like the twist in the lines of a caricature in a political cartoon. A serious play would call for less exaggerated or less comic scenery.

As an illustration of what is called for in scene design, let us consider two plays by the Spanish playwright Federico García Lorca. His *Blood Wedding* is the story of a young bride-to-be who runs away with a former lover on the day she is to be married. The two flee to a forest. In the forest, allegorical figures of the Moon and a Beggar Woman, who represents Death, seem to echo the fierce emotional struggle taking place within the characters, who are torn between duty to their families and passion for each other. For this part of the play, the scenery and costumes must have the same sense of mystery, of the unreal, which rules the characters. The forest should not have real trees but should represent the thicket of emotions in which the man and woman are entangled; the costumes of the Moon and the Beggar Woman should not be realistic but should suggest the forces that endanger the lovers.

Another play by García Lorca, *The House of Bernarda Alba,* is a contrast in style: it has no fantasy or symbolic characters. This play concerns a woman and her five daughters. The mother has grown to hate and distrust men, and so she locks up her house, like a closed convent, preventing her daughters from going out. From a design point of view, it is important to convey the closed-in, cloistered feeling of the house in which the daughters are held as virtual prisoners. The walls of the house and its furniture should all have solid reality, creating an atmosphere that will convey a sense of entrapment.

Scene design is especially important in indicating to the audience whether a play is realistic or departs from realism. **Realism** in theater means that everything connected with a production conforms to our observation of the world around us. This includes the way characters speak and behave, the clothes they wear, the events that occur in the play, and the physical environment. Characters presented in a living room or a bar, for example, will look and act as we expect people in those settings to look and act.

On the other hand, *nonrealism* or *departures from realism* means all types of theater that depart from observable reality. A musical in which characters sing and dance is nonrealistic because people do not ordinarily go around singing and dancing in public places. A play like Shakespeare's *Macbeth* is unrealistic because it has witches and ghosts—two types of creatures not encountered in everyday existence. Also, the language of the play is poetry, and there are soliloquies in which characters speak thoughts out loud—again, these are elements that depart from the reality we see in our daily lives. Nonrealistic elements are, of course, highly theatrical and can increase our pleasure and excitement. Moreover, they often indicate a deeper reality than we see on the surface. Thus *departures from realism* does not imply that something is not genuine or not true; it simply means that something is a departure from what we see around us.

The terms, then, are simply ways of categorizing aspects of theater; and they are particularly important in scene design, because scenery can quickly signal to an audience which type of theater we are viewing.

Establishing Locale and Period.   Whether realistic or not, a stage set should tell the audience where and when the play takes place. Is the locale a saloon? A bedroom? A courtroom? A palace? A forest? The set should also indicate the time period. A kitchen with old-fashioned utensils and no electric appliances sets the play in the past. An early radio and an icebox might tell us that the period is the 1920s. A spaceship or the landscape of a faraway planet would suggest that the play is set in the future.

In addition to indicating time and place, the setting can also tell us what kinds of characters a play is about. For example, the characters may be neat and formal or lazy and sloppy. They may be kings and queens or members of an ordinary suburban family. The scenery should suggest these things immediately.

Developing a Design Concept.   In order to convey information, the scene designer frequently develops a *design concept.* Such a concept should be arrived

REALISM AND NONREALISM IN SCENIC DESIGN

Scene design helps indicate whether a production is realistic or a departure from realism. Shown here are good examples of the two approaches. One scene (above) is an example of nonrealistic scenery designed by Robert Wilson for his rock opera POEtry, about Edgar Allen Poe. There is no attempt to portray reality, but rather the surrealistic presentation of images and ideas. In contrast we see a scene from Robert Harling's play Steel Magnolias, *on Broadway at the Lyceum Theater, which featured (from left) Delta Burke as Truvy, Rebecca Gayheart as Shelby, Christine Ebersole as M'Lynn, and Lily Rabe as Annelle. The scenic design was by Anna Louizos, and the costume designs were by David Murin.*
(© Hermann and Clärchen Baus) (Sara Krulwich/The New York Times)

CENTRAL DESIGN CONCEPT

In certain productions, the scene designer attempts to create a strong central visual image or metaphor that gives unity and focus to the whole. Shown here is the designer Ming Cho Lee's use of a giant head of Buddha, which hovers over the setting for a production of Antony and Cleopatra *at the Guthrie Theater in Minneapolis. The design element, which is ever-present, establishes a visual focus for the production but does not interfere with the action onstage.* (© T. Charles Erickson)

at in consultation with the director and should complement the directorial concept (discussed in Chapter 8). The design concept is a unifying idea carried out visually. For García Lorca's *The House of Bernarda Alba,* for example, such a concept would be a claustrophobic setting that sets the tone for the entire play.

A strong design concept is particularly important when the time and place of a play have been shifted. Modern stage designs for Shakespeare's *A Midsummer Night's Dream* illustrate this point. In most productions, this play is performed in a palace and a forest, as suggested by the text. But for a production done in the early 1970s, the director Peter Brook wanted to give it a modern, clean, spare look so that the audience would see its contemporary implications. Accordingly, the scene designer, Sally Jacobs (1932–), fashioned a single set consisting of three bare white walls, rather like the walls of a gymnasium. This single set was used as the background for all the scenes in the play, giving visual unity to the production and also creating a modern, somewhat abstract atmosphere. As part of the action, trapezes were lowered onto the stage at various times, and in some scenes the performers actually played their parts suspended in midair.

Providing a Central Image or Metaphor. The design concept is closely related to the idea of a *central image* or *metaphor*. Stage design not only must be consistent with the play; it should have its own integrity. The elements of the design—lines, shapes, and colors—should add up to a complete visual universe for the play. Often, therefore, the designer tries to develop a central image or metaphor.

In a production of Stephen Sondheim's *Sweeney Todd* in 2005, the designer, John Doyle, who was also the director, created a vast wooden cabinet in the center of the back wall. The subtitle of this musical is *The Demon Barber of Fleet Street;* and the cabinet, some 18 or 20 feet tall, had shelves for razors and all the tools of the barber trade as well as other bric-a-brac. A black coffin, which served other functions as well as its original purpose, stood at center stage throughout. But it was the menacing presence of the towering cabinet that dominated the scene and served as a central design image for the entire production.

In his design for the original Broadway production of *Death of a Salesman*, Jo Mielziner (1901–1976) created a set that combined various elements inherent in the play. On the one hand, there was the real home of Willy Loman, including a kitchen with a refrigerator, a table, and chairs. At the same time, surrounding the house was a skyline consisting of apartment houses closing in on Willy's world. When Willy moved from the present to his memory of the past, the lights would shift so that the audience could see through transparent walls of his house to the world around him. From the real world, Willy moved, as if by magic, through the walls of his home into the past. In these scenes, the hope and promise of Willy's youth, when his world was full of fresh, growing things, was symbolized by projections of green leaves thrown over the entire set, hiding the surrounding apartments. Mielziner's set provided a central metaphor for the play, with Willy's home as the constant, and the green plants—depicting youthful hope—ultimately blocked out by the encroaching skyline.

Coordinating Scenery with the Whole. Because scenic elements have such strong symbolic value and are so important to the overall effect of a production, the designer needs to provide scenery consistent with the playwright's intent and the director's concept. If the text and acting are highly stylized, the setting should be stylized too. If the text and acting are realistic, the setting should also be realistic, rather than some kind of fantastic or overpowering spectacle. As with other elements, the setting should contribute to the overall effect of a production.

Solving Practical Design Problems. Finally, the scene designer must deal with practical problems of design. Many of these involve physical elements of stage design, to which we'll now turn.

Elements of Scene Design

Five Elements of Scene Design. As the scene designer proceeds, he or she makes use of the following elements:

1. *Line,* the outline or silhouette of elements onstage; for example, predominantly curved lines versus sharply angular lines.
2. *Mass,* the overall bulk or weight of scenic elements; for example, a series of high, heavy platforms or fortress walls versus a bare stage or a stage with only a single tree on it.
3. *Composition,* the balance and arrangement of elements; the way elements are arranged: for example, mostly to one side of the stage, in a vertical or horizontal configuration, or equally distributed onstage.
4. *Texture,* the "feel" projected by surfaces and fabrics; for example, the slickness of chrome or glass versus the roughness of brick or burlap.
5. *Color,* the shadings and contrasts of color combinations.

The designer will use these elements to affect audiences, in conjunction with the action and other aspects of the production.

Physical Layout: The Playing Area. A playing area must, obviously, fit into a certain stage space and accommodate the performers. A designer cannot plan a gigantic stage setting for a theater where the proscenium opening is only 20 feet wide and the stage is no more than 15 feet deep. By the same token, to design a small room in the midst of a 40-foot stage opening might be ludicrous.

The designer must also take into account the physical layout of the stage space. If a performer must leave by a door on the right side of the stage and return a few moments later by a door on the left, the designer must obviously provide space for crossing behind the scenery. If performers need to change costumes quickly offstage, the scene designer must make certain that there is room offstage

GROUND PLAN
To aid the director, performers, and stage technicians, the designer draws a ground plan or blueprint, of the stage, showing the exact locations of furniture, walls, windows, doors, and other scenic elements.

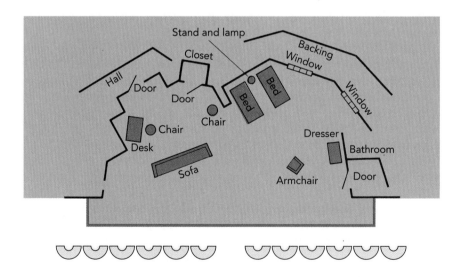

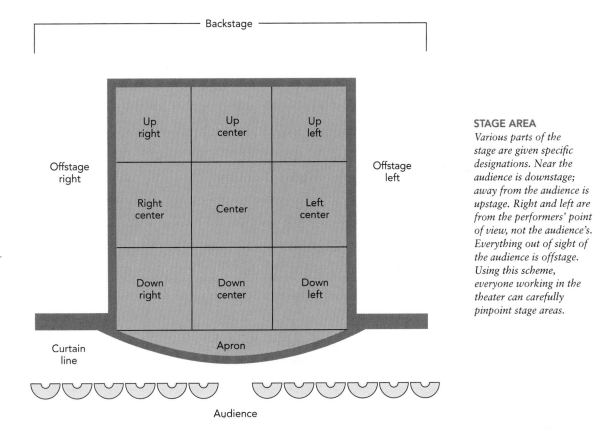

Backstage

Up right	Up center	Up left
Right center	Center	Left center
Down right	Down center	Down left

Offstage right

Offstage left

Curtain line

Apron

Audience

STAGE AREA
Various parts of the stage are given specific designations. Near the audience is downstage; away from the audience is upstage. Right and left are from the performers' point of view, not the audience's. Everything out of sight of the audience is offstage. Using this scheme, everyone working in the theater can carefully pinpoint stage areas.

for changing. If there is to be a sword fight, the actors must have space in which to make their turns, to advance and retreat.

Any type of physical movement requires a certain amount of space, and the scene designer must allow for this in his or her ground plan. A ***ground plan*** is a blueprint, or floor plan, outlining the various levels on the stage and indicating the placement of all scenery, furniture, doors, windows, and so on. The designer, working in conjunction with the director, is chiefly responsible for ensuring a practical ground plan.

How doors open and close, where a sofa is placed, at what angle steps will lead to a second floor—all these are important. Performers must be able to execute stairs easily and to sit in such a way that the audience can readily see them, and they must have enough space to interact with each other naturally and convincingly. If a performer opens a door onstage and is immediately blocked from the view of the audience, this is obviously an error on the part of the scene designer.

To designate areas of the stage, scene designers, directors, performers, and technicians use terminology peculiar to theater. *Stage right* and *stage left* mean the right side and the left side of the stage, respectively, as seen from the position of a performer facing the audience. (In other words, when spectators in the auditorium look at the stage, the area to their left is known as *right stage* and the area to their right as *left stage.*) The stage area nearest the audience is known as *downstage;* the area farthest away from the audience is *upstage.* The designations *downstage* and *upstage* come from the eighteenth and nineteenth centuries, when the stage was raked—that is, it sloped downward from back to front. As a result of this downward slope, the performer farthest away from the audience was higher, or "up," and could be seen better. Also, performers downstage from—below—an upstage performer would be forced to turn their backs on the audience when addressing him or her. This is the origin of the expression *to upstage someone.* Today the term is used whenever one performer grabs the spotlight from everyone else or calls attention to himself or herself by any means whatever. At first, however, it meant simply that one performer was in a better position than the others because he or she was standing farther back on the raked stage and hence was higher.

Materials and Devices of Scene Design. In creating a stage set, a designer begins with the stage floor. At times, trapdoors are set into the floor; through them, performers can enter or leave the stage. For some productions, tracks or slots are set into the stage floor, and set pieces or wagons are brought onstage in these tracks. A *wagon* is a low platform set on wheels. Wagon stages are brought onstage electronically or by stagehands hidden behind them. This type of scene change is frequently used in musical comedy. Another device used along the stage floor is a *treadmill,* which can carry performers, furniture, or props from one side of the stage to the other. Sometimes the stage floor includes a *turntable*—a circle, set into the floor, which is rotated mechanically or electronically to bring one set into view as another disappears.

Formerly, equipment such as turntables, wagons, and treadmills would be moved mechanically or by hand. In recent years, however, these operations have been computerized. Complicated scene changes can be controlled by computer so that they take place efficiently and simultaneously. Computers can also control the turning and shifting of scenic elements. For instance, panels, screens, and scenic flats (discussed below) not only can be moved on- and offstage but also can be shifted or rotated while onstage. In addition, safety features are built into the new computerized equipment. When performers are on a moving treadmill, for example, light beams or pressure-sensitive plates can detect a malfunction and shut the system down before anyone is hurt.

Instead of coming from the sides, scenery can be dropped from the *fly loft; to fly* is the term used when scenery is raised into the area above the stage, out of sight of the audience.

From floor level, ramps and platforms can be built to any height desired. To create walls or divisions of other kinds, for many years the most commonly used element was the *flat,* so named because it is a single flat unit, consisting of canvas stretched on a wood frame. The side of the flat facing the audience was painted to look like a solid wall, and flats used in conjunction were made to look like a complete room.

SPECIAL SCENIC EFFECTS: THE SCRIM

Scene designers use various materials and devices to achieve their effects. One popular scenic element is the scrim, which can be transparent when light comes from behind it and opaque when light comes from the front. It is especially effective for scenes of memory and fantasy. Shown here, in front of a scrim, is a character from a production at the Huntington Theatre entitled 36 Views. *The designers were Adam Stockhausen, scenery; Teresea Snider-Stein, costumes; and Chris Parry, lighting.* (© T. Charles Erickson)

Today scene designers and shop technicians have turned more and more to the *hard flat,* sometimes called a *movie* or *Hollywood* flat; it consists of a thin, solid material, called *luan,* mounted on a wooden or hollow metal frame. A hard flat can be painted, and three-dimensional plastic moldings can be attached to it, creating cornices, chair rails, and other interesting features. Other vertical units are *cutouts*—small pieces made like flats or cut out of plywood. These too can be painted.

A special type of scenery is the **scrim**—a gauze or cloth screen. A scrim can be painted like a regular flat; however, the wide mesh of the cloth allows light to pass through. When light shines on a scrim from the front—that is, from the audience's point of view—it is reflected off the painted surface, and the scrim appears to be a solid surface. When light comes from behind, the scrim becomes transparent and the audience can see performers and scenery behind it. Scrims are particularly effective in scenes where ghosts appear or when eerie effects are desired. Scrims are also useful in memory plays or plays with flashbacks: the audience sees the scene in the present in front of the scrim; then, as the lights in front fade and the lights behind come up, a scene with a cloudy, translucent quality appears through the gauzelike scrim, indicating a scene taking place in someone's memory or in the past.

SCENIC PROJECTIONS
Effective scenic supplements to traditional scenery are video and screen projections—either still images or moving images. Visual effects can be superimposed or used in the background of stage action. The musical The Woman in White *used nothing but projections throughout the production to create both interior scenes and outdoor landscapes. The projections were thrown on a large white semicircular background that encompassed the action. Changes were carried out entirely by computer. Shown here is the designer William Dudley, standing in front of a projection of a waterfall.* (Sara Krulwich/The New York Times)

Another scenic device is *screen projection*. A picture or drawing is projected on a screen either from in front—as in an ordinary movie theater—or from behind. The advantage of projection from behind is that the performers will not be in the beam of light, and thus there will be no shadows or silhouettes. Obviously, projections offer many advantages: pictures can change with the rapidity of cinema, and vast scenes can be presented onstage in a way that would otherwise require tremendously elaborate scene painting. In Andrew Lloyd Webber's musical *Woman in White*, scenic projections replaced scenery for the entire production. On a semicircular white background were projected scenes of stately homes, the English countryside, and moving trains.

In recent years, many avant-garde artists have also incorporated video screens and video projections into production design, frequently to draw stark parallels or contrasts between the live performance and something captured on video.

Special Effects. Scrims and projections bring us to a consideration of *special effects*. These are effects of scenery, lighting, sound, and props that seem unusual or even miraculous. (The term *prop* comes from the word *property;* it refers to any object that will be used onstage but is not a permanent part of the scenery or costumes. Props are such things as lamps, mirrors, computers, walking sticks, umbrellas, and fans.) Special effects include fog, ghosts, knives or swords that appear to stab victims, walls and windows that fall apart, and so on. Today, films and television—because of their technical capabilities—have very realistic special effects, like burning buildings and exploding cars. Also, computers can create the world of dinosaurs or storms at sea. Special effects onstage, however, are almost as old as theater itself. From the Greeks on, theater has tried to create the illusion of the miraculous or extraordinary.

A modern version occurs in *The Phantom of the Opera,* when a huge chandelier falls from the top of the auditorium onto the stage. In Chapter 11, we will see that there are also many special effects of lighting and sound.

The Process of Scene Design: Steps in the Design Process

In meeting the objectives described above, how does the scene designer proceed? Although every designer has his or her own method, usually the same general pattern is followed.

The designer reads the script and develops ideas about scene designs and a design concept. He or she may even make a few rough sketches to illustrate thoughts about the designs. Meanwhile, the director also has ideas about the scenery. These ideas may vary considerably, depending on the director: they may be vague, or they may be an exact picture of what the scenery should look like.

Director and designer meet for a preliminary conference to exchange ideas about the design. During these discussions, they will develop and discuss questions of style, a visual concept for the production, the needs of the performers, and so on.

Next, the designer develops preliminary sketches, called *thumbnail sketches,* and rough plans to provide a basis for further discussions about the scenic elements.

As the designer proceeds, he or she attempts to fill out the visual concept with sketches, drawings, models, and the like. Sometimes the designer will bring the director sketches showing several possible ideas, each emphasizing different elements to achieve different results.

When the director and the designer have decided on an idea and a rough design, the designer will make a more complete sketch, usually in color, called a *rendering.* If the director approves of the rendering, the designer will make a small-scale three-dimensional *model* that the director can use to help stage the show. There are two types of models. One shows only the location of the platform and walls, with perhaps some light detail drawn in; it is usually all white. The other is a complete, finished model: everything is duplicated as fully as possible, including color and perhaps moldings and texture.

Today, more and more designers are using computers and computer graphics to develop not only ground plans but also three-dimensional models of sets.

Because computer design is so flexible, a designer can make instantaneous changes in what appears on the screen. The director can be shown easily and quickly alternative plans and features of a stage set.

The Scene Designer's Collaborators

As with every element of theater, the visual elements of a production are created collaboratively. A number of important people, in addition to the scene designer, are required to develop scenic effects.

First, there may be people who help the scene designer draw the architectural plans for platforms, ramps, flats, and other scenery. These plans require exact measurements that conform to the stage space, and to the proscenium opening if there is one. They must be drawn precisely to scale, like the blueprints used by architects and engineers in constructing buildings. Today, computers can assist in this drafting.

Once a rendering, model, or computer design is complete and has been approved, it is turned over to the *technical director* of the production, who is also given all the necessary ground plans. Together with building and painting crews, the technical director sees that the necessary elements are built, painted, and installed onstage.

Stage carpenters—people who understand materials and methods of construction—build the platforms, set pieces, flats, and other scenic elements; then scene painters paint them. Scene painting often requires both talent and technique—to create, for instance, the feeling of rare old wood in a library, or of bricks, or of a glossy wall in an expensive living room. There are also people who find fabric for draperies, slipcovers for furniture, and other items that "dress" the stage set.

When the time comes for technical rehearsals, dress rehearsals, and actual performances, a production requires stagehands and a stage manager to coordinate scene changes, to remove and replace scenery and furniture, and to see that each setting is correct and is put into place quickly.

It is clear from all this that a scene designer works closely with others: first with the director—to develop a concept and a visual approach consistent with the overall production—and then with the many people who build, paint, and dress the set and "run" the show after it opens. (To *dress a set* means to add all the furniture and details: draperies, rugs, cushions, and the like.)

Designing a Total Environment

Sometimes, in addition to all these duties, a designer goes farther, designing not only scenery and special effects but the entire theater space. For example, a designer might decide to rearrange the position of the stage and the audience seating area around it. Seats might be removed to make way for additional stage space; or, in a flexible area without fixed seating, the stage might be put in one corner rather than in a central position.

COSTUME DESIGN

Of all the visual elements in theater, costumes are the most personal because they are worn by the performers. Visually, performer and costume are perceived as one; they merge into a single image onstage. At the same time, costumes have a value of their own, adding color, shape, texture, and symbolism to the overall effect. Closely related to costumes are makeup, hairstyles, and masks.

Outside the theater, most people think of costumes in terms of a holiday parade, a masquerade ball, an occasion like Halloween or Mardi Gras, or a historical pageant. Costumes, however, also play a significant role in daily life. People wear clothes not only for comfort but to convey information about themselves. If we look around us, we are actually surrounded by costumes: the formal, subdued uniform of a police officer; the sparkling outfits of a marching band at a football game; sports gear, such as hockey and baseball uniforms; caps and gowns at a graduation; a priest's cassock; brightly colored bathing suits at a swimming pool.

Clothes have always suggested a number of things about the wearer:

Position and status

Gender

Occupation

Flamboyance or modesty

Independence or regimentation

Occasion—work or leisure, a routine event or a special event

As soon as we see what people are wearing, we receive a great many messages and impressions about them; we instantaneously relate those messages to our own experiences and preconceptions; and we form judgments, including value judgments. Even if we have never before laid eyes on people, we feel we know a great deal about them when we first see the clothing they wear.

In theater, clothing also sends us signals; but, as with other elements of theater, there are significant differences between theatrical costumes and costumes in everyday life. Although stage costumes, like ordinary clothes, communicate information about gender, status, and occupation, this information is magnified onstage because it is in the spotlight. Also, of course, stage costumes must meet other requirements, not normally imposed on everyday clothing.

DESIGNING AN ENVIRONMENT
In addition to creating a specific space, such as a kitchen or a bedroom, the designer often creates an "environment," meaning the entire physical landscape in which a production takes place. A good example would be the house and yard in Mexico that are the setting for this production of Tennessee Williams's play The Night of the Iguana. *The tropical atmosphere creates an entire ambience in which the action takes place. The production shown here was directed by John Miller-Stephany at the Guthrie Theater in Minneapolis. The performers are Armand Schultz, Joel Friedman, and Kate Forbes. The designers included James Youmans, set; and Mathew LeFebvre, costumes. At the moment of this scene, Marcus Dilliard's lighting and Scott Edward's sound combined with the set to create a fierce tropical storm. (© T. Charles Erickson)*

Jess Goldstein: Costume Designer

Jess Goldstein has designed costumes for Broadway (The Most Happy Fella, A Streetcar Named Desire, and Love! Valour! Compassion!); for off-Broadway (The Substance of Fire, Other People's Money, Proof, Dinner with Friends, and Take Me Out); for many major regional theaters; and for the New York City Opera. He teaches costume design at the Yale Drama School.

Growing up in the New Jersey suburbs right outside New York City, I began seeing Broadway theater at a relatively early age. I think I was always most impressed with the costume and set design, possibly because I had no talent for performing yet seemed to show some aptitude for drawing and painting. But the world of theatrical design, from my naive perspective, seemed far too exotic and unattainable, so I enrolled as a commercial art major at Boston University. But I continued to see a lot of theater in Boston, which in the early 1970s was still an important tryout stopover for Broadway shows.

At B.U. I met students who were majoring in design in the theater school. Somehow, the fact that one could earn a degree in theater design seemed to endow it as a career choice with some validity and security. Well, talk about "naive"! Nevertheless, I switched majors, and really found school and classwork exciting for the first time in my life.

But it was going to the theater and seeing those Hal Prince, Bob Fosse, Gower Champion, and Michael Bennett musicals that really inspired me. The stars of those shows were terrific, but my heroes were Irene Sharaff, Raoul Pene duBois, Patricia Zipprodt, and Florence Klotz. Watching the way colors and shapes might be manipulated in a scene or the way a skirt would move to the choreography was a significant part of my early training.

I soon began seeking out other kinds of theater: plays off-Broadway, the Shakespeare festivals in New York and Stratford, Connecticut, as well as opera and ballet; and by the time the off-off-Broadway theater movement was in full swing in New York in the late 1970s, I had just completed my M.F.A. at the Yale School of Drama and was ready as a designer to be a part of it.

The Costume Designer

The person responsible for creating costumes for performers is the ***costume designer.*** Like a scene designer, a costume designer must develop visual ideas with the director and communicate those ideas through drawings. Drawings by a costume designer are frequently accompanied by swatches of material. It is the costume designer's responsibility to determine how costumes will actually look on performers in front of an audience. Obviously, all this requires both training and talent.

The costume designer should begin with a thorough knowledge of the play—its subject matter, period, style, and point of view—and with an intimate understanding of the characters. The costume designer must also be aware of the physical demands of the text—what is called for in terms of sitting, moving, dancing, fighting, and so on. Finally, the designer must be acquainted with the physical characteristics of the performers themselves in order to create costumes accommodating their individual physiques and patterns of movement.

THE COSTUME DESIGNER AT WORK
The costume designer is responsible for the look of each performer onstage: the shape, color, and style of what the performer wears; the accessories that accompany the clothes; and the way the costumes of various characters blend together and offset one another. Here the designer William Ivey Long is fitting Robin Givens's costume as Roxie in Chicago. (© Alessandra Petlin/Edge)

THE COSTUME DESIGNER: SKETCHES
One of the most active costume designers of recent times is William Ivey Long. Like many costume designers, he often sketches the costumes of the characters in the play, indicating the style of the clothes, the fabrics, the colors, and the silhouette. Long developed a collage board for all the characters in the "grand finale" of the musical Hairspray, not only sketching the costumes themselves but—below the sketches— adding swatches of fabric indicating colors and other qualities of the fabrics. Shown here are several of the costumes taken from the full cast of the finale, giving an indication of how Long developed the final costumes. (Sketches courtesy of William Ivey Long Studios)

COSTUMES INDICATE TIME AND PLACE
Designers indicate many things, for example, time and place, and whether the characters are upper-class or ordinary people. Seen here are the period costumes (early nineteenth century) designed by Mathew J. LeFebvre for a production of Pride and Prejudice *at the Guthrie Theater in Minneapolis. John Lee Beatty designed the sets. Note the finery and details of the costumes, the frills, and the formality, which let us know this is the scene of a special occasion.* (© Michal Daniel)

Additionally, the costume designer must decide whether the costumes are to be *pulled* or *built*. *Pulling* costumes means renting them from a costume warehouse or choosing them from an inventory owned by a theater company. *Building* costumes means creating them in a costume shop under the supervision of the designer. Built costumes must be sewn, fitted, and completed with accessories and ornamentation. Sometimes, a designer will pull some costumes for a production but build the more unusual ones.

The Costume Designer's Objectives

Stage costumes should meet six requirements:

1. Help establish the tone and style of a production
2. Indicate the historical period of a play and the locale in which it is set
3. Indicate the nature of individual characters or groups in a play: their stations in life, their occupations, their personalities
4. Show relationships among characters: separate major characters from minor ones, contrast one group with another
5. Meet the needs of individual performers: make it possible for an actor or actress to move freely in a costume; allow a performer to dance or engage in a sword fight, for instance; when necessary, allow performers to change quickly from one costume to another
6. Be consistent with the production as a whole, especially with other visual elements

Let us look at these objectives one at a time.

Setting Tone and Style.   Along with scenery and lighting, costumes should inform the audience about the style of a play. For a production taking place in outer space, for instance, the costumes would be futuristic. For a Restoration comedy set in the late 1600s, the costumes would be elegant, with lace at the men's collars and cuffs, and elaborate gowns for the women. For a tragedy, the clothes would be somber and dignified; seeing them, the audience would know immediately that the play itself was somber and its tone serious.

Indicating Time and Place.   Costumes indicate the period and location of a play: whether it is historical or modern, set in a foreign country or the United

States, and so on. A play might take place in ancient Egypt, for instance; in seventeenth-century Spain; or in modern Africa. In some productions, the director and designers want to indicate timelessness, in which case the costumes should not suggest any one period.

Sometimes, as we have already seen, a costume designer and a director decide to shift the period of a play. Such a shift may come as a shock to the audience, and it is up to the costume designer to help the audience adjust to it. For example, if *Hamlet* is to be performed in modern dress, the costume designer in certain scenes might have Hamlet wear a tuxedo and Gertrude an evening gown.

For most historical plays, the director and the costume designer actually have a range of choices. For example, depending on the directorial concept, costumes for Shakespeare's *Julius Caesar* could indicate the time and place in which Caesar lived—ancient Rome—and would include togas and soldiers' helmets. Or the costumes could be Elizabethan, since we know that in Shakespeare's day stage costumes were a heightened version of contemporary English clothes. Or the designer could use costumes from an entirely different period, including the present.

Indicating Characterization.

Just as everyday clothes often do, costumes tell us whether their wearers are aristocrats or ordinary people, blue-collar workers or professionals. In the theater, such signals must be clear and unmistakable. For example, a person in a long white coat could be a doctor, a laboratory technician, or a hairdresser. A stage costume must indicate the exact occupation, and so it may be necessary to add accessories, such as a stethoscope for a doctor.

Costumes also tell us about characters' personalities: a flamboyant person will be dressed in flashy colors; a shy, retiring person will wear subdued clothes.

Costumes can also be used to create symbolic or nonhuman characters. Many plays call for special costumes, denoting abstract ideas or giving shape to fantastic creatures. Here the costume designer must develop an outfit that has the appropriate imaginative and symbolic qualities. A good example would be the Moon and Beggar Woman in *Blood Wedding*.

Indicating Relationships among Characters.

Characters can be set apart by the way they are costumed. Major characters, for example, will be dressed differently from minor characters. Frequently, a costume designer will point up the major characters by dressing them in distinctive colors, in sharp contrast to the

COSTUMES INDICATE SOCIAL RELATIONSHIPS
Along with their many other properties, costumes can signal relationships and contrasts among characters in a production. The lead character may be dressed more vividly than those surrounding her or him; opposing forces such as the two families in Romeo and Juliet *may be dressed in different colors. A good example is shown in this scene from a production of David Mamet's play* Boston Marriage, *at the Public Theater, with costumes designed by Paul Tazewell. The woman on the left (Martha Plimpton) is upper-class, as is indicated by the refinement of fabric and cut of her dress. The actress on the right (Arden Myrin) is in a maid's outfit.* (© Michal Daniel)

COSTUMES: COLOR AND STYLE
Color and style are two elements that costumes add to the visual aspect of a theater production. An example is the pajama fashion show in the musical Pajama Game, *directed and choreographed by Kathleen Marshall, with sets by Derek McLane and costumes by Martin Pakledinaz.* (Sara Krulwich/The New York Times)

colors worn by other characters. Consider, for instance, Shaw's *Saint Joan,* a play about Joan of Arc. Obviously, Joan should stand out from the soldiers surrounding her. Therefore, her costume might be bright blue while theirs are steel-gray. In another play of Shaw's, *Caesar and Cleopatra,* Cleopatra should stand out from her servants and soldiers.

Costumes also underline important differences between groups. In *Romeo and Juliet,* the Montagues wear costumes of one color; the Capulets wear another color. In a modern counterpart of *Romeo and Juliet,* the musical *West Side Story,* the two street gangs are dressed in contrasting colors: the Jets might wear various shades of pink, purple, and lavender; the Sharks might wear green, yellow, and chartreuse.

Meeting Performers' Needs. Virtually every aspect of theater has practical as well as aesthetic requirements, and costume design is no exception. No matter how attractive or how symbolic a costume may be, it must work for the performer. A long flowing gown may look beautiful; but if it is too long and the actress wearing it trips every time she walks down a flight of steps, the designer has overlooked an important practical consideration. If an actor is called on to engage in hand-to-hand combat or fight a duel, his costume must stand up to this wear and tear; and his arms and legs must be free to move, not constrained by the costume. If performers are to dance, they must be able to turn and leap freely.

STYLE, FABRIC, AND CUT IN COSTUMES

The type of fabric, the line and shape of an outfit, the ornateness of the trim and finishing: these tell us a great deal about the characters in a play. Shown here are the costumes designed by Miguel Angel Huidor for a production of Shakespeare's Twelfth Night *at the Public Theater in New York. Note the white of Olivia's costume, contrasting with the red military uniforms of the others. The piping, buttons, and other elements of the uniforms, along with the boots, clearly indicate the military. The soft outline and flowing fabric of Olivia's dress sets her character apart. (© Michal Daniel)*

Ensuring Consistency with the Whole. Finally, costumes must be consistent with the entire production, especially with the other visual elements. A realistic production set in the home of everyday people calls for down-to-earth costumes. A highly stylized production requires costumes designed with flair and imagination.

Elements of Costume Design

Resources of the Costume Designer. Among the resources a costume designer works with are:

Line, shape, and silhouette

Color

Fabric

Accessories

Line. Of prime importance is the cut or line of a costume. Do the lines of the outfit flow, or are they sharp and jagged? Does the clothing follow the lines

ORNAMENTATION IN COSTUME

Those who create costumes, wigs, and hairstyles often use a wide variety of objects and accessories: feathers, fabrics, jewelry, and the like. A vivid example is found in the elaborate costume, wig, and hairpiece for the actress Patricia O'Connell (seen here with Remak Ramsay) in a production of She Stoops to Conquer *at the Irish Repertory Theatre, with costumes by Linda Fisher. (© Carol Rosegg)*

of the body, or is there some element of exaggeration, such as shoulder pads in a man's jacket or a bustle at the back of a woman's dress?

Color. A second important resource for costume designers is color. Earlier, we saw that major characters can be dressed in a color that contrasts with the colors worn by minor characters, and that the characters in one family can be dressed in a different color from those in a rival family. Color also suggests mood: bright, warm colors for a happy mood; dark, somber colors for a more serious mood.

Fabric. Fabric is a third resource of the costume designer. In one sense, fabric is the medium of the costume designer, for it is in fabric that silhouette and color are displayed. Texture and bulk of a fabric are also important. Does a fabric have a smoothness or sheen that reflects light? Or is it rough, so that it absorbs light? How does it drape on the wearer? Does it fall lightly to the floor, outlining the body, or does it hide the body? Does it wrinkle naturally, or is it smooth? Beyond its inherent qualities, fabric has symbolic values. Burlap or other rough-textured cloth, for example, suggests peasants or earthy people. Silks and satins, on the other hand, suggest elegance, refinement, and perhaps even royalty.

In terms of fabric, a number of improvements have been made in recent years, just as they have in other fields of design. William Ivey Long (1947–) is an award-winning designer who designs for Broadway, off-Broadway, and the long-running outdoor drama *The Lost Colony* in North Carolina. In an interview, Long explained the improvements in fabric: "We're actually using more accurate fabrics. When I was growing up, polyester was what was available, and blends. Flax is now available—wool, silk, cotton, linen, flax. We are able to use more plastics (to support the costumes), and we have better products for maintaining the costumes that are fabric-, people- and environment-friendly."

Accessories. Ornamentation and accessories are another resource for costume designers. Fringe, lace, ruffles, feathers, belts, and beads can add to the attractiveness and individuality of a costume. Walking sticks, parasols, purses, and other items that are carried or worn can give distinction and definition. Using the combined resources of line, color, fabric, and accessories, the costume designer arrives at individual outfits that tell us a great deal about the characters who wear them and convey important visual signals about the style and meaning of the play as a whole.

Related Elements. Three elements that are closely related to costumes are makeup, hairstyles, and masks.

Makeup. Makeup—the application of cosmetics such as paints, powders, and rouges to the face and body—helps a performer personify and embody a character. Makeup can be particularly useful if there are age or ethnic differences between the performer and the character.

MAKEUP

Makeup is frequently applied so that facial features will not be washed out by bright theater lights, or to change the look of a performer. In traditional Asian theater, makeup has always been a key element in the performer's appearance. Often it is applied quite heavily and becomes almost like a mask, with colors, lines, and designs. Shown here is an actor in Cantonese opera applying stage makeup. (© Bob Krist/Corbis)

Makeup used to be more popular in the theater than it is today. In a modern small theater, performers playing realistic parts will often simply go without makeup of any consequence. But makeup has a long and important history in theater, and sometimes it is still a necessity—a good example being makeup to highlight facial features that would not otherwise be visible in a large theater. Even in a smaller theater, bright lights tend to wash out cheekbones, eyebrows, and so on. Makeup is often essential because the age of a character differs from that of the performer. If a 19-year-old performer is playing the part of a 60-year-old, the appropriate age can be suggested with makeup, such as a little gray in the hair or simulated wrinkles. Makeup is also necessary in creating fantastic or other nonrealistic creatures.

Asian theater frequently relies on heavy makeup. For instance, Japanese kabuki, a highly stylized theater, uses completely nonrealistic makeup. The main characters must apply a base of white covering the entire face; over this base, bold patterns of red, blue, black, and brown are painted. These colors and patterns symbolize the character. In Chinese theater, too, the colors of makeup are

WIGS AND HAIRSTYLES

Hairstyle indicates social status and other facts about a character; it also provides information about when a play is taking place. Shown here in the exaggerated hairstyles of the 1960s are Laura Bell Bundy as Amber Van Tussle, Clarke Thorell as Corney Collins, and Linda Hart as Velma Van Tussle in the Broadway production of Hairspray. *Wig and hair design by Paul Huntley; costume design by William Ivey Long.* (Sara Krulwich/The New York Times)

symbolic: all white means treachery; black means integrity; red means loyalty; green indicates demons; yellow stands for hidden cunning; and so forth.

Hairstyles.   Closely related to makeup are hairstyles. Outside the theater, hairstyles have varied a great deal in different historical periods and among different social classes. In certain periods, for example, men have worn wigs: the time of the American Revolution is a good example, and judges in England still wear wigs today. In theater, such styles can be used to indicate a historical era or social status.

In the middle of the nineteenth century, women often wore ringlets like Scarlett O'Hara's in the film *Gone with the Wind*. A few decades later, near the turn of the twentieth century, women piled their hair on top of the head in a pompadour; this was referred to as the "Gibson girl" look. In the 1920s, women wore their hair in waves, sometimes slicked down close to the head.

Today, women tend to wear their hair in more natural styles, but actually there is tremendous variety. Some women have short curly hair; some have short straight hair; some have frizzy hair; others have long hair, perhaps even down to the waist, and again, this can be straight or quite curly.

MASKS

Almost from the beginning of theater, in both the west and the east, masks have been an integral part of theater presentations. Masks can change the appearance of a performer, make the face and head larger than life, and freeze the face into a fixed expression. They can also be fanciful and imaginative, suggesting animals or otherworldly creatures, or they can be frightening. Seen here are two examples. In the first we see Ruben Santiago-Hudson (Caesar), the figure in the mask, center, surrounded by John Earl Jelks (Citizen Barlow) and Phylicia Rashad (Aunt Ester) in August Wilson's Gem of the Ocean, *directed by Kenny Leon at the Huntington Theatre. The costume design was by Constanza Romero. In the second example, we see Bakary Sangare in a lion mask in a production of Robert Wilson's* The Fables of La Fontaine. *Céline Samie plays Circea. The masks and costumes were by Robert Wilson. (© T. Charles Erickson) (© Martine Franck/Magnum Photos)*

Masks.   Masks seem to be as old as theater. They were used in ancient Greek theater and in the drama developed by primitive tribes. In one sense, a mask is an extension of a performer: a face on top of a face. There are several ways to interpret masks. They remind us, first, that we are in the theater, that the act going on before our eyes is not real in a literal sense but is rather symbolic or artistic. Second, masks allow a face to be frozen in one expression—a look of horror, perhaps—which we see throughout a production.

The Costume Designer's Collaborators

Like the scene designer, the costume designer works closely with a number of other people. There are, for example, experts at making wigs and masks, and people who specialize in makeup. The actual costumes must be sewn and fitted to the performers by professionals. Sometimes the making and sewing of a costume can be an extremely complicated affair, especially if sequins, feathers, a special corset, or other items are required. Accessories and other personal properties such as hats, umbrellas, and walking canes must be made or found. A costume designer must work closely with these specialists at the same time that he or she is realizing the overall concept developed with the director.

In Chapter 11 we turn to two other important contributors to the visual and aural elements of theater productions: the light and sound designers.

SUMMARY

Two important visual elements of theater are scenery and costumes. These elements are used both to convey information and for aesthetic effect. Scene and costume designers create and organize these visual aspects of theater production.

The scene designer's goals are to help set the tone and style of the production, establish locale and period, develop a design concept, coordinate scenery with other production elements, and solve any practical design problems. Basic elements used by the scene designer are line, mass and composition, texture, and color.

The costume designer also helps establish tone, style, historical period, and locale. In addition, the costume designer helps indicate the personality and social status of individual characters and shows relationships between characters. Costumes—like settings—must be designed so that performers can use them safely and easily. Related to costume are hairstyles and masks, which must also be appropriate and functional.

Scene and costume designers work closely with people who construct sets, props, and costumes and see that they function properly during productions.

KEY TERMS

Build To create a costume from scratch in a costume shop.

Costume designer The person responsible for the appearance of each performer onstage.

Downstage Front of the stage toward the audience.

Flat Single piece of flat, rectangular scenery, used with other similar units to create a set.

Fly loft Space above the stage where scenery may be lifted out of sight by means of ropes and pulleys.

Ground plan Blueprint or floor plan of stage design that outlines the various levels on the stage and indicates the placement of scenery, furniture, doors, windows, and other necessary scenic elements.

Left stage Left side of the stage from the point of view of a performer facing the audience.

Props Properties; objects that are used by performers onstage or are necessary to complete a set.

Pull To choose a costume from an inventory owned by a theater company.

Realism Broadly, an attempt to present onstage people and events corresponding to those in everyday life.

Right stage Right side of the stage from the point of view of a performer facing the audience.

Scrim Thin, open-weave fabric which is nearly transparent when lit from behind and opaque when lit from the front.

Technical director Person who oversees all technical aspects of a theater production, especially the building, painting, and installation of scenery and related elements.

Upstage At or toward the back of the stage, away from the front edge of the stage.

Wagon Low platform mounted on wheels or casters by means of which scenery is moved on- and offstage.

THEATER ON THE WEB

For more research and to learn more about the topics in this chapter, please visit the Online Learning Center at **www.mhhe.com/livelyart6.**

Designers: Lighting and Sound

◀ **THE MAGIC OF STAGE LIGHTING**

Lighting can define a stage area, create mood, indicate changes of scene, and contribute a host of other effects to a theatre production. In the scene here, lights above frame the four singers in the musical Jersey Boys. *The men are shown in silhouette. Lighting is especially effective for such dramatic tableaux as the one here. For this production the lighting design was by Howell Binkley, the sets were designed by Klara Zieglerova, the costumes were designed by Jess Goldstein, and the sound was by Steve Canyon Kennedy. (© Joan Marcus)*

STAGE LIGHTING

In Chapter 10, we explored the work of scene and costume designers. In this chapter, we turn to two other important aspects of theatrical design: lighting and sound. We begin with lighting, which must be coordinated closely with scene design. We'll consider how lighting has been used in earlier periods of theater history, what its aesthetic functions and qualities are, and how a lighting designer works. Next, we discuss sound design and its use. Finally, we'll look at special effects in lighting and sound design.

Lighting in Theater History

For the first 2,000 years of its recorded history, theater took place mostly outdoors during the day, one important reason being the need for illumination—the sun, after all, is an excellent source of light.

Since artificial lighting was unavailable, playwrights used the imagination to suggest nighttime, or shifts in lighting. Performers would bring on torches—or a candle, as Lady Macbeth does—to indicate night. Playwrights also used language in place of lighting. When Shakespeare has Lorenzo say, in *The Merchant of Venice* (1596–1597), "How sweet the moonlight sleeps upon this bank," this is not just a pretty line of poetry but also serves to remind us that it is nighttime. The same is true of the eloquent passage in which Romeo tells Juliet that he must leave because dawn is breaking:

> Look, love, what envious streaks
> Do lace the severing clouds in yonder East:
> Night's candles are burnt out, and jocund day
> Stands tiptoe on the misty mountain tops.

Around 1600, theater began to move indoors. Candles and oil lamps were used for illumination until 1803, when a theater in London installed gaslights. With gas, lighting became more manageable, allowing some control of intensity and color, but it remained crude, primitive, and limited in its effectiveness. In addition, gas and other lighting systems of the time involved open flames and thus posed a constant threat of fire. During this period, there were several tragic and costly fires in theaters, in both Europe and the United States.

In 1879, Thomas Edison invented the incandescent lamp—the electric lightbulb—and the era of technological theater lighting began. Not only are incandescent lamps safe, but their intensity can be controlled by means of rheostats and other devices. Brightness can be increased or decreased, so that the same lighting instrument can produce the full light of noon or the dim light of dusk. Also, the color of the light can be controlled by putting a colored film over the source.

Beyond the power and versatility of electric light, there have been numerous other advances in controls and equipment over the past 50 years. Lighting instruments have been constantly refined to become more powerful, as well as more subtle, and to throw a more concentrated, more sharply defined beam. Moreover, miniaturization and computerization have been incorporated into lighting more

Peggy Eisenhauer: Lighting Designer

Peggy Eisenhauer is a lighting designer whose credits include concert designs for David Bowie's and Linda Ronstadt's tours, and the Broadway shows Will Rogers Follies; Angels in America; Grand Hotel; Twilight: Los Angeles, 1992; Bring in 'da Noise, Bring in 'da Funk; Ragtime; Cabaret; *and many others.*

I grew up in the New York Metropolitan area, the lucky child of parents who exposed me to the thrill and excitement of live performance. By the time I was 10, I had seen the New York City Ballet, Bill Baird, Ringling Brothers, and Broadway shows, as well as local concerts and theater. By working in community theater in my high school years, I became familiar with all theatrical crafts and became especially interested in lighting design.

The Broadway production of *Pippin,* with direction by Bob Fosse and lighting by Jules Fisher, was the deciding factor in my choice of career. Jules's unique musicality expressed through lighting design spoke to me, and I tried to see as much of his work as I could. I went on to study lighting design at his alma mater, Carnegie-Mellon University, and met Jules there.

After graduation, and after gaining working experience with other designers on and off Broadway, I saw my dream come true: I assisted Jules on a Broadway project, and we've been working together ever since. Our second production together was Bob Fosse's final musical, *Big Deal,* which opened nearly 10 years to the day after I saw *Pippin.* Our recent joint designs include *Tommy Tune Tonight; Twilight: Los Angeles, 1992;* the *Whitney Houston Bodyguard Tour;* and *A Christmas Carol.*

---

successfully than into any other element of theater. After all, costumes must still be sewn individually, and scenes on flats must still be painted by hand. Lighting, however, is controlled by electricity and therefore offers a perfect opportunity to take advantage of innovations in electronics and technology. First came resistance systems, then thyratron vacuum tubes, and after that a series of technologies with names such as *magnetic amplifiers* and *silicon-controlled rectifiers.*

Applied to lighting, these innovations allowed for increasingly complex and sophisticated controls. For a large college theater production, 200 to 300 lighting instruments may be hung around and above the stage; for a large Broadway musical, there may be 800 or more, depending on the type of show and the technology being used. Each of these instruments can be connected to a central computer board, and light settings—the level, direction, and color of the lighting instruments—can be stored in the computer. By pushing a single button, an operator can bring about a shift in literally dozens of instruments in a split second. The resulting flexibility and control are a remarkable tool for achieving stage effects.

Objectives of Lighting Design

The following are the functions and objectives of stage lighting:

1. Provide visibility
2. Help establish time and place
3. Help create mood

LIGHTING ESTABLISHES TIME AND PLACE
By the use of color, direction, and intensity, lighting can help establish the time and place of a story. Here Anne Newhall as Aaronetta Gibbs in Morning's at Seven *is bathed in late evening light. The production was by the Utah Shakespearean Festival. The lighting designer was Lonnie Rafael Alcaraz.* (© Utah Shakespearean Festival. Photo by Karl Hugh.)

4.   Reinforce the style of the production
5.   Provide focus onstage and create visual compositions
6.   Establish rhythm of visual movement

Providing Visibility.   The chief practical function of lighting is, of course, illumination or visibility. First and foremost, we must be able to see the performers' faces and actions. Occasionally, lighting designers, carried away with the atmospheric possibilities of light, will make a scene so dark that we can hardly see what is happening. Mood is important, of course, but seeing the performers is obviously more important. At times, a script does call for the lights to dim; in a suspense play, for instance, the lights in a haunted house might go out. But these are exceptions. Ordinarily, if you cannot see the performers, the lighting designer has not carried out his or her first assignment.

Establishing Time and Place.   The color, shade, and intensity of lighting can suggest time of day, giving us the pale light of dawn, the bright light of midday, the vivid colors of sunset, or the muted light of evening. Lighting can also indicate the season of the year, because the sun strikes objects at very different angles in winter and summer. Lighting can also suggest place—indoor or outdoor light, for instance.

Creating Mood.   Light, together with scenery and costumes, can help create a certain mood. Rarely, however, can lighting alone create mood. For example, if a stage is filled with blue light, it might be inviting, romantic moonlight, but it could also be a cold, dark, evil setting. When action, scenery, and words are combined with light, they tell us exactly what the mood is. In general, a happy, carefree play calls for bright, warm colors, such as yellows, oranges, and pinks. A more somber piece will lean toward blues, blue-greens, and muted tones.

Reinforcing Style.   With regard to style, lighting can indicate whether a play is realistic or nonrealistic. In a realistic play, the lighting will simulate the effect of ordinary sources, such as table lamps and sunlight. In a nonrealistic production, the designer can be more imaginative: shafts of light can cut through the dark, sculpturing performers onstage; a glowing red light can envelop a scene of damnation; a ghostly green light can cast a spell over a nightmare scene.

Providing Focus and Composition.   In photography, the focus has to do with adjusting the lens of a camera so that the picture recorded on the film is sharp and clear. In theater lighting, *focus* means that beams of light are aimed at, or "focused on," a particular area. Focus in theater lighting directs our attention to one part of the stage—generally the part where the important action is occurring—and away from other areas.

Furthermore, lights should illuminate the playing area, not the scenery. If more light is on the scenery than on the performers, the audience's attention will be drawn to the scenery and away from the actors and actresses. Therefore, the first objective of focus is to aim the light at the right place. A good example of the use of focus occurs when there is a split stage, with half the action on one side and half on the other side. The lights can direct our attention from side to side as they are dimmed in one area and come up in another.

Composition is the way lighted areas are arranged onstage in relationship to one another—which areas are dimmed, which are brightly lit, and what the overall stage effect is with regard to light. By means of focus, light can create a series of visual compositions onstage. The effects can vary from turning the stage into one large area to creating small, isolated areas.

Establishing Rhythm.   Since changes in light occur over a time continuum, they establish a rhythm running through a production. Abrupt, staccato changes with stark blackouts will convey one rhythm; languid, slow fades and gradual cross-fades will convey another.

Lighting changes are timed in coordination with scene changes. The importance of this coordination is recognized by directors and designers, who take great care to "choreograph" shifts in light and scenery, like the movements of dancers.

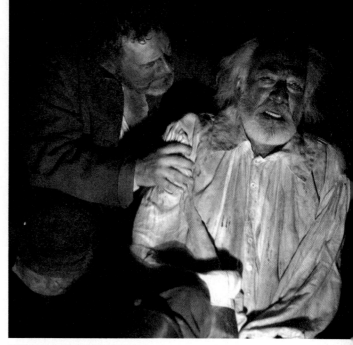

LIGHTING CREATES MOOD
No element is more effective than lighting at creating mood onstage. In this scene from King Lear *in a production at Lincoln Center, the lighting casts an eerie glow on Lear (Christopher Plummer), who is alone on the heath, comforted only by Kent (Benedict Campbell). The lighting design is by Robert Thomson, with costume design by Clare Mitchell.* (© Joan Marcus)

Elements of Stage Lighting

A *lighting designer* knows which elements or qualities of light will achieve the objectives we have just been discussing. Let's consider these qualities.

Intensity.   First of all, light has brightness, or *intensity.* Intensity is controlled by an electronic device called a *dimmer,* which can make a scene brighter or darker. Dimmers allow a scene at night to take place in very little light and a daylight scene to take place in bright light.

Color.   Another quality, a very powerful aspect of light, is *color.* Theater lights can be changed very easily to any one of several hundred colors simply by putting colored material in slots at the front of the lighting instruments. This material is

LIGHTING CREATES FOCUS

Lighting helps create focus and powerful visual arrangements onstage. An example is this scene from Caryl Churchill's Far Away. *Note how lighting isolates the two figures: Alan Drake (playing Todd) on the left, and Kirsty Bushell (as Joan) on the right. This dramatic use of lighting increases the dramatic impact of the scene. The lighting design is by Rick Fisher.* (© Donald Cooper/Photostage)

usually called *gel*—short for *gelatin,* the cellophane of which it was originally made. Today, however, these color mediums are generally made of plastic mylars and acetates. With modern technology, color can even be changed electronically without gels (the special equipment is described below, in the section on the lighting designer's resources).

Color is mixed so that the strong tones of one shade will not dominate, creating an unnatural appearance. Warm lights (amber, straw, gold) are mixed with cool (blue, blue-green, lavender) to produce depth, texture, and naturalness. One exception to the usual mixing of angles and colors of light, however, would be a scene calling for special effects: for example, we would expect stark shadows and strange colors—such as an eerie blue—in a suspenseful scene in a graveyard.

Direction.   A third quality of light is direction, that is, the way lights are placed on or near the stage so that illumination comes from a particular angle. In earlier days, footlights—a row of lights across the front of the stage floor—were popular. However, because the light source was below the performers, footlights had the disadvantage of casting ghostly shadows on their faces. Footlights also created a barrier between performers and audience. With the development of more powerful, versatile lights, footlights have been eliminated.

Today, most lighting hits the stage from above, coming from instruments in front of the stage and at the sides. The vertical angle of the light beams is frequently close to 45 degrees, to approximate the average angle of sunlight. The lights converge from different sides to avoid the harsh shadows that result when light hits only one side of a performer's face.

Once performers are properly illuminated by lights from the front and sides and from above, other lighting is added—***downlighting*** from directly overhead

LIGHTING AIDS COMPOSITION
Lighting can create arrangements onstage that in themselves are striking visual pictures. These can serve the play by emphasizing certain characters, and they can also be aesthetically pleasing and exciting. A striking example is this scene from Tony Kushner's Caroline, or Change, *on Broadway. Note the arrangements of the characters in various isolated tableaux. Jules Fisher and Peggy Eisenhauer designed the lighting; Riccardo Hernandez designed the sets; Paul Tazewell was responsible for the costumes. (© Michal Daniel)*

and *backlighting* from behind—to give further dimension and depths to figures onstage.

Form.   The *form* or *shape* of light is a fourth quality. It can be a single shaft of light, like a nightclub spotlight, a single beam of moonlight through trees, or general lighting. Light can also create a pattern, such as dappled sunlight through the leaves of trees in a forest. The edges of the light can be sharp and clearly defined, or soft and diffused. To accomplish either kind of definition, light can be shaped by special shutters that close in at the edges and give it an outline as it hits the stage area.

Movement.   A fifth quality of light is movement. With various types of dimmers, light can shift its focus from location to location and can also change from color to color. In addition, light can move to suggest changing time of day, sunsets, and so on, providing more information for the audience.

For an example of how these qualities function, consider the lighting for a production of *Hamlet*. To emphasize the somber, tragic quality of this play, with its

COLOR IN LIGHTING

One important quality of stage lighting is color. By the use of gels and other electronic means, an almost infinite variety of colors can be created and combined. Two examples are shown here: a production of the musical Aida, *with figures silhouetted against a red background by the lighting designer Natasha Katz; and the Broadway production of* The Lion King, *with figures, human and animals, featured against a yellow-orange background created by the lighting designer Donald Holder.* (© Joan Marcus/Walt Disney Theatrical Productions)

murders and graveyard scene, the lighting would be generally cool rather than warm. In addition to lighting from the front of the stage, there might be lighting angled down from above and backlighting to give a sculptured, occasionally unreal quality to the characters. In terms of movement, the lights would change each time there was a shift in locale. This would create a rhythm of movement through the play and would also serve to focus the audience's attention on particular areas of the stage.

The Lighting Designer's Resources

Among the resources of the lighting designer are various kinds of lighting instruments and other kinds of technical and electronic equipment.

Types of Stage Lights. Most stage lights have three key elements: a lamp that is the source of the light, a reflector, and a lens through which the beams pass. Basic types of stage lights include the following:

SOFT-EDGED SPOTLIGHT (SELECON 1200 FRESNEL)

1. *Soft-edged spotlights.* The most popular soft-edged spotlight (top right) is the *fresnel* (pronounced "fruh-NEL"). All spotlights illuminate limited areas of the stage with a concentrated beam of light; they precisely define a particular area to be lighted and leave other areas in darkness. The fresnel spotlight has a spherical reflector and a special lens that is flat on one side and has ridges of concentric circles on the other, an arrangement that allows for a thinner, lighter lens that softens the edges of the beam. The lens of the fresnel spotlight produces a soft-edged beam and allows for a variable beam spread. It is especially useful for area lighting where a feathered or undefined edge is desirable. Many lighting designers use this instrument for toplighting and backlighting. The fresnel is generally used in positions near the stage —behind the proscenium opening, or mounted close to the action on an arena or thrust stage.

2. *Sharp, concentrated spotlights.* The best-known sharp spotlight is the *ellipsoidal reflector spotlight*, which most lighting designers consider the "workhorse" of contemporary practice (bottom right).

ELLIPSOIDAL REFLECTOR SPOTLIGHT

FLOODLIGHT (SELECON ACCLAIM FLOOD)

MOVING LIGHT OR AUTOMATED LIGHT
(VARI*LITE VL6 SPOT LUMINAIRE)

Generally the ellipsoidal reflector lighting instrument is more efficient than a fresnel because it can throw a stronger beam of light much farther. Most spotlights of this type have an ellipsoidal-shaped reflector that partially surrounds the lamp and sends a strong beam through two plano-convex lenses. It is used when the distance between the instrument and the stage area is greatest—for example, from positions outside the proscenium opening in the auditorium. It affords greater control of light than the fresnel and allows for shaping the edges of the beam with shutters. This instrument will also project patterns of light through the use of *templates* or **gobos.** In recent years the standard ellipsoidal spotlight has undergone revisions that have resulted in a brighter unit using nearly 50 percent less energy because of improved reflectors as well as new lens systems. A mobile spotlight, which an operator can shift to follow a performer across the stage, is called a ***follow spot.*** The instrument shown here is a zoom spotlight.

3. *Floodlights, "scoops," strip lights,* and *border lights.* These lights bathe a section of the stage or scenery in a smooth, diffused wash of light. Above left is a ***floodlight.*** Floodlights are used, singly or in groups, to provide general illumination for the stage or scenery. The light from floods can be blended in acting areas, or used to "tone" settings and costumes. They are also used to illuminate cycloramas at the rear of the stage, or ground rows along the floor of the stage.

4. *Automated or moving light.* The fourth light (left) is the newest and most versatile instrument of the group. Sometimes known as an ***automated light*** or a ***moving light,*** it can do the work that in the past would have had to be carried out by several lighting instruments. This light can carry our various alterations—changing the angle of the light, or its color, or the shape of its beam—automatically when commanded from a computer. It can change colors (to any of nearly 1,000 hues or shades), change focus by swiveling in place, and shift beams. All this is done remotely

and has been made possible by advances in the technology of computers, electronics, and other elements. This instrument is particularly useful in elaborate musical productions and is widely used in rock concerts.

Lighting Controls.   Among the visual elements of theater, lighting is by far the most technologically developed. Lighting instruments can be hung all over a theater and beamed at every part of the stage; and all these instruments can be controlled by one person sitting at an electronic panel, or computer board.

Lighting changes—or *cues,* as they are called—can be arranged ahead of time. In a complicated production (a musical, say, or a Shakespearean play), there may be several hundred light cues. A cue can range from a *blackout* (all the lights are shut off at once); to a *fade* (the lights dim slowly, changing the scene from brighter to darker, or, with a *fade-in,* from dark to light); to a *cross-fade* (one set of lights comes down while another comes up). Moreover, with today's modern equipment, such changes can be timed automatically so that a cross-fade will take exactly the number of seconds called for and all guesswork is eliminated.

Using contemporary technology, all cues can be prearranged by computer so that during a performance, the operator at the console pushes a button and an entire change occurs automatically.

New Technology in Lighting.   Stage lighting has benefited from technological advances that were originally developed for rock musicians and others who perform before vast audiences and for whom light and sound are essential elements. Huge banks of lights are focused on the stage; sometimes there are banks of lights behind the performers, forming part of the stage picture.

With the instruments known as automated lights or moving lights, not just one element can be controlled, but three: color, direction, and movement. Without a follow-spot operator, these lighting instruments can *pan* (move from side to side) and *tilt* (move up and down) to create movement and change the angle of the beam and therefore the focus onstage. And it is no longer necessary to change color by putting a gel over a beam by hand; instead, by means of dichoric filters these instruments can change to any one of hundreds of colors, shades, and hues.

The sharpness and width of the beam, as well as the pattern it projects, can be changed instantaneously in each instrument because both the *iris* (which controls the size of the pool of light) and the gobo or template (which determines patterns of light) are variable and changeable. All these adjustments are made not manually but remotely, from a central computer panel by an operator pushing a switch or button. Everything is preset on the computer: each movement of the light, each change in color, each alteration in direction or size of the beam. This is done for what are sometimes hundreds of instruments. At a given moment, at the touch of a button by an operator at the central lighting computer, dozens of lights go off, dozens more come on as they swivel in a different direction and change color—and all of this occurs simultaneously.

The Lighting Designer's Collaborators

A number of people work closely with the lighting designer. When the lighting designer has determined what instruments, colors, and so on will be used, he or she develops a *light plot*—a detailed outline or diagram showing where each instrument is placed in relation to the stage. The designer may have experts assist in drawing up light plots.

When the time comes to put the lights in place, they are *hung*, which means that they are attached to pipes—or *battens,* as these pipes are sometimes called —backstage and in various other places throughout the theater. This requires technicians who are familiar with the instruments and the pipes. These same technicians will assist the designer in focusing the lights. (To *focus* lights, as we have seen, means to aim them at a certain area onstage.)

During a performance, experts are required to *run* the lights—that is, to operate the computer or whatever device executes light changes and light cues. These experts take cues from the stage manager and coordinate their work with the other technical aspects of the production. The follow spot (a moving spotlight) requires an operator who aims the beam at the proper person or area of the stage.

SOUND DESIGN

Sound—which has become an increasingly important element in theater productions—may be said to include all sound effects, recordings, and electronic enhancement. Audiences have become increasingly aware of sound as such, partly because of concerts by groups whose members attach microphones to themselves and their instruments and use huge banks of speakers to project their music to the audience.

In recent years, sound, in addition to having its own *sound designer,* has developed its own artistry and technology.

The Sound Designer

A counterpart to designers for visual aspects of theater is the sound designer. Like other designers, he or she reads the script to see what the sound requirements will be. Understandably, the needs of a musical theater production will be different from those of a nonmusical drama. In the former, the orchestra and all singing voices must be heard and carefully blended.

After reading the script and noting all requirements, the sound designer meets with the director to discuss those requirements and to take note of special requests that the director might have. Following this, the sound designer plans how he or she will go about meeting the needs of the production with regard to sound.

Objectives of Sound Design

Basically, the objectives of sound design are twofold: (1) to provide all background or other aural effects called for in the production, and (2) to reinforce spoken and musical sounds.

SOUND EFFECTS
Sound in the theater is created in a number of ways, such as by actual mechanical means (like a gunshot) and by tape or disk recording. In the scene here, from a production of Chekhov's Uncle Vanya, *Derek Jacobi, as Vanya, fires a gun at a professor he finds unbearable. The gunshot goes astray (perhaps on purpose), but the sound of the firing is crucial to the scene, underscoring Vanya's rage. Sound for the production was created by David Van Teighem.* (Sara Krulwich/ The New York Times)

Sound Reproduction and Sound Reinforcement

Reproduction is the use of motivated or environmental sounds. **Motivated sounds** would be, for instance, a car crunching on gravel, a car motor turning off, and a door slamming—a sequence that could announce the arrival of a character at a house where a scene is taking place. Motivated sounds, then, are those called for by a script. **Environmental sounds** are noises of everyday life that help create verisimilitude in a production: street traffic in a city, crickets in the country, loud music coming from a college dormitory. Such sounds are usually heard as background.

One form of sound reproduction is *sound effects,* which can be defined as any sounds produced by electronic or human means to create for the audience a noise associated with the play.

In earlier years—for several centuries, in fact—various devices were developed to create such sounds. A noise sounding like a howling wind, for example, can be produced by a wooden drum made from slats being turned. For a slamming door, a miniature door or even a full door in a frame can be placed just offstage and opened and shut. Two pieces of wood slammed shut can also simulate the sound of a closing door, and in some cases this device can sound like a gunshot. A gunshot can also be created by firing a gun using blank cartridges. (Real guns—those which fire ammunition—should never be used onstage; and in some states there are also laws forbidding the purchase of blank guns.) Thunder can be simulated by hanging a large, thick metal sheet backstage and gently shaking it.

In recent years, however, most sound effects can be reproduced on audiotape, on disks, or digitally on computers. Virtually every sound—from birds singing

SOUND TECHNOLOGY

The audio side of theater has made great advances in recent years. It has become pervasive, especially in musical theater. Here, for example, we see Jamyl Dobson and Benton Greene in The Seven, *wearing personal microphones connected by a remote arrangement with a central sound control system. These microphones worn by actors are similar to those worn by rock performers and reflect the influence of rock. The production was at the New York Theater Workshop, with sound by Darron L. West. (© Carol Rosegg)*

to dogs barking to jet planes flying—can be re-created electronically or digitally. These are available not only to expensive professional productions but to college, university, and community theaters.

Reinforcement is amplification of sounds produced by a performer or a musical instrument. In recent decades, with the growth of electronics in music, more and more instruments are amplified. In today's theater, this is also true of the voices of actors and singers.

Elements of Sound: Sound Technology

Microphones and Loudspeakers. Speech reinforcement involves using microphones to pick up dialogue and songs. Several types of microphones are used for this. A *shotgun mike* is highly directional and is aimed from a distance at a specific area. A *general mike* picks up sounds in the general area toward which it is aimed. A *body mike* is popular today in musicals. At first, body mikes were small microphones attached in some way to performers' clothing; a wire ran from the mike to a small transmitter concealed on the performer, and from the transmitter the sound was sent to an offstage listening device that fed it into a central sound-control system.

In today's lavish musical productions, the microphone worn by a performer is often a small instrument—hardly larger than a small piece of wire—worn, perhaps, over one ear alongside the temple, or under a wig. In some musicals, such as *Rent,* performers wear microphones that resemble a telephone operator's headset.

Microphones not worn by performers are placed in various locations. One position is alongside the downstage edge of the stage, where the footlights used to be located. Another position is in the air, with microphones placed near the overhead lights.

Any type of microphone must be hooked up to an amplifier that increases the electronic energy of the sound and sends it through speakers. The placement of loudspeakers is both an art and a science. It is necessary to determine the correct speakers for the size and shape of the theater, and to position them so that they carry sound clearly and evenly into the auditorium—to the upper levels of the balcony, to the side seats, and to the areas underneath the balcony as well as the first few rows of the orchestra. Also, sound must reach the sides and back of the theater at the proper interval. One problem in this regard is that sound travels much more slowly than light. The speed of sound is only 1,100 feet per second—which means that for a spectator seated at the back of a large theater, sound from

a speaker at the rear of the auditorium will be heard before the human voice from the stage. Developments in digital electronics have led to devices that process, sample, and synthesize sound for various effects; and one useful device addresses this problem, delaying the electronic sound so that it arrives through a loud-speaker at the same time as the much slower live sound.

Placing microphones and speakers in a theater and on the stage is a complicated process. The goal is clear but unobtrusive sound. When electronic sound is not properly modulated, it can become an artificial barrier between performers and audience and can seriously interfere with the actor-audience relationship.

Sound Recordings. The process of assembling sound recordings is similar for professional and nonprofessional productions. First, a list is made of all nonmusical sound effects required. This list is usually developed by the sound designer in consultation with the director, and possibly with a composer: for a show with a great deal of sound or music, there may be both a sound designer and a music composer. Once the list is drawn up, a master recording is made and the sounds are arranged in their order of appearance in the script. This process is called *editing*. When the production moves into the theater, there is a technical rehearsal without performers, during which each sound cue is listened to and the volume is set. When rehearsals with the performers start in the theater, more changes will be made. Depending on the action and the timing of scenes, some cues will be too loud and others too soft; some will have to be made shorter and others made longer.

During an actual performance of a production using sound reinforcement, an operator must sit at a complex console "mixing" sound—that is, combining all elements from the many microphones and from the master sound recording —so that there is a smooth, seamless blend of sound. Also, the operator must make certain not only that all sound is in balance but that sound does not intrude on the performance or call attention to itself, away from the stage and the performers.

New Technologies in Sound.   As with lighting, in recent years we have seen frequent advances and breakthroughs in sound equipment and technology. The new body microphones and a device that delays the delivery of electronic sound have already been mentioned. But there are other developments as well.

Analog reel-to-reel tape decks, which were standard only a few years ago, have given way to digital technology such as digital audiotape (DAT), recordable compact discs, minidiscs, and direct playback from a computer's hard drive. Sound is now recorded and edited at digital audio workstations, based on personal computers. Such stations allow easier editing of sound, more complex effects, and higher-quality sound. Digital playback systems allow very easy and precise cueing of shows, as well as greatly improved sound quality.

It should be clear that sound is rapidly taking its place alongside other design aspects as a key feature of theater productions.

The Sound Designer's Collaborators

Like all designers, the sound designer has a number of people with whom he or she collaborates. There are technicians who understand the intricacies of sound equipment; there are specialists in the art of hanging and coordinating speakers around the stage and in the auditorium; there are experts at *running* sound in a production. This list includes managing the sound console at the back of the auditorium or in the sound booth. Among other things, this involves handling the complexities of the many microphones required in a large musical presentation; some of these microphones are on the performers, and others are in the orchestra pit or offstage. It would detract enormously from a performance if a body microphone were turned on when it was supposed to be off, or if the reverse occurred.

SPECIAL EFFECTS IN LIGHTING AND SOUND

As in scene design, some effects of lighting and sound can seem unusual or even miraculous.

There are several special lighting effects that can be used to create interesting visual pictures. One simple effect is to position a source of light near the stage floor and shine the light on the performers from below. This creates shadows under the eyes and chin and gives performers a ghostly or horrifying quality. Another common special effect is ultraviolet light, a very dark blue light that causes phosphorus to glow; when the stage is very dark, or completely dark, costumes or scenery that have been painted with a special phosphorus paint will "light up."

An effect of slow motion or of silent movies—where the performers seem to be moving in jerks—is created by a *strobe light,* a very powerful, bright gas-discharge light that flashes at rapid intervals. As we saw earlier, technological advances in lighting have made it possible to create even more spectacular effects.

There are also a number of special sound effects. Sometimes speakers are placed completely around the audience so that the sound can move from side to side. Echoes can be created by a machine that causes reverberations in sound waves. Expanding audio technology also allows for more complex sound effects. Computerized noises and electronic music can be used to create special sounds for various situations, and compact discs give instantaneous access to any element of the sound design. Also, with computerized synthesizers, a few musicians can replace a large orchestra.

Finally, we should add that lighting and sound, like scenery and costumes, are means to an end: they add to and complement the artistic and aesthetic aspects of a production, thereby contributing to the overall experience.

In Chapters 10 and 11, we have looked at the design of scenery, costumes, lighting, and sound. To create theater, these must be coordinated and integrated with acting and directing—and with the text—into a single unified whole, a process we will examine in Chapter 12.

SUMMARY

Lighting—historically the last of the visual elements of theater to be fully developed—is today the most technically sophisticated of all. Once the incandescent electric lamp was introduced, it was possible to achieve almost total control of the color, intensity, and timing of lights. Lighting controls have also benefited from computerization; extensive light shifts can now be hooked up to computer boards and controlled by an operator at a console.

Lighting design is intended to provide illumination onstage, to establish time and place, to help set the mood and style of a production, to focus the action, and to establish a rhythm of visual movement. Lighting should be consistent with all other elements. The lighting designer uses a variety of lighting instruments and controls to achieve effects and works closely with a group of collaborators to place lighting instruments in the theater and to see that lighting changes are carried out effectively during a performance.

Another design element in theater is sound. In today's theater, sound is reproduced and reinforced by various means, many of them technologically advanced. For example, sound effects can be created by primitive mechanical means—such as pieces of wood slapped together to simulate a closing door—or by sophisticated computer and digital technology. These techniques are continually improving and affect the way sound is created, reproduced, and conveyed throughout a theater auditorium.

Special effects in lighting and sound include such things as ultraviolet light, strobe lights, echo effects, and computerized synthesizers.

KEY TERMS

Automated lights (moving lights) Generic term for a new type of lighting instrument that can tilt, pan, rotate, change colors, and change focus—all electronically by computerized remote control.

Backlighting Lighting that comes from behind.

Batten Pipe or long pole suspended horizontally above the stage, upon which scenery, drapery, or lights may be hung.

Blackout Total darkening of the stage.

Composition How lighted areas are arranged onstage relative to each other.

Cue Any prearranged signal, such as the last words in a speech, a piece of business, or any action or lighting change, that indicates to a performer or stage manager that it is time to proceed to the next line of action.

Dimmer Device for changing lighting intensity smoothly and at varying rates.

Downlighting Lighting that comes from directly overhead.

Environmental sounds Noises from everyday life that provide background sound in a production.

Fade Slow dimming of lights, changing from brighter to darker, or vice versa.

Focus Aiming light on a particular area of the stage.

Floodlight Lighting instrument used for large or general area lighting.

Follow spot Large, powerful spotlight with a sharp focus and narrow beam that is used to follow principal performers as they move about the stage.

Fresnel (fruh-NEL) Type of spotlight used over relatively short distances with a soft beam edge that allows the light to blend easily with light from other sources; also, the type of lenses used in such spotlights.

Gobo Template in a theater lighting instrument that determines the shape and arrangement of the beam or pool of light thrown by the instrument. For example, a pattern created by a gobo or template could result in stripes, leaves on trees, the outline of a windowpane, or the like.

Light plot Detailed outline or diagram showing where each lighting instrument is placed in relationship to the stage.

Motivated sounds Sounds called for in the script that usually come from recognizable sources.

Pan Term used in theater lighting when a beam of light from a lighting instrument moves horizontally, from side to side.

Reinforcement Amplification of sounds in the theater.

Reproduction The use of motivated or environmental sounds.

Tilt Term in theater lighting used when a beam of light from an instrument moves vertically, up and down.

For additional research and to learn more about the topics in this chapter, please visit the Online Learning Center at **www.mhhe.com/livelyart6.**

CHAPTER 12

Profile of a Production

◀ **PROFILE OF A PRODUCTION:**
GREAT EXPECTATIONS

The production being examined in this chapter is Great Expectations, *a new musical based on the novel by Charles Dickens. In the first scene, shown here, an escaped convict hiding in a graveyard grabs Pip by the throat and demands food and a file. Pip is the main character in the musical, which follows his journey from being an orphan in a small village to trying to better himself in London. The convict, Magwitch, is played by Ed Sala; and Pip, seen here as a young boy, is played by Maggie Matteson.*

All photos in this chapter © Stephanie Klein-Davis/Freelance

In Chapters 4 through 11, we have looked at the separate elements that go into a theatrical production. In this chapter we examine how these elements are combined, step by step, to create an actual production.

The one we have chosen is the first full production of a new musical version of the novel *Great Expectations* by Charles Dickens. The authors—Edwin Wilson, who wrote the book and lyrics; and Doug Katsaros, who composed the music—began working on the musical several years before it was given a full staging. (Wilson is the coauthor of this volume.) In a series of readings with professional actors in New York City and elsewhere, the authors revised and improved the script: adding new songs, eliminating songs that seemed to impede the action, editing dialogue, experimenting with the sequence of scenes. By the spring of 2005, they felt that they had a script ready to be mounted in a full production.

Great Expectations, set in England in the 1850s, is the story of Pip, an orphan raised by a stern older sister and her kind husband, Joe. On Christmas Eve, while visiting the graves of his parents, Pip is accosted by an escaped convict who demands that Pip bring him a file and food, which Pip does. (The file is for the purpose of cutting the chains on the convict's legs.) Through a series of adventures and misadventures, Pip moves from boyhood to manhood. Along the way, he encounters an eccentric, reclusive woman, Miss Havisham—with whose young ward, Estella, he falls in love.

Pip is given money by an unknown benefactor to go to London and become "a gentleman." As a grown-up, he meets Estella once more, only to lose her to a rival. Another blow comes when he discovers that his benefactor is not Miss Havisham, as he had supposed, but the criminal he had befriended many years before. Later, after a long separation, Pip and Estella meet once again. Both admit that they have made mistakes in their lives, and both vow to make a new beginning with more insight and humility than before.

Jere Lee Hodgin, the producing artistic director of the Mill Mountain Theatre in Roanoke, Virginia, had read the script and heard the music of the new version of *Great Expectations.* In the early summer of 2005, it was decided that this work would fill an early spring slot for 2006 in the Mill Mountain schedule. This is a slot in which a classic is usually presented, not only as part of the regular season, but also for special daytime performances for the high school and middle school students in the area.

Mill Mountain Theatre has a 400-seat main stage and excellent shop and rehearsal facilities. As a member of LORT, it is a fully professional resident theater, employing primarily Equity actors. The theater had been operating for 42 years, with Hodgin serving as artistic director for 19 years. During the summer and fall of 2005, preliminary work on the production began. Hodgin chose his designers: Robert Croghan (from North Carolina State University at Charlotte) to design the sets; Jennie Ruhland to design the costumes; and for lights and sound, the staff designers Genny Wynn and Timothy Stanley. Croghan, in particular, had long experience in working at the theater and collaborating with Hodgin.

Because Roanoke is in the mountains of western Virginia, and is not a large city, Mill Mountain generally casts actors from New York City. In a series of auditions in the fall of 2005, over 200 actors were interviewed, from which eleven Equity actors were cast. Also chosen were two non-Equity actors; and young local girls to play the young Estella; and a female college student who had played young boys before, to play the young Pip.

As we discussed in Chapter 8, the director's job is to develop a concept for the production, cast the show, and collaborate with the designers to develop unified sets, costumes, and lighting. The director, during rehearsals, also works closely with the actors to help them develop their characterizations, deal with specific physical expectations, understand their blocking, and recognize how each character fits into the overall concept. The process from rehearsal studio to theater is an arduous one. Actors begin by working in a space without the elements that will bring the production to life; they must use their imagination to prepare for the incorporation of all the elements we have previously discussed in this volume.

Set designers must find ways to communicate to the director. Designers usually create renderings of the set to provide a sense of visual concept, layout, and organization. In order to give the director a clearer sense of the set as it will exist onstage, many designers also create detailed models. In **Photo 1**, we see the designer, Robert Croghan (right), showing the model of his set for *Great Expectations* to the director, Jere Lee Hodgin (left), and to the cast. He is explaining how various scenes will work: both exteriors, such as a graveyard scene, which he is

PHOTO 1
Director meets with set designer.

PHOTO 2
Set model.

demonstrating here; and interiors, such as Miss Havisham's dining room and the law office of Mr. Jaggers in London.

In **Photo 2** we see the actual model itself. For *Great Expectations,* Croghan designed a unit set, built of timbers and planks, which remained in place throughout the show. Various cutouts of buildings and churches were flown in from the fly loft, and furniture, such as tables and desks, was brought onstage by cast members and others. Note the various levels: an upper level and raised platforms, upstage on the main floor of the set, which was slightly raked (meaning slanted from higher in back to lower in the front). **Photo 3** shows the master carpenter of Mill Mountain, Karen Gierchak, constructing portions of the set, which is being built on the stage itself. The illusion of planks and timbers was created over the top of the basic framework shown here. This view is from one side and above.

For most theater productions, costumes are either pulled from stock or built. Through costume renderings, the costume designer communicates to the director what each character will wear. These renderings help create a sense of how the characters will appear and how their costumes relate to each other. The director can see whether the costumes capture the sense of the character within the context of the specific production.

In **Photo 4,** we see the costume designer, Jennifer Ruhland (right), showing the costume that will be worn by Miss Havisham to the actress who is playing the role: Noelle McGrath. Miss Havisham's costume, which required special features, was designed, built, and sewn in the Mill Mountain costume shop. Many of the other costumes, typical of England in the 1850s, were rented from costume houses. Jennifer Ruhland spent two days in the Costume Collection of the Theatre Development Fund in New York City, selecting over forty costumes to be used. Other costumes were lent by various college costume collections.

Photo 5 shows the costume for Miss Havisham being constructed by Beth Christensen. In her final scene, Miss Havisham gets too close to the flames in her

PHOTO 3
Carpenter constructing set.

PHOTO 4
Costume designer showing Miss Havisham's costume.

PHOTO 5
Costume construction.

PHOTO 6
Lighting designer.

PHOTO 7
Musical director playing the piano.

fireplace, and her dress catches fire. The red in the costume was underneath, and when the dress was raised it created the effect of the dress being on fire. Note the spools of colored thread on the wall above the sewing machine table.

In preparing a production, the lighting designer needs to communicate to the director and to the technicians what the lighting for the production will be like. In order for the lights to be hung before the technical and dress rehearsals, a detailed light plot must be created. Light plots are extremely complicated, providing a sense of where instruments are to be hung in the theater, what types of instruments are to be used, and many other technical details. In **Photo 6,** we see the lighting designer, Genny Wynn (right), testing lighting patterns onstage and creating a light plot. Sitting to the left of her is Eric Tysinger, the stage manager, who will call the 310 light cues during the running of performances.

While the process of designing, constructing, and creating sets, costumes, and lights was going on, the actors and the director begin rehearsals. As rehearsals get under way, **Photo 7** shows the musical director, John B. DeHaas, playing through the score for the composer, Katsaros; the librettist, Wilson; and the director, Hodgin (left to right). DeHaas will accompany the actors throughout the rehearsal period and during performances. He will also rehearse and conduct the seven-piece orchestra. Katsaros, in addition to composing the score, also created the vocal and orchestral arrangements.

Photo 8 shows the first day of rehearsals. The director, Hodgin, has gathered the cast around tables in the rehearsal studio to read throught the script, and to hear the score played. After the initial read-through, rehearsals begin. In **Photo 9,** we see six cast members preparing a musical number. In **Photo 10,** Jason W. Shuffler, in the role of the adult Pip; and Justin R. G. Holcomb, as his brother-in-law, Joe, rehearse a scene.

Along with general rehearsals, there are rehearsal calls for special needs such as choreography or dealing with other issues such as dialects. For *Great Expectations,* for example, Professor Patricia Raun served as dialect coach, teaching the actors both the country accents used by characters in Kent, and the city accent used by the upper class in London. Before the show

PHOTO 8
Cast meeting.

PHOTO 9
Rehearsals.

PHOTO 10
Pip and Joe in rehearsal.

223

PHOTO 11
Lobby of the Mill Mountain Theatre.

opens, there are technical rehearsals that focus on all the design and technical elements; and then there are dress rehearsals, when costumes are added and the show is run as if it were actually in performance.

In addition to the actors, director, and designers, there are many individuals who work behind the scenes to bring productions to life: stage managers, running crew members, literary advisers (dramaturgs), the production management staff, box office personnel, and the house management staff. These people are rarely seen by the general public, yet without their assistance productions could not be staged successfully. In **Photo 11,** we see part of the "front of the house" at Mill Mountain Theatre—the lobby area—where some of these administrative people have prepared the display panels that advertise the play, show pictures of the cast members, and offer other information.

Opening night arrives. **Photo 12** shows the scene in the theater as the audience members have assembled just before the play begins. **Photo 13** depicts the Prologue to the musical itself. The actor Ed Sala, in the center, plays the leader of a traveling theater troupe, who welcomes the audience to the production and invites them to use their imagination to help create the theatrical event that will follow.

PHOTO 12
The audience arrives.

PHOTO 13
Prologue.

PHOTO 14
Jaggers has news.

PHOTO 15
Pip in a gentleman's club.

In **Photo 14,** Lawyer Jaggers (Ed Sala) arrives at the home of the blacksmith (Pip's brother-in-law, Joe) to announce that he has news for young Pip. Greeting him in this scene is Pip's older sister, Mrs. Joe (Carey Van Driest). During the scene that follows, Pip will be told that he has "Great Expectations"—he will be given money to go to London and become "a gentleman." **Photo 15** shows Pip

PHOTO 16
Production shot: Miss Havisham with Estella.

(Justin W. Shuffler), in the chair at the left, being initiated into a gentleman's club in London, known as the Finches. Others in the photo (left to right) are Fielding (David Howard), Drummle (Sal Sabella), Hargrove (Justin Holcomb), and Pocket (Matt Leisy).

Photo 16 shows a scene near the end of the play. Miss Havisham (Noelle McGrath) confronts her ward, the grown Estella (Katie E. Tomlinson), who is leaving her to get married. Miss Havisham argues that Estella has not shown her the proper affection and appreciation; Estella responds that however she behaves, it is behavior learned from Miss Havisham.

After 3 ½ weeks of rehearsals, the production of *Great Expectations* ran at the Mill Mountain Theatre for three weeks. During the run, several daytime performances were given for middle and high school students in the Roanoke area.

Theater Tradition and Theater Today

PART 3

In Part Three we explore the theater of the past and theater today. The two are inextricably linked: contemporary theater builds on theater from the past—both the western tradition, which began in Greece and Rome; and the eastern tradition, which began in India, China, and Japan many centuries ago. Seen here is a modern musical version of a play from the western tradition, Shakespeare's *Two Gentlemen of Verona*. This adaptation, presented at the New York Shakespeare Festival, was by John Guare and Mel Shapiro and was directed and choreographed by Kathleen Marshall.
(© Michal Daniel)

Greek and Roman Theaters

◀ **GREEK THEATER:**

THE FOUNTAINHEAD

Western drama began with Greek theater and continued with Roman theater. One of the best-known tragedies from Greek theater is Oedipus *by Sophocles. Seen here is a modern version of* Oedipus *by Ellen McLaughlin at the Guthrie Theater, with Peter Macon as Oedipus and Isabel Monk O'Conor as his mother, Jocasta, whom he mistakenly marries. The production was directed by Lisa Peterson. (© T. Charles Erickson)*

The ancient civilizations of Greece and Rome have had a profound impact on western civilization. Their innovations in the arts, architecture, culture, science, philosophy, law, engineering, and government shaped much of later thought and practice in the western world. The theaters of Greece and Rome laid the foundations of many traditions of today's western theater. Although Greek and Roman theater, like Greek and Roman society, were quite distinct, the theatrical practices of both influenced later generations of theater artists. Before turning to these two remarkable eras, however, we should first briefly discuss some of the possible origins of theater.

ORIGINS OF THEATER

No one knows exactly how theater began, or where or when it originated. We do know, however, that the impulse to create theater is universal among humans. There is evidence that in every culture and every historical period, people have used elements of theater to communicate, to educate, and to entertain.

Two elements of theater are storytelling and imitation: these, along with other elements, are an important part of religious observances and rituals—formal, repeated ceremonies—in cultures around the world. An example is found in ancient Egypt, where there was an elaborate ritual concerning the god Osiris. Osiris became a ruler of Egypt, married his sister Isis, was murdered by his brother, and was eventually avenged and resurrected. The ceremony retelling the story of Osiris was performed over a period of nearly 2,000 years, from around 2500 B.C.E. to 550 B.C.E., at a sacred place called Abydos.

Another recurring theatrical element is costuming. Throughout central and western Africa, for example, striking and imaginative costumes and masks are

ORIGINS OF THEATER
Most ceremonies—whether in Africa, for instance, or among Native Americans, or in southeast Asia—have a strong theatrical component. This includes masks, costumes, repeated phrases, music, and dancing. Shown here are Dogon dancers performing a ceremony in Bamoko, Mali. Note especially the elaborate masks and colorful costumes. (© Jacky Naegelen/Corbis)

used in a variety of ceremonies. Among the Kuba people in Zaire, there is a dance that marks the initiation into manhood. The central figure in this ceremony is the Woot, a mythical hero who wears an enormous headdress and a mask made of feathers, plumes, shells, and beads.

In certain societies, rituals, religious ceremonies, imitation, and storytelling have been combined and transformed into theatrical events. In western culture, the first place where this occurred was ancient Greece.

GREECE

Background: The Golden Age of Greece

There are times in history when many forces come together to create a remarkable age. Such a time was the fifth century B.C.E. in Athens, Greece, when there were outstanding achievements in politics, philosophy, science, and the arts, including theater. This era has come to be known as the *classical period* and also as the *golden age* of Greece. There are good reasons for calling it a golden age, because important accomplishments were made in many fields.

For example, Greece was then a collection of independent city-states, and Athens—the most important—is credited with being the birthplace of democracy (although only male citizens had a voice in politics and government). There were advances in other areas as well. Greek philosophers, such as Socrates and Plato, tried to explain the world around them; Herodotus transformed history from a simple account of events into a social science. Also, a number of important mathematical and scientific discoveries were made: for instance, the Greek mathematician Pythagoras formulated a theorem that remains one of the cornerstones of geometry; and Hippocrates formulated an oath for physicians that is the one still taken today. Moreover, the classical Greeks were remarkable artists and architects: Greek sculpture from this period is treasured in museums around the world, and buildings such as the Parthenon—the temple that sits atop the Acropolis in Athens—remain models for architects.

Theater and Culture: Greek Theater Emerges

Of particular importance to Greek theater were the ceremonies honoring Dionysus—the god of wine, fertility, and revelry. Later, Greek drama was presented in honor of Dionysus, and most (though not all) historians believe that Greek drama originated out of the dithyrambic chorus, a group of fifty men who sang and danced a hymn praising Dionysus.

A performer named Thespis is customarily credited with transforming these songs into drama in the sixth century B.C.E., by stepping out of the **chorus** and becoming an actor. He moved from simply reciting a story to impersonating a character and engaging in dialogue with members of the chorus. The contribution of Thespis is reflected in the term **thespian,** which is often used as a synonym for "stage performer."

GREEK THEATER AND RELIGION

Throughout its history, theater has often had a close association with religion. This is true of both western and eastern theater. Greek and Roman theater events were often associated with religious festivals, and an important segment of medieval theater dealt directly with religious subjects. The chief Greek theater festival honored the god Dionysus, who was the subject of the play by Euripides called Bacchai. *The scene here is from a production of the play by the National Theatre in London. The performers, left to right, are William Houston (Agave), Greg Hicks (Dionysus), and David Ryall (Cadmus). (© Donald Cooper/Photostage)*

Theater and Religion.   Greek theater was intimately bound up with Greek religion. Over the centuries, the Greeks had developed a religion based on worship of a group of gods, of whom Zeus and his wife, Hera, were the leaders. Annual festivals were held in honor of the gods, and theater became a central feature of certain Greek festivals. In Athens, a spring festival called the **City Dionysia,** honoring the god Dionysus, incorporated tragic drama in 534 B.C.E. and comedy c. 487 B.C.E. This festival lasted several days, including three days devoted to tragedies, and had time set aside for five comedies. **Satyr plays** were also performed. (A description of the satyr play appears in Key Terms at the end of the chapter.) A few days after the festival, awards were given, the festival operation was reviewed by a representative body, and people who had behaved improperly or disrespectfully were judged and penalized.

Since theater was a religious and civic event, the organization of dramatic presentations was undertaken by the government. Eleven months before a festival, an appointed official of the city-state would choose the plays to be presented and would appoint a *choregus*—the equivalent of a modern-day producer—for each of the selected playwrights. In the early days of Greek dramatic festivals, the tragic playwrights themselves functioned as directors. A playwright would choose the actors and supervise the production, working with the chorus and conferring with the actors about their roles.

Theater and Myth.   What kind of stories were told in the plays written for the festivals? Where did the writers find these stories? The answer in most cases is Greek myths.

A *myth* is a story or legend handed down from generation to generation. Frequently, myths are attempts to explain human and natural phenomena: the changing of the seasons, for example, and cataclysmic occurrences like earthquakes and civil wars. Myths also deal with extreme family situations: one branch of a family opposing another, or a difficult relationship between a husband and wife or between parents and children. In every culture, certain myths have a strong hold because they seem to sum up a view of human relationships and of the problems and opportunities life presents to individuals. Greece had a multitude of myths. One good example is found in the ninth century B.C.E., in the works of the poet Homer. Homer recounts the war between the Greeks and the Trojans in the *Iliad* and the return from the war of the Greek hero Odysseus in the *Odyssey*. These and other myths furnished the stories for Greek drama.

Greek Tragedy

The most admired form of drama at the Greek festivals was tragedy. Approximately 900 tragedies were produced in Athens during the fifth century B.C.E., of which thirty-one have survived—all by three dramatists: Aeschylus, Sophocles, and Euripides.

Tragic Dramatists: Aeschylus, Sophocles, and Euripides.   Aeschylus (525–456 B.C.E.) is considered the first important Greek dramatist, and therefore the first important western dramatist. He began writing at a time when a theater presentation would be performed by a large chorus of fifty men and a single actor. In his own dramas, however, Aeschylus called for a second actor, who could play different parts when he put on different masks. This made possible a true dramatic exchange between characters and was the start of drama as we know it. (It should be noted that all performers were men; women's roles were played by men.) In another innovation, Aeschylus reduced the size of the chorus to twelve, making it more manageable.

The dramas of Aeschylus dealt with noble families and lofty themes and were praised for their lyric poetry as well as their dramatic structure and intellectual content. He was the acknowledged master of the *trilogy*—three tragedies that make up a single unit. The best-known of his trilogies is the *Oresteia* (458 B.C.E.): the saga of Agamemnon, a hero of the Trojan war who, when he returns home, is murdered by his wife, Clytemnestra. She in turn is killed by their children, Electra and Orestes.

GREECE
Year, B.C.E.

Theater	Year	Culture and Politics
	800	Age of Homer (800 B.C.E.)
Arion, harpist and poet, develops the dithyramb (c. 600 B.C.E.)	600	
		Thales of Miletus begins natural philosophy (physics) (c. 585 B.C.E.)
	575	
		Peisistratus, tyrant of Athens (560 B.C.E.)
Thespis, supposedly first "actor" in dithyramb (mid-sixth century)	550	Pythagoras flourishes; Doric temples of southern Italy and Sicily (c. 525 B.C.E.)
Play contests begin in Athens (534 B.C.E.)		Athenian democracy (510 B.C.E.)
	525	Pindar begins to write odes (500 B.C.E.)
Comedy introduced to City Dionysia (487 B.C.E.)		Persian Wars (499–478 B.C.E.) Battle of Marathon (490 B.C.E.)
Aeschylus introduces second actor (c. 471 B.C.E.)	500	Socrates born (470 B.C.E.)
Sophocles introduces third actor (c. 468 B.C.E.)		Pericles begins rise to power: age of Pericles (462–429 B.C.E.)
Aeschylus's *Oresteia*; introduction of skene (458 B.C.E.)	475	Hippocrates born (460 B.C.E.)
Prizes for tragic acting awarded (449 B.C.E.)		Beginning of Parthenon; Herodotus flourishes (447 B.C.E.)
Dramatic activities incorporated into Lenaia (c. 442 B.C.E.)	450	Phidias dies (500–435 B.C.E.)
Sophocles's *King Oedipus* (c. 430 B.C.E.)	425	Peloponnesian Wars (431–404 B.C.E.)
Euripides's *Trojan Women* (415 B.C.E.)		Athenian fleet destroyed (404 B.C.E.)
Aristophanes's *Lysistrata* (411 B.C.E.)		Spartan hegemony begins (404 B.C.E.)
	400	Trial and execution of Socrates (399 B.C.E.)
		Aristotle born (384–322 B.C.E.)
Professional actors replace amateurs at City Dionysia (c. 350 B.C.E.)	375	Plato's *Republic* (c. 375 B.C.E.)
Aristotle's *Poetics* (c. 335–323 B.C.E.)		Spartan hegemony ends (404–371 B.C.E.)
Theater of Dionysus completed (c. 325 B.C.E.)	350	Theban hegemony ends (371–362 B.C.E.)
		Philip II, king of Macedonia (352 B.C.E.)
From this period to c. 100 B.C.E., Greek theaters built throughout Mediterranean (320 B.C.E.)	325	Alexander succeeds Philip II; in 335 B.C.E., occupies Greece
Menander's *Dyskolos* (316 B.C.E.)		Hellenistic culture spreads throughout eastern Mediterranean (c. 320 B.C.E.)
Artists of Dionysus recognized (277 B.C.E.)	300	
	275	

Sophocles (c. 496–406 B.C.E.), who lived through most of the fifth century B.C.E., built on the dramatic form that Aeschylus had begun. He raised the number in the chorus to fifteen, where it was to remain. More important, he realized that an additional, third actor—who, again, might play several parts—would allow enormous flexibility. Because each actor, by wearing different masks in turn, could play two or three parts, the use of three actors meant that a play could have seven or eight characters: an actor who was a messenger in one scene, for example, could be the king's daughter in a second scene and a soldier in a third.

With this newfound flexibility, Sophocles became particularly adept at dramatic construction, introducing characters and information skillfully and building swiftly to a climax. (We will see a good example when we look more closely at *King Oedipus*.) In fact, Sophocles has rarely, if ever, been surpassed at plot construction.

The third great dramatist of the period, Euripides (c. 484–406 B.C.E.), was more of a rebel and has always been considered the most "modern" of the three. This results from several factors: his sympathetic portrayal of female characters; his increased realism; his mixture of tragedy with melodrama and comedy; and his skeptical treatment of the gods.

Tragic Structure.   Let's look now at the structure of Greek tragedy, and at the plot of one tragedy—*King Oedipus*—in particular.

Pattern and Plot in Greek Tragedy.   Though there are variations among the surviving thirty-one plays of the three great dramatists, the structure in most of them follows the same pattern. First comes the opening scene, after which the chorus enters. This is followed by an episode between characters; then comes the first choral song. From that point on, there is an alternation between character episodes and choral songs until the final episode, which is followed by the exit of all the characters and the chorus.

Clearly, the chorus was a key element of Greek drama. It was also a unique element: after the period of classical Greek theater, it was never again used in the same way. The characters portrayed by the chorus usually represented ordinary citizens, and they had several functions. First, they reacted the way people in the audience might react and thus became surrogates for the audience. They were a group with which the audience members could identify. Second, the chorus often gave background information necessary for an understanding of the plot. Third, the chorus represented a moderate balance between the extreme behaviors of the principal characters. Fourth, the chorus frequently offered philosophical observations and drew conclusions about what had happened in the play. It is important to note that the choral passages were sung and danced, though we do not know what the music sounded like or how the movements were choreographed.

Whether representing men or women, chorus members were always male—as were all performers in Greek theater.

The Plot of *King Oedipus*.   In Chapter 6, we discussed two basic plot arrangements developed in western drama: climactic and episodic construction. Climactic

THE TRAGEDY *OEDIPUS REX*
One of the most famous Greek tragedies is Oedipus Rex *by Sophocles. Oedipus becomes king of Thebes after unwittingly killing his father and marrying his mother. When a plague strikes Thebes, Oedipus decides to find the killer. He eventually discovers what he has done, blinds himself, and is exiled. Here is a scene from a production at the Stratford Festival at Stratford, Ontario, of a version of the play by W. B. Yeats, the famous Irish poet and dramatist. It was directed by Douglas Campbell. The figure in the center is Jocasta (Diane D'Aquila), both mother and wife of Oedipus. (Cylla von Tiedemann)*

structure, like so much else in theater, got its start in Greek drama, and Sophocles's play *King Oedipus* (c. 430 B.C.E.) is a good example.

The story of Oedipus begins long before the opening of the play, when Oedipus—the son of King Laius and Queen Jocasta of Thebes—is born. When he is an infant, it is prophesied that he will kill his father and marry his mother, and so he is left on a mountaintop to die. A shepherd saves him, however, and takes him to Corinth, where he is raised by the king and queen of Corinth as their own son.

When Oedipus grows up, he learns of the oracle that prophesied that he would kill his parents. Thinking that the king and queen of Corinth are his true parents, he flees Corinth and heads for Thebes. As he approaches Thebes, he encounters, at a crossroads, a man whom he kills in a fight, not realizing that the man is his natural father, the king of Thebes. Oedipus proceeds on to Thebes and, after correctly answering the riddle of the Sphinx, he becomes king of Thebes; he also marries the queen, Jocasta, not realizing that she is his mother. After a time, a plague hits Thebes.

This is when the play begins. The action takes place on one day in one place: in front of the palace at Thebes. After the play opens, there is an alternation of choral sections and episodes. The plot has many twists and turns, as well as ups and downs for the characters. First, it is revealed that an oracle has said that the plague will not be lifted until the murderer of the former king is found and punished. Oedipus, not knowing that he himself is the murderer, vows to find the guilty party. After that, Jocasta says Oedipus should ignore the oracle because it stated that her husband, the king, would be killed by his son, but he was killed at a crossroads. Then Oedipus says he killed a man at a crossroads. Next, a messenger arrives from Corinth saying that the king there is dead. Jocasta points out that this proves that Oedipus did not kill his father, because the father died while Oedipus was away. But then the messenger reveals that the king of Corinth was not the real father of Oedipus, and so forth, until the final revelations and conclusion—when Oedipus puts out his eyes and Jocasta kills herself.

Thematically, *King Oedipus* raises questions that have provoked philosophical discussions for centuries: questions about fate, pride, and the ironic nature of human events.

Greek Comedy

As we've noted, part of the seven-day City Dionysia was devoted to comedy, and comedies by five playwrights were presented during the festival. Later in the fifth century, a separate festival in the winter was devoted solely to comedy.

Greek comedy of this period has come to be known as **Old Comedy** to distinguish it from a different kind of comedy that took hold at the end of the fourth century B.C.E. and is called **New Comedy.** The only surviving Old Comedies were written by Aristophanes (c. 448–c. 380 B.C.E.).

Old Comedy always makes fun of social, political, or cultural conditions, and its characters are often recognizable personalities; the philosopher Socrates is only one of a number of prominent figures satirized in the plays of Aristophanes. The modern counterpart of Old Comedy is political satire in films; in television programs such as *Saturday Night Live, Mad TV,* and *The Daily Show* with Jon Stewart; and in the routines of "insult" comedians in nightclubs and on television.

In Old Comedy, the satire is underlined by fantastic and improbable plots; this is an aspect of the comic premise, discussed in Chapter 7. In *Lysistrata,* for instance, Aristophanes condemns the Peloponnesian war, which Greece was then fighting; the women in the play go on a sex strike, refusing to sleep with their husbands until the men stop the war.

Unlike tragedies, most Old Comedies do not have a climactic structure. For example, they do not take place within a short span of time or in one locale, and they often have a large cast of characters. They also have two scenes not found in tragedy. One is a debate, called an **agon,** between two forces representing opposite sides of a political or social issue. The other is a choral section, known as a

Antigone

Athens, 441 B.C.E. The year is 441 B.C.E. It is a morning in late March in Athens, Greece, and the citizens of Athens are up early, making their way to the Theater of Dionysus, an open-air theater on the south side of the Acropolis, the highest hill in Athens. On the Acropolis are several temples, including the Parthenon, a magnificent new temple dedicated to the goddess Athena, which is under construction at this very time.

The Theater of Dionysus has semicircular seating built into the slope of the hill on the side of the Acropolis. At the foot of the seating area is a flat, circular space—the orchestra—where the actors will perform. Behind the orchestra a temporary stage house has been built, from which the performers will make entrances and exits. The facade of the stage house for the performance today represents the temple at Thebes, where the action will take place.

Priests of various religious orders are sitting in special seats at the edge of the circle opposite the stage house. Other dignitaries, such as civic and military officials, are arranged around them in the first few rows; above them sit both citizens and slaves. No one—not even those sitting in the top row—will have any trouble hearing the performers; the acoustics are so good that a whisper by an actor in the orchestra will carry to the upper reaches of the amphitheater.

The plays performed for the citizens of Athens are part of the City Dionysia festival, an annual series of events lasting several days. During this festival, all business in Athens—both commercial and governmental—comes to a halt. On the day before the plays, there was a parade through the city, which ended near the theater at a temple dedicated to the god Dionysus, for whom the festival is named. There, a religious observance was held at the altar.

Today is one of three days of the festival devoted mainly to tragedies. On these days, one playwright will present three tragedies and a satyr play. The three tragedies are sometimes linked to form one long play, called a *trilogy*; but sometimes they are three separate pieces—as they are today.

The play about to begin is *Antigone* by Sophocles. Its subject comes from a familiar myth: Antigone is the daughter of King Oedipus. After her father's death, her two brothers, Eteocles and Polynices, fight a war against each other to see who will become king of Thebes; during the war, they kill one another. Antigone's uncle, Creon, then becomes king of Thebes. Creon blames Polynices for the conflict and issues an edict that Polynices is not to be given an honorable burial. Antigone decides to defy Creon's order and bury Polynices. The audience members know this myth well and are curious to see how Sophocles—one of their favorite dramatists— will deal with it.

As the play begins, two actors, each wearing the mask and costume of a woman, appear in the playing area: they represent Antigone and her sister, Ismene. Antigone tells Ismene that she means to defy their uncle, the king, and give their brother Polynices an honorable burial. Ismene, unlike Antigone, is timid and frightened; she argues that women are too weak to stand up to a king. Besides, Ismene points out, Antigone will be put to death if she is caught. Antigone argues, however, that she will not be subservient to a man, even the king.

When the two female characters leave the stage, a chorus of 15 men enters. These men represent the elders of the city, and throughout the play—in passages that are sung and danced—they will fulfill several functions: providing background information, raising philosophical questions, and urging the principal figures to show restraint. The choral sections alternate with scenes of confrontation between Antigone, Creon, and the other main characters.

As the play continues, Antigone attempts to bury Polynices, but she is caught and brought before the king. In their confrontation, Antigone defies Creon. She is sentenced to death and put into a cave to die. By the end of the play, not only is Antigone dead; so too are Creon's wife and son, who have killed themselves. In the final scene, we see Creon standing alone, wearing his tragic mask, bereft of all those whom he held dear.

parabasis, addressed directly to the audience; it makes fun of the spectators in general and of specific audience members.

During the Greek Hellenistic era, which began in the fourth century B.C.E., Old Comedy gave way to New Comedy. Instead of the political, social, and cultural satire of Old Comedy, New Comedy dealt with romantic and domestic problems. We will study this kind of drama when we look at Roman comedy—a direct outgrowth of Greek New Comedy.

Theater Production in Greece

Greek drama, as we have noted, was staged in *amphitheaters.* An amphitheater was cut out of the side of a hill and probably held between 15,000 and 17,000 spectators. At the base of the hillside was a circular playing area called the *orchestra* (recent excavations suggest that the earliest orchestra may have been rectangular). Behind the playing area was a scene house. The chorus made its entrances and exits on each side of the scene house through an aisle called a *parodos.* This is the first recorded example of the thrust stage, discussed in Chapter 9. The standard scenic setting for Greek tragedy was a palace, and simple devices were used to indicate locales and to move characters on- and offstage. The audience sat in the *theatron.* During the classical period the hillside theatron probably had temporary wooden bleachers, but these were replaced by stone seats during the later Hellenistic era.

All the characters in Greek drama, male and female, were portrayed by men. The performers, particularly the chorus members, had to be accomplished at singing and dancing as well as vocal projection. The actors may have been paid, and after 449 B.C.E. an acting contest was introduced.

The major element in Greek costuming was the mask, worn by all performers. The mask covered the entire head and included hairstyle and distinctive facial features such as a beard. Masks indicated the emotional state of the characters and also made it possible for male actors to play female characters.

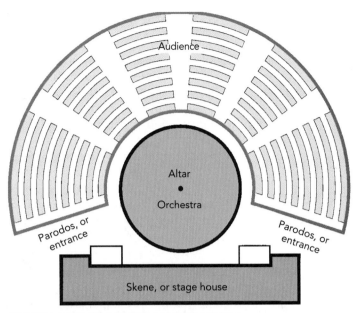

GROUND PLAN OF A TYPICAL GREEK THEATER
The theaters of ancient Greece were set into hillsides, which made natural amphitheaters. At the base of the seating area was a circular space (orchestra) in which the chorus performed; at the center of the orchestra was an altar (thymele). Behind the orchestra was a temporary stage house (skene), at each side of which was a corridor (parodos) for entrances and exits.

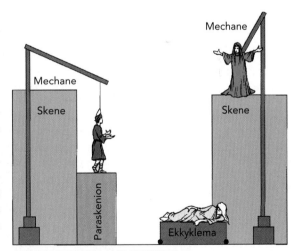

GREEK MECHANE AND EKKYKLEMA
A conjectural reconstruction of Greek stage machinery. On the left, a crane used for flying in characters located on a side wing (paraskenion) of the scene building. On the right, a mechane higher up on the roof of the skene. The ekkyklema below was a platform on wheels used to bring out characters from inside the building.

Dramatic Criticism in Greece: Aristotle

In the fourth century B.C.E., roughly 100 years after Sophocles was at the height of his powers as a playwright, the first significant work of dramatic criticism—*The Poetics*—appeared. Its author was Aristotle (384–322 B.C.E.). Aristotle, like Socrates and Plato, was an important Greek philosopher; he was also a scientist who described and cataloged the world he saw around him, and he took the same approach in analyzing tragedy. *The Poetics* is loosely organized and incomplete, and the version we have may have been based on a series of lecture notes. It is so intelligent and so penetrating, however, that it remains the single most important piece of dramatic criticism in existence.

In *The Poetics* Aristotle describes six elements of drama: (1) plot (arrangement of dramatic incidents), (2) character (people represented in the play), (3) thought or theme (ideas explored), (4) language (dialogue and poetry), (5) music, and (6) spectacle (scenery and other visual elements). It will be noted that these correspond roughly to the elements of theater we explore in Chapters 5 through 11, except that Aristotle does not include the performers or the audience. Tragedy, Aristotle suggests, deals with the reversals in fortune and eventual downfall of a royal figure.

Later Greek Theater

In the two centuries after Aristotle—referred to as the *Hellenistic age*—there were several developments in Greek theater.

The period of great original drama was over, and revivals of plays from the past were increasingly presented. As original drama became less important, there was a shift of focus to acting and the actor. The theater of this period saw the introduction of enlarged masks, exaggerated headdresses, and platform shoes that made the performers taller. Also, larger, more permanent stages were built, and these too directed more attention toward the actors. Emblematic of this new status for performers was the creation in 277 B.C.E. of a guild known as the Artists of Dionysus, which was the ancient equivalent of today's Actors Equity Association.

Theater buildings proliferated throughout the Hellenistic world. We know of at least forty theaters built during this period from Asia Minor in the east to Italy in the west, many of them still standing. These were permanent structures, with both the seating area and the stage house built of stone, in contrast to the less permanent wooden structures of earlier times.

Theater continued to flourish in Greece long after the second century B.C.E., but it was no longer purely Greek theater—it was influenced by the omnipresent Roman civilization.

ROME

Background: Rome and Its Civilization

As ancient Greece declined in power and importance, another civilization began to emerge in Europe, on the Italian peninsula. Its center was the city of Rome, from which it took its name. While Greece is noted for its creativity and imagination—in art, philosophy, and theater, for example—Rome is recognized more for its practical achievements: law, engineering, and military conquest. And just as these achievements were more down-to-earth than those of Greece, so too was Roman theater. Instead of high-minded tragedy, it focused on comedy and other popular entertainments, comparable to our movies, television, and rock concerts.

Rome was founded, according to legend, around 750 B.C.E., and for over 200 years it was ruled by kings. Around 500 B.C.E. the kings were overthrown, and a republic—which was to last nearly 500 years—was established.

During the third century B.C.E., Rome engaged in a lengthy conflict with Carthage known as the Punic Wars and finally emerged victorious. As a result, Rome controlled large parts of the central and western Mediterranean. It was at this period of conquest that Rome also came into contact with Greece and saw firsthand Greek art and culture, including theater.

During the first century B.C.E., the Roman republic began to show signs of serious strain in attempting to govern so vast an area. In the midst of general turmoil, Julius Caesar made himself dictator. He was subsequently assassinated by a group led by Brutus, who in turn was defeated in battle by Mark Antony and Octavius. The republic could not survive these shocks, and in 27 B.C.E. Rome became an empire with one supreme ruler. This form of government continued for several centuries, during which most of the civilized western world was unified under Roman rule.

Throughout their long history, the Romans were always practical. Their laws dealing with property, marriage, and inheritance have continued to influence western civilization to the present day; in addition, the Romans were great engineers and architects, building important aqueducts and roadways. Religion was also of utmost importance to the Romans, who worshipped gods that were counterparts of the Greek deities, as well as a large number of other divinities.

Theater and Culture in Rome

When the Romans turned to theater, they were strongly influenced by the Greeks, just as they were in sculpture and architecture. They borrowed freely from Greek theater—particularly Greek New Comedy, from which they developed their own form of popular comedy. We should note that the Romans' popular entertainments were also influenced by Etruria, a civilization northwest of Rome that flourished from 650 to 450 B.C.E.

In 240 B.C.E., a festival called the *Ludi Romani* dedicated to Jupiter (the Roman counterpart of Zeus), became the first major Roman festival to incorporate theater. Five more official festivals eventually incorporated theater; in addition, an increasing number of days were set aside for minor festivals and theatrical activities.

Popular Entertainment in Rome

Throughout the course of theater history, all civilizations have developed popular entertainments for the masses. Popular entertainments appeal to all levels of society, and no educational, social, or cultural sophistication is required to appreciate

ROME
Year, B.C.E.–C.E.

Theater		Culture and Politics
	750	Traditional date for the founding of Rome (753 B.C.E.)
Regular comedy and tragedy added to *Ludi Romani* (240 B.C.E.)	250	First Punic Wars (Greek influence on Roman culture) (264–241 B.C.E.)
Plautus's *Pseudolus* (191 B.C.E.)	200	Second Punic Wars (218–201 B.C.E.); Hannibal's victories (218–216 B.C.E.)
Terence's *Phormio* (161 B.C.E.)		Rome defeats Philip V of Macedonia (200–197 B.C.E.)
	150	Censorship of Cato; 1,000 talents spent on sewers (184 B.C.E.)
Vitruvius's *De architectura* (90 B.C.E.)	100	Roman citizens freed of direct taxation (167 B.C.E.)
First permanent theater in Rome (55 B.C.E.)		Rome annexes Macedonia (147 B.C.E.)
	50	First high-level aqueduct in Rome (144 B.C.E.)
Horace's *Art of Poetry* (24 B.C.E.)		Slave revolts in Sicily (135 B.C.E.)
	0	Pompey suppresses piracy (67 B.C.E.)
Romans build theaters and amphitheaters throughout the empire (c. 30–200 C.E.)		Golden age of Roman literature (c. 58–50 B.C.E.)
	50	Caesar's conquest of Gaul (55 B.C.E.)
Seneca (c. 4 B.C.E.–65 C.E.) writes Roman tragedies		Jesus crucified (30 C.E.)
	100	
	150	Marcus Aurelius rules (161–180 C.E.)
		Severan dynasty; Augustan order disintegrates (193–235 C.E.)
	200	
Theatrical presentations approximately 100 days per year	250	Extensive persecution of Christians (c. 250–300 C.E.)
	300	Constantine rules; empire reunited (324–337 C.E.)
		St. Augustine born (354 C.E.)
	350	Julian the Apostate restores paganism (361 C.E.)
Council of Carthage decrees excommunication for those who attend theater rather than church on holy days; actors forbidden sacraments (398 C.E.)		Theodosius I forbids pagan worship (391 C.E.)
	400	Sack of Rome by Visigoths (410 C.E.)
	450	Death of Attila the Hun (453 C.E.)
		Fall of western Roman empire (476 C.E.)
	500	

POPULAR ENTERTAINMENTS IN ROME
Large arenas were constructed by the Romans for the presentation of popular entertainments, including gladiator battles, chariot races, and animal battles. Seen here is the Roman Colosseum, an amphitheater originally built in 70 to 82 C.E., that still stands today. It was the scene of many spectacular events, including bloody combats. (Royalty-Free/Corbis)

them. Many popular entertainments are theatrical in nature, using live performers. Some historians say that twentieth-century American culture, with its highly developed popular entertainments—television, film, rock concerts, and other less sophisticated dramatic arts—was much like Roman culture. The reason for this is that many Roman entertainments correspond to modern ones. The Romans, for example, greatly enjoyed chariot racing, equestrian performances, acrobatics, wrestling, prizefighting, and gladiatorial combats—though the gladiatorial combats were not simulated but actual battles to the death.

To house these spectacles, the Romans constructed special buildings, counterparts to our modern football and baseball stadiums. The Circus Maximus in Rome, first laid out in 600 B.C.E. for chariot races and frequently remodeled thereafter, eventually seated over 60,000 spectators. The most renowned amphitheater constructed by the Romans was the Colosseum, built in 80 C.E.

The Romans also developed popular entertainments that were more closely connected to theater. Roman mime, like Greek mime, included gymnastics, juggling, songs, and dances. Short comedic skits, which were often risqué (that is,

ROMAN COMEDY

Roman comedy, which was based on Greek New Comedy, stressed domestic travails. Roman comedy has been the basis for comedy running through the entire western tradition, right up to today's television situation comedies. One of the most popular adaptations of ancient Roman comedy is the musical A Funny Thing Happened on the Way to the Forum, *with music and lyrics by Stephen Sondheim. The scene here is from a production directed by Edward Hall at the Royal National Theatre in London. The Performers (left to right) are David Schneider, Shamus McColl, Desmond Barritt, and Sam Kelly.* (© Geraint Lewis)

sexually suggestive), were also presented. A unique Roman stage presentation was *pantomime.* Roman pantomime used a single dancer, a chorus, and musical accompanists and was somewhat akin to modern ballet; its performers were often sponsored by emperors and members of the nobility.

Roman Comedy: Plautus and Terence

Although theater flourished in Rome for nearly seven centuries, the works of only three playwrights survive: the comedies of Plautus and Terence and the tragedies of Seneca.

Plautus (c. 254–184 B.C.E.), who based almost all his comedies on Greek New Comedy, dealt exclusively with domestic situations, particularly the trials and tribulations of romance. His characters are recognizable, recurring stock types, the most popular being the parasite who lives off others and is motivated mainly by sensuality. Courtesans, lovers, and overbearing parents were also favorite characters. Most of the dialogue was meant to be sung. Plautus's comedies are farces, and they use such farcical techniques as mistaken identity. A good example of mistaken identity is found in *The Menaechmi.*

The Roman comic writer who followed Plautus was Terence (c. 185–159 B.C.E.). Although Terence's plots are as complicated as those of Plautus, his style is more literary and less exaggerated. Terence's *Phormio* (161 B.C.E.) dramatizes the attempts of two cousins, named Antipho and Phaedria, to overcome their fathers' objections to their lovers. The plot complications and stock characters are

The Menaechmi

Rome, 184 B.C.E. It is 184 B.C.E., and many of the inhabitants of the city of Rome are on their way to attend performances at a spring festival in honor of Jupiter. Their mood today is happy and ebullient, because they are about to see a comedy by Plautus, whose plot twists and comic invention have made his works favorites with everyone.

The Romans are heading toward a large, temporary wooden theater building, seating several thousand, that has been erected next to a temple of Jupiter. All theater productions in Rome now take place during religious festivals, and all the theaters are near temples. A Roman theater—unlike the Greek theaters in the lands Rome has conquered—is a single unit, built on level ground, with the stage house attached directly to the ends of a semicircular audience area. In front of the stage house is a long platform stage; and in front of that is a half-circle surrounded by the audience.

The group converging on the theater consists of people from all walks of life. Plautus himself has remarked that a Roman audience is a genuine mixture: in addition to well-to-do middle- and upper-class citizens, it includes government officials and their wives; children with nurses; prostitutes; slaves—in short, virtually every social group. Because this is a state festival, admission is free.

Magistrates of the state have received a grant to produce today's plays and have engaged acting troupes to present individual plays. Each troupe is under the direction of a manager, and one of these managers has bought from Plautus a play called *The Menaechmi* and has arranged for the costumes, music, and other production elements.

As the Romans enter the theater, they see two doors onstage: one opens on the house of Menaechmus of Epidamnus (the Greek city in which Plautus has set his play); the other is the door to the house of Erotium, a woman with whom Menaechmus is having a love affair that he is trying to keep secret from his wife. The stage represents the street in front of the two houses; at one end is an exit to the port, and at the other end is an exit to the center of town.

An actor comes onstage to deliver a prologue. He asks the audience members to pay careful attention to what Plautus has to say, and then he outlines the background of the story: how the Menaechmi twins were separated when they were infants and how the twin who grew up in Syracuse is just now returning to try to find his long-lost brother. As in many of Plautus's plays, most of the dialogue is sung, somewhat like the musical numbers in twentieth-century musical comedies.

When the play opens, Menaechmus is shown to be the despair of his jealous wife. He confides to "Sponge," a parasite, that he has stolen his wife's dress, hiding it under his own clothes—and is going to give it to his mistress, Erotium. At Erotium's house he suggests that in return for the dress, she invite them to dinner. Menaechmus exits.

Meanwhile, the twin from Syracuse has arrived with his slave, Messenio. His master gives Messenio a purse full of money for safekeeping. At that point, Erotium steps out of her house and, mistaking the Syracuse twin for Menaechmus, makes advances to him, by which he is totally confused. Not knowing he is a twin, she is equally confused by his odd behavior. Meanwhile, the two servants of the twins are constantly confused with one another as well.

Finally, the Syracuse twin does enter the house of Erotium to have dinner, and later leaves with the dress that his twin brother Menaechmus had previously given her. Menaechmus comes back just in time to have his wife demand that he return her dress. He goes to Erotium to retrieve the dress, only to be told by her that she has already given it to him. In short, he is rebuffed by both his wife and his mistress.

The play continues like this, with the two brothers constantly being confused for one another by everyone, including the wife, the mistress, the father, and the two servants. Confusion and slapstick comedy abound until the end of the play, when everything is resolved.

similar to those found in *The Menaechmi,* but *Phormio* is less farcical and slapstick and gives more emphasis to verbal wit. Also, whereas much of Plautus's dialogue was meant to be sung, most of Terence's dialogue was spoken.

Roman Tragedy: Seneca

The most notable tragic dramatist of the Roman period was Seneca (c. 4 B.C.E.–65 C.E.). Seneca's plays appear to be similar to Greek tragedies but in fact are quite distinct. His chorus is not integral to the dramatic action; and—unlike Greek dramatists, who banished violence from the stage—Seneca emphasizes onstage stabbings, murders, and suicides. In addition, supernatural beings often appear in the dramatic action.

Although his plays were probably not performed for large public audiences, Seneca's influence on later periods is noteworthy. Shakespeare, for example, was greatly influenced by Seneca's dramatic style; in fact, *Hamlet*—which has much onstage violence and includes a supernatural character (the ghost of Hamlet's father)—is often described as influenced by a Senecan revenge tragedy.

Dramatic Criticism in Rome: Horace

Like Roman drama, Roman dramatic criticism was based on the work of others, especially Aristotle. Horace (65–8 B.C.E.), sometimes called the "Roman Aristotle," outlined his theory of correct dramatic technique in *Ars poetica (The Art of Poetry)*. Horace argued that tragedy and comedy must be distinct genres, or types, of drama, and that tragedy should deal with royalty, while comedy should depict common people. He also stressed that drama should not just entertain but also teach a lesson.

Theater Production in Rome

Roman production practices differed slightly from those of Greece. Roman festivals were under the jurisdiction of a local government official who hired an acting troupe. The *dominus,* or head, of a troupe—who was usually the leading actor—made financial arrangements, bought dramas from playwrights, hired musicians, and obtained costumes. Acting companies had at least six members, all male; and the Romans ignored the three-actor rule of Greek theater. Roman acting technique emphasized detailed pantomime and broad physical gestures, necessitated by the size of Roman theaters; it also stressed beautiful vocal delivery. The Romans did not greatly value versatility in actors; rather, they admired performers who specialized in one type of role and refined the characterizations of stock figures. Facial expression was unimportant, since full linen head masks were worn—only mime performers appeared without masks.

As we've seen, Roman theaters were based on Greek models. The Romans did not construct a permanent theater until 55 B.C.E. Thus there were no permanent spaces for presenting the works of Plautus and Terence, the best-known Roman playwrights. Instead, elaborate temporary wooden structures, probably similar to the later permanent ones, were erected.

THE ROMAN THEATER AT ORANGE
The Romans built theaters throughout their empire, which circled the Mediterranean Sea. One of the best-preserved, built in the first or second century C.E., is at Orange in France, near the center of town. Note the semicircular orchestra, the large stage area, and the stage house at the back, with its ornate facade with niches for statues and other adornments. (© Vanni/Art Resource, N.Y.)

A Roman theater had the same three units as a Greek theater: (1) a semicircular, sloped seating area; (2) an orchestra; and (3) a stage house, called the *scaena*. The Roman structures, however, were different from classical Greek theaters in that they were freestanding buildings with the tiered audience section connected to the stage house to form a single unit. The sloped, semicircular audience seating area was often larger than its Greek counterpart; the average capacity of a Roman theater was around 25,000.

The Roman orchestra, which was also semicircular (rather than circular as in Greek theaters), was rarely used for staging; rather, it was used for seating government officials or, in some theaters, was flooded for sea battles.

In front of the stage house was a large raised stage about 5 feet high whose area varied from approximately 100 feet by 20 feet to 300 feet by 40 feet. The stage house itself was a unique feature of the Roman theater structure. Two or three stories high, it was used for storage and dressing space, and a roof extended from the scene building over the stage to protect the actors from the weather.

Making Connections

Greek & Roman Popular Arts

GLADIATOR BATTLES
Shown here is a Roman mosaic depicting a gladiator battling a leopard. Such battles between human combatants and animals were extremely popular, particularly during the Roman empire. (© Archivo Iconografico, S.A./Corbis)

While we focus on the great dramas and comedies created during the Greek and Roman eras, we should not forget that there was a great tradition of popular entertainment during these time periods. The types of popular arts that flourished during these eras were to have a great influence on popular culture through our own times.

During the classical and Hellenistic Greek eras, we know that there were traveling mimes who per-formed throughout the Greek world. Historians believe that mime may have developed in the fifth and fourth centuries B.C.E., but there is a great deal of debate over how to define the form. Greek mime is often described as dealing with domestic and sexual situations in a popular and highly bawdy manner, though it may have first been a form that parodied mythological figures and stories.

Mimes sometimes performed by themselves, but by the Hellenistic era they were usually organized into troupes. Mime was never introduced into the festivals and was seen as a lower form of theatrical art. Women eventually were performers in mime troupes, and frequently the actors in this type of popular entertainment, especially in the Hellenistic era, appeared without masks. In order to survive economically, mime troupes traveled extensively. For that rea-son, it is often argued that Greek mime performers influenced the development of Roman theater and popular entertainments.

Roman theater had great competition in the popular arts that were available to the Roman public. Mime troupes continued to perform in Roman times. The Romans also developed a form referred to as *pantomime*, in which a single male dancer interpreted classical literature, sometimes accompanied by a chorus that chanted, and by musicians.

But the Romans also organized even greater spectacles. As we have noted, they created huge circuses, stadiums, and amphitheaters for popular arts. Some of the circuses, for example, had tracks for chariot races. Stadiums held animal battles, battles between gladiators, and fights between humans and animals; the Circus Maximus and the Colosseum were erected for just such events.

In modern times, we can see many similarities to the popular arts of Greece and Rome. Stand-up comedians and small troupes of comics entertain us regularly in events that are very reminiscent of the early mimes. Sports arenas, indoors and outdoors, house gladiator-like battles, such as football and boxing. And many of these events are highly theatrical, mixing pregame, half-time, and postgame performances into already highly theatricalized sports.

Two side wings connected the stage house to the audience area. The facade of the stage house—the *scaena frons*—was elaborate and ornate, with statuary, columns, recesses, and three to five doorways. Because of its emphasis on the raised stage and the facade behind it, the Roman theater moved to a point somewhere between the thrust stage of the Greek theater and later proscenium stages.

Decline of Roman Theater

In the fourth century C.E., it was clear that the Roman empire was beginning to fall apart. In 330, Emperor Constantine established two capitals for the empire: Rome in the west and Constantinople in the east. From that point on, the center of gravity shifted to Constantinople, and the city of Rome became less and less important.

The downfall of Rome was marked in 476 C.E. by the unseating of the western Roman emperor by a barbarian ruler. It had probably been caused by the disintegration of the Roman administrative structure and the sacking of Roman cities by northern barbarians; but in any case the fall of the empire also meant the end of western Roman theater.

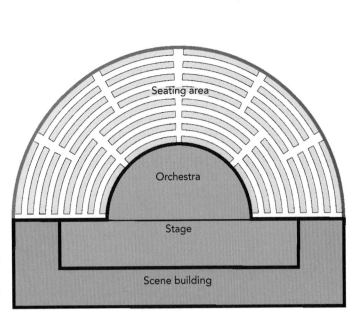

GROUND PLAN OF A TYPICAL ROMAN THEATER
Roman theaters, in contrast to Greek theaters, were freestanding structures—all one building—with the stone stage house connected to the seating area, known as the cavea. The orchestra was a semicircle instead of a full circle as in Greek theaters. The stage was long and wide, and the stage house was several stories high with an elaborate facade.

Another important factor in the decline of Roman theater was the rise of Christianity. From the outset, the Christian church was opposed to theater because of the connection between theater and pagan religions and because the church fathers felt that evil characters portrayed onstage taught immorality to audiences. In addition, the sexual content of Roman entertainments offended church leaders. As a result, the church issued various edicts condemning theater and in 398 C.E. decreed that anyone who went to the theater rather than to church on holy days would be excommunicated.

After the invaders from the north had plundered the cities of the Roman empire, no large centers of culture remained. People scattered, and in many places the buildings that had housed government offices, schools, and performing spaces were abandoned. The plays of the Greek and Roman dramatists and the writings of Aristotle and Horace were lost or forgotten. The tradition of theater that had stretched virtually unbroken for nearly 1,000 years—from the Greeks in the fifth century B.C.E. through the early centuries of the Christian era—was at an end. In the western world, theater as an organized activity would not appear again until the medieval period, many centuries later.

SUMMARY

The impulse to create theater is universal. Elements of theater exist in rituals and ceremonies in Africa, in Asia, in Europe, and wherever else human society develops.

On the European continent, Greek theater set the stage for all western theater to follow, with the tragedies of Aeschylus, Sophocles, and Euripides and the dramatic form known as climactic structure. Aristotle's *Poetics* marked the development of serious criticism of drama and theater. With Aristophanes's Old Comedies, the Greeks were leaders in comedy as well. Classical Greek theater buildings were large outdoor spaces built into hillsides, which accommodated audiences attending religious festivals. All the performers were male, and the chorus was an integral element of all classical Greek drama and theater. During the later Hellenistic period in Greece, New Comedy, which was concerned with domestic and romantic situations, prepared the way for almost all subsequent popular comedy.

The Romans borrowed many Greek conventions, including the introduction of drama and theater into religious and civic festivals, but they emphasized domestic and romantic comedies, as in the plays of Plautus and Terence. The tragedies of Seneca are noteworthy because of their influence on later playwrights.

Roman theaters were usually huge outdoor buildings. In Roman playhouses (unlike Greek theaters), all the structural elements were connected, and the most significant element was a large raised stage with an ornate facade.

KEY TERMS

Agon (AG-ohn) In classical Greek Old Comedy, a scene with a debate between the two opposing forces in a play.

Amphitheater Large oval, circular, or semi-circular outdoor theater with rising tiers of seats around an open playing area; also, an exceptionally large indoor auditorium.

Choregus (koh-REE-guhs) Wealthy person who financed a playwright's works at an ancient Greek dramatic festival.

Chorus In ancient Greek drama, a group of performers who sang and danced, sometimes participating in the action but usually simply commenting on it. In modern times, performers in a musical play who sing and dance as a group.

City Dionysia (SIT-ee digh-eh-NIGH-see-uh) The most important Greek festival in honor of the god Dionysus, and the first to include drama.

Dominus Leader of a Roman acting troupe.

New comedy Hellenistic Greek and Roman comedies that deal with romantic and domestic situations.

Old comedy Classical Greek comedy that pokes fun at social, political, or cultural conditions and at particular figures.

Orchestra A circular playing space in ancient Greek theaters; in modern times, the ground-floor seating in a theater auditorium.

Pantomime Originally a Roman entertainment in which a narrative was sung by a chorus while the story was acted out by dancers. Now used loosely to cover any form of presentation that relies on dance, gesture, and physical movement without dialogue or speech.

Parabasis (puh-RAB-uh-sihs) Scene in classical Greek Old Comedy in which the chorus directly addresses the audience members and makes fun of them.

Parodos (PAR-uh-dohs) In classical Greek drama, the scene in which the chorus enters. Also, the entranceway for the chorus in Greek theater.

Satyr play One of the three types of classical Greek drama, usually a ribald takeoff on Greek mythology and history that included a chorus of satyrs, mythological creatures who were half-man and half-goat. On festival days in Athens, it was presented as the final play following three tragedies.

Scaena (SKAY-nah) Stage house in a Roman theater.

Theatron Where the audience sat in an ancient Greek theater.

Thespian Synonym for "performer"; from Thespis, who is said to have been the first actor in ancient Greek theater.

Trilogy In classical Greece, three tragedies written by the same playwright and presented on a single day; they were connected by a story or thematic concerns.

THEATER ON THE WEB

For more research and to learn more about the topics in this chapter, please visit the Online Learning Center at **www.mhhe.com/livelyart6**.

Asian and Medieval Theaters

◀ **KABUKI THEATER**

Traditional kabuki theater, with its stylized movements, elaborate costumes, and painted facial makeup on the actors, continues to be popular in Japan today. Seen here is Kankuro Nakamura performing on a special stage set up on a beach at the break of the New Year in Naruto, Japan. (© Reuters/Corbis)

Chapter 14 Asian and Medieval Theaters

255

After the fall of Rome, the highly developed theater of Greece and Rome disappeared. Wandering players kept some kind of theatrical tradition alive in western society for 500 years after the fall of the Roman empire. However, it was not until the period between 1000 and 1500 c.e. that new types of theater, many connected to the church, developed.

At the same time, in the Asian world various classical forms of theater arose, many of which had strong connections to Asian religions.

ASIA

Background: Asian Theater

When we turn to the theater of Asia, we have moved half a world away from the theater of Greece and Rome as well as the later Middle Ages. These two cultures —east and west—knew nothing of each other at the time. Nevertheless, theater had begun in parts of Asia during a period of nearly 1,000 years—from roughly 350 to 1350 c.e.—when there was little organized theater in Europe.

Each of the three great Asian traditions—Indian, Chinese, and Japanese— reached a high point at a time when religion and philosophy were central in the culture. As a result, the focus of these traditional theaters has remained to some extent religious and philosophical, even though the societies themselves changed and were modernized. In addition, the three great cultures created and sustained forms of theater in which there was a unique synthesis of many facets of theatrical art—acting, mime, dancing, music, and text. We will understand the development of Asian theater more clearly as we examine these three theaters in turn, beginning with the theater of India.

Theater in India

Indian history has been described as a succession of immigrations into the Indian subcontinent from the north. Though early traces of civilization in Indian history go back to 3000 b.c.e., it was 1,000 years later, when the Aryans came into southern India and left behind works in Sanskrit, that the basis of the great Indian literary traditions was established.

Around 400 b.c.e., Buddhism, the religion of eastern and central Asia that follows the teachings of Buddha, reached a peak of development. By roughly 240 b.c.e., India was united under Buddhist rule, but a period of disorder and confusion followed for several centuries, until around 320 c.e., when the Guppy dynasty began to reunite the nation. Hindu culture entered its golden age at this time, and it was during the next centuries that the great Sanskrit dramas were written and performed.

Sanskrit Drama. What remains from the tradition of this golden age is a group of plays written in Sanskrit—the language of the noble classes—for performance in various court circles. These plays draw on themes from Indian epic lit-

KATHAKALI: INDIAN DANCE DRAMA
Much Asian drama includes a large element of dance. A prime example is kathakali, a dramatic form found in southwestern India. In kathakali, stories of strong passions, the furies of gods, and the loves and hates of extraordinary human beings are told in dance and mime. Notice the makeup and stylized costumes and headdresses. Also note the peacock feathers underneath the bottom of the costumes. (© David Ball/Index Stock Imagery)

erature. The most famous play of the classic period is *Shakuntala*, a long love idyll on various classic themes, by Kalidasa (c. 373–415 C.E.).

Although their texts have been preserved, no information remains on how the Sanskrit plays were acted. We do, however, have descriptions of a typical theater in which they were performed. It was 96 feet long and 48 feet wide, divided equally into stage and auditorium, and the seating capacity was probably between 200 and 500. There were four pillars in the auditorium—one white, one yellow, one red, and one blue—indicating where members of different castes were to sit. A curtain divided the stage into two parts: one part for the action and the other for dressing rooms and a backstage area. Scenery was evidently not used, although elaborate costumes probably were. Dance, symbolic gestures, and music played an important part in the productions. The plays often use fixed characters, such as a narrator and a clown.

Not only playwriting but also dramatic criticism reached a peak during the great period of Sanskrit theater. The best-known work of criticism is the *Natyasastra*, probably written sometime between 200 B.C.E. and 100 C.E. In addition to discussing the content and philosophy of Sanskrit drama, it also serves as a dictionary of theatrical practices.

Later Indian Drama. By the end of the ninth century, the golden age of Hindu culture had faded. By the twelfth century, the Arabs had begun to invade India; and with that series of invasions, the Hindu Sanskrit tradition disappeared. However, folk dramas and dance dramas, based on epic materials from Sanskrit drama and Indian myths, remained popular.

In more recent times—during the past three centuries—an interesting form of dance drama, called *kathakali,* has been prominent in southwestern India. It is produced at night by torchlight, on a stage approximately 16 feet square covered with a canopy of flowers. Kathakali heightens certain elements of Sanskrit drama, presenting violence and death onstage in dance and pantomime. The stories revolve around clashes between good and evil, with good always winning. A language of 500 or more gestural signs has been developed to tell these stories.

Theater in China

Chinese civilization can be traced back to at least 2000 B.C.E., when a unified culture spread over large parts of what is now the People's Republic of China. By 200 B.C.E., a centralized imperial system had been developed; and China was provided with a central government that continued to remain effective, through many long periods of stability, until modern times.

The early development of theater, like that of many other forms of art in China, was linked to the patronage of the imperial court. Records of court entertainments go back as far as the fifth century B.C.E., and ancient chronicles mention other theatrical activities such as skits, pantomimes, juggling, singing, and dancing—early Chinese versions of popular entertainments.

Later, the court of the emperors during the Tang period (618–906 C.E.) was one of the high points of world culture. At this time there was in the capital a kind of actors' training institute known as the Pear Garden, which firmly established a tradition of training theatrical performers. During the Song dynasty (960–1279)—the last dynasty before the coming of the Mongols—various court entertainments contributed to the development of a form called *variety plays.* Documents record the existence of traveling theatrical troupes, some permanent playhouses, and theatrical activity that involved not only performers, dancers, and singers but also shadow puppets and marionettes.

Chinese Theater in the Yuan Dynasty. A synthesis of art and popular tradition came in the dramas of the Yuan period which became well known in the west through the writings of the Italian explorer Marco Polo. Beginning in 1167, China was faced with an invading army from the north led by the Mongol

ASIA
Year, C.E.

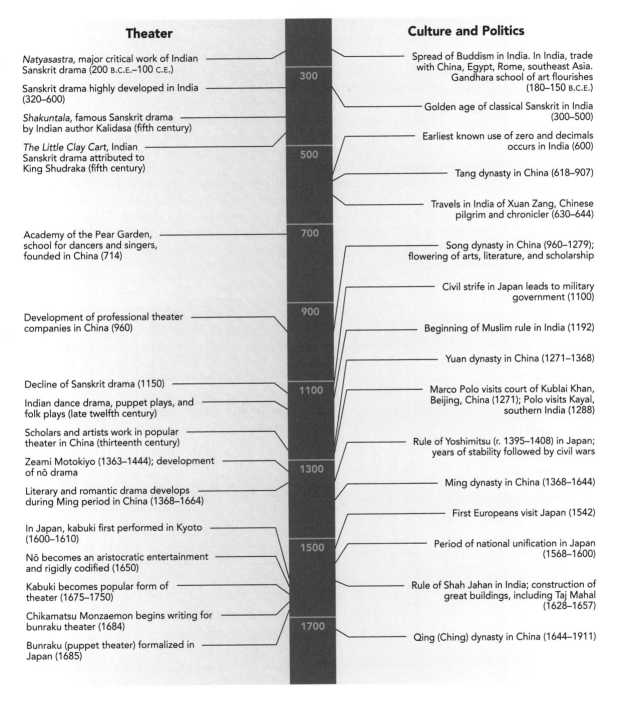

Theater

Natyasastra, major critical work of Indian Sanskrit drama (200 B.C.E.–100 C.E.)

Sanskrit drama highly developed in India (320–600)

Shakuntala, famous Sanskrit drama by Indian author Kalidasa (fifth century)

The Little Clay Cart, Indian Sanskrit drama attributed to King Shudraka (fifth century)

Academy of the Pear Garden, school for dancers and singers, founded in China (714)

Development of professional theater companies in China (960)

Decline of Sanskrit drama (1150)

Indian dance drama, puppet plays, and folk plays (late twelfth century)

Scholars and artists work in popular theater in China (thirteenth century)

Zeami Motokiyo (1363–1444); development of nō drama

Literary and romantic drama develops during Ming period in China (1368–1664)

In Japan, kabuki first performed in Kyoto (1600–1610)

Nō becomes an aristocratic entertainment and rigidly codified (1650)

Kabuki becomes popular form of theater (1675–1750)

Chikamatsu Monzaemon begins writing for bunraku theater (1684)

Bunraku (puppet theater) formalized in Japan (1685)

Culture and Politics

Spread of Buddism in India. In India, trade with China, Egypt, Rome, southeast Asia. Gandhara school of art flourishes (180–150 B.C.E.)

Golden age of classical Sanskrit in India (300–500)

Earliest known use of zero and decimals occurs in India (600)

Tang dynasty in China (618–907)

Travels in India of Xuan Zang, Chinese pilgrim and chronicler (630–644)

Song dynasty in China (960–1279); flowering of arts, literature, and scholarship

Civil strife in Japan leads to military government (1100)

Beginning of Muslim rule in India (1192)

Yuan dynasty in China (1271–1368)

Marco Polo visits court of Kublai Khan, Beijing, China (1271); Polo visits Kayal, southern India (1288)

Rule of Yoshimitsu (r. 1395–1408) in Japan; years of stability followed by civil wars

Ming dynasty in China (1368–1644)

First Europeans visit Japan (1542)

Period of national unification in Japan (1568–1600)

Rule of Shah Jahan in India; construction of great buildings, including Taj Mahal (1628–1657)

Qing (Ching) dynasty in China (1644–1911)

Timeline (center)
- 300
- 500
- 700
- 900
- 1100
- 1300
- 1500
- 1700

general Genghis Khan. Gradually, the Mongols took control of China; and though the Song dynasty lasted until it was finally defeated in 1279, by 1271 the Mongols had effectively taken control of the country and the dynasty under the rule of Genghis Khan's son, Kublai Khan, had begun. It was known as the Yuan dynasty and lasted until 1368.

In the Yuan dynasty—the late thirteenth and early fourteenth centuries, the fusion of popular culture with the high culture of literary intellectuals resulted in an outpouring of drama. Yuan drama was usually written in four acts—or four song sequences, since these plays used a great deal of music. Rather than writing an original drama, a playwright would compose a dramatic text to suit the rhythms and meter of familiar popular music. Usually, the leading character—the protagonist—sang all the music in any given act. Unfortunately, none of the music has survived.

The poetic content of these plays was considered the central factor in their success. Because of its lyrical nature, Yuan drama had only a small number of characters, and subplots and other complexities were avoided. The topics chosen by Yuan playwrights ranged from love and romance to religion, history, and even crimes and lawsuits.

GROUND PLAN OF A TRADITIONAL CHINESE THEATER

Diagrammed here is the arrangement for seating in Chinese theaters for the period from the seventeenth through the nineteenth centuries. Before that, performances were held in teahouses; when permanent theaters were built, tables with chairs around them were retained in the section nearest the stage. Women and commoners sat at the sides and back.

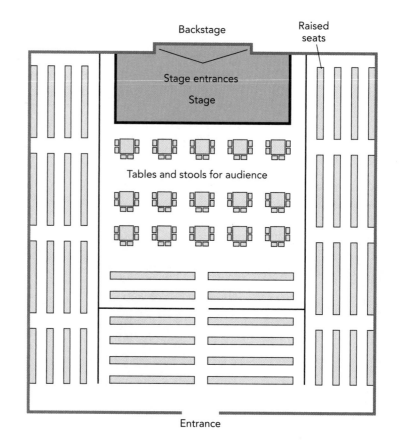

Perhaps the most famous of the plays that have survived from this period is *The Romance of the Western Chamber,* actually a cycle of plays, by Wang Shifu (fl. late thirteenth century). These dramas chronicle the trials of two lovers—a handsome young student and a lovely, well-born girl—who became the models for thousands of imitations down to the present century.

Relatively little is known about how Yuan plays were produced, but it is thought that the actors and actresses were professionals, and that performers of each sex occasionally played both male and female roles. The performers were organized into troupes, some of which were run by women. Most of the theater buildings seem to have been built for outdoor use and were not roofed over. Curtains and such properties as swords and fans were used, but there is no evidence of scenery. Much of the color of the performances came from elaborate costumes and stylized makeup.

Chinese Theater in the Ming Dynasty.   By the end of the Yuan period, theater in China had reached a very high level. However, with the overthrow of the Mongols and the establishment of the Ming dynasty (1368–1644), a Chinese emperor was restored to the throne, and he reinstated traditional patterns of social behavior. This meant that dramatists reverted to writing only for the elite, and theater lost contact with the broad public.

Still, a new dramatic form, which expanded the structure of Yuan drama, emerged in the Ming period. One of the best-known plays of this type was *Lute Song* by Gao Ming (c. 1301–1370), which dealt with questions of family loyalties; its main character is a woman whose husband has abandoned her.

By the middle of the sixteenth century, Manchu peoples would begin to advance southward into northern China; and in the middle of the seventeenth century, they—like the Mongols before them—would conquer the country. This period of foreign rule was to last until the dissolution of the empire in 1912. The Manchu rulers enjoyed Chinese culture, including theater, and continued to support the sort of lavish literary productions that had become a tradition among the elite. On the other hand, popular theater was often suppressed, and its scripts were destroyed, for political or moral reasons.

Peking (Beijing) Opera.   In the nineteenth century, elements of folk theater and other genres popular among ordinary people formed the basis for a new form of popular theater that in the west was called *Peking opera* or—more recently—*Beijing opera.* (The city whose name is now transliterated as Beijing was for many years known to westerners as Peking. Peking opera is also called by other Chinese names, including *jingju* and *xiqu*. Although mindful of the rationale for each of these, we will use the traditional term: Peking opera.) Peking opera is not like the grand opera we know in the west; though it combines music and theater, it is also based on dance and even acrobatics.

The theater space traditionally used for Peking opera is something like a modern dinner theater: audience members are seated at tables and eat and drink during performances. In its staging, Peking opera stresses symbolism. The only

BEIJING (PEKING) OPERA

A highly formalized theater, Beijing (or Peking) opera was developed in China in the nineteenth century. It is not like western grand opera; rather, it is a popular entertainment. Beijing opera is filled with song, dance, and acrobatics. It makes wide use of symbols—with, for instance, a table standing for a mountain—and is performed in highly colorful, stylized costumes like the ones shown here. Also, note the theatrical headdress and makeup. The production being enacted is The Monkey King. *(© Dean Conger/Corbis)*

furniture onstage is usually a table and several chairs, but these few items are used with imagination. The table and chairs, for instance, may represent a dining hall, a court of justice, a cloud, or a mountain. A tripod holding incense indicates a palace. When a script calls for a long journey, the performers walk around the stage in a circle. Costumes and makeup are highly lavish, ornate, and colorful, and they too serve symbolic functions. The colors and patterns of makeup, for example, signal to the audience what type of character a performer is playing. Performance style emphasizes symbolic movement and piercing vocal patterns.

Theater in Japan

Although the civilization of Japan is younger than that of China, its heritage is long and complex. By the fifth century C.E., the southern portions of the country were consolidated and a series of capitals were established in the vicinity of present-day Kyoto. By that time, the Japanese had developed a religion called Shinto ("Way of the Gods"), which was closely bound to nature and spirit worship. With the growing influence on the Japanese aristocracy of the Tang dynasty in China (618–907 C.E.), Buddhism became a prevailing influence in Japan, first in court circles and then in the country as a whole. Both Shinto and Buddhism had a strong influence on the development of theater in Japan. The first great period in the history of Japanese theater occurred in the fourteenth century, not long after similar developments in China. The sudden and remarkable development of *nō*—one of three great traditional forms of Japanese theater—came about when popular stage traditions and high learning joined forces.

Nō. In the fourteenth century in Japan, there were a number of roving troupes of actors who performed in a variety of styles, some popular and even vulgar but others having genuine artistic merit. One of the artistic troupes was directed by the actor Kan'ami (1333–1384), whose son Zeami Motokiyo (1363–1443) was one of the finest child actors in Japan. A performance by the troupe was seen by Ashikaga Yoshimitsu (1358–1408), the shogun of Japan, a man of wealth, prestige, and enormous enthusiasm for the arts. Fascinated by what he saw, he arranged for Zeami to have a court education to develop his art.

When Zeami succeeded his father as head of the troupe, it remained attached to the shogun's court in Kyoto. With a patron of this caliber, Zeami was able to devote himself to all aspects of theater: composing plays, training actors (there were no actresses in Zeami's theater), and constantly refining his own acting style. Under Zeami's direction, nō became the dominant form of serious theater in his own time, and it would remain dominant for 200 years—well past 1600. In fact, the elegance, mystery, and beauty of nō have continued to fascinate the Japanese, and the tradition, passed on from teacher to disciple, is still carried on today.

The stories on which nō plays were based often came from literary or historical sources. One particularly notable source was a famous novel, Lady Murasaki's *The Tale of Genji*, written around 1000; it depicted court life during the Heian period (794–1185). Many nō dramas show a strong influence of Buddhism. *Sotoba Komachi,* written by Kan'ami and revised by his son Zeami, is one in which this influence is most pronounced (this was the play performed by Zeami at the Kitano temple in 1413). In fact, its title indicates a Buddhist connection: *Sotoba Komachi* can be translated as "Sotoba on the Stupa," and a stupa is a monument to Buddha.

NŌ PERFORMANCE TODAY

Traditional nō theater is still performed in Japan and other parts of the world, and it still features stylized acting, minimalist settings, ornate costumes, and distinctive masks. Shown here is Otoharu Sakai performing Hagoromo, *("Angel's Robe") in Tokyo in 2004. The elaborate, colorful costume is typical of those worn by nō performers for centuries.* (© Toshiyuki Aizawa/Reuters/Corbis)

Sotoba Komachi

1413, Kitano temple, Japan The year is 1413. In Japan, at the Kitano temple, a platform stage, with a floor of polished wood, has been set up. There is also a wooden walkway, or bridge, on which actors can move to the stage from a dressing room set up in one of the temple buildings. The spectators are on three sides of this platform stage.

The actor performing today is Zeami. He is 50 years old and has been under the patronage of the shogun of Japan since he was 12. Zeami's father, Kan'ami, was a renowned actor before him, and Zeami has carried his father's art to even greater heights. He has studied different acting styles, perfected his own technique, trained other actors, and written plays for them to perform.

The theater he has fashioned from all this is called *nō*; it has elements of opera, pantomime, and formal, stylized dance. In nō theater, the main character, who wears a beautifully carved, hand-painted wooden mask, recites his or her adventures to the constant accompaniment of several on-stage musicians. Toward the end of the play, the chief actor will perform a ritualistic dance that includes symbolic gestures of the head and hands and stomps of the feet on the wooden floor.

The crowd is gathered today for a special reason. Usually, Zeami performs only in a restricted theater space for the shogun and members of his court, or at a temple for a select audience. But here at the Kitano temple, performances will go on for seven days and will be open to everyone; as one later commentator will explain: "All were admitted, rich and poor, old and young alike."

As with all nō performances, several plays will be presented each day. The play the audience awaits now, *Sotoba Komachi*, was written by Zeami's father. In it, Zeami portrays a woman. (As in ancient Greek theater, all the performers in nō are men.) The legend of Komachi is as well-known to the audience as the story of Antigone was to the Greeks. Komachi, a beautiful but cruel woman, is pursued by a man named Shii no Shōshō. She tells him that he must call on her for 100 nights in a row, and for 99 nights he comes, in all kinds of weather. But on the hundredth night he dies. On that night a snowstorm is raging and he falls exhausted, to die on her doorstep.

When the play begins, we see two priests enter. As they discuss the virtues of following Buddha, they come upon an old woman. This is Zeami in the mask and wig of Komachi in old age. She is a wretched woman approaching her hundredth birthday. Komachi tells how she was once beautiful but has lost her beauty and grown old. She argues with the priests about religion and then reveals who she is. She recounts the story of what she did to Shōshō.

As the play progresses, the audience watches Zeami's performance with rapt attention. At one point, his character becomes possessed: the spirit of Shōshō takes over Komachi, and Zeami acts this out in pantomime, to a musical accompaniment. At times, he acts out Komachi's part while her lines are chanted by a chorus of 10 or 12 men sitting at the side of the stage. At another point, Komachi is dressed as Shōshō and becomes him, feeling his death agony. Zeami performs this sequence as a mesmerizing, frightening dance. At the end of the play, the spirit of Shōshō leaves Komachi, and she prays to Buddha for guidance and for a peaceful life in the hereafter.

The audience members, who have heard a great deal about Zeami but have never before seen him perform, watch in awe. Throughout, he plays the various parts with astounding grace, subtlety, and understatement, developed through years of training and performance. The segments when he lets go—as in Shōshō's death agony—are all the more effective because of their contrast with the measured quality of the rest. For the audience, the play is a revelation of how moving a theatrical performance can be—an experience unlike any they have had before.

The nō stage has remained roughly the same since the time of Zeami and his successors. The stage has a bridge, called a *hashigakari,* which leads from the actors' dressing room off-stage to the stage proper. The bridge is normally around 20 feet long, depending on the size of the theater; the main playing space is about 18 feet square, is roofed, and has a ceremonial pine tree painted on the rear wall. At the back of the playing space is a narrow section for four or five musicians, who accompany the play. Nō theaters were originally outdoors, but a modern nō theater is placed inside a larger shell as though it were a giant stage set.

Nō actors move in a highly stylized way that has important elements of both dance and pantomime. During the performance of a nō text, the actors alternate sections of chanting with a heightened speech that might best be compared to recitative in western opera.

Costumes made for nō are usually of great elegance, and the masks worn by the chief character are among the most beautiful, subtle, and effective ever created for any theater.

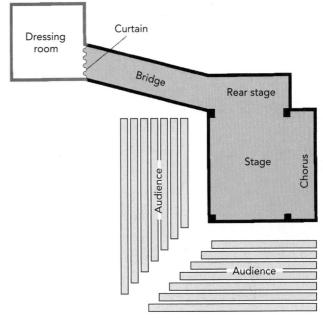

GROUND PLAN OF A TRADITIONAL NŌ THEATER
Nō theater of Japan—a stylized theater originally for the upper classes—began nearly 600 years ago. It was performed outdoors; a ramp at the left led from a dressing room to the wooden platform stage. Spectators sat on two sides of the stage, to the left and in front.

Bunraku: Puppet Theater. Nō remained the most popular theatrical form during Japan's long medieval period. Civil wars and other disturbances, however, caused increasing political disarray until in 1600 a general, Tokugawa Ieyasu, unified the country. All through the long Tokugawa period (1600–1868), Japan was unified and at peace, but this period of calm was purchased at a price. Alarmed at the political maneuvering of Japan's growing number of Christians—who had been converted by European missionaries—the Tokugawa family outlawed Christianity and cut Japan off from any extensive contact with either China or Europe until the middle of the nineteenth century. Peace did bring, however, a rapid development of commerce and trade and a growing merchant class, which demanded its own entertainment.

The first of the new popular forms of theater to flourish was a puppet theater known as *bunraku.* Bunraku is a highly unusual type of theater featuring musicians and a chanter who tells the story and creates the voices of all the characters. The puppets that enact the drama are today approximately two-thirds of human size and are operated by men dressed in black who move each puppet's head, arms, and body. The puppeteer's black outfit is a convention: it signifies that the audience should consider him invisible. Bunraku first became popular in the early seventeenth century and is still performed in Japan today.

JAPANESE BUNRAKU: PUPPET THEATER

Bunraku—puppet theater—became a popular form in Japan in the 1600s. In bunraku, unlike traditional western puppet theater, the puppeteers are in full view of the audience and are always dressed in black. Often, the story is delivered by a chanter, with the puppets dramatizing the action. Because the puppets today are very complex, there may be more than one puppeteer controlling each of them, as in the photo shown here, with the men in black to the right and left of the two characters. The play being performed is One Thousand Cherry Trees. *(© Michael S. Yamashita/Corbis)*

The first and undoubtedly the best of the writers for bunraku, Chikamatsu Monzaemon (1653–1725), contributed enormously to the transformation of this popular theater into a true art form. Chikamatsu wrote both historical plays and domestic dramas dealing with life in his own day; his domestic dramas have remained popular to the present time. His emphasis on ordinary people was new to the Japanese stage and foreshadowed later developments in European theater. Because of his great talent and the wide-ranging subject matter of his many dramas, he is sometimes spoken of as the "Shakespeare of Japan."

Kabuki. Shortly after bunraku had become established, another form of popular theater—*kabuki*—developed, in the early and middle seventeenth century. Legend has it that kabuki was originated by an actress, Okuni, who lived around the end of the sixteenth century. Kabuki drew its material from plays written for nō and bunraku; the exaggerated gestures of kabuki are often attributed to the fact that in its early phases a conscious attempt was made to imitate puppets. Despite these exaggerated and stylized gestures, kabuki was less formal and distant than nō, which remained largely the theater of the court and nobility. Kabuki quickly became a tremendously popular form of theater, and it remains a favorite of Japanese audiences today.

Kabuki was performed first by all-female troupes, then by boys, and finally—beginning in 1652—by all-male companies. Kabuki actors are trained from childhood in singing, dancing, acting, and physical dexterity. The actors who play women's parts are particularly skillful at suggesting the essence of a feminine personality through stylized gestures and attitudes. The costumes and makeup are elegant as well as colorful. Musicians—sometimes onstage, sometimes offstage—generally accompany the stage action.

The stage used for kabuki performances underwent various changes during the history of the art, but the same principles were observed after the middle of the nineteenth century. The stage is long and has a relatively low proscenium. Kabuki features elaborate and beautiful scenic effects, including the revolving stage, which was developed in Japan before it was used in the west. Another device used in kabuki is the *hanamichi*, or "flower way," a raised narrow platform connecting the rear of the auditorium with the stage. Actors often make their entrances on the hanamichi and occasionally perform short scenes there as well.

KABUKI PERFORMANCE TODAY

According to legend, Japanese kabuki was developed around 1600 by a woman named Okuni. Today, all roles in kabuki are performed by men; most of the actors are descended from generations of kabuki performers and train for years. In the scene shown here, note the heavy, stylized makeup, which covers the entire face; the ornate costumes; and the highly theatrical wigs. The costumes, makeup, gestures, and stage configuration are part of a long tradition. (© Charles and Josette Lenars/Corbis)

Southeast Asia: Shadow Plays

Though we have focused on theater in India, China, and Japan, it is important to remember that considerable theater activity has occurred in other parts of Asia, such as Korea and the southeastern countries of Burma, Cambodia, Laos, Indonesia, Malaysia, Thailand, and Vietnam. Each of these southeastern nations has its own theatrical history and tradition, but all of them share certain characteristics. Most of their theatrical styles were influenced by the theater of India, and in some instances by that of China. In virtually every one of these countries we note the influence of two epics from India, the *Ramayana* and the *Mahabharata*. These stories and others are almost always performed as dance drama, classical dance, or puppet theater. As is true in other Asian countries, theatrical presentations combine dance, song, movement, and recited text with elaborate costumes. It is worth noting that most of these countries do not even have a word in their language that denotes a dramatic form which is only written or spoken.

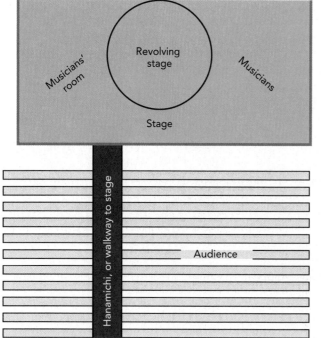

A KABUKI THEATER

Kabuki, a 400-year-old Japanese theater, is performed today in elaborate spaces with staging devices that include onstage turntables for shifting scenery. As shown in this ground plan, the stage covers the entire front of the theater and is approached by a ramp—the hanamichi—on which performers make dramatic entrances and exits.

One type of theatrical activity that came to prominence in southeast Asia in the eleventh century is particularly significant. This was the *shadow play,* which is widely performed in Thailand, Malaysia, and Indonesia. It appears to have been developed most fully in Java, an Indonesian island.

A shadow play uses flat puppets made of leather. These figures are intricately carved to create patterns of light and shadow when their image is projected on a screen. The puppets are manipulated by sticks attached to the head, the arms, and other parts of the body. The person manipulating the puppets also narrates the drama and speaks the dialogue of the characters. Shadow plays usually take place at night—sometimes they last all night long—and are accompanied by music and sound effects.

In various places, other theatrical forms have been developed from shadow puppets. One variation uses three-dimensional doll puppets; another uses human performers wearing masks.

THE MIDDLE AGES

Background: Medieval Europe

The period from 500 to 1500 C.E. in western history is known as the *Middle Ages* or the *medieval* era. The first 500 years are referred to as the early Middle Ages, and the next 500 years as the later Middle Ages.

At the start of the early Middle Ages in Europe, following invasions from the north and the dissolution of Roman civilization, cities were abandoned and life throughout southern and western Europe became largely agricultural. The nobility controlled local areas, where most people worked as vassals. Gradually, several hundred years after the fall of the Roman empire, towns began to emerge, and with them trade and crafts. Learning also slowly revived. The strongest force during this period was the Roman Catholic church, which dominated not only religion but education and frequently politics as well.

We should also note that theatrical activity did continue in the eastern Roman empire, known as Byzantium, until 1453, when the region was conquered by the Islamic Turks. The theater of Byzantium was reminiscent of theater during the Roman empire. The Hippodrome, a large arena in Constantinople, was the Byzantine equivalent of the Circus Maximus or the Colosseum, and popular entertainments like those of Rome flourished in the east. One contribution of the Byzantine empire to the continuity of theater consists of these popular presentations; another important contribution lies in the fact that Byzantium was the preserver of the manuscript of classical Greek drama: the plays of Aeschylus, Sophocles, and Euripides and the criticism of Aristotle were saved because eastern scholars recognized their importance and made certain that they were not destroyed. When the eastern empire fell in 1453, these manuscripts were transferred to the western world and became part of the rediscovery of the past that influenced the Renaissance.

Theater and Culture in the Middle Ages

During the early part of the Middle Ages there were some scattered traces of theatrical activity, mostly based on the popular entertainments of Greece and Rome—traveling jugglers, minstrels, and mimes. In the late tenth century a nun in a convent in Germany, Hrosvitha of Gandersheim (c. 935–1001), wrote religious plays based on the dramas of the Roman writer Terence. Though her plays were probably not produced, it is still remarkable that she created drama almost in a vacuum. (Hrosvitha has recently been rediscovered by feminist critics and others.)

Essentially, though, theater had to be reborn in the west during the latter part of the Middle Ages. Interestingly, key elements of the new theater first appeared in the church, which had suppressed theater several hundred years earlier. In certain portions of the church service, priests or members of the choir chanted the lines of characters from the Bible. Gradually these small segments, which were delivered in Latin, were enlarged, and became short dramas—known as *liturgical dramas*—enacted in the church.

Also, during this early period of the Middle Ages, a German nun named Hildegard von Bingen (1098–1179) wrote short musical plays that were probably performed in the convent, which she oversaw. Hildegard wrote liturgical songs that were accompanied by texts. These dramatic musical pieces honored saints and the Virgin Mary and were written for performance on religious days. Hildegard also created a play in Latin, *Ordo Virtutum (Play of Virtues)*, that seems to foreshadow the later vernacular morality plays.

MEDIEVAL MYSTERY PLAYS

Interest in medieval mystery plays is still strong. Shown here is Pauline Malefane as the Virgin Mary in one such play, The Mysteries, *being presented by the Broomhill Opera Company, a South African theater troupe based in London. (© Donald Cooper/Photostage, England)*

MIDDLE AGES
Year, C.E.

Theater		Culture and Politics
Traveling performers (c. 500–925)	475	"Dark ages" (476–1000)
	525	Justinian becomes Byzantine emperor (527)
Byzantine theater (similar to Roman theater) (fifth through seventh centuries)	575	Muhammad born (c. 570)
Trulian Synod attempts to end performances in Byzantium (692)	675	Charles Martel defeats Muslims near Poitiers (732)
	725	
Traveling performers on European continent (500–975)	775	Charlemagne crowned Holy Roman Emperor (800)
	825	Beginning of Romanesque architecture (c. 830)
	875	
Quem quaeritis trope (c. 925)	925	Earliest European reference to a collar in the harness of a horse that would allow the drawing of heavy loads and plow (920)
Hrosvitha, a nun, writes Christian comedies based on Terence (c. 970)	975	Beowulf (1000)
	1025	Norman Conquest (1066)
		First Crusade (1095)
	1075	Beginning of Gothic architecture (1140)
	1125	
	1175	English Magna Carta (1215)
		Oxford University flourishes (c. 1260)
Vernacular religious drama flourishes: Peak of medieval theater (c. 1350–1550)	1225	Roger Bacon's De computo naturali (1264)
	1275	Black death apparently originates in India (1332)
Second Shepherds' Play (c. 1375)		Boccaccio's Decameron (1353)
Pride of Life (c. 1400)	1325	Urban VI in Rome; Clement VII at Avignon (1378)
The Castle of Perseverance (c. 1425)		Peasant revolt in England (1381)
Actor playing Judas at Metz almost dies while being hanged (1437)	1375	Chaucer dies (1400)
Pierre Patelin (c. 1470)	1425	Gutenberg invents printing by movable type (c. 1450)
Hans Sachs born (1494)		Constantinople falls to the Turks (1453)
Everyman (c. 1500)	1475	Copernicus born (1473)
Jean Bouchet, pageant master, directs cycle at Poitiers (1508)		Martin Luther born (1483)
Cycle staged at Mons (1510)	1525	Columbus crosses the Atlantic (1492)
John Heywood's Johan Johan (1533)		

Later in the Middle Ages, *vernacular drama* developed. The language of these later plays was not Latin but the everyday speech of the people. Everyday speech is referred to as the *vernacular,* hence the name of the drama. Like the brief church plays, vernacular dramas dealt with biblical stories and other religious stories. Vernacular dramas, however, were more elaborate and were usually presented as a series of one-act dramas. Also, they were presented not inside churches but in town squares or other parts of cities. Historians continue to debate whether vernacular drama evolved from liturgical drama or developed independently.

Medieval Drama: Mystery and Morality Plays

Two types of religious vernacular plays were popular in the medieval period. *Mystery* or *cycle plays* dramatized a series of biblical religious events that could stretch from Adam and Eve in the garden of Eden, Noah and the flood, and Abraham and Isaac to the stories of Christ in the New Testament as well as the lives of the saints. *Morality plays* such as *Everyman* (c. 1500) used religious characters and religious themes to teach a moral lesson. Virtually all the plays were short—the equivalent of a one-act play today—and mystery plays were often strung together to form a series, known as a *cycle.*

The best-known mystery play is *The Second Shepherds' Play,* produced in England in the late fourteenth century. It concerns three shepherds who, according to the Bible, went to visit the Christ child just after his birth in a manger. The first section of the drama comically depicts the stealing of a sheep from the shepherds by a rogue, Mak. When the three shepherds search for the missing sheep in Mak's home, his wife Gil pretends that the sheep is her newborn child. When the shepherds return a second time to offer gifts to Mak's "child," they discover that the infant is the stolen sheep, and they proceed to toss Mak in a blanket. In the second section of the play, the shepherds are called by an angel to visit the newborn Christ child, to whom they also bring gifts.

The Second Shepherds' Play illustrates most of the standard dramatic techniques of medieval cycle plays. One technique is to take things out of their actual time period. Though this is a Bible story, the shepherds are not biblical characters but people of the Middle Ages who complain about their lords and feudal conditions. And even though Christ is not born until the close of the play, they pray to him and to various saints throughout the initial section. Another technique is to mix different types of drama. Though the play dramatizes the birth of the Christian savior, this serious event is preceded by an extended comic section, reflecting the influence of secular farce on medieval religious drama. In the later Middle Ages, a tradition of nonreligious folk comedies made a significant contribution to the theatrical activity of the period.

In Chapter 6, we discussed the two major dramatic structures of western theater—climactic and episodic. The seeds of episodic form are found in medieval religious drama. This structure has numerous episodes and is expansive rather than restrictive in terms of time, place, and numbers of characters. In *The Second Shepherds' Play,* a forerunner of this form, the action shifts abruptly from a field

PAGEANT WAGONS

One form of staging for medieval religious plays was the pageant wagon, which could be rolled into a town or field nearby. The wagon—or wagons—served as a stage, contained scenery, and had a backstage area for costume changes. We do not know exactly how a pageant wagon worked, but shown here are two suggestions or speculations. At the top is a model of a pageant wagon in a town square. The wagon has a platform with a cloth covering its lower part (from which characters could emerge). The bottom drawing shows a cutaway view of two wagons; one serves as a stage platform while the other, behind it, provides a place for scenery, changing costumes, and hiding special effects. (Model: Cleveland State University, Theater Arts Area)

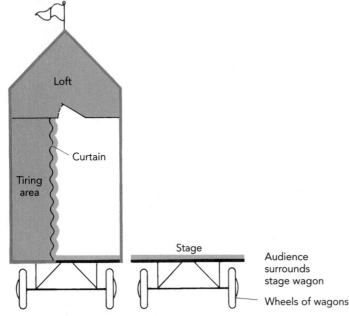

Side view of possible arrangement of medieval pageant wagon behind a second wagon

to Mak's hut and to Christ's manger some distance away; also, comic and serious elements are freely intermingled.

We should mention that *secular* theater and drama also existed during the Middle Ages. In France and Germany, for example, many popular farces were written and performed. They are a continuation of the tradition of popular entertainment discussed in Chapter 13. It is medieval religious drama, however, which is most remembered today.

Noah's Ark

1501, Mons The year is 1501. In a large town square in Mons—in the area that will much later become Belgium—a row of small stage houses called *mansions* have been erected. They serve as the setting for a series, or cycle, of plays based on the Old and New Testaments: dramatized Bible stories that move from the creation to the crucifixion. In the biblical plays at Mons this year, about 150 actors will perform 350 roles. They have held 48 rehearsals, and it will take four days to present all the plays in the cycle.

The mansions set up across the stage area are changed to suit whatever play is being performed. More than 60 different mansions—representing the garden of Eden, the manger in Bethlehem, the temple where Christ drove out the money changers, and so forth—will be used during these four days. At each end of the stage area are two permanent mansions, symbolic of the opposing sides in this great religious drama: one is heaven and the other hell. Hell is represented by the large mouth of a monster, out of which devils and smoke pour forth at appropriate moments.

This kind of religious drama is the chief theatrical presentation in the medieval period. It takes forms that vary in theatrical setting and in staging, but in both England and continental Europe, it is widespread and popular. The church encourages it because most people cannot read or write, and this is an excellent way for them to become familiar with stories from the Bible. The only other form of entertainment in this era is traveling troupes of jugglers, singers, dancers, and mimes. They go from place to place, performing brief dramatic sketches along with musicals and other pieces.

A good percentage of the people who live in Mons and the surrounding areas are present at the four-day cycle of religious plays. They represent a cross section of the community. The spectators either sit in temporary wooden bleachers or stand in the town square, trying to get the best possible view of the acting area and the various "mansions" from which the action of each episode begins.

The audience members have already seen dramas about Adam and Eve and about Cain slaying his brother Abel; now they will see a play about Noah, who is commanded by God to build an ark to save his family and the animals from the flood.

In the play, Noah is warned by God that it will rain for 40 days and 40 nights, and that he must build an ark into which he will take his family and two animals of every kind. As Noah begins building, his neighbors make fun of him, and his shrewish wife argues with him.

The wife does not want to go aboard the ark; she feels that Noah is foolish. She chides and criticizes her husband, and it is only when the rain begins to fall that she agrees to board the ark.

The spectators enjoy this byplay, but the moment they are waiting for is the deluge of rain, which is expected to be spectacular. At last the moment arrives, and the audience is not disappointed. On the roofs of houses behind the stage area, water has been stored in wine barrels and men are standing by, waiting for a signal to open the barrels. Now the signal is given, and the deluge begins: torrents of water fall onto the stage. The audience is completely in awe; enough water has been stored to provide a steady rain for five minutes. Water rises all around, but Noah, his family, and his animals are safe in the ark. Soon after, a dove comes, indicating that Noah can leave the ark.

During the remaining days of the cycle of plays, the spectators will see a continuing series of biblical stories, which trace episodes from both the Old Testament and the New Testament, including many events from the life of Christ. When the entire cycle has concluded, audience members will recall many highlights, but none, perhaps, more spectacular than the sensational flood in the play about Noah and his family.

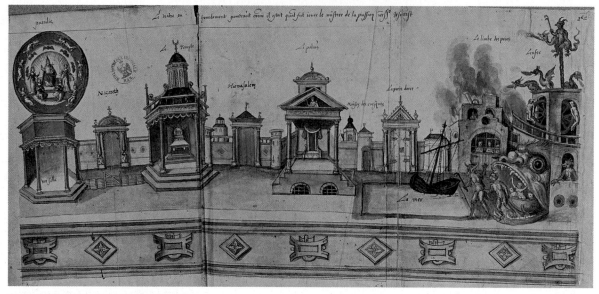

OUTDOOR STAGES AT VALENCIENNES

A popular form of medieval staging, especially on the European continent, was a series of stage areas set alongside each other. In the one at Valenciennes, France, shown here in a color rendering of the original stage set, the action would move from one area to the next. At the far left is heaven or paradise; at the right is hell, with a mouth out of which devils came. In between are other "mansions" representing various locales. (Bibliothèque Nationale de France)

Medieval Theater Production

Large-scale productions of mystery plays took place in what is now Spain, France, the Netherlands, Belgium, and England. In some cases, most often on the continent of Europe, stages were set up in a large town square, behind which were placed the individual scenic units—the *mansions*—one for each of the plays in a cycle. In other cases, particularly in England and Spain, portable *wagon stages*—whose appearance and mode of operation are still debated by scholars— moved through towns and stopped at points along the way to present one of the plays. (We should note that a few historians even question whether the wagons actually stopped to present the plays at different points or simply paraded through the town to one central location.)

The performers, who prepared for a few weeks for their roles, were amateurs. Only men performed in England, but women were performers in some continental European countries. *Craft guilds*—silversmiths, leather workers, carpenters, and so forth—or laypeople who belonged to religious organizations were responsible for producing individual plays, which were presented as part of annual festivals. Frequently, they provided their own costumes, which for the most part were contemporary dress rather than historically accurate clothing. Sometimes these presentations became extremely prolonged and elaborate; a series of plays presented in Valenciennes, France, in 1547 lasted for 25 days. Because of the complexity of cycle plays, there developed, both on the continent and in England, a practice of having one person organize and oversee a production. In England, there are records of someone referred to as a *pageant master,* who supervised the mounting of plays on wagons. This might include advance preparations—both for the wagons and for the rehearsals of plays to be presented on them—and the logistics of seeing that the plays unfolded on schedule.

To accommodate the abrupt changes in location that characterized the plots of mystery plays, medieval theaters used a neutral *platform stage,* set up either in a town square or on one of the wagon stages. This platform was not a specific locale, like a palace in Greek drama, but an unidentified space that could become whatever was designated. If the performers or the script indicated that a scene was set in a field, the platform instantaneously became a field; if it was supposed to be a ship at sea, it became a ship. This freedom of movement, based on the imagination, later became the basis of theatrical techniques perfected by Renaissance playwrights in Spain and England.

Toward the end of the Middle Ages, there was a gradual decline of religious theater. One reason was a weakening of the church, culminating in the Protestant Reformation; a second reason was that the secular qualities of drama finally overcame the religious material.

In Chapter 15, we will turn to the Renaissance. During the Middle Ages, religious plays had become increasingly sophisticated, and this growing professionalism was also seen in nonreligious comedies and farces. Thus theater in the west was poised for the important developments that would take place during the Renaissance, both in theatrical production—in acting, theater buildings, scenery, and costumes—and in playwriting.

SUMMARY

The traditional theaters of Asia originated with religious ceremonies and ideas. Most are highly theatrical and stylized, and they fuse acting, mime, dance, music, and text. Among the important Asian theaters are Sanskrit drama in India; the popular Peking opera in China; and the stylized nō drama, bunraku (puppet theater), and kabuki in Japan.

In Europe during the period from 500 to 1000 C.E.—the early Middle Ages—touring minstrels kept the theatrical tradition alive. Later in the Middle Ages, theater was reborn, primarily in the Roman Catholic church. Dramatic interpolations that had been added to religious services grew into plays—written in Latin and dramatizing biblical events—which were staged in churches by the clergy. In the fourteenth century, plays in the everyday language of the people developed. Mystery or cycle plays, which depicted a series of biblical tales—and which established the basis for extensive plot structure—were staged and acted outdoors by amateurs.

KEY TERMS

Bunraku (buhn-RAH-koo) Japanese puppet theater.

Hanamichi (hah-nah-MEE-chee) In kabuki theater, a bridge running from behind the audience (toward the left side of the audience) to the stage. Performers can enter on the hanamichi; important scenes may also be played on it.

Hashigakari (ha-shee-gah-KAH-ree) Bridge in nō theater on which the performers make their entrance from the dressing area to the platform stage.

Kabuki Form of popular Japanese theater combining music, dance, and dramatic scenes.

Kathakali Traditional dance-drama of India.

Liturgical drama Early medieval church drama, written in Latin and dealing with biblical stories.

Mansions Individual scenic units used for the staging of religious dramas in the Middle Ages.

Morality play Medieval drama designed to teach a lesson. The characters were often allegorical and represented virtues or faults.

Mystery plays Also called *cycle plays*. Short dramas of the Middle Ages based on events of the Old and New Testaments and often organized into historical cycles.

Nō Rigidly traditional form of Japanese drama combining music, dance, and lyrics.

Pageant master During the Middle Ages, one who supervised the mounting of mystery plays.

Peking (Beijing) opera Popular theater of China that developed in the nineteenth century.

Platform stage Elevated stage with no proscenium.

Shadow play A play performed widely in Thailand, Malaysia, and Indonesia involving intricately carved flat leather puppets that create patterns of light and shadow when their image is projected on a screen.

Vernacular drama Drama from the Middle Ages performed in the everyday speech of the people and presented in town squares or other parts of cities.

Wagon stage Low platform mounted on wheels or casters by means of which scenery is moved on- and offstage.

For more research and to learn more about the topics in this chapter, please visit the Online Learning Center at **www.mhhe.com/livelyart6.**

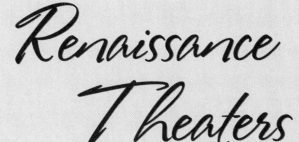

CHAPTER 15

Renaissance Theaters

◄ SHAKESPEARE: MASTER
DRAMATIST OF THE RENAISSANCE

The plays of William Shakespeare, the leading English Renaissance dramatist, continue to be immensely popular. There are frequent productions of his plays, and many have been adapted into films. Stage and film directors often set his work in a contemporary context in order to engage their audiences. Seen here is Mark Rylance as Olivia in Shakespeare's Twelfth Night. Rylance, the artistic director of the reconstructed Globe Theatre in London, decided to present the play as it was performed in Shakespeare's day, that is, with men playing all the women's parts. (© Donald Cooper/Photostage)

Renaissance is a term that means "rebirth"; it refers to an awakening of the arts and learning in the western world, which occurred during the period stretching roughly from the late fourteenth through the early seventeenth century. The center of activity was Italy, which at this time was made up of a group of independent city-states. The Renaissance was also prevalent a short time later in England, Spain, and France. During the Renaissance, theater blossomed in these countries. Before we discuss the theatrical innovations of this time period, however, let us first examine social and cultural changes.

ITALY

Background: The Renaissance Era

European politics changed markedly during the Renaissance. There was a rise of kings and princes, and merchants became key economic figures. As these people's wealth increased, they had leisure time to fill and also became eager to display their fortunes; consequently, they often hired artists to create lavish works for them.

Renaissance art is noticeably different from medieval art. During the Middle Ages, painting and sculpture had religious subjects. Renaissance artists, on the other hand, treated their subjects as human beings with whom we can identify. A good example is the statue of David by the Italian sculptor Michelangelo: the figure of David looks like a real person, not an otherworldly religious image. Painting also became more realistic through the use of oils and perspective, a technique that gives the illusion of three-dimensional depth on a flat canvas. In Renaissance literature, the major movement was *humanism,* which imitated the Greeks and Romans and focused on human beings rather than the gods. The printing press, which appeared in Europe in the 1450s, made this literature available to great numbers of people.

The Renaissance was also a period of exploration and invention. Discoveries in North and South America brought new wealth to Europe; at the same time, scientific advances revolutionized western ideas about of the position of humanity in the universe. For example, the Italian astronomer Galileo proved that the sun, not the earth, is the center of the solar system.

The Renaissance also saw remarkable developments in theater, especially in Italy, England, Spain, and France.

Italian Theater: Commedia dell'Arte

Italy, which led the way in Renaissance painting and sculpture, also saw radical transformations in its theater between 1550 and 1650. These were chiefly in improvisational theater, acting, dramatic criticism, theater architecture, and scene design. The written drama of the Italian Renaissance is less significant: much of it was modeled after Greek and Roman plays and presented at academies or at the homes of wealthy patrons, and almost none of it left a lasting mark. Two other dramatic forms that were developed in the Renaissance and were influenced by classical subject matter and dramatic techniques were intermezzi and pastorals.

ITALIAN RENAISSANCE
Year, C.E.

Theater		Culture and Politics

Death of Dante (1321)

1325

Antonio Laschis, *Achilles* (c. 1390)

Manuel Chrysoloras opens Greek classes in Florence; beginning of revival of Greek literature in Italy (1396)

1400

Cosmo de Médicis rules Florence (1432)

Founding of Platonic Academy in Florence (1440)

1425

Twelve of Plautus's lost plays rediscovered (1429)

Gutenberg invents movable type (c. 1450)

Leonardo da Vinci born (1452)

1450

Manuscripts of Greek plays brought to Italy after fall of Constantinople (1453)

Lorenzo de Médicis rules Florence (1469)

Michelangelo born (1475)

1475

Vitruvius's *De architectura* published (1486)

Birth of Venus by Botticelli (1484)

Plays by Aristophanes published by Aldine Press in Venice (1498)

Columbus discovers America; Leonardo da Vinci draws a flying machine (1492)

Ariosto's *I Suppositi* (1509)

1500

Machiavelli's comic play *Mandragola* (c. 1513)

Italian wars spread Italy's cultural influence but weaken Italy politically (1494)

Bibbiena's *La Calandria* (1513)

Leonardo da Vinci's *Mona Lisa* (1503)

Beolco begins writing and performing (c. 1520)

1525

Michelangelo's *David* (c. 1504)

Serlio's *Architettura* (6 vols.) (1545)

Sistine Chapel (c. 1512)

Peak of commedia dell'arte (1550–1650)

Machiavelli's *The Prince* (1513)

1550

First performances of I Gelosi (the Andreinis) (c. 1569)

Leonardo da Vinci dies (1519)

Castelvetro requires unities (1570)

Verrazano discovers New York Bay and Hudson River (1524)

1575

Teatro Olimpico built (1584)

Uffizi Museum at Florence founded (1560)

Sabbioneta Theater built (1588)

Galileo born; Michelangelo dies (1564)

Peri's *Dafne* (1597)

1600

I Gelosi troupe disbands upon the death of Isabella Andreini (1604)

Palladio's *I quattro libri dell'architettura* (1570)

Aleotti uses flat wing (c. 1606)

Catherine de Médicis, queen mother of France, dies (1589)

Teatro Farnese built (1618)

1625

Sabbatini's *Manual for Constructing Theatrical Scenes and Machines* (1638)

Mannerism begins to appear in Italy (1600)

Galileo dies (1642)

Torelli's pole-and-chariot system (c. 1645)

1650

Intermezzi were short pieces depicting mythological tales; they were presented between the acts of full-length plays and were often thematically related to the full-length works they accompanied. Intermezzi often required spectacular scenic effects. Although popular in the 1500s, this form disappeared in the 1600s.

The Italians also imitated Greek satyr plays—short, ribald comic pieces that had been presented as a follow-up to Greek tragedies—in a form they called a *pastoral.* The subject matter of a Renaissance pastoral is romance; the characters are usually shepherds and mythological creatures. Unlike Greek satyr plays, the Italian pastorals were not overtly bawdy or sexual. These pastorals usually deal with lovers who are threatened and often at odds with each other; while the action is serious, the endings are happy.

Opera, of course, is of great significance: it was invented during the Italian Renaissance by people who believed they were re-creating the Greek tragic style, which had fused music with drama; and in fact it is the only Italian Renaissance theatrical form that has survived. However, opera is usually considered a part of music because the *libretto*—its text—is often secondary to the music.

If, however, the Italian Renaissance is not distinguished for its written drama, it did originate an important and immensely popular form of improvisational theater, closely related to many of our popular performance forms today. This was *commedia dell'arte*—"comedy of professional artists." Commedia dell'arte flourished in Italy from 1550 to 1750.

In commedia, performers had no set text; they invented words and actions as they went along. *Scenarios*—short plot outlines without dialogue—were written by company members.

Commedia companies, usually consisting of 10 performers (seven men and three women), were traveling troupes; the most successful companies were often organized by families. Commedia companies were adaptable: they could perform in town squares, in theater spaces, in the homes of wealthy merchants, or at court.

Commedia performers played the same stock characters throughout most of their careers. Among the popular comic personages were a lecherous, miserly old Venetian man, Pantalone; a foolish scholar, Dottore; a cowardly, braggart soldier, Capitano; and sometimes foolish servants known as *zanni,* of whom Arlecchino, or Harlequin, was the most popular. Commedia scenarios also included serious young lovers. All commedia characters used standard *lazzi*—repeated bits of comic business, usually physical, and sometimes bawdy and obscene.

Commedia characters wore traditional costumes, such as Harlequin's patchwork jacket and Dottore's academic robes. A significant addition to Harlequin's costume was the *slapstick,* a wooden sword used in comic fight scenes; today, we still use the term *slapstick* for comedies emphasizing physical horseplay. Masks, usually covering part of the face, were a significant element of commedia costumes. The young lovers, however, did not wear masks.

Italian Dramatic Rules: The Neoclassical Ideals

In terms of drama, critics rather than playwrights proved influential in the Italian Renaissance. Italian critics formulated dramatic rules—known as the *neoclassi-*

STOCK CHARACTERS

Comedy in particular features stock or stereotypical characters who have clearly identifiable traits, gestures, styles of dress, and qualities. This was particularly true in Italian commedia dell'arte. Certain characters always had the same traits, which identified them, such as a pompous professor, a charlatan doctor, or a clever servant. A favorite of commedia, the servant Harlequin, is shown here, seated, wearing the patchwork costume that identifies him. On either side are other stock characters from commedia, in a painting of a scene from "Le tombeau de Maître André." (© Erich Lessing/Art Resource, N.Y.)

cal ideals—which were to dominate dramatic theory through much of Europe for nearly 200 years.

One overriding concern of the neoclassicists was *verisimilitude,* by which they meant that drama should be "true to life." Their verisimilitude, however, was not the kind of realism we find in modern drama. Though the neoclassicists insisted that these be recognizable and verifiable from real life, nevertheless they permitted stock dramatic situations and stock characters.

Another concern of the neoclassicists—in fact, their most famous mandate—was their insistence on three **unities:** unity of *time,* of *place,* and of *action.* The unities grew out of the desire for verisimilitude. Unity of time required that the dramatic action in a play should not exceed 24 hours. Unity of place restricted the action of a play to one locale. Unity of action required that there be only one central story, involving a relatively small group of characters; this meant that there could be no subplots. The three unities are often mistakenly attributed to Aristotle, though in fact he had suggested only one unity: the unity of action.

Commedia dell'Arte

1500s, Rome The time is the late 1500s; the place is a town square in Rome. Set up in the square is a wooden platform stage with a backdrop at the rear. This backdrop, or curtain, not only forms the scenic background of the action on the platform but also provides a hidden space in which the performers can adjust their costumes and from which they can make their entrances and exits.

A crowd is beginning to gather, and people are trying to get the best position to see the performance that is about to begin. In front of the stage, people are already standing several rows deep; at the sides the audience members push closer, but they won't be facing the stage directly. As the spectators look around, they can see that the audience represents a cross section of Roman citizens.

There is great anticipation in the air, because the performers are members of one of the best-known theater companies in Italy —a troupe called I Gelosi, led by Francesco and Isabella Andreini. The 10 members of the company have perfected commedia dell'arte, a form of improvisational comedy that has become the most popular type of theater in Italy.

Commedia is different from many other kinds of theater. There is no script in the usual sense. There is an outline of the action— the characters portrayed in a scene, what happens, how the scene develops—but the dialogue is not written out. The lines the characters speak are not provided.

The performers, therefore, improvise their speeches—that is, they make the dialogue up as they go along. This, plus the fact that the movements also are improvised, adds a great air of immediacy to the production. It is most challenging to the performers, and this makes the presentation all the more exciting for those now assembled to watch.

Soon the performance is under way, and the fun begins. The story is partly about an actress who is pursued by every man—unmarried or married—in town, and partly about the adulterous intrigues of her pursuers' wives. There are insults, cases of mistaken identity, and plans gone wrong, and people's misbehavior is exposed.

The characters are stock figures: an old Venetian merchant, a foolish pedant, a cowardly braggart soldier, comic servants, and young lovers. All the characters except the lovers wear masks, most of which are half masks covering the upper part of the face. Each character wears a costume that makes him or her easily recognizable: the pedant, for instance, wears academic robes; the captain wears a uniform; the young lovers are fashionably dressed. One source of great pleasure in watching the performance is seeing these pompous, self-important characters get their comeuppance during the course of the action.

The servants are a special delight. They are known as *zanni* and are usually of two types. The first, called Buffetto and various other

names, is a clever, domineering intriguer who motivates the plot through various schemes. The other, even better known, is Arlecchino, or Harlequin. He wears a patchwork outfit of many colors, is given to pratfalls, and is often the victim of knockdown physical humor. Frequently, the servants outwit their masters and help the young lovers get together.

One plot twist operates around the notion that older characters attempt to thwart the desires of the young lovers, and it is only at the conclusion that the lovers achieve their objective.

The spectators crowded around the platform, knowing that the performers are improvising, are amazed at how quick on their feet the performers are and how readily they respond to the dialogue thrown at them.

The interaction of the performers is very physical. In one scene, a master beats a servant with a stick, which is hinged with a flap to make an exaggerated sound when it hits the servant's backside. In another scene, a soldier challenges a lover to a duel and becomes hopelessly entangled with his own sword; at times his sword sticks out from between his legs, taking on a sexual connotation. The more entangled he becomes, the louder the audience laughs.

At the end of the play, as they make their way home, audience members talk among themselves, sometimes laughing out loud as they recall highlights of the performance.

TEATRO OLIMPICO

Completed in 1584, the Teatro Olimpico in Vicenza, Italy, is the oldest surviving theater from the Renaissance. The stage attempted to duplicate the facade of the Roman scene house and had five alleyways leading off it. Down each alleyway, small models of buildings were created to give the illusion of disappearing perspective. This photo shows the ornate facade, a holdover from Roman theaters, with the five alleyways, two on each side of the central alleyway. (© Dennis Marsico/Corbis)

The neoclassicists interpreted genre very narrowly. For many of them, tragedy dealt with royalty, comedy with common people; tragedy must end sadly and comedy happily; and the two genres must never be mixed.

The function of all drama, the neoclassic critics insisted, was to teach moral lessons. Also, they held, characters must be morally acceptable to the audience.

There were numerous other rules. Onstage violence was forbidden, for instance; and the neoclassicists banished the chorus and supernatural characters. They were also opposed to the *soliloquy*—a monologue through which a character reveals thoughts by speaking them aloud.

While there were significant differences among the various Italian critics, they were all highly *prescriptive,* telling authors how to write in order to create great drama. The rules of the neoclassical critics were to have particular influence on playwrights in France during the seventeenth century.

Theater Production in Italy

Another significant contribution of the Italian Renaissance was made by architects who revolutionized theater construction. Two buildings in particular illustrate the gradual development of Italian theater architecture, and fortunately both are still standing.

The oldest surviving theater built during the Italian Renaissance—the Teatro Olimpico in Vicenza, completed in 1584—was designed as a miniature indoor Roman theater. Its auditorium, accommodating approximately 3,000 spectators, had curved benches connected to the *scaena,* or stage house; this arrangement

TEATRO FARNESE

created a semicircular *orchestra*. There was a raised stage, about 70 feet wide by 18 feet deep, in front of the scaena. The ornate facade of the scene house, patterned after the Roman scaena frons, was designed to look like a street. There were five openings in the facade—three in the back wall and one on each side. Behind each opening was an alleyway or street scene that seemed to disappear in the distance. To achieve an effect of depth, in each alleyway there were three-dimensional buildings—houses and shops—which decreased in size as they were positioned farther and farther away from the opening onstage.

The most renowned theater building of the Italian Renaissance was the Teatro Farnese in Parma, completed in 1618. The Farnese had a typical court, or academic, theater auditorium, with raised horseshoe seating that accommodated about 3,500 spectators. What was revolutionary in the Teatro Farnese was its *proscenium-arch* stage. Despite the term *arch*, a proscenium opening is usually a rectangular frame. Realistic scenery can be placed much more effectively behind such a frame than in any other type of theater; thus the proscenium arch, along with Renaissance innovations in scene design, became an impetus for greater theatrical realism. (See Chapter 9 for a fuller discussion of the proscenium-arch theater.)

When we move from the stage to the auditorium, we find that the major changes occurred in the public opera houses of Venice. These were proscenium-arch houses, but—unlike court or academy theaters—they were commercial ventures that needed as many paying customers as possible; thus they required a larger audience area. Opera houses were therefore designed with "pit, boxes, and galleries," which had already been used in France, England, and Spain. It was their combination of a "pit, box, and gallery" auditorium with a proscenium-arch stage that made the Venetian opera houses innovative. This kind of

proscenium-arch theater with pit, box, and gallery seating would later become the standard theater space throughout the western world and would remain so for over 300 years.

The *pit,* in which audience members stood, was an open area on the house floor extending to the side and back walls. Built into the walls were tiers of seating. The lower tiers were usually the most expensive; they were divided into separate private *boxes* and were frequented by the upper classes. The upper tiers, which were called *galleries,* had open bench seating. The pit—a raucous area where the spectators ate, talked, and moved around—and the galleries were the least expensive accommodations.

Advances in scene design during the Italian Renaissance were no less impressive than architectural innovations. *Perspective* drawing, which creates an illusion of depth and which had become an important feature of Renaissance art, was introduced into theater.

The earliest painted-perspective scenery was clumsy and not easy to shift; as a result, by the early 1600s flat wings were used to create painted-perspective settings. In this arrangement, a series of individual wings on each side of the stage, parallel to the audience, were placed in a progression from the front to the back of the stage and enclosed at the very back by two shutters that met in the middle. The final element in these perspective settings was provided by overhead borders —strips across the top of the stage that completed the picture.

The method of scene shifting used with settings of this kind is often referred to as the *groove system* because the wings and shutters were placed in parallel grooves on and above the stage floor. The major problem with this system was coordinating the removal of the flat wings by scene shifters at each groove position. This problem was solved with an innovative scene-changing system

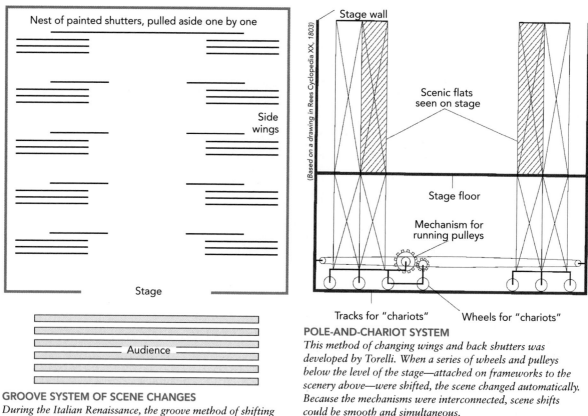

Nest of painted shutters, pulled aside one by one

Side wings

Stage

Audience

(Based on a drawing in Rees Cyclopedia XX, 1803)

Stage wall

Scenic flats seen on stage

Stage floor

Mechanism for running pulleys

Tracks for "chariots"   Wheels for "chariots"

GROOVE SYSTEM OF SCENE CHANGES

During the Italian Renaissance, the groove method of shifting scenery was perfected. Along the sides of the stage, in parallel lines, scenery was set in sections. At the back, two shutters met in the middle. Together, these pieces formed a complete stage picture. When one set of side wings and back shutters was pulled aside, a different stage picture was revealed.

POLE-AND-CHARIOT SYSTEM

This method of changing wings and back shutters was developed by Torelli. When a series of wheels and pulleys below the level of the stage—attached on frameworks to the scenery above—were shifted, the scene changed automatically. Because the mechanisms were interconnected, scene shifts could be smooth and simultaneous.

developed by Giacomo Torelli (1608–1678) and known as the ***pole-and-chariot*** system. Poles attached to the flats continued below the stage floor, where they were connected to wheels ("chariots") in tracks. In this way, the flats could be moved offstage smoothly; by connecting a series of ropes and pulleys, the entire set could be removed by turning a single winch. The pole-and-chariot system was adopted and used throughout much of the world for over two centuries.

ENGLAND

Background: Elizabethan England

The English Renaissance is often called the *Elizabethan* period, because its major political figure was Elizabeth I, who reigned during the 45 years from 1558 to 1603. Throughout the English Renaissance, explorations abroad were undertaken, and language and literature flourished. The English were intrigued by language—Queen Elizabeth herself was an amateur linguist—and at the heart of the English Renaissance in literature and the arts was theater.

Elizabethan Drama

Christopher Marlowe and the "Mighty Line". One of the most important of the Elizabethan playwrights was Christopher Marlowe (1564–1593), who advanced the art of dramatic structure and contributed a gallery of interesting characters to English drama; he also perfected another element that was to prove central to later Elizabethan plays: dramatic poetry. Critics speak of Marlowe's "mighty line," by which they mean the power of his dramatic verse. The meter of this verse is iambic pentameter, which has five beats to a line, with two syllables to each beat and the accent on the second beat. In Marlowe's hands, dramatic verse in iambic pentameter developed strength, subtlety, and suppleness, as well as great lyric beauty.

Marlowe wrote several important plays, including *Doctor Faustus* (c. 1588), *Tamburlaine* (Parts 1 and 2; c. 1587), and *Edward II* (c. 1592), but his promising career as a dramatist was unfortunately cut short when he was stabbed to death in a tavern brawl in 1593 at the age of 29.

William Shakespeare: A Playwright for the Ages. William Shakespeare (1564–1616) appeared on the theater scene around 1590, just after Marlowe had made his debut. Shakespeare was a native of Stratford-upon-Avon (a town about 85 miles northwest of London); his father was a prosperous glove maker and town alderman, and his mother—Mary Arden—was the daughter of a prominent landowner and farmer. Shakespeare was educated in Stratford; he then married Anne Hathaway, who was several years older than he and who bore him three children.

TWO PLAYWRIGHTS OF THE ELIZABETHAN ERA *Christopher Marlowe (left) and William Shakespeare (right) are the most renowned playwrights of an era that produced many great dramatists.* (Marlowe: Hulton Deutsch Collection Ltd. Shakespeare: Victoria and Albert Museum, London)

ENGLISH RENAISSANCE
Year, c.e.

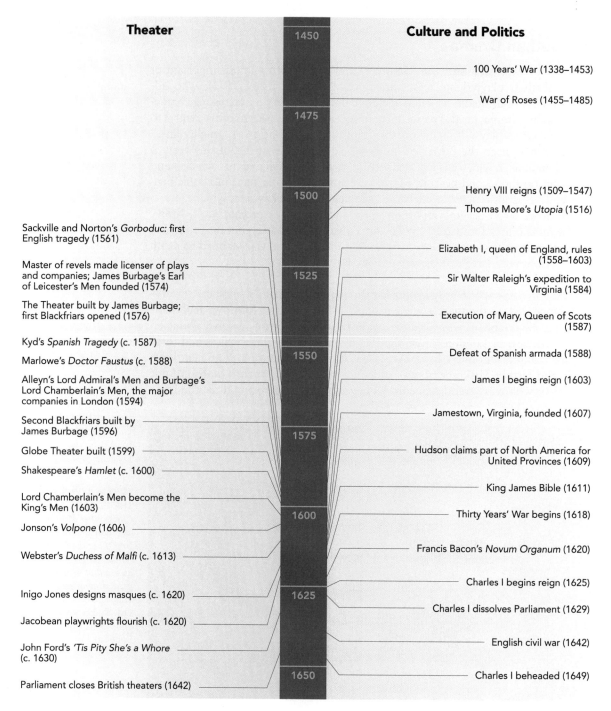

Theater

Culture and Politics

1450

100 Years' War (1338–1453)

War of Roses (1455–1485)

1475

1500

Henry VIII reigns (1509–1547)

Thomas More's *Utopia* (1516)

Sackville and Norton's *Gorboduc:* first English tragedy (1561)

Elizabeth I, queen of England, rules (1558–1603)

Master of revels made licenser of plays and companies; James Burbage's Earl of Leicester's Men founded (1574)

1525

Sir Walter Raleigh's expedition to Virginia (1584)

The Theater built by James Burbage; first Blackfriars opened (1576)

Execution of Mary, Queen of Scots (1587)

Kyd's *Spanish Tragedy* (c. 1587)

Marlowe's *Doctor Faustus* (c. 1588)

1550

Defeat of Spanish armada (1588)

Alleyn's Lord Admiral's Men and Burbage's Lord Chamberlain's Men, the major companies in London (1594)

James I begins reign (1603)

Second Blackfriars built by James Burbage (1596)

Jamestown, Virginia, founded (1607)

Globe Theater built (1599)

1575

Hudson claims part of North America for United Provinces (1609)

Shakespeare's *Hamlet* (c. 1600)

Lord Chamberlain's Men become the King's Men (1603)

King James Bible (1611)

1600

Thirty Years' War begins (1618)

Jonson's *Volpone* (1606)

Webster's *Duchess of Malfi* (c. 1613)

Francis Bacon's *Novum Organum* (1620)

Charles I begins reign (1625)

Inigo Jones designs masques (c. 1620)

1625

Charles I dissolves Parliament (1629)

Jacobean playwrights flourish (c. 1620)

John Ford's *'Tis Pity She's a Whore* (c. 1630)

English civil war (1642)

1650

Charles I beheaded (1649)

Parliament closes British theaters (1642)

At some point after the third child was born, Shakespeare left his family and went to London, where he worked first as an actor and shortly after that as a playwright. As a dramatist, he worked with elements that had been established in early Elizabethan drama—Senecan dramatic devices; the platform stage; powerful dramatic verse; source material from English history, Roman history and drama, and Italian literature; and the episodic plot structure that had its roots in medieval theater. He fused these elements into one of the most impressive bodies of plays ever created.

Shakespeare was an expert in many aspects of theater. As an actor and a member of a dramatic company, the Lord Chamberlain's Men (which was London's leading troupe), he understood the technical and business elements of theater. As a writer, he excelled in several genres, including tragedy, comedy, and history. His tragedies include *Romeo and Juliet* (1595), *Julius Caesar* (1599), *Hamlet* (1601), *Othello* (1604), *Macbeth* (1605–1606), and *King Lear* (1605–1606). His comedies include *The Comedy of Errors* (1592), *A Midsummer Night's Dream* (1595), *As You Like It* (1599), and *Twelfth Night* (1601). Among his well-known histories are *Richard III* (1592–1593); *Henry IV, Parts 1 and 2* (1597–1598); and *Henry V* (1599).

His verse, especially the power of his metaphors and the music of his language, is extraordinary; and his characters are so well-rounded and carefully detailed that they often seem like living people. He was also a master of plot construction, notably episodic plot structure—which, as we have seen, stands alongside climactic

SHAKESPEARE'S PLAYS
Shakespeare's plays have given us many memorable characters. One of his most popular comic creations is Falstaff, a bumbling, egotistical drunkard with a heart of gold. Seen here is a scene from a production of The Merry Wives of Windsor *at the Utah Shakespearean Festival in 2000. Dennis Robertson is Sir John Falstaff and Libby George is Mistress Quickly.* (© Utah Shakespearean Festival. Photo by Karl Hugh)

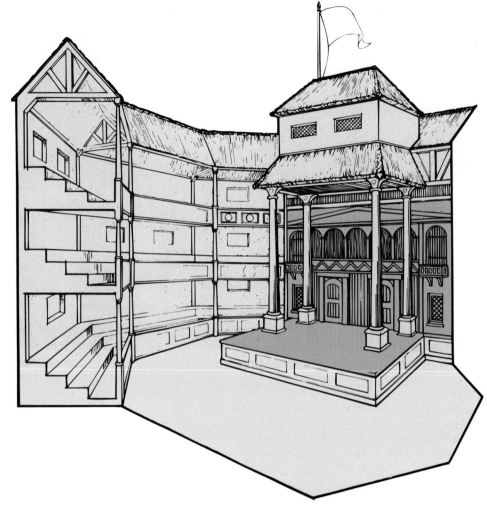

AN ELIZABETHAN PLAYHOUSE
This drawing shows the kind of stage on which the plays of Shakespeare and his contemporaries were first presented. A platform stage juts into an open courtyard, with spectators standing on three sides. Three levels of enclosed seats rise above the courtyard. There are doors at the rear of the stage for entrances and exits and an upper level for balcony scenes.

structure as one of the two main forms that have been predominant throughout the history of western theater.

The Globe Theater, where his plays were produced, burned in 1613; after that, Shakespeare retired to Stratford and became one of its leading citizens. He died three years later.

Elizabethan Theater Production

Public or Outdoor Theaters. The plays of Shakespeare, Marlowe, and their contemporaries were performed primarily in *public theaters*. Between the 1560s

Hamlet

1600, London It is early afternoon on a day around the year 1600. In London, England, people from many parts of the city are gathering along the north bank of the Thames River to be carried by boat across to its south bank. There is a special excitement in the air because most of those crossing the Thames are headed for the Globe Theater, to see the first public performance of a new play by William Shakespeare called *Hamlet.*

The Globe is one of the newest and finest playhouses serving London. The reason it is on the other side of the Thames, outside city limits, is that officials in London have forbidden theatrical performances inside the city. The first permanent theaters in England have been built to the north of London or across the Thames to the south, outside the jurisdiction of city officials.

When the spectators arrive at the theater—well over 2,000 people all together—they can pay a penny at the main door to get in, or they can use another entrance for the more expensive accommodations. Those who use the main door move into a central courtyard, open to the sky, where they will stand during the performance around three sides of a platform stage at one end of the courtyard. Those who can afford to pay more enter one of three levels of covered gallery seats surrounding the stage and courtyard on three sides.

By paying even more, the nobility can sit on cushioned seats in boxes next to the stage. Food and drink —apples, nuts, water, ale—are being sold throughout the playhouse.

As the audience gathers, there is a great deal of conversation about the play. Some audience members already know something about *Hamlet;* they are familiar with earlier versions of the story, and they know that *Hamlet* will be a revenge play—one of their favorite types of drama. There is keen interest, too, because *Hamlet* is by William Shakespeare, a favorite playwright; and its star is Richard Burbage, who is considered by many people the finest actor in England.

At two o'clock, the play begins. Two sentinels standing watch on the parapet of a castle appear onstage, soon to be joined by Horatio, a friend of Hamlet's; the three men discuss a ghost that has been appearing every night. All of a sudden, the ghost is there: it is the ghost of Hamlet's father, and it is played by Shakespeare himself, who is also an actor with the company. Horatio and the sentinels are frightened; the ghost stays briefly and then disappears.

The scene shifts to the interior of the castle: King Claudius enters. He is the brother of Hamlet's father, the dead king, and he has married Hamlet's mother, Queen Gertrude. Onstage, too, are the other principals of the play, includ-

ing Hamlet, who is dressed in black and stands apart from the others.

The action of the play is full of twists and turns. In the next scene, Hamlet himself sees the ghost of his father, who says that Hamlet must avenge his murder at the hands of his brother, Claudius. Hamlet later has a group of strolling players present a drama which proves that Claudius did murder Hamlet's father. In a later scene, Hamlet thrusts his sword through a curtain in his mother's bedroom, thinking that Claudius is hiding behind it, but the person concealed there turns out to be someone else.

As the plot continues to unfold, the audience is enthralled—all the way to the end, when almost everyone is killed: Hamlet and Laertes in a duel, Gertrude by poisoning, Claudius by stabbing. Throughout the play, the audience enjoys not only the action and suspense but also the memorable lines and speeches. Several times Hamlet stands alone onstage delivering a soliloquy.

On the way back across the Thames, after the play is over, and all evening, the audience members will continue to discuss *Hamlet.* They would like to see it again because there is more to it than they were able to take in at one viewing; they want to live through it once more to feel the thrill of the action and to sort out their thoughts about what it means.

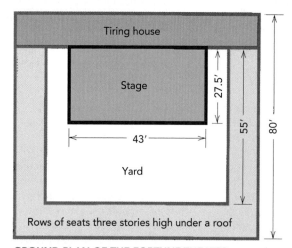

Tiring house

Stage

27.5'

43'

Yard

55'

80'

Rows of seats three stories high under a roof

GROUND PLAN OF THE FORTUNE THEATER

The only English Renaissance theater for which we have a number of specific dimensions is the Fortune. From the builder's contract we know the size of the stage, the standing pit, the audience seating area, and the theater building itself. The building was square; the backstage area ran along one side; the stage was rectangular; and the audience—both standing and sitting—was on three sides.

and 1642, at least nine open-air public theaters were built just outside the city of London. The reason for their being located just outside the city limits was to avoid government restrictions. All levels of society attended productions at the public theaters. The most famous public theater was the Globe, because it was the home of Shakespeare's plays.

In recent years, sections of the foundations of the Globe and another theater, the Rose, have been rediscovered and excavated. Also, a replica of the original Globe was erected near the site of the original theater. It opened for performances in 1997.

The stage of a public theater—a raised platform surrounded on three sides by the audience—was closer to a contemporary thrust stage than to a proscenium stage. This platform stage was a neutral playing area that could become many different places in quick succession: a room in a palace, a bedroom, a street, a battlefield. When one group of characters left the stage and another group entered, this generally signaled a change of scene. Sometimes the characters announced where they were; at other times, the location was apparent from the action.

In the stage floor were trapdoors. Behind the raised platform was the stage house, known as the *tiring house.* This three-story building served as a place for changing costumes as well as for storing properties and set pieces. The stage house was also the basic scenic piece in an Elizabethan public theater.

There is a great deal of debate over the configuration of the tiring house, but it is usually argued that the first level had two doorways, one on each side; and that entrances and exits through these doors indicated scene changes. For plays with scenes in which characters were concealed, there was probably an inner stage on the first level, either as part of the tiring house or within a freestanding structure. If such a special area did not exist, possibly one of the doors provided a place for concealment.

Another feature of the Elizabethan playhouse was an upper playing area for balcony scenes. No one knows for certain what the upper playing area looked like, but it might have been an inner area on the second level of the tiring house or part of a freestanding structure at the rear of the stage. The third level of the stage house, referred to as the *musicians' gallery,* probably housed the musicians who provided accompaniment for the plays. A roof, which protected the stage, extended out from the stage house. In some theaters it was supported by pillars; in others, it was suspended from the back. A flag was flown from the top of the stage house on days when a performance was taking place.

The exact shape of public theaters varied. It is estimated that their audience capacity was between 1,500 and 3,000—the larger number is now more widely accepted. Spectators were accommodated in the *yard, boxes,* and *galleries.* On the ground floor, in front of and on the sides of the stage, was the standing area, known as the *yard,* the front half of which sloped from the back to the stage. The lower-class audience members who stood in the yard were known as *groundlings.* The galleries were usually three tiers of seating ranged on three sides around the stage. One tier was divided into boxes, known as *lords' rooms* because they were frequented by the wealthy; the undivided tiers were equipped with bench seating. Spectators—even those at the back wall of the galleries—were never very far from the actors.

Private Theaters. Elizabethan *private theaters* were indoor spaces, lit by candles and high windows. The term *private* in this context often causes confusion, because today it would imply that certain classes were excluded. In Elizabethan England, however, private theaters were open to the general public, though they were usually smaller (seating about 600 to 750 spectators) and therefore more expensive than public theaters.

The pit of a private theater, which faced the stage in only one direction, had backless benches. The platform stage extended to the side walls, with galleries and boxes facing the stage on three sides.

Scenery and Costumes in Elizabethan Theaters. The Elizabethans did not use painted scenery in their public or private theaters, and the stage space did not represent a specific locale. Instead, the extensive, episodic nature of Elizabethan drama required scenes to be changed rapidly. Sometimes actors coming onstage would bring out minimal properties, such as a throne, to suggest a locale.

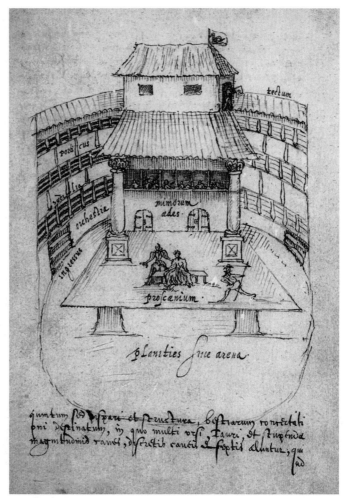

THE SWAN THEATER
This drawing of an Elizabethan playhouse is a copy of a sketch made by a Dutch visitor to London in 1596. While the sketch shows the platform stage, tiring house, and galleries, controversial questions remain. Is the sketch complete? If so, where is the space for concealed characters? Who are the people in the "gallery"? Is this a rehearsal or a performance? (University Library, Utrecht)

Costuming followed the conventions and traditions of medieval English theater. While their dramas exhibit a great deal of historical and geographical variety, the Elizabethans were not overly concerned with accuracy; most costumes were simply contemporary clothing, reflective of the social classes being depicted.

English Actors and Acting Companies. Throughout the English Renaissance, the monarchy exerted considerable legal control over theater, and the number of acting companies was restricted by law.

JACOBEAN DRAMA

Following Shakespeare and other Elizabethan dramatists, the dramatists in the period of James I (1603–1625) wrote more melodramatic tragedies. A good example is The White Devil *by John Webster, a revenge tragedy filled with intrigue and bloody retribution. Seen here in a production from the Sydney Theatre Company of Australia are Marcus Graham and Angie Milliken.* (© Richard Termine)

Elizabethan acting companies—each of which had approximately twenty-five members—were organized on a *sharing plan.* There were three categories of personnel in a company: *shareholders, hirelings,* and *apprentices.* Shareholders, the elite members of the company, received a percentage of the troupe's profits as payment. Hirelings were actors contracted for a specific period of time and for a specific salary, and they usually played minor roles. Apprentices—young performers training for the profession—were assigned to shareholders. There were no female performers; women's roles were played by boys. Since the plays had many characters, doubling of roles was common.

What style of acting was used by the Elizabethans continues to be debated, particularly how "realistic" it was—that is, how close to the speech and gestures of everyday life. Many of the conventions of the period, such as dramatic verse, seem to suggest a departure from realistic style.

An English company would rarely perform the same play on two consecutive days, and each company had to be able to revive plays in its repertoire on very short notice. Thus the primary concern was not so much a carefully realized production as expert delivery of lines. Actors were provided with *sides,* which contained only their own lines and cues rather than the full script, and improvisation must have been used frequently. *Plots*—outlines of the dramatic action of the various plays—were posted backstage so that performers could refresh their memories during performances. Rehearsals were run by playwrights or leading actors; and since rehearsal time was minimal, the prompter (who stood just offstage) became an indispensable part of the productions.

Theater after Elizabeth's Reign

After Elizabeth I died in 1603, the great Elizabethan dramatists, including Shakespeare and Ben Jonson (1572–1637), continued to write plays. Ben Jonson's comic masterpiece *Volpone,* for example, was staged in 1606. In contrast to Shakespeare, Jonson championed a more literary approach to drama.

James I succeeded Elizabeth; his reign is known as the *Jacobean* period. *The Duchess of Malfi* (c. 1613–1614), by John Webster (c. 1580–c. 1630), is probably the most renowned Jacobean tragedy. These later tragedies were usually very melodramatic and emphasized violence and spectacle.

Another development in English drama in the early 1600s was a mixing of serious and comic elements. Such plays generally had many of the qualities of tragedy but ended happily. Francis Beaumont (c. 1584–1616) and John Fletcher (1579–1625), two playwrights who often collaborated with each other, excelled at this form.

An elaborate type of entertainment featured at court during the reign of James I and his successor Charles I, and not found in either public or private theaters, was the *masque.* Masques were ornate, professionally staged, mythological allegories intended to praise the monarch; they were embellished by music and dance, and they frequently used amateur performers from the court. In the first decade of the seventeenth century, Inigo Jones (1573–1652), a designer who had studied in Italy, began to introduce the Italian style of theater architecture and scene design into English court masques.

James I was succeeded by Charles I in 1625. Though Charles I was not deposed—and beheaded—until 1649, the English Renaissance ended in 1642. By then, a civil war had begun between supporters of Charles I and the Puritan-backed Parliament. The Puritans were vehemently opposed to theater; they believed that playgoing was an inappropriate way to spend one's leisure time and that theater was a den of iniquity, teaching immorality. In 1642, the Puritans outlawed all theatrical activity.

THE SPANISH GOLDEN AGE
The two major playwrights of the Spanish golden age were Calderón de la Barca and Lope de Vega. It was a period—partly coinciding with the Elizabethan era in England—in which theater flourished in Spain. Here, Joaquin Notario appears in La Vida Es Sueño (Life Is a Dream) *by Calderón de la Barca, in a production by the Compañia Nacional de Teatro Clásico of Almagro, Spain.* (Ros Ribas)

SPAIN

Background: The Spanish Golden Age

The period from about 1550 to 1650 is known as the Spanish golden age. During this rich period, Spain, which had a formidable navy, became a leading world power, primarily because of its exploration and conquest of the new world. Spain also remained a devoutly Catholic nation in the face of the Protestant Reformation,

Making Connections

The Popular Arts of Shakespeare's Time

When we review the history of English Renaissance theater, we often forget that Shakespeare and his contemporaries had to battle with the popular arts for London's audiences. Two of the most popular were bearbaiting and cockfighting.

Bearbaiting consisted of a bear being chained in the middle of an arena and then attacked by trained mastiff dogs. Points were scored depending on where the dogs struck the bear. The entertainment was probably developed out of the Roman animal entertainments and the tradition of baiting bulls during the Middle Ages.

In the 1500s, bearbaiting became a commercial entertainment in London. Up until 1574, there were two baiting rings in that city. During Shakespeare's time, there was one extremely popular arena: the Bear Garden. The Bear Garden was allowed to present bearbaiting on Sundays, when the theaters were closed. Sunday attendance was so great that in 1583, parts of the building collapsed because of the large number of spectators.

Shakespeare comments on the popularity and theatricality of bearbaiting in his comedy *The Merry Wives of Windsor* (1600). The comedic character Slender comments about how much he loves the sport of bearbaiting and the audience's admiration for the great bear Sackerson:

> I love the sport well, but I shall as soon quarrel at it as any man in England. You are afraid if you see the bear loose, are you not? . . . I have seen Sackerson loose twenty times, and have taken him by the chain; but I warrant you, the women have so cried

POPULAR ARTS IN SHAKESPEARE'S TIME
Bearbaiting was a popular entertainment during Shakespeare's lifetime. Arenas were constructed for this form of entertainment, in which bears were attacked by trained dogs. Remarkably, bearbaiting continued to attract audiences in the early nineteenth century. Shown here is an illustration of bearbaiting in Westminster, London, in the 1820s. (© Hulton-Deutsch Collection/Corbis)

and shrieked at it, that it passed.

This form of entertainment remained popular through the English Restoration and was not made illegal until 1835.

The Cockpit, also known as the Phoenix, was opened in 1609 as an indoor space to house cockfights, another animal entertainment. Spectators would watch and bet on cocks, which were trained to fight with each other. The Cockpit became one of the best-known private, or indoor, theaters in the late English Renaissance after it was remodeled in 1616.

The popularity of cockfighting continued into the eighteenth-century English world. For that matter, the sport was popular in the early American colonies. George Washington, in his diaries, comments on attending cockfights in the new world.

Given the great competition for audiences, it is clear that the stage fights, violence, and slapstick comedy that abound in English Renaissance drama were techniques used to combat the popularity of these other forms of entertainment.

which had swept much of the rest of Europe. In order to keep Spain Catholic, the church instituted the Inquisition, a type of court that punished any seeming religious heresy. During this period a popular theater, which incorporated both religious and popular secular forms, flourished.

Spanish Drama

Spain was one of England's chief rivals in the late sixteenth century and the early seventeenth. At the same time that the two nations competed with each other, there were many similarities in their theaters. One important difference, however, is that the Spaniards—unlike the English—adopted the techniques of medieval religious drama and continued to produce religious dramas throughout their golden age and beyond: until 1765, in fact.

Secular drama, which flourished between 1550 and 1700, developed in Spain side by side with religious drama and was created by the same artists. Full-length secular plays, known as *comedias,* usually dealt with themes of love and honor; the leading characters were often minor members of the nobility. Comedias were written in three acts, and like English Renaissance plays, they were extensive or episodic in form. Comedias mix serious and comic subject matter and are very similar to modern melodrama. Thus if Spanish plays of the golden age are very close to Elizabethan drama in their dramatic form, they seem closer in their subject matter to the swashbuckling films of the 1940s, to romantic novels, and to television soap operas.

Besides full-length plays, the Spaniards developed many popular, short, farcical forms. A short farce of this kind would be presented on the same program with a comedia.

The major playwrights of this period were Lope de Vega (1562–1635) and Calderón de la Barca (1600–1681). Lope de Vega was born within a year of Shakespeare and was a remarkable playwright—one of the most prolific dramatists of all time. He is said to have written 1,500 plays (although 800 is a more realistic figure); 470 of them survive, one of the best-known being *The Sheep Well* (c. 1614). One of Calderón's most famous plays is *Life Is a Dream* (c. 1636).

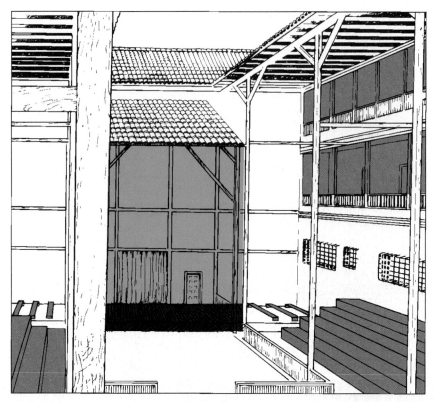

A SPANISH CORRAL

This drawing is based on John J. Allen's research on the corral del Principe in Madrid. Note the various elements of the corral: the yard (patio), the seating areas (boxes and galleries), and the platform stage with the tiring house behind it. Note also that in front of the yard there were benches or stools and that seats are set up at the side of stage. In addition, notice how similar the face of the building behind the stage was to the facade of the Elizabethan tiring house.

There were also a number of female playwrights in Spain during the seventeenth century, though most of their works were not produced. However, recent scholarship has shown that these women wrote texts subverting many of the traditions of the comedias and calling into question the traditional views of gender roles, love and honor, and political authority. Female playwrights of the Spanish golden age whose works have gained significant scholarly attention are Angela de Azevedo, Ana Caro Mallén de Soto, Leonor de la Cueva y Silva, Feliciana Enríquez de Guzmán, María de Zayas y Sotomayor, and Sor Juana Inés de la Cruz.

Theater Production in Spain

The Corrales.   Nonreligious plays by writers like Lope de Vega and Calderón were staged in public theaters known as *corrales* (the plural of *corral*). Corrales were constructed in existing courtyards; like Elizabethan public theaters, they were open-air spaces with galleries and boxes protected by a roof. These courtyard theaters were

SPANISH GOLDEN AGE
Year, C.E.

Theater		Culture and Politics
		Spain united under Ferdinand and Isabella (1469)
	1475	Inquisition established in Spain (1481)
		Jews expelled from Spain; Columbus discovers America; conquest of Granada (1492)
Juan del Encina's *The Eclogue of Placida and Victoriana* (1513)	**1500**	Cortés conquers Aztecs (1519)
		Pizzaro takes Peru (1530)
Bartolomé de Torres Naharro's *Propalladia* (1517)		Opening of Potosí mines in Bolivia (1545)
Lope de Rueda, Spain's first popular playwright (c. 1545)	**1525**	Jesuits begin missionary work in South America (1549)
		Felipe II (rules 1556–1598)
City councils assume responsibilities for the staging of autos (c. 1555)	**1550**	Netherlands revolt against Spain (1567)
Corral de la Cruz, first permanent theater in Spain (1579)		Victory against Turks at Lepanto (1571)
		El Greco arrives from Greece (1575)
Corral del Principe (1583)	**1575**	Felipe II annexes Portugal (1580)
Women licensed to appear onstage (c. 1587)		Defeat of Spanish armada (1588)
		Felipe III (rules 1598–1621)
Strict censorship of plays (1608)	**1600**	Cervantes's *Don Quixote*, Part 1 (1605)
Lope de Vega's *The Sheep Well* (1614)		Expulsion of Moors (1609)
Philip IV brings designer Cosme Lotti from Florence (1626)		Felipe IV (rules 1621–1665)
	1625	Velázquez completes painting *Vulcan's Forge* (1630)
Cofradia de la Novena (actors' guild) established (1631)		Revolt of Catalans and Portuguese (1640)
Calderón's *Life Is a Dream* (c. 1636)	**1650**	Defeat of Spanish army by French at Rocroi (1643)
Coliseo, court theater with proscenium arch, built (1640)		Peace of the Pyrenees; Spain's power declines (1659)
Public theaters closed (1646–1651)	**1675**	Carlos II (rules 1665–1700)
Number of carros for autos increased from two to four (1647)		Murillo's *Immaculate Conception* (Murillo used this subject thirty times) (1678)
First reference to Spanish designer José Caudi (1662)	**1750**	*Publication of Spanish Colonial Code (1680)*
Autos sacramentales prohibited (1765)		Murillo dies (1617–1682)

The King, the Greatest Alcalde

1620, Madrid It is four o'clock on a lovely spring afternoon in 1620. In Spain, a new full-length play by the Spanish playwright Lope de Vega is about to be performed at the Corral del Principe, one of two public theaters in Madrid. The audience has paid two entrance fees, one to the company presenting the play and the second to a charity supporting the city's hospital. The fee to the charity is one reason why government and church officials allow theater in Madrid.

As the audience gathers inside the *corral,* there is great excitement about the performance that will soon begin. Those standing in the patio are a bit noisy. Many of the spectators have bought nuts, fruit, and spiced honey from the *alojero* (refreshment stand). People in the pit are jostling for the best vantage point; people in the galleries are exchanging pleasantries, speaking to friends, and looking around the theater to see who is here this afternoon.

The audience is particularly excited to attend a new play by Lope de Vega. Some years ago, in 1609, Lope argued, in an essay titled "The New Art of Writing Plays in This Age," that the most important measure of success in theater is the audience's enjoyment. He has certainly passed his own test, for he is the most popular playwright of the day. The play about to be seen, *The King, the Greatest Alcalde,* promises to be filled with thrilling episodes.

Now the performance begins. First, before the actual play, there is a comic prologue. Then comes the play itself. It is a *comedia:* in Spain, this is the term for any full-length nonreligious play, serious or comic. *The King, the Greatest Alcalde* is serious, but it also has comic elements. It is about a farmer who promises his daughter Elvira to a peasant, Sancho. Sancho seeks approval for the marriage from his lord, Don Tello. Don Tello agrees, but when he sees Elvira, he wants her for himself. He postpones the wedding and kidnaps Elvira. As the play unfolds, it seems to have all the ingredients of a sparkling drama: a clash between peasants and the nobility, a wronged peasant, a kidnapping, a beautiful maiden in distress. The boisterous spectators in the pit are especially vocal in responding to each twist and turn of the plot and to the mixture of comedy and suspense, but the entire audience finds itself caught up in the story.

The actors and actresses in the theater company play 15 speaking roles and some nonspeaking parts, and the audience responds enthusiastically to the performances. Though the play has 13 scenes in different locations, all the action takes place on the platform stage. It is easy to follow the action, because—through a combination of dialogue and properties, such as a throne—the playwright and the performers let the spectators know exactly where they are in every scene. The scenes are divided into three acts; during intermissions between the acts, the spectators are also entertained by short comic pieces and musical interludes.

As the play continues, Sancho appeals to the king to help him regain Elvira from Don Tello; after several complications, the king arrives, in disguise. When the king discovers that Don Tello has forcibly seduced Elvira, he orders Don Tello to marry her and then has him executed so that Elvira will be honorably widowed and can marry Sancho. At this conclusion, everyone in the audience—in the galleries as well as the pit— is pleased that justice has been done.

The corrales were outdoor courtyard theaters used for the presentation of secular drama during the Spanish golden age. These playhouses were similar to the public theaters of the English Renaissance. A corral uncovered accidentally in Almagro, Spain, in 1955 is shown here. A theater festival is staged in this space every year. (Courtesy Festival d'Almagro)

temporary at first but later became permanent spaces. The two most famous were both in Madrid: the Corral de la Cruz (1579) and the Corral del Principe (1583).

The stage in a corral was a platform erected opposite the entrance to the yard. Access to the yard was usually through a street building; there were also several entranceways for other seating areas. The yard floor or *patio* was primarily an area for standing and, like the pit of an Elizabethan public theater, was a raucous area. At the front of the yard, near the stage, a row of stools—later, a few benches—were set up, separated from the rest of the yard by a railing.

In the back wall opposite the stage, above the main entranceway in the yard, was a gallery for unaccompanied women known as the *cazuela;* it had its own separate entrance and was carefully guarded to prevent men from entering. Above the cazuela, there was a row of boxes for local government officials; above these boxes was a larger gallery for the clergy. Along the side walls of the yard were elevated benches and above them windows, protected by grills, from which a play could be viewed. On the next level were boxes that extended out from the buildings around the courtyard. A fourth floor had cramped boxes with low ceilings. At the back of the yard, on one side of the main entrance, was a refreshments box, the *alojero,* from which food and drinks were sold.

A corral held about 2,000 spectators: 1,000 places for men, 350 for women, and the rest reserved boxes and other accommodations for government officials and the clergy.

Scenic conventions in Spain were similar to those in England. A two-story facade behind the platform stage was the basic scenic construction; a curtain, props, and flats might be used in conjunction with this facade. There were three openings for entrances, exits, and scenes of concealment, as well as an upper playing area. The facade, therefore, served the same function as the Elizabethan tiring house. Spoken dialogue was also used to indicate locale.

Spanish Acting Companies. In Spain during the golden age, acting troupes consisted of 16 to 20 performers. Unlike Elizabethan companies, these Spanish companies included women. In many places on the European continent—in contrast to England—women had been allowed to act in medieval religious drama, and the inclusion of women in Spanish companies during the Renaissance was an outgrowth of this custom. The church, though, did not support the use of female performers; as a result, the Spanish government was forced to impose stringent restrictions on women working in the theater—for instance, only a woman who was married or otherwise related to an actor in a troupe could be employed. Most Spanish acting troupes were *compañías de parte*—sharing companies, like those of Elizabethan England. Some companies, however, were organized by a manager who contracted performers for a specific period of time.

FRANCE

Background: France in the Seventeenth Century

Renaissance theater did not reach its zenith in France until the seventeenth century, later than in Italy, England, or Spain. This was partly due to a religious civil war taking place in France between Catholics and Protestants, a war that was finally brought to an end in 1594 when Henry IV formulated the Edict of Nantes, which offered religious tolerance to Catholics and Protestants. With religious and political stability established in the seventeenth century, French society was able to flourish under Louis XIV, who ruled from 1643 to 1715. Among France's significant accomplishments during this period was exploration of the new world, particularly in Canada and the Louisiana Territory of the United States.

During this period, French society was greatly influenced by the innovations of the Italian Renaissance. As we shall see, French theater in the seventeenth century adopted and adapted many of the Italian theatrical innovations.

French Drama: The Neoclassical Era

The most important seventeenth-century French dramatists were Molière, noted for his comedies; and two authors known for tragedy: Pierre Corneille and Jean Racine.

Among all the French neoclassical playwrights, the one who exerts the most influence on modern theater is Molière (Jean-Baptiste Poquelin; 1622–1673). Molière was not only a dramatist but also an actor and the leader of a theatrical troupe. His first theater venture in Paris was a failure, and so he toured the provinces for 12 years, learning firsthand the techniques of theater and perfecting his craft as a dramatist. He then returned to establish himself as France's leading actor-manager and playwright, specializing in comedies of character.

Molière's work was strongly influenced by Italian commedia dell'arte. In plays like *Tartuffe* (1664), *The Misanthrope* (1666), *The Miser* (1668), and *The Imaginary Invalid* (1673), he creates exaggerated character types and makes fun of their eccentricities. The title character in *The Miser*, for example, is a man so greedy and so possessive of his money that he becomes paranoid when he thinks anyone knows where he has hidden it; in protecting his treasure, he even turns against his children. Molière was a master of slapstick as well as more subtle kinds of comedy, and he frequently used a *deus ex machina* to resolve his contrived plots.

Pierre Corneille (1606–1684) began his career writing comedies but soon turned to tragedy. His play *The Cid*, which opened in 1636, became a huge success. It aroused opposition from intellectuals because it did not follow the neoclassic rules established by Italian critics; despite this, it remained enormously popular and was presented frequently not only in France but in other European countries. Corneille, however, stopped writing plays for four years. Because of the controversy, when he resumed playwriting, he adhered more closely to the neoclassical rules.

Jean Racine (1639–1699) was the other great writer of tragedy in seventeenth-century France. Unlike Corneille, he was comfortable with the neoclassic rules from the start; all of Racine's tragedies adhere to these rules.

One of Racine's best-known tragedies, *Phaedra* (1677), is based on a play by Euripides. In Racine's version, Phaedra, queen to King Theseus, falls in love with her stepson, Hippolytus. Upon hearing that Theseus has died, she admits her love to Hippolytus, who reacts with disgust. When Phaedra discovers that Theseus is not dead, she allows her maid to spread the rumor that it was Hippolytus who made amorous advances to Phaedra, rather than the other way around. Hearing the rumor and believing it, Theseus invokes a god to kill his son Hippolytus, after which a heartbroken Phaedra takes poison—before she dies, however, she reveals the truth.

Racine's *Phaedra* is a perfect example of climactic plot structure: it has only a few characters, and the action takes place in one room at one time. Furthermore, Racine's masterful handling of poetry and emotion established a model to be followed in France for the next three centuries.

Theater Production in France

The French were probably the first Europeans after the Romans to construct a permanent theater building. This was the Hôtel de Bourgogne, completed in

THE MISER BY MOLIÈRE
The most famous comic playwright of the French Renaissance—and one of the best comic playwrights of all time—was Molière. He was particularly masterful at creating characters who carried an idea or obsession to excess. Seen here are Sarah Agnew (Élise) and Steven Epp (Harpagon) in a coproduction of The Miser *by A.R.T.-Theatre de la Jeune Lune. (© Richard Feldman)*

FRENCH NEOCLASSICAL DRAMA

The two major playwrights of French neoclassic drama were Pierre Corneille and Jean Racine. Both, in their separate ways, perfected a French version of classic tragedy. Racine's Phaedra *is probably the best-known neoclassic tragedy. It is the story of a woman who falls in love with her stepson, with the result that everyone involved, including these two, as well as Phaedra's husband, meets a tragic ending. Shown here is Joanna Roth, in the title role, with Toby Stephens in a production in London. (© Robbie Jack/ Corbis)*

1548. The Bourgogne was built by the Confraternity of the Passion, a religious order that had been granted a monopoly for the presentation of religious drama in Paris. When religious drama was outlawed—in the same year that the Bourgogne was completed—the Confraternity rented its space to touring companies.

The Hôtel de Bourgogne, a long, narrow building with a platform stage at one end, was the sole permanent indoor theater building in Paris for nearly a century, until the Théâtre du Marais opened in 1634. The Marais was a converted indoor tennis court. Such indoor courts were long and narrow—like the Bourgogne—and had galleries for spectators (court tennis was a popular sport); thus they could be transformed into theaters very easily.

The Italian influence on French theater architecture became evident in 1641, when Cardinal Richelieu, a leading political figure, erected the Palais Cardinal, renamed the Palais-Royal after his death. This is the theater that Molière's troupe eventually used. The Palais Cardinal was the first proscenium-arch theater in France and also had Italian-style machinery to shift scenery. Following the construction of Richelieu's theater, the Théâtre du Marais and the Hôtel de Bourgogne were remodeled in the 1640s into proscenium-arch theaters. Painted-perspective wing-and-shutter scenery—shifted by the pole-and-chariot system—was used in the two remodeled theaters.

Early French proscenium-arch theater buildings differed slightly from those of the Italian Renaissance: in the back wall opposite the stage was an *amphithéâtre*, an undivided gallery with inexpensive bleacherlike seating. In both the Marais and the Bourgogne, there was probably a small upper stage, raised 13 feet above the main stage, which was used for special effects such as flying. At the close of the seventeenth century, upper-class audience members were frequently seated onstage.

In the 1650s, Louis XIV's interest in ballet brought this form of entertainment back into prominence at court. To satisfy the royal taste for elaborate ballets and to prepare for Louis's marriage, a new court theater was built, known as the Salle des Machines ("Hall of Machines"). It was completed in 1660 and was the largest playhouse in Europe: 52 feet wide and 232 feet long. The auditorium took up only 92 feet of the 232-foot length, leaving 140 feet for the stage and its machinery. The backstage equipment included one piece of machinery on which the entire royal family and all their attendants—well over 100 people—could be "flown" into the space above the stage. Because of its unsatisfactory acoustics, its size (especially backstage), and the expense of producing spectacles, the Salle des Machines was rarely used after 1670.

NEOCLASSICAL FRANCE
Year, c.e.

Theater		Culture and Politics

1500

Confraternity of the Passion (founded 1402) given monopoly of Paris theater (1518)

1525

Exploration of Gulf of St. Lawrence by Jacques Cartier (1534–1535)

Religious plays prohibited; Hôtel de Bourgogne opens; perspective scenery used for first time at Lyon for performance celebrating marriage of Henri II and Catherine de Médicis (1548)

Henri II (rules 1547–1559)

Outbreak of civil war between Protestants and royal troops (1562)

1550

Alexandre Hardy, first professional playwright, flourishes (1597)

St. Bartholomew's Day massacre; Protestants killed (1572)

Valleran le Comte (King's Players), first important theatrical manager (1598)

Montaigne's *Essays* (1580)

1575

Farce players, Turlupin, Gaultier-Garguille, Gros-Guillaume popular (1610–1625)

Assassination of Henri III; Henri IV reigns (1589)

Henri IV abjures Protestantism (1593)

Théâtre du Marais (1634)

Edict of Nantes (1598)

Corneille's *Le Cid* (1636)

1600

Richelieu's Palais Cardinal opens (later renamed Palais-Royal) (1641)

Permanent French outpost in Quebec (1608)

New Marais with proscenium arch (1644)

Henri IV assassinated (1610); Louis XIII (rules 1610–1643)

1625

Torelli brings Italianate innovations to France (1645)

Richelieu enters royal council (1624)

Bourgogne remodeled (proscenium added) (1647)

Descartes's *Discourse on Method* (1637)

Richelieu's death (Mazarin's takeover) (1642)

Vigarini comes to France (1659)

1650

Death of Louis XIII; Louis XIV (rules 1643–1715)

Molière's troupe given Palais-Royal (1660)

Molière's *The Miser* (1668)

Civil war (1648–1652)

1675

Jean-Baptiste Lully given monopoly of musical performances in Paris (1672)

Louis XIV ("Sun King") personal reign (1661)

After Molière's death, Marais and his company amalgamated by Louis XIV (1673)

Founding of the French Academy of Science (1666)

Racine's *Phaedra* (1677)

1700

Revocation of Edict of Nantes (1685)

Comédie Française founded (1680)

Anglo-Dutch coalition wars against France (1689–1713)

Comédie Française gets new theater, to be used until 1770 (1689)

1725

Louis XIV dies (1715)

Paris commedia troupe expelled (1697)

Tartuffe

1669, Paris The date is February 9, 1669. At the Palais-Royal theater in Paris, France, spectators are eagerly awaiting a performance of *Tartuffe*, written by France's best-known comic playwright and actor, Molière.

Tartuffe has already been the cause of an enormous controversy. Molière first read it four years ago to King Louis XIV at his palace at Versailles; the king liked it, but before it could be presented publicly, it provoked an uproar. The reason is its subject matter. The title character of the play, Tartuffe, is a religious hypocrite. He pretends to be very pious and wears clothing that looks like a religious habit, but he is actually interested in acquiring money and seducing women. He has come to live in the house of Orgon, a wealthy man who has been completely taken in by Tartuffe's false piety.

The people who oppose the presentation of *Tartuffe* include a number of religious figures (one of them is the archbishop of Paris) who say that it is an attack on religion. Molière, however, insists that his play is not an attack on religion, but rather an attack on people who hide behind religion and exploit it.

The audience is aware that until now the opposition has been successful in keeping *Tartuffe* out of theaters; the king did not dare authorize its presentation as long as the forces against it were so strong. So far, the play has been presented only once, in the summer of 1667, and then for only one night. The king was out of the country at that time, and in his absence the religious authorities had it closed down. Now, however, *Tartuffe* has finally been given royal approval, and today's performance is to be its official public unveiling.

The Palais-Royal theater, where Molière's troupe performs, is a rectangular space with a stage at one end and galleries on three sides around it. It accommodates almost 1,500 people: 300 stand in a "pit" in front of the stage, about 700 sit in a raised amphitheater behind the pit, about 330 sit in the galleries, 70 stand at the very back, and 50 wealthy nobles sit on the sides of the stage itself. Having spectators onstage is customary in French theaters but makes things very difficult for the performers.

The stage is fitted with wings and shutters, like Italian Renaissance theaters, and scenery can be changed with a pole-and-chariot system. For *Tartuffe*, however, there will be no scene changes: the entire action takes place in the drawing room of Orgon's house.

Well aware of all the scandal and debate, the audience feels a rush of anticipation as this performance of *Tartuffe* begins. Once it is under way, though, the spectators realize that the controversial figure of Tartuffe does not even make an appearance for two full acts. Rather, it is the figure of Orgon, played by Molière himself, on whom they first concentrate. The spectators see that Orgon is thoroughly duped and pays no attention to the members of his family when they tell him how dishonest and disreputable Tartuffe is.

Finally, in the third act, Tartuffe makes his entrance. He is challenged by Orgon's family, but Orgon remains loyal to him. Only when Orgon learns for himself the awful truth about Tartuffe does he realize his error. This occurs in a scene in which Orgon, hiding under a table, hears Tartuffe try to seduce his wife. The wife has led Tartuffe on, and he exposes himself as a genuine scoundrel. As the audience members watch the scene, they think it is one of the funniest they have ever seen.

Orgon's discovery of Tartuffe's true nature seems to come too late: at this point, Orgon has already handed his house and his fortune over to Tartuffe, disinheriting his own children. At the end of the play, though, the king intervenes. This is the same Louis XIV who in real life has intervened on Molière's behalf so that the play can be presented.

A few weeks from now, both king and playwright will be vindicated: *Tartuffe* will be performed 28 times in a row—an unprecedented number—and will show every sign of becoming a classic comedy.

Another major theater building of the French neoclassical period was the Comédie Française, which housed the national theater. The French national theater had been founded by Louis XIV in 1680, but the company did not move into its own building until 1689. The interior of the Comédie Française featured a horseshoe-shape construction, which meant that the sight lines were significantly better than those in other French spaces of the time.

Acting companies in French neoclassical theaters were organized under a sharing plan and had women members who could become shareholders. Rehearsals were supervised by the playwright or a leading performer or both, but troupes spent little time on rehearsals. Once a play was introduced, the troupe was expected to be able to revive it at a moment's notice, and the bill at theaters was changed daily.

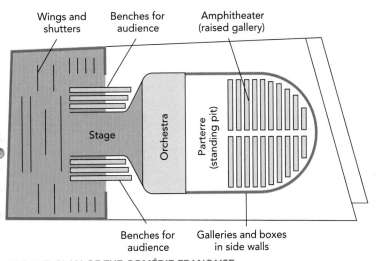

Wings and shutters | Benches for audience | Amphitheater (raised gallery)

Stage | Orchestra | Parterre (standing pit)

Benches for audience | Galleries and boxes in side walls

GROUND PLAN OF THE COMÉDIE FRANÇAISE
The French national theater company performed in this playhouse for 81 years, beginning in 1689. The theater had a procenium-arch stage with machinery for scene shifts, and a horseshoe-shaped auditorium for improved sight lines. The parterre was where audience members stood; the amphitheater contained bleacherlike seating.

The Renaissance in Italy, England, Spain, and France saw significant—even revolutionary—changes in theatrical practices. Many of these practices will be built on as we look at developments in theater from the Restoration through romanticism, in Chapter 16.

SUMMARY

During the Italian Renaissance, the neoclassical rules for drama were formulated. Commedia dell'arte developed as a popular theater, based on stock characters, repeated pieces of comic business, and recognizable costumes. Painted-perspective scenery, which could be changed easily, and the proscenium-arch theater were both introduced, leading to greater verisimilitude—true to life—in theater.

During the English Renaissance—the Elizabethan age—the great plays of Shakespeare and his contemporaries were being staged. Outdoor public theaters and indoor private theaters accommodated these extensive-form dramas through the use of an unlocalized platform stage and a flexible tiring house, or stage house. Brilliant poetic language also helped set the action.

In Spain during its golden age, the secular dramas of Lope de Vega and Calderón de la Barca were performed in corrales, theaters built in courtyards. Corrales used many of the same staging conventions as Elizabethan theaters.

In French neoclassical theater, the tragic dramas of Corneille and Racine and the comedies of character by Molière were clearly patterned after traditions established in the Italian Renaissance. French theater architecture and design were also based on Italian models.

KEY TERMS

Apprentice Young performer training in an Elizabethan acting company.

Box Small private compartment for a group of spectators built into the walls of traditional proscenium-arch and other theaters.

Cazuela (cah-zoo-EHL-ah) Gallery above the tavern in the back wall of the theaters of the Spanish golden age; the area where unescorted women sat.

Comedia (koh-MAY-dee-ah) Full-length (three-act) nonreligious play of the Spanish golden age.

Compañías de parte (cahm-pa-NYEE-ahs day PAHR-teh) Acting troupes in the Spanish golden age, organized according to a sharing system.

Corral Theater of the Spanish golden age, usually located in the courtyard of a series of adjoining buildings.

Gallery In theater buildings, the undivided seating area cut into the walls of the building.

Groove system System in which tracks on the stage floor and above the stage allowed for the smooth movement of flat wings onto and off the stage; usually there were a series of grooves at each stage position.

Hireling Member of an Elizabethan acting troupe who was paid a set salary and was not a shareholder.

Lazzi (LAHT-zee) Comic pieces of business used repeatedly by characters in Italian commedia dell'arte.

Masque Lavish, spectacular court entertainment primarily during the late English Renaissance.

Neoclassical ideals Rules developed by critics during the Italian Renaissance, supposedly based on the writings of Aristotle.

Patio In the theater of the Spanish golden age, the pit area for the audience.

Perspective Illusion of depth in painting, introduced into scene design during the Italian Renaissance.

Pit Floor of the house in Renaissance theaters. It was originally a standing area; by the end of the eighteenth century, backless benches were added in most countries.

Plot The sequence and patterned arrangement of events in a drama, with incidents selected and arranged for maximum dramatic impact.

Pole and chariot Giacomo Torelli's mechanized means of changing sets made up of flat wings.

Private theaters Indoor theaters in Elizabethan England.

Public theaters Outdoor theaters in Elizabethan England.

Shareholders In Elizabethan acting troupes, members who received part of the profits as payment.

Sides Script containing only a single performer's lines and cues. Elizabethan actors learned their roles from sides.

Slapstick A type of comedy or comic business that relies on exaggerated or ludicrous physical activity for its humor.

Soliloquy Speech in which a character who is alone onstage speaks inner thoughts.

Tiring house Elizabethan stage house.

Unities Term referring to the preference that a play's plot occur within one day (unity of time), in one place (unity of place), and with no action irrelevant to the plot (unity of action).

Yard Pit, or standing area, in Elizabethan public theaters.

Zanni (ZAH-nee) Comic male servants in Italian commedia dell'arte.

THEATER ON THE WEB

For more research and to learn more about the topics in this chapter, please visit the Online Learning Center at **www.mhhe.com/livelyart6.**

CHAPTER 16

Theaters from the Restoration through Romanticism

◀ **THEATER: RESTORATION THROUGH ROMANTICISM**

The period covered in this chapter was ushered in by the Restoration theater in England, so named because at that time the English monarchy was restored, after the civil war. Restoration comedy was aimed at the upper class and focused on satirizing upper-class people: their manners, their mores, and particularly their pretension. Wit, urbanity, and sensual innuendo were hallmarks of Restoration comedy. A prime example was The Rivals *by Richard Brinsley Sheridan. Shown here in a production at the Huntington Theatre are Cheryl Lynn Bowers (as Lydia Languish) and Scott Ferrara (as Captain Jack Absolute).*
(© T. Charles Erickson)

The period from 1660 to 1875 saw radical transformations in western society. Revolutions and nationalism led to changes in governments and the establishment of new nations. Mechanization and new technology transformed work, the workplace, and economic classes. Innovations in modes of transportation made travel easier, both within nations and internationally. Theater mirrored the social, political, and economic issues of the times, and it too was transformed. In this chapter, we will examine the theater of England in the late seventeenth century as well as developments in worldwide theater in the eighteenth and nineteenth centuries.

THE ENGLISH RESTORATION

Background: England in the Seventeenth Century

After a bitter civil war lasting from 1642 to 1649, Charles I of England was removed from the throne by the Puritans and beheaded. For the next 11 years, England was a Commonwealth, governed by Oliver Cromwell with a Parliament that had been purged of all his opponents.

When Cromwell died in 1658, his son was unable to keep control of the government; and in 1660 Charles II, who had been living in exile in France, was invited by a newly elected Parliament to return and rule England. The monarchy was thus restored, and this period in English history—usually dated from 1660 through 1700—is therefore called the *Restoration.*

During the period of the Commonwealth, many members of the English nobility had been exiles in France; when the English monarchy returned, these people took back with them the theatrical practices they had seen there.

Restoration Drama: Comedies of Manners

The theaters that reopened in England represented a fusion of Elizabethan, Italian, and French stage conventions. This gave a unique flavor to every aspect of Restoration theater: texts, theater buildings, and set designs.

The best-known Restoration comedies, many of which were influenced by the French dramatist Molière, are referred to as **comedies of manners**. They poked fun at the social conventions of the upper class of the time and satirized the preoccupation of English aristocrats with reputation: most of the upper-class characters in these plays are disreputable. Emphasizing witty dialogue and filled with sexual intrigue and innuendo, the plays took an amoral attitude toward human behavior, including sex. Audiences consisted primarily of members of the nobility and the upper class, the same people whom the playwrights were satirizing.

In their dramatic structure, Restoration comedies combine features of Elizabethan theater and the neoclassical theater of Italy and France. For example, in *The Country Wife* by William Wycherley (1640–1715), the action is far more unified than in a Shakespearean play, with fewer scene shifts. But it does move from place to place, involves many characters, and even has a subplot. The characters in Wycherley's play are stock types, with names that usually describe their distinctive

FEMALE PLAYWRIGHTS IN THE RESTORATION
There were a number of significant women playwrights during the Restoration. Among them was Aphra Behn, whose works are frequently revived today. Seen here is a production of her most famous comedy of intrigue, The Rover, *as staged at Illinois State University.* (© Peter Guither)

personality traits. Fidget and Squeamish are nervous about their reputations; Pinchwife is a man who doesn't want his wife pinched by other men; and Sparkish is a fop who mistakenly believes himself to be a real "spark," witty and fashionable.

Other types of Restoration comedies included comedies of humors and comedies of intrigue. Comedies of humors followed the tradition of Ben Jonson, in which characters have one trait overshadowing all others. Comedies of intrigue featured daring exploits of romance and adventure and had complicated plots. One of the most successful writers of this type of comedy was a woman, Aphra Behn (1640–1689), whose most famous play is *The Rover* (1677).

Another well-known comic playwright of the Restoration is William Congreve (1670–1729). Congreve's *The Way of the World* (1700) is often considered a bridge between Restoration comedy and the later, more traditional morality of eighteenth-century English sentimental comedy. In eighteenth-century English comedy, as we will see, the sinful are punished and the virtuous are rewarded.

ENGLISH RESTORATION
Year, C.E.

Theater	Year	Culture and Politics
Parliament closes theaters (1642)	1640	English civil war (1642)
	1645	
	1650	Execution of Charles I (1649)
		Hobbes's *Leviathan* (1651)
Davenant's *The First Day's Entertainment at Rutland House; Siege of Rhodes* (designer John Webb) (1656)	1655	Anglo-Dutch Wars (1652–1674)
		Protectorate under Oliver Cromwell (1653–1658)
Davenant's and Killigrew's companies granted patents (women in companies) (1660)		Cromwell dies (1658)
Lincoln Inn Fields Theater (1661)	1660	Restoration of Charles II; Navigation Acts (1660)
Thomas Betterton foremost actor (c. 1662)		Royal Society founded (science) (1662)
	1665	
		Milton's *Paradise Lost* (1667)
Dorset Garden (1671)	1670	Treaty of Dover between Charles II and Louis XIV (1670)
New Drury Lane opens (1674)		
Wycherley's *The Country Wife* (1675)	1675	
Dryden's *All For Love* (1677)		
Aphra Behn's *The Rover* (1677)		Habeas Corpus Act (1679)
Otway's *Venice Preserved* (1682)	1680	Wren's Tom Tower, Christ Church, Oxford (1681)
Actress Nell Gwynn (1650–1687)		
	1685	James II rules (1687)
		Newton's laws of gravity (1687)
		William and Mary; Glorious Revolution (1688)
	1690	Locke's *Essay Concerning Human Understanding* (1690)
		Bank of England established (1694)
Mary Pix's *The Innocent Mistress* (1697)	1695	
Collier's *Short View of the Immorality and Profaneness of the English Stage* (1698)		
Congreve's *The Way of the World* (1700)	1700	

Like Restoration comedy, *The Way of the World* has a number of characters involved in adulterous affairs, as well as the traditional stock characters; but its two young lovers, Mirabell and Millamant, are united, while the wicked characters, Fainall and Marwood, are punished.

Following the lead of Aphra Behn, women playwrights emerged at this time. The London season of 1695–1696 saw productions by seven female playwrights. Three women dramatists, known as the "female wits," were active in the period that marked the end of the Restoration and the beginning of the eighteenth century. They included Mary Pix (1666–1706), Delarivière Manley (c. 1663–1724), and Catherine Trotter (1679–1749).

Many Restoration comedies, including *The Country Wife,* indicate that audiences of that era, unlike today's audiences, were quite spirited during theatrical presentations. The fop Sparkish in *The Country Wife* describes how audience members bought fruit from the "orange wenches" (some of whom were prostitutes), spoke back to the performers, arranged assignations, and attended theater to be seen rather than to see the play. These extratheatrical activities increased attacks on theater by religious leaders, who were generally opposed to theater anyway.

Theater Production in the Restoration

Performers and Acting Companies. In theater production, the most obvious difference between the English Renaissance and the Restoration was the appearance of women on the English stage for the first time.

Another change was that in London the sharing plan followed by companies like Shakespeare's almost disappeared during the Restoration. Instead, London performers were hired for a specific period of time at a set salary. In order to increase the set wage, an actor or actress was provided with a yearly *benefit,* a performance of a play from which he or she kept all the profits. The benefit system was used in English theater from the Restoration through the nineteenth century.

The Restoration also saw the emergence of theatrical entrepreneurs who were often part owners of theater buildings and companies. The rise of the entrepreneur as a powerful theatrical force was, of course, a step in the development of modern theater business, with its independent theater owners and producers.

Government and Theater. When English theater was restored in 1660, Charles II issued patents to two entrepreneurs, William Davenant and Thomas Killigrew (1612–1683), which in effect gave them a monopoly on presenting theater in London.

By the early eighteenth century, this monopoly would become unenforceable, however; and in 1737 Parliament was to pass the Licensing Act, a new attempt to regulate London theater. Under this act, only two theaters—Drury Lane and Covent Garden—were authorized to present drama for "gain, hire, or reward," and the lord chamberlain became responsible for licensing plays.

The Country Wife

1675, London, England It is a raw, overcast day in January 1675, and two young men—members of the nobility—have set forth to the theater in London. They are making their way to the new Drury Lane Theater. Another theater once stood at the site of the Drury Lane, but it burned in 1672; the new theater, designed by the architect Christopher Wren and erected on the same spot, opened only a year ago, in 1674.

The play they will see is a new one, by William Wycherley, called *The Country Wife*. They anticipate that they will hear witty, rapier-like exchanges between the characters, and doubtless many double-entendres: clever lines which operate on two levels, one ordinary and the other decidedly sexual.

It is just after two o'clock in the afternoon. The play will not begin until 3:30, but the young men want to arrive at the theater early—to talk to their acquaintances, to flirt with the attractive young women who sell oranges and other things to eat, and even to go backstage to try to see the actresses. As they arrive at the playhouse, the young men join a carefree, pleasure-loving crowd.

The new Drury Lane—a building 58 feet wide by 140 feet long—seats 650 people, some in a pit facing the stage, others in boxes and galleries along the sides and back. Its stage is a platform about 34 feet deep; the front half of the stage is open, and the back half—

framed by a proscenium—contains the scenic elements.

When the performance begins, the first person onstage is an actor named Charles Hart, who delivers a prologue; then the play itself starts. Hart plays a character called Horner, who spreads the rumor that he has been rendered impotent by a venereal disease he contracted while abroad. Horner's doctor, Quack, substantiates the rumor, and Horner uses this "cover story" to gain access to his acquaintances' wives; because of his supposed condition, the husbands will regard him as no threat. The wife he most desires is Margery Pinchwife, a naive woman whose husband usually keeps her locked away in the country and tries to disguise her as a boy when they are in town. Coming upon Pinchwife and the disguised Margery in the street, Horner realizes that the "boy" is a woman in a man's clothing and takes advantage of the situation to make amorous advances, hugging and kissing her in front of her husband, who can do nothing. During the course of the dramatic action, a subplot develops: Horner's friend Harcourt steals Pinchwife's sister Alithea away from her intended husband, Sparkish.

The young male spectators are particularly taken with Elizabeth Bowtell, who plays Margery. In France and Spain, women have appeared onstage for some time; but England forbade actresses until 1660—only a few years ago—

and seeing them now is a novelty that strongly appeals to the men in the audience. Moreover, ever since women have been allowed to perform onstage in England, a favorite dramatic device is to have a woman dress as a man; parts that require this kind of cross-dressing are called *breeches roles*. Seeing a woman's legs—which are usually hidden under wide skirts—has a strong sexual fascination.

The audience is also titillated by the sexual references, especially by a scene which is to become famous—the "china closet" scene. In this scene, Horner and Lady Fidget are in a room offstage while Lady Fidget's husband is onstage listening to their conversation. Horner and Lady Fidget are supposed to be examining Horner's collection of china, but the audience soon realizes that though Horner is speaking about china, he is actually making love to Lady Fidget while her husband stands by in ignorance. Then another woman, Mrs. Squeamish, arrives, and she too asks to see Horner's china. When Horner tells Mrs. Squeamish he has no more, the audience knows that china has become a code word for sex and that Horner is unable at that moment to make love.

At the conclusion of the play, Horner's scheme has been successful: he has made love not only to Margery but to the other wives as well.

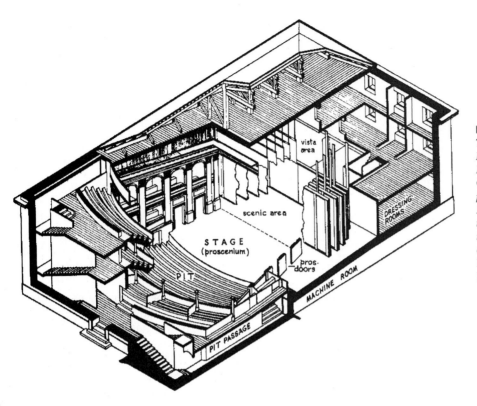

Theater Architecture. During the Restoration, there were three theaters of note in London: Drury Lane (1663); Lincoln Inn Fields (1661), a converted tennis court; and Dorset Garden (1671). Though the interiors of these theaters were distinct, all three showed a unique fusion of Italian and Elizabethan features.

All Restoration theaters were indoor proscenium-arch buildings. The area for the audience was divided into pit, boxes, and galleries and had a total seating capacity of about 650. The pit, which had backless benches to accommodate spectators, was raked—or slanted—for better sight lines.

The Restoration stage was highly unusual in that it was divided into two equal halves by the proscenium arch. In the seventeenth century, only English theaters had this extended apron, and most historians believe that it was a vestige of the Elizabethan platform stage. The deep apron was a major performance area in Restoration theaters; the upstage area housed the scenery. The entire stage was raked to improve the spectators' sight lines.

Another unique element of the Restoration stage was the proscenium doors, with balconies above them. On each side of the stage there were two proscenium doors leading onto the forestage. These doors were used for exits and entrances, and for concealment scenes—scenes in which one character listens from out of sight, a popular device in Restoration comedy. The balconies above these doorways could be used for balcony and window scenes.

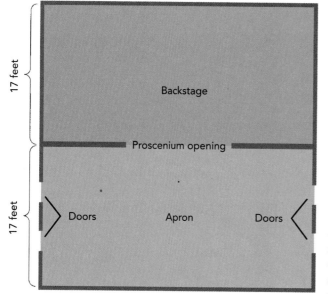

17 feet

17 feet

Backstage

Proscenium opening

Doors   Apron   Doors

GROUND PLAN OF A RESTORATION STAGE

This stage was an unusual combination of English and Italian Renaissance stages. The Restoration saw the introduction of the Italianate proscenium arch into public playhouse in England. However, the extended apron, equal in depth to the rear stage area, and the two proscenium doors on each side of the stage were vestiges of the Elizabethan platform stage and tiring house.

Scenery, Lighting, and Costumes. Restoration scenery and lighting also illustrate a fusion of Italian and English stage practices. The basic scenic components were wings, shutters—sometimes replaced by rolled backdrops—and borders for masking. The English rarely used the pole-and-chariot system for scene changes; instead, they used the groove system. Throughout the Restoration, companies kept collections of stock sets, painted in perspective; these were reused frequently, partly because it was expensive to have new scenery painted.

Because Restoration theaters were indoors, lighting was a major concern. During the late seventeenth century, theater performances were normally given in the afternoon so that the windows could provide some natural lighting. Candles were the source of artificial light; these were placed in chandeliers above the stage and the audience, and also in brackets attached to the fronts of the boxes. The stage and audience area were always lit, and footlights—candles on the floor along the front of the stage—were also used.

Restoration costuming followed the traditions of the English Renaissance and the French neoclassical era: contemporary clothing was used rather than historically accurate costuming.

THE EIGHTEENTH CENTURY

Background: A More Complex World

Throughout Europe, the eighteenth century was a time of transition. As the world was slowly transformed into a global community, homogeneous, self-contained societies began to disappear. Increased manufacturing and international trade affected populations worldwide. The major eighteenth-century mercantile powers were England and France, and decisions made in these two nations directly affected people in such places as North America, India, and Africa. One effect on Africa, for example, was a marked increase in the slave trade.

Because of the growth in trade, western Europe prospered more than ever before. Profits from colonial trade filtered down to the emerging middle class, which included merchants and others in commercial enterprises and which now became a social as well as a political force.

There were so many new developments in learning and philosophy that the eighteenth century is called the *age of enlightenment*. Two major political and social upheavals, the American Revolution (1775–1783) and the French Revolution (1789–1799), were based on ideals of the enlightenment. Unfortunately, the ideals of the French Revolution were compromised by the Reign of Terror, instead of liberty, equality, and fraternity, the French in 1799 wound up with Napoléon.

Much of the new knowledge that characterized this era had practical applications. Inventions of the late eighteenth century facilitated the industrial revolution in the nineteenth century. The flying shuttle, the spinning jenny, and the cotton gin revolutionized the textile industry; James Watt's improved steam engine revolutionized manufacturing and transportation.

In the arts of the late seventeenth century and early eighteenth century, the predominant style was *baroque.* Baroque painters emphasized detail, color, and ornamentation to create a more total visual illusion. Renowned baroque composers achieved unity of mood and continuity of line, but their music—like baroque painting—was filled with movement and action.

The complexity of eighteenth-century society was mirrored in an extremely complex theater that crossed many national boundaries and saw the rise of many new theatrical forms.

Eighteenth-Century Drama: New Dramatic Forms

The eighteenth century did not produce outstanding drama; rather, this was a time when new dramatic forms began to appear.

In terms of genre, for instance, many eighteenth-century plays deviated from traditional definitions of tragedy and comedy. The *drame,* a new French form, was a serious play that did not fit the neoclassical definition of tragedy. *Bourgeois* ("middle-class") *tragedy* and *domestic tragedy* are eighteenth-century examples of drame. Bourgeois and domestic tragedies ignored the neoclassical requirement that the chief characters

RESTORATION DRAMA: COMEDIES OF MANNERS
During the period of the English Restoration, beginning in 1660, the most popular plays were comedies that satirized the upper classes—their gossip, emphasis on dress and decorum, infidelity, sexuality, and conspiracies. In the scene here from William Congreve's The Way of the World, *Lee Mark Nelson plays the servant Waitwell and Sandra Shipley plays Lady Wishfort. In Restoration comedy of manners, which put a premium on language (including sexual double meanings), even the characters' names, such as Waitwell and Wishfort, indicated proclivities or features of the characters. This production was at the Yale Repertory Theatre. (© T. Charles Erickson)*

be kings, queens, or nobles; their new tragic heroes and heroines were members of the emerging middle class. These plays were frequently sentimental and melodramatic, and they usually reflected eighteenth-century middle-class morality, with the virtuous being rewarded and the wicked punished. By the close of the century, such melodrama was being written in France, Germany, and England.

SENTIMENTAL COMEDY

In the eighteenth century in England a type of comedy emerged that was much less amoral than Restoration comedy. Called sentimental comedy, it satirized social pretensions but upheld middle-class values. A good example of the form is The School for Scandal *by Oliver Goldsmith, which contains one of the famous comic scenes of all time, the "screen scene," in which Joseph Surface's shenanigans with the ladies are exposed by a screen falling and revealing all. In the scene here Margaret Welsh is Lady Teazle and Robert Cuccioli is Joseph. The production was at the McCarter Theatre in Princeton, New Jersey.* (© T. Charles Erickson)

The English and the French originated additional dramatic forms during this period. In England these included the satirical *ballad opera,* popularized by the success of *The Beggar's Opera* (1728) by John Gay (1685–1732); and *sentimental comedy.* Sentimental comedy of eighteenth-century England, like Restoration comedy, was comedy of manners, except that it reaffirmed middle-class morality. The major examples of this later form are *The Rivals* (1775) and *The School for Scandal* (1777) by Richard Brinsley Sheridan (1751–1816). In the emerging American theater, *The Contrast* (1787) by Royall Tyler (1757–1826) was patterned after Sheridan's sentimental comedies.

There were opponents of sentimental comedy, the best-known being the English dramatist Oliver Goldsmith (c. 1730–1774), who wrote two plays: *The Good Natur'd Man* (1768) and *She Stoops to Conquer* (1773). Goldsmith advocated "laughing comedy," which would force audiences to laugh at their own eccentricities and absurdities.

In the late eighteenth century, many German playwrights revolted against the neoclassical ideals. The playwright and critic Gotthold Ephraim Lessing (1729–1781), for example, was a leader in the *Sturm und Drang* (**storm and stress**) movement, in which dramatists patterned their works on Shakespeare's extensive episodic structure, his mixture of genres, and his onstage violence. "Storm and stress"—which included such plays as *Goetz von Berlichingen* (1773) by Johann Wolfgang von Goethe (1749–1832) and *The Robbers* (1782) by Friedrich Schiller (1759–1805)—was the forerunner of nineteenth-century romanticism.

In Italy during the mid-eighteenth century, there was a struggle between the playwrights Carlo Goldoni (1707–1793) and Carlo Gozzi (1720–1806) over what direction commedia dell'arte should take: Goldoni wanted to make it less artificial, while Gozzi wanted to make it even more fantastic.

Theater Production in the Eighteenth Century

Government and Theater. In certain countries—such as England, France, and the independent German states—the eighteenth century was marked by governmental attempts to regulate theater. We noted earlier that in 1737 the English Parliament issued the Licensing Act, which restricted the presentation of drama in London to the Drury Lane and Covent Garden theaters and made the lord chamberlain responsible for licensing plays. Frequently, however, ingenious

theatrical entrepreneurs found ways to outwit the government and get around its restrictions.

In eighteenth-century France, the government restricted what types of plays could be produced and granted monopolies to certain theaters: the Opera, the Comédie Française (the home of nonmusical drama), and the Comédie Italienne (the home of commedia dell'arte and, later, of comic opera) were the three major Parisian theaters. In 1791, the leaders of the French Revolution abolished the earlier theatrical restrictions.

In Germany, government intervention in theater was of a somewhat more positive nature. Eighteenth-century Germany was not unified but consisted of several independent states, and German theater became an important artistic force in the last part of the century. Subsidized theaters were organized in several German states; and this practice provided stability for theater artists, though it also meant that the government could wield control over the content of plays.

Eighteenth-Century Theater Architecture. The basic configuration of eighteenth-century continental theaters followed the Italian Renaissance tradition; but to accommodate the new middle-class audiences, both continental and English theaters became larger. The interiors were usually egg-shaped, to improve sight lines. In England, playhouses moved more toward the continental model: the apron shrank to about 12 feet, and the area behind the proscenium became much deeper.

Throughout Europe—in such countries as Germany, Russia, and Sweden—theater buildings proliferated during the eighteenth century. One of the most

EIGHTEENTH CENTURY
Year, C.E.

Theater

Culture and Politics

Theater	Year	Culture and Politics
Ferdinando Bibiena introduces angle perspective (c. 1703)	1700	War of Spanish Succession in France (1701–1714)
		Peter the Great begins westernization of Russia (c. 1701)
Susanna Centlivre's *The Busy Body* (1709)		
	1710	*The Spectator* begun by Addison and Steele (1711)
		Louis XIV dies (1715)
Gottsched and Neuber meet (1727)		Defoe's *Robinson Crusoe* (1719)
Gay's *The Beggar's Opera* (1728)	1720	Baroque music flourishes (Bach and Handel) (c. 1724)
Lillo's *The London Merchant* (1731)		
Voltaire's *Zaire;* London's Covent Garden Theater built (1732)		Swift's *Gulliver's Travels* (1726)
	1730	John Key's "flying shuttle" loom patented (1733)
English Licensing Act (1737)		
Voltaire's *Mahomet;* Macklin's Shylock—an attempt at costume reform (1741)		Rococo style flourishes (1737)
		Frederick the Great of Prussia, "enlightened despot" (1740)
Garrick becomes actor-manager at Drury Lane (1747)	1740	
Goldoni's *The Comic Theater* (1750)		
Hallams in Virginia (1752)		*Encyclopédie* begun (c. 1750)
Voltaire's *Orphan of China* (1755)	1750	French and Indian War (1754)
Spectators banished from French stage (c. 1759)		Seven Years' War begins (1756)
Boulevard theaters begin to develop in France (c. 1760)		Voltaire's *Candide* (1759)
	1760	Rousseau's *Social Contract;* Catherine the Great of Russia begins reign (1762)
Piranesi continues to paint his "prison drawings" using chiaroscuro (1761)		James Watt patents a steam engine (1769)
Gozzi's *Turandot* (1762)		
Drottningholm completed; Southwark Theater in Philadelphia (1766)	1770	Declaration of Independence (American Revolution, 1775–1783); Adam Smith's *Wealth of Nations* (1776)
John Street Theater in New York (1767) Lessing's *Hamburg Dramaturgy* (1767–1769) Hamburg National Theater (1767–1769) "Storm and stress" movement (1767–1787)		Goya's *Don Manuel de Zuniga;* James Watt patents a locomotive (1784)
	1780	Mozart's *Don Giovanni* (1787)
Goethe's *Goetz von Berlichingen;* Goldsmith's *She Stoops to Conquer* (1773)		French Revolution (1789)
		David's *Murder of Marat* (1793)
Sheridan's *The School for Scandal* (1777)	1790	Consulate of Napoleon (1799)
Goethe "directs" Weimar court theater; Schiller assists (1798)		
Schiller's *Mary Stuart* (1800)	1800	

significant theater buildings of this period is Drottningholm in Sweden, erected in 1766 outside Stockholm. Drotttningholm was boarded up in the 1790s and remained closed until the twentieth century, when it was reopened. Today tourists there can explore a perfect working example of an eighteenth-century theater.

In the United States, during the colonial era and after the American Revolution, permanent theaters were constructed following the English model.

Scenery, Lighting, and Costumes. In the eighteenth century, as in the Renaissance, Italy was the birthplace of many scenic innovations. The most influential Italian designers and theater architects of

The Marriage of Figaro

1784, Paris, France It is a brisk spring day in May 1784. In Paris, the Comédie Française is giving a performance in its new theater building, which opened two years ago. With great expectations, Parisians depart early so that they can arrive at the theater before the starting time, 5:30. Tonight they are to see Beaumarchais's new play *The Marriage of Figaro*.

The Comédie Française is noted not only for traditional neoclassical drama but also for new drama by French authors. At this performance, there will be dance presentations between the acts of the play and also a short, comic afterpiece following *The Marriage of Figaro*. Not since *Tartuffe* has there been such controversy over a play.

The Marriage of Figaro—set in Spain—is about an older man's attempt to seduce a servant girl, and its key character is a comic servant; Beaumarchais introduced his characters several years ago, in *The Barber of Seville*. The real point of *The Marriage of Figaro* is social and political satire, and it is this that is controversial. Because of the controversy, the king, Louis XVI, has refused to give his permission for its production. Despite this, however, it has been performed continuously since its opening in April and is clearly a success. People who were present on the opening night have reported that the theater was filled hours beforehand and that some of the audience members had brought food

with them so that they would not have to risk losing their seats by leaving the theater to eat.

As the spectators enter the theater, they are struck by its size and beauty. Remarkably, everyone in the audience now has a place to sit. In earlier French theaters, the pit in front of the stage had no seats, and people in that area stood during performances; in fact, people in the old seatless pits would move about and socialize. The new seats are controversial—Parisians enjoyed the social ambience of the old pit, and one of the leading playwrights of the day, Louis Sébastian Mercier, has publicly criticized the addition of benches. The audience area is egg-shaped; this configuration, at least, will be welcome, making it easier for everyone in the audience to see the action onstage. Like older theaters, the new Comédie Française has three rows of boxes with a row of galleries above those. Spectators who cannot afford the more expensive sections take their place in the pit, sitting on the new benches.

When the curtain rises, the spectators are impressed at once by the stage, which is large and very deep. However, it has a smaller apron than the company's previous theaters had: the actors and actresses must all perform behind the proscenium arch. The scenery is painted and will be changed by wings and shutters. As the play begins, the spectators are

very excited, because they are seeing performers they have heard much about.

The plot of *The Marriage of Figaro* is full of intrigue, unexpected twists, and great comic moments. Figaro, the servant, is engaged to marry Suzanne, who is also a servant; but his master, Count Almaviva, wants to sleep with her himself. The count has been unfaithful to his wife, and we watch with great enjoyment the various complications that develop as he tries to conquer another woman but is thwarted. At the end of the play, the count is exposed in his plotting and is humiliated; he pledges fidelity to his wife, and Figaro and Suzanne are brought together.

As the Parisians walk home, they relive many of the comic moments in the play. Yet they also understand why this seemingly simple, farcical work has caused such a political furor. It is the master who is ridiculed and frustrated: despite his social rank, his machinations are futile and his clever servants outwit him. Clearly, Beaumarchais is questioning the social structure of France. Some people are saying that this play threatens society with the same kind of revolution that has taken place in the new world. Are these people right? Was the king right to be concerned about the political implications of this comedy? These questions remain long after the evening at the Comédie Française.

SET DESIGN BY ONE OF THE BIBIENAS
During the eighteenth century, one family dominated scene design in Europe: the Bibiena family, whose second, third, and fourth generations carried on the tradition begun by Giovanni Bibiena. This engraved stage design by Giuseppi Bibiena (1696–1757) is typical of the family's work, with its vast scale, ornateness, and elegance, and its perspective vista disappearing in several directions. (Victoria and Albert Museum, London)

the period were the Bibienas—an extended family that included several generations of designers. One innovation by the Bibienas was *angular* or *multipoint perspective*. Previously, the painted sets used during the Italian Renaissance pulled the eye to a central vanishing point and appeared to be totally framed and enclosed by the proscenium arch. In the Bibienas' designs, the eye was attracted to various vanishing points, and the set seemed to extend beyond the proscenium. Typically, the Bibienas' designs were grandiose, lavish, and ornate.

Elsewhere, Italian influence was pervasive in eighteenth-century scene design. Most continental theaters used wing-and-shutter settings, painted in perspective and shifted by Torelli's pole-and-chariot mechanism. Additional elements occasionally incorporated into the painted designs included (1) borders at the top; (2) *ground rows* (cutouts along the stage floor); (3) large scenic cutouts, such as painted trees; (4) rolled backdrops; and (5) *act drops*—curtains at the front of the stage.

A few historians have argued that sometime between the Renaissance and the eighteenth century, Italian designers also introduced the *box set,* in which flats are used to create three sides of a room onstage. We will look at the development of the box set more closely when we discuss nineteenth-century theater.

There were also experiments with stage lighting in the late 1700s, including attempts to mask lighting sources, to use silk screens for coloring, and to replace candles with oil lamps and other sources. These lighting sources were not easily controlled, however, and the auditorium as well as the stage had to remain lit.

Unlike scenery and lighting, theatrical costuming remained undeveloped throughout most of the eighteenth century. Actors and actresses believed that the chief criterion for a costume was to show the performer off to the best advantage. Daring theater artists throughout Europe experimented with historically accurate costuming, but their attempts rarely resulted in the kind of historical reconstructions we see today.

Acting in the Eighteenth Century. If many of the plays of the eighteenth century were not noteworthy, the performers often were. This was an age that glorified star performers. All across Europe, successful actors and actresses developed dedicated followings.

The predominant approach to acting in the eighteenth century was *bombastic,* emphasizing the performer's oratorical skills. More often than not, performers addressed their lines to the audience rather than the character to whom they were supposed to be speaking. Standardized patterns of stage movement were necessary because rehearsal time was limited and bills were changed frequently.

In the midst of these conventional practices, however, there were some innovators. Among those who rebelled against the bombastic, conventionalized style were the English actors Charles Macklin (c. 1700–1797) and David Garrick (1717–1779). Macklin and Garrick rejected formal declamation, stereotyped patterns of stage movement, and singsong delivery of verse.

The Emergence of the Director. In terms of the future, possibly the most significant development during the eighteenth century was the first emergence of the modern director. Before then, playwrights or leading performers normally doubled as directors of stage business, and actual directing was minimal; furthermore, little time was spent on preparing a production in rehearsal. What was missing in theater was someone to oversee and unify stage productions, assist performers, and ensure the appropriateness of visual elements. Two eighteenth-century figures are often considered the forerunners of the modern stage director: the English actor David Garrick and the German playwright, poet, and novelist Johann Wolfgang von Goethe.

Between 1747 and 1776, David Garrick was a partner in the management of the Drury Lane Theatre and was therefore responsible for all major artistic decisions. He championed a more natural style of acting and argued for careful development of characters' individual traits as well as for thorough preparation and research. In contrast to the usual eighteenth-century custom, Garrick's rehearsals were quite extended. Garrick was also a strict disciplinarian: he required his performers to be on time, to know their lines, and to act—not simply recite—during rehearsals. As part of his reform of stage practices, Garrick also banished spectators from the stage.

Goethe, unlike Garrick, was not restricted by commercialism; nor was he an actor in the company he directed. In 1775, Goethe—by then a famous author—was invited to oversee the court theater at Weimar in Germany. Initially, Goethe did not take his theater duties seriously, but by the 1790s he had become enthusiastic about the theater and had become a *régisseur,* or dictatorial director. (*Régisseur* is the French term for "director.")

Goethe rehearsed for long periods and expected his performers to work as an ensemble. He established rules for stage movement and vocal technique, and he also set rules for his performers' behavior in their personal lives. He even laid down rules for the conduct of his audiences; the only appropriate audience reactions, he insisted, were applause and withholding applause.

Goethe did not advocate a completely natural style of acting; he believed, for instance, that performers should speak facing the audience rather than each other. He used routine blocking patterns, although he did emphasize careful stage composition. Goethe oversaw settings and costumes and believed in historical accuracy.

DAVID GARRICK
The eighteenth century was an era of great stars, some of whom paid close attention to details of performance and costuming to achieve a greater sense of reality. David Garrick was an outstanding example of this approach to acting, and also a strong manager of his theater company. In the portrait here (by Nathaniel Dance) he is shown in the title role in Shakespeare's Richard III. (Stratford Town Council, Stratford-upon-Avon)

THE NINETEENTH CENTURY

Background: A Time of Social Change

Major social changes took place in the period from 1800 to 1875, including the industrial revolution—which involved technological advances such as steam power, expanded means of transportation, and new modes of communication. Another major development was the rise of nationalism.

There was also intellectual ferment. Two especially significant theoretical works were Charles Darwin's *On the Origin of Species* (1859) and Karl Marx's *Das Kapital* (*Capital*; 1867). Darwin's work, which dealt with evolution by natural selection, questioned traditional religious concepts; Marx's work questioned the capitalist system, which was the driving economic force of the industrial revolution.

These societal transformations had a major impact on the nature of theater. Nineteenth-century theater built on the innovations of the eighteenth century and paved the way for modern theater.

Theater in Nineteenth-Century Life

Before examining specific transformations in drama and production techniques during the nineteenth century, we should look at the unique place theater held at that time. Between 1800 and 1875, the dramatic arts exploded. The working and middle classes who filled the fast-growing cities demanded theater; it was a passion, a fad, and also a seeming necessity for these new audiences. Nineteenth-century theater, therefore, was a true popular entertainment that attracted huge numbers of spectators and helped audiences to forget—momentarily, at least—the cares and drudgery of daily life.

Nonliterary forms of entertainment also attracted the masses. The American public, for example, supported such popular arts as the *minstrel show, burlesque, variety, the circus, wild west shows,* and *medicine shows*. Throughout the nineteenth century, concert halls, saloons, and playhouses presented collections of entertainments—including songs, dances, acrobatics, and animal acts—on one bill; these developed into the popular variety and vaudeville presentations at the turn of the century and in the early twentieth century. The renowned popularizer of the circus, P. T. Barnum (1810–1891), merits special mention. Barnum developed the art of spectacular advertising to attract audiences to his entertainments; when he became involved with the circus in the 1850s, he advertised it as the "greatest show on earth." The wide variety of attractions to which audiences responded in the nineteenth century is a prime example of the tradition of popular entertainments of which we have spoken in earlier chapters.

The increase in numbers of spectators and types of entertainments resulted in the construction of more and larger playhouses throughout the western world. With improvements in rail transportation, the dramatic arts were also brought to new places and new audiences.

The passion that audiences felt for theater helps to explain several infamous theater riots. One of these episodes, the "Old Price Riots," took place when London's Covent Garden Theatre was remodeled in 1809 and prices for admission were raised by the actor-manager John Philip Kemble (1757–1823). Another theater riot took place in Paris in 1830, when *Hernani* by Victor Hugo (1802–1885) premiered at the Comédie Française.

The most violent of the nineteenth-century riots occurred outside New York's Astor Place Theater in lower Manhattan and grew out of rivalry between the

NINETEENTH CENTURY, 1800 TO 1875
Year, C.E.

Theater		Culture and Politics

Talma foremost actor in France (c. 1800)

1800

Louisiana Purchase (1803)

Goethe's *Faust,* Part I (1810)

Napoléon I, emperor of France (1804)

Kleist's *The Prince of Homburg* (1810)

Fulton's paddle steamer *Clermont* navigates on Hudson (1807)

Pixérécourt and French melodrama flourish (1810)

Latin American independence (1808–1826)

Edmund Kean's London debut (1814)

1810

Mme. de Stael's *Of Germany,* published in France (1810)

Chestnut Street Theater in Philadelphia becomes first totally gaslit theater (1816)

Beethoven's *Fifth Symphony* (1810)

Daguerre exhibits diorama (1822)

Battle of Waterloo; Metternich system (1815)

Charles Kemble's historically accurate *King John;* Shchepkin member of Moscow troupe (1823)

1820

First Factory Act, England (1819)

Greek war of independence (1821)

Forrest's New York debut (1826)

Monroe Doctrine (1823)

Hugo's *Hernani* (1830)

Decembrist uprising in Russia (1825)

Madame Vestris's management of Olympic Theater begins (1831)

1830

Comte's positivism (1830)

Upper middle class enfranchised in England (1832)

Gogol's *Inspector General;* Büchner's *Woyzeck* (1836)

Davy Crockett killed at the Alamo (1836)

Macready manages Covent Garden (1837)

Victoria of England (rules 1837–1901)

Scribe's *A Glass of Water* (1840)

1840

Dickens's *Oliver Twist* (1838)

England's Theater Regulation Act (1843)

Second French Empire; Napoléon III (1852)

Astor Place Riot (1849)

Crimean War (1853–1865)

Dumas *fils's Camille;* first production of *Uncle Tom's Cabin;* Charles Kean's *King John* (1852)

Perry in Japan (1854)

1850

Flaubert's *Madame Bovary* (c. 1857)

Adolphe Montigny innovates in directing at Gymnase (c. 1853)

Darwin's *On the Origin of Species* (1859)

Sardou's *A Scrap of Paper* (1860)

American Civil War (1861–1865); proclamation of the kingdom of Italy

Edwin Booth's *Hamlet* runs 100 nights in New York (1864)

1860

Bismarck becomes Prussian prime minister (1862)

Duke of Saxe-Meiningen begins reforms (1866)

Dostoyevsky's *Crime and Punishment* (1866)

Booth Theatre (1869)

Marx's *Das Kapital;* extension of suffrage in Great Britain (1867)

Henry Irving at Lyceum (1871)

1870

Tolstoy's *War and Peace* (c. 1869); American transcontinental railway (1869)

Zola's *Thérèse Raquin;* preface discussed naturalism (1873)

German empire founded; Paris commune (1871)

Paris Opéra building completed (1874)

1880

Making Connections

Nineteenth-Century Popular Theatrical Arts

POPULAR ARTS
During the nineteenth century, a number of highly theatrical popular entertainments developed. Among these was the circus. The American entrepreneur P. T. Barnum was a significant innovator in developing the circus as we know it today. Seen here are female trapeze artists, performing in 1890. (Library of Congress)

As we have noted, it is hard to distinguish between the popular entertainments of the nineteenth century and the theater of that era. Many of the popular forms were presented in theaters, and many traditional dramas were adopted for spaces that usually held mass audience entertainments.

The nineteenth century saw an explosion of museums, musical halls, and circuses. The American who was world-renowned for his ability to draw mass audiences was P. (Phineas) T. (Taylor) Barnum (1810–1891), who in 1841 opened the American Museum, in which he exhibited human curiosities and also staged concerts and plays, including many temperance melodramas. Later, in the early 1870s, Barnum was also instrumental in developing the three-ring circus as we know it today. But even before Barnum, there were circus rings that housed clowns, equestrian performances, trained animal acts, and pantomimes. In the early nineteenth century, dramas staged on horseback were presented in many of these spaces.

The music halls of England served food and drink and had a small platform stage for popular song and dance presentations. A master of ceremonies moved the show along, providing comic interludes. By the end of the 1800s, these early music halls evolved into theatrical spaces dedicated exclusively to the presentation of these musical performances.

The nineteenth century also saw the development of many other forms of popular entertainments, including wild west shows, vaudeville, and minstrelsy. *Wild west* shows (or exhibitions), popular in the last quarter of the nineteenth century, presented heroic figures of the west as well as Native Americans, most often to audiences in the eastern United States who had little real contact with that world.

Minstrel shows were variety shows that featured white performers wearing blackface, and caricaturing African Americans. Later in the nineteenth century, there were African American minstrel troupes. Vaudeville was a series of variety acts—music, sketches, juggling, animal acts—that made up an evening's entertainment.

The intertwining of the popular arts and theater made the two

almost indistinguishable. Furthermore, many of the popular forms
developed in the nineteenth century
continue to have an impact on our

performance arts. For example, the
well-known Canadian circus troupe
Cirque du Soleil stages productions
that break the boundaries between

popular art and theater. Television
has incorporated the tradition of
vaudeville and variety.

English star William Charles Macready (1793–1873) and the American star Ed-win Forrest (1806–1872). Forrest, who was noted for his portrayals of melodra-matic heroes, had made an unsuccessful English tour; he blamed its failure on Macready, whose performance style was more subtle and realistic. When Mac-ready appeared at the Astor Place Theater on May 8, 1849, Forrest's working-class fans prevented the performance.

Macready was persuaded by his aristocratic admirers to appear again two nights later, on May 10, but this performance brought out a mob of 15,000 who assembled outside the playhouse and began to attack it. The infantry was called out to disperse the mob, and by the time the riot ended, twenty-two people had been killed.

The popularity of theater between 1800 and 1875 has not been equaled in modern times. Partial parallels could be drawn to movies and television, which present similar kinds of entertainment, attract mass audiences, and feature popu-lar stars. Still, the passion of nineteenth-century audiences has rarely been aroused by other forms of entertainment. In our own time, the only equivalent might be the emotional intensity of audiences at rock concerts.

ASTOR PLACE RIOT BY C. M. JENKES
This riot, which happened in New York City in 1849, was a result of nationalistic fervor and the passionate involvement of theater audiences. It broke out when working-class fans of the American star Edwin Forrest attacked the theater in which the English actor William Charles Macready, who had supposedly insulted Forrest, was performing. (The Metropolitan Museum of Art, The Edward W. C. Arnold Collection of New York Prints, Maps, and Pictures, Bequest of Edward W. C. Arnold, 1954.)

GOETHE'S *FAUST*
The greatest nineteenth-century romantic drama was Goethe's Faust, *which is written in two parts. It follows the pattern of episodic Shakespearean drama and deals with the temptation of Faust by Mephistopheles. Shown here is a scene from Peter Stein's full-length production staged in Germany in 2000.* (© Ruth Walz)

The Astor Place Riot and the subject matter of much popular drama also reflected growing nationalism. For example, Anna Cora Mowatt, one of America's first significant female playwrights, wrote a comedy of manners, *Fashion* (1845), that depicted the values of hardworking America as more honest than the social pretensions of Europe. The character Adam Trueman in *Fashion* was a descendant of an earlier popular stock figure in American melodramas and comedies—the "stage Yankee," a representative of diligent, unpretentious, rural America.

Nineteenth-Century Dramatic Forms

Two major forms of drama that came to the fore between 1800 and 1875 were romanticism and melodrama.

Romanticism. *Romanticism,* influenced by the German "storm and stress" movement, was a revolutionary literary trend of the first half of the nineteenth century. The most noted romantic dramas of the period were Goethe's *Faust* (Part 1, 1808; and Part 2, 1831) and Victor Hugo's *Hernani* (1830).

The romantics rejected all artistic rules, believing that genius creates its own rules. Since many of the romantics adopted Shakespeare's structural techniques, their plays were episodic and epic in scope; but unlike Shakespeare, they were often more interested in creating dramatic mood and atmosphere than in developing believable plots or depth of character. The romantic hero was frequently a social outcast—a bandit, for example—who sought justice, knowledge, and truth.

Melodrama.   Another dramatic form that came to the forefront in the nineteenth century was melodrama. As was discussed in Chapter 7, *melodrama* literally means "song drama" or "music drama"—a reference to the background music that accompanied these plays.

In nineteenth-century melodrama, the emphasis was on surface effects, such as effects evoking suspense, fear, nostalgia, and other strong emotions in the audience. The conflict between good and evil was clearly established: melodramatic heroes and heroines stood in sharp contrast to villains, and the audiences sympathized with the good characters and despised the bad ones. Virtue was always victorious.

To hold the audience's interest, melodramas had suspenseful plots, with a climactic moment at the end of each act (the modern equivalent would be a television drama that has a car crash or a sudden confrontation just before a commercial break). Since melodrama is primarily an escapist form, visual spectacle and special effects were important.

The Well-Made Play.   Many popular melodramas of the nineteenth century had a structure described by the term *well-made play.* Characteristic of such plays were tightly constructed cause-and-effect development, and action revolving around a secret known to the audience but not to the characters. The opening scenes carefully spell out the necessary background information, or *exposition.* Throughout the play, the dramatic action is clearly foreshadowed, and each act builds to a climax. In the major scene, known as the *obligatory scene,* the opposed characters confront each other in a showdown. The plot is carefully resolved so that there are no loose ends.

The two most famous writers of well-made plays were both French: Eugène Scribe (1791–1861) and Victorien Sardou (1831–1908).

Theater Production in the Nineteenth Century

Performers and Acting.   Even more than the eighteenth century, the nineteenth century was an era of great stars; performers throughout the world were idolized

THE WELL-MADE PLAY
A type of drama that came to prominence in the nineteenth century was the well-made play. The term means a play that was carefully constructed and featured unity of action and often unity of time and place as well. It incorporated a tightly managed plot with a strong cause-and-effect sequence of events. An example is The Heiress, *adapted by Ruth and Augustus Goetz from a novel by Henry James. Shown here is Eve Best in the title role in a London production at the Royal National Theatre, directed by Philip Franks. (© Donald Cooper/Photostage)*

EDWIN BOOTH

*An outstanding actor of the nineteenth century
was Edwin Booth, famous for his portrayal of
Hamlet, shown here, and other Shakespearean
characters, as well as for building his own
theater. As a performer, he was renowned for
depth of character, grace, and freedom from
mannerisms. In an age of posturing onstage,
he took a more natural approach to his roles.*
(Bettmann/Corbis)

by the audiences who flocked to see them. Some of these performers amassed—and frequently lost—fortunes, and a number of them were not only national but international figures.

During the nineteenth century, the traditional *repertory company,* a troupe of actors and actresses performing together for a set period of time in a number of plays, gradually disappeared. As transportation improved, not only stars but full productions—known as *combination companies*—began to tour, replacing the local repertory troupes. At about the same time, the long run became more common: popular plays might run for more than 100 consecutive performances.

Most performers of the period acted in the classical, romantic, and melodramatic styles. Many, however, moved toward modern realism. Among such more realistic performers were the American Edwin Booth (1833–1893) and the Italian Eleonora Duse (1858–1924).

Nineteenth-Century Developments in Directing. The art of directing, pioneered by David Garrick and Johann Wolfgang von Goethe in the eighteenth century, was refined and developed in the nineteenth century. The goal of innovative nineteenth-century directors was to create a unified stage picture, particularly by allotting more time for rehearsal and paying more attention to production details. Many of them also experimented with historical accuracy in scenery and costuming.

In England and the United States, numerous performer-managers took great interest and care in creating stage productions. On the European continent, a number of people significantly developed the art of directing, including two Germans—the opera composer Richard Wagner (1813–1883) and George II (1826–1914), duke of Saxe-Meiningen—who were not actors within their companies and thus were closer to our modern idea of the director.

Wagner's concept of a totally unified artwork—the *Gesamtkunstwerk*—controlled by one person influenced twentieth-century theories of "total theater" and directing. Wagner believed that an opera, which is made up of many musical and theatrical elements, needs a controlling figure to unify it. At his Bayreuth Festspielhaus, he put this theory into practice, becoming its *régisseur,* or "director." Wagner's innovations for increasing stage illusion are particularly important. Musicians were forbidden to tune their instruments in the orchestra pit, and audiences were not supposed to applaud during the course of a presentation. Wagner is also often credited with being the first director to extinguish the house lights in order to focus the audience's attention on the stage.

In 1866, the duke of Saxe-Meiningen—a small state in northwestern Germany—took control of his court theater; and between 1874 and 1890 he made

NINETEENTH-CENTURY THEATER ARCHITECTURE

Significant changes took place in theater architecture in the 1800s. The illustration of Covent Garden in London (above) shows a typical "pit, box, and gallery" theater of the era. The illustration of Wagner's Bayreuth Festspielhaus (next page), however, shows that by 1876 significant transformations were occurring. Wagner's theater is much more like a modern proscenium theater, with comfortable seating in the orchestra area, a small balcony, and a sunken orchestra pit. (Historical Picture Archive/Corbis) (© Victoria and Albert Museum, London)

the Meiningen Players the most renowned company in the world and revolutionized stage production. He rehearsed for extensive periods of time, refusing to open a show until he believed it was ready. He was opposed to the star system and employed mostly young performers. His productions were especially famous for intricately planned crowd scenes and were also admired for their historically accurate settings and costumes. Because his company toured frequently to other countries, the duke's theatrical innovations became well known throughout Europe.

Nineteenth-Century Theater Architecture.   Between 1800 and mid-century, many playhouses, with the traditional proscenium arch and "pit, box, and

**ELEONORA DUSE, PORTRAIT BY
E. GORDIGIANI**

*Duse was the great Italian actress of the late
nineteenth century and the early twentieth
century. She was known for her more
realistic acting style. The English playwright
George Bernard Shaw considered her a
greater performer than Sarah Bernhardt.*
(Photo Studio Humberto N. Serra)

gallery" arrangement, were enlarged to meet the demands of the expanding lower-class urban audiences. By the 1860s, however, there was a shift away from the construction of huge theaters.

In the United States, the Booth Theater, completed in 1869 for the renowned American Shakespearean actor Edwin Booth, is often cited as the first modern theater in New York City. Instead of a pit and galleries, it had a modern orchestra area and balconies, and the seats were individual armchairs. The stage in Booth's theater was revolutionary: it was not raked, and it had no grooves. Rather, scenery could be raised from the basement by elevators or dropped in ("flown in") from above, and scenic pieces were often supported by braces.

Another innovative nineteenth-century theater building, the Bayreuth Festspielhaus, built for Richard Wagner, opened in 1876. Wagner wanted seating that would not emphasize class distinctions, and so his theater had 1,300 individual seats in thirty raked rows, forming a fan-shaped auditorium. Audiences exited at the ends of the rows, an arrangement known as *continental seating*.

Scenery, Costumes, and Lighting. Eighteenth-century experiments with realistic devices and conventions in scenery and costuming were carried even farther in the nineteenth century. Historical accuracy in sets and costumes became more common with the increasing availability of works of historical research. This new knowledge about the past—combined with the fascination with antiquity that characterized the nineteenth century—led various theater artists, including the duke of Saxe-Meiningen, to mount historically accurate productions.

Wing-and-shutter settings shifted by pole-and-chariot or groove systems gradually disappeared during the nineteenth century. The most significant alternative was the *box set,* an arrangement in which flats are cleated together at angles—rather than set up parallel to the audience—to form the walls of a three-dimensional room. As noted previously, the box set may have been introduced as early as the Renaissance, but it was in the nineteenth century that box sets revolutionized scene design.

During this same period, the technology of the industrial revolution was introduced into theater. New means of scene shifting were developed: by the close of the century, the *elevator stage* (which allows sections of a stage floor, or even the entire floor, to be raised or lowered) and the *revolving stage* were perfected. The latter is a large turntable on which scenery is placed; as it moves, one set turns out of sight and another is brought into view.

Nineteenth-century technology also revolutionized stage lighting. In 1816, Philadelphia's Chestnut Street Theater became the world's first playhouse to be completely gaslit. Gaslight allowed control of the intensity of lighting in all parts of the theater; and by the middle of the century, the *gas table*—the equivalent of a modern dimmer board—enabled one stagehand to control all the stage lighting.

Thomas Edison's incandescent lamp, invented in 1879, further revolutionized stage lighting. Electricity, of course, is the most flexible, most controllable, and safest form of theater lighting. By 1881, London's Savoy Theatre was using incandescent lighting, though some other playhouse may actually have used it earlier.

By 1875, theater was about to enter the modern era: the seeds of theatrical realism—as well as of reactions against realism—had been gradually planted since the Renaissance. In Chapter 17, we turn to the beginnings of the modern era: the development of realism and early reactions against the new realistic theater. In Chapter 18, we explore these and other developments in modern theater.

SUMMARY

The theater of the English Restoration combined aspects of English and continental Renaissance theater. Restoration drama had elements of both Elizabethan theater and the French theater of Molière. The Restoration stage also had native and continental elements: its modified proscenium came from French and Italian practice, but its elongated apron came from Elizabethan theaters.

In the eighteenth century, there were many attempts throughout Europe to break away from the Italianate tradition. Theaters were still constructed as proscenium-arch spaces, but their shapes and sizes changed. Revolutionary authors—especially the "storm and stress" dramatists of the late 1700s—abandoned the neoclassical ideals. Many new genres that ignored the Italian Renaissance rules were developed, including bawdy Restoration comedy, sentimental comedy, middle-class tragedy, drame, and ballad opera.

There were also attempts in the 1700s to develop unity in production; these included some primitive experiments with historical accuracy, and—especially notably—the directorial controls instituted by David Garrick and Johann Wolfgang von Goethe.

The nineteenth century was the bridge to our modern era. Comfortable modern proscenium-arch theaters, such as Booth's Theater and the Bayreuth Festspielhaus, were built. Principles of modern directing were developed and were clearly manifested in the work of the duke of Saxe-Meiningen. Historical accuracy in costuming and settings as well as expanded use of the box set added to theatrical illusionism. Theater was also affected by technological advances, such as gas lighting.

KEY TERMS

Ballad opera Eighteenth-century English form that burlesqued opera.

Box set Interior setting using flats to form the back and side walls and often the ceiling of a room.

Comedy of manners Form of comic drama that became popular in seventeenth-century France and the English Restoration, emphasizing a cultivated or sophisticated atmosphere and witty dialogue.

Drame (DRAHM) Eighteenth-century French term usually denoting a serious drama that dealt with middle-class characters.

Exposition Imparting of information necessary for an understanding of the story but not covered by the action onstage; events or knowledge from the past, or occurring outside the play, which must be introduced so that the audience will understand the characters or plot.

Gesamtkunstwerk Richard Wagner's theory of a unified work of theatrical art.

Melodrama Dramatic form, made popular in the nineteenth century, which emphasized action and spectacular effects and also used music; it had stock characters and clearly defined villains and heroes.

Minstrel show Type of nineteenth-century production featuring white performers made up in blackface.

Régisseur (ray-zhee-SUHR) Continental European term for a theater director; it often denotes a dictatorial director.

Repertory, repertoire Acting company that at any given time can perform a number of plays alternately; also, the plays regularly performed by a company.

Romanticism Movement of the nineteenth century that sought to free the artist from rules and considered unfettered inspiration the source of all creativity.

Storm and stress Antineoclassical eighteenth-century German movement that was a forerunner of romanticism; in German, *Sturm und Drang*.

Well-made play Dramatic form popular in the nineteenth century and early twentieth century that combined apparent plausibility of incident and surface realism with a tightly constructed plot.

THEATER ON THE WEB

For more research and to learn more about the topics in this chapter, please visit the Online Learning Center at **www.mhhe.com/livelyart6**.

CHAPTER 17

Early Modern Theater Movements

◀ **REALISTIC DRAMA**

The first controversial movement of the late nineteenth century was realistic drama. The pioneers were Ibsen, Strindberg, and Chekhov, but a prominent later practitioner was the Spanish playwright Fcderico García Lorca. A prime example of his realistic work was The House of Bernarda Alba, in which an overbearing mother keeps her daughters imprisoned at home. In the secene here—from a new English version of the play, by David Hare—the mother, played by Sally Hawkins, is struggling with one of the daughters, played by Penelope Wilton. The production was at the Royal National Theatre in London.

(© Geraint Lewis)

In the modern era, usually defined as 1875 to the present, the arts have, as always, mirrored changes occurring in society; in theater, these developments have been reflected in a great diversity of types of theater. Theater in the modern period has become increasingly eclectic and experimental. Avant-garde theater appears alongside more conventional theater, and new plays are produced while classics from the past also enjoy great popularity.

In the theater of the modern era, four major strands stand out. The first strand is realism; the second is departures from realism; the third is a continuation of traditional theater from the past—comedies, tragedies, melodramas, and spectacular extravaganzas that nineteenth-century audiences applauded—and the fourth is postmodern experimentation and forms, which seem to defy traditional categorization. In Chapters 17, 18, and 19 we will discuss all four of these strands as they developed chronologically.

In this chapter, we will begin our examination of how these four approaches developed in modern theater between 1875 and 1945.

THE BIRTH OF REALISM

Background: The Modern Era

Modern theater began with the plays of three dramatists: the Norwegian Henrik Ibsen; the Swede August Strindberg; and the Russian Anton Chekhov. Their works also reflect the period when they were written—the *modern era*, which began in the late nineteenth century and continues to this day. Their plays also ushered in the techniques and the outlook that characterized western theater throughout most of the twentieth century.

In the mid-nineteenth century, profound changes began to occur in religion, philosophy, psychology, and economics. Ideas were put forth that were to challenge long-held beliefs about who we are and how we relate to the world around us. In 1859, Charles Darwin published *On the Origin of Species*, which challenged the concept that human beings are special and created by God in his own image. In 1867, Karl Marx's *Das Kapital* questioned the fundamentals of capitalism. In 1900, Sigmund Freud's *Interpretation of Dreams* suggested that we are not in complete control of our actions or even our thoughts: frequently, Freud claimed, the subconscious as much as the conscious mind influences our behavior. In 1905, Albert Einstein presented the first part of his theory of relativity, which stated that many aspects of the universe that we consider fixed and immutable are subject to variation and change; by extension, people questioned whether other aspects of life are also relative rather than absolute or permanent. One result of this series of intellectual, religious, and moral challenges was that societies that had been unified now became fragmented.

Along with fragmentation, the first half of the twentieth century was marked by tremendous unrest, in both Europe and Asia. This era of unrest was ushered in by World War I, which lasted from 1914 to 1918 and resulted in 8.5 million deaths. Unrest also contributed to the Russian Revolution of 1917, which led to the establishment of the Soviet government and a costly civil war.

1875 TO 1915
Year

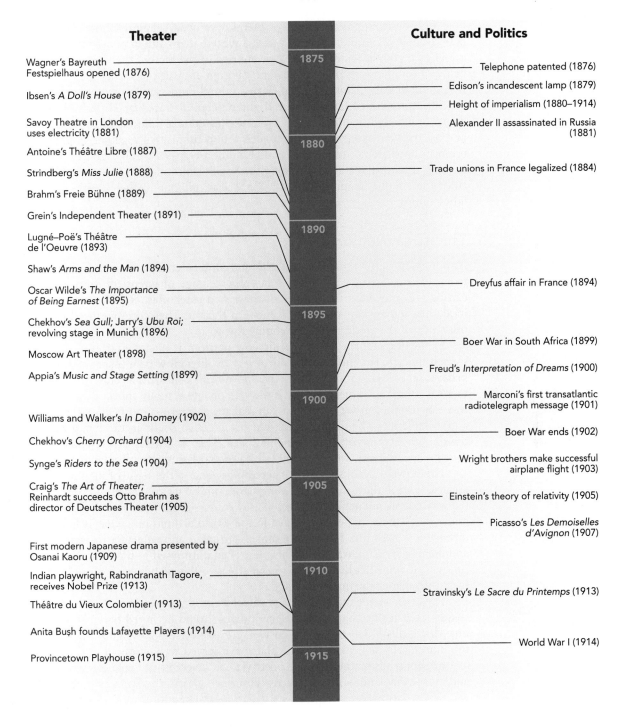

Theater

Wagner's Bayreuth Festspielhaus opened (1876)

Ibsen's *A Doll's House* (1879)

Savoy Theatre in London uses electricity (1881)

Antoine's Théâtre Libre (1887)

Strindberg's *Miss Julie* (1888)

Brahm's Freie Bühne (1889)

Grein's Independent Theater (1891)

Lugné–Poë's Théâtre de l'Oeuvre (1893)

Shaw's *Arms and the Man* (1894)

Oscar Wilde's *The Importance of Being Earnest* (1895)

Chekhov's *Sea Gull;* Jarry's *Ubu Roi;* revolving stage in Munich (1896)

Moscow Art Theater (1898)

Appia's *Music and Stage Setting* (1899)

Williams and Walker's *In Dahomey* (1902)

Chekhov's *Cherry Orchard* (1904)

Synge's *Riders to the Sea* (1904)

Craig's *The Art of Theater;* Reinhardt succeeds Otto Brahm as director of Deutsches Theater (1905)

First modern Japanese drama presented by Osanai Kaoru (1909)

Indian playwright, Rabindranath Tagore, receives Nobel Prize (1913)

Théâtre du Vieux Colombier (1913)

Anita Bush founds Lafayette Players (1914)

Provincetown Playhouse (1915)

Culture and Politics

1875

Telephone patented (1876)

Edison's incandescent lamp (1879)

Height of imperialism (1880–1914)

Alexander II assassinated in Russia (1881)

1880

Trade unions in France legalized (1884)

1890

Dreyfus affair in France (1894)

1895

Boer War in South Africa (1899)

Freud's *Interpretation of Dreams* (1900)

1900

Marconi's first transatlantic radiotelegraph message (1901)

Boer War ends (1902)

Wright brothers make successful airplane flight (1903)

1905

Einstein's theory of relativity (1905)

Picasso's *Les Demoiselles d'Avignon* (1907)

1910

Stravinsky's *Le Sacre du Printemps* (1913)

World War I (1914)

1915

Chapter 17 Early Modern Theater Movements   **345**

When World War I ended, it was hoped that peace would come to the western world, but severe economic problems developed in Europe and the United States. In Europe, there was rampant inflation followed by a depression; economies were destroyed and monetary systems devalued. A famous photograph of the period shows a German citizen pushing a wheelbarrow full of paper money to buy a loaf of bread. Economic troubles were one of the factors that led to the emergence of totalitarianism in Europe and the rule of fascist dictators such as Benito Mussolini in Italy, Adolf Hitler in Germany, and Francisco Franco in Spain.

The extremes of fascism were frighteningly illustrated by Hitler's Nazi Germany, in which individual liberty was suppressed and millions of Jews, Gypsies, and others were exterminated in concentration camps. All together, Hitler's government murdered 6 million Jews and 1 million Gypsies. Similar abuses occurred in other totalitarian states, including the Soviet Union, where Joseph Stalin (who ruled the country from 1928 until 1951) sent millions to their deaths in slave-labor camps.

Theatrical Realism

As noted above, two major strands of modern theater are realism and departures from realism. Broadly speaking, a large percentage of twentieth-century drama can be put into one or the other of these two categories. *Realism* was the first modernist movement, ushering in modern theater. Therefore, we need to begin our study of the modern era by defining this form.

In theater, *realism* has a specific connotation. It means that everything onstage is made to resemble observable, everyday life. How people speak, dress, and behave; what kinds of rooms they live in—all this conforms as closely as possible to what we in the audience know is the way people actually speak, dress, act, and live. For instance, if we see a family in realistic theater—a mother, a father, a son, and a daughter—the action of the play is likely to occur in the living room of their home or some other identifiable space. They will dress as we would expect such people to dress, and they will talk to each other in everyday language.

The power of realism lies in its credibility and in the sense of identification it creates. If we in the audience can verify from our own experience and observation the way people are acting onstage, we say to ourselves: "Yes, this must be true. I know that's the way people behave in the world around me; what is happening onstage is true to life. I suffer the same heartaches and entertain the same hopes and dreams as the characters in this play. I can put myself in their place and identify with them." Realistic theater is so effective that it has been a predominant form throughout the modern period.

The other major movement we call *departures from realism*. This will be discussed later in this chapter, but a few points should be noted here. At the same time that realism was becoming pervasive, there were playwrights who found it too limiting. In fact, many devices that have served well throughout theater history are not realistic: they include poetry (a characteristic of Shakespearean drama and most other drama before recent centuries), ghosts and witches (like those in

Macbeth), songs, fantasies, and dream sequences. Such devices do not correspond to our experience of everyday life and hence are generally excluded from realism. The division between realism and departures from realism therefore creates something of a dilemma: with realism we can have strong audience recognition and identification; but we need these departures if we want to use a whole range of poetic and imaginative devices that make theater richer.

Of course, realism and departures from realism can be and frequently are combined. For that matter, some contemporary critics argue that these divisions may be artificial; that all texts contain within them their own individual reality and their own theatricality. These critics suggest that rather than place works in broad categories, every theater text should be examined for its own unique approach to creating a dramatic world.

Still, these divisions are a useful, if somewhat artificial, way of beginning to examine our modern theater. Realism was the first of these two forms to become firmly established, and so we will look at it first.

Realistic Playwrights

Henrik Ibsen. The Norwegian playwright Henrik Ibsen (1828–1906) is often considered the founder of modern realistic drama. Ibsen did write nonrealistic works at certain times in his career: as a young man he wrote romantic dramas, and near the end of his life (as discussed below) he experimented with abstract symbolist drama. He is best known, however, for his realistic works—plays like *A Doll's House* (1879), *Ghosts* (1881), and *Hedda Gabler* (1890).

As a realistic playwright, Ibsen sought to convince his audiences that the stage action in his dramas represented everyday life. But he went farther than that: he felt that drama should tackle subjects that had been taboo onstage—such as economic injustice, the sexual double standard, unhappy marriages, venereal disease, and religious hypocrisy. Ibsen and the realistic dramatists who followed him often insisted that the purpose of drama was to call attention to social problems in order to bring about change.

Realists like Ibsen refused to make simple moral judgments or resolve their dramatic action neatly. Unlike popular melodramas, realistic plays frequently implied that morality and immorality were relative and not clearly distinct or easily defined. Not surprisingly, Ibsen and other realists met a great deal of opposition in producing their plays and were constantly plagued by censorship.

August Strindberg. A second major figure ushering in the era of modern realism was the Swedish playwright August Strindberg (1849–1912). Strindberg, who was 20 years younger than Ibsen, took realism another step in plays like *The Father* (1887) and *Miss Julie* (1888): he personalized and intensified Ibsen's realism.

AUGUST STRINDBERG
Along with Ibsen, the Swedish dramatist August Strindberg was a pioneer in developing modern realistic drama. These playwrights revolutionized the theater of the late nineteenth century by dealing with taboo subject matter in a manner that mirrored everyday life. Much of their work was controversial and could not be produced in state or commercial theaters. (Theatre Collection, Museum of the City of New York)

MISS JULIE

An early, important realistic play by Strindberg was Miss Julie. *The daughter of an aristocrat, Julie is a driven, neurotic woman, torn between the conventional life in which she was brought up and her desire for total freedom. She is fatally attracted to Jean, an ambitious servant in her father's house. In this production at the Two River Theatre Company, Heather Lea Anderson is Julie and Ed Onipede Blunt is Jean.* (© T. Charles Erickson)

Instead of focusing on people in a social context—on conflicts between individuals and a restrictive society—Strindberg concentrated on individuals at war with themselves and with each other. In both *The Father* and *Miss Julie*, there is a war between the sexes: men and women vie with each other and attempt to dominate one another. In the end, one of them is destroyed—the man in *The Father* and the woman in *Miss Julie*. Also, Strindberg's characters are subject to the neuroses and anxieties that characterized so much of twentieth-century life.

Strindberg took realistic drama closer to naturalism, a type of realism we will discuss shortly. In a famous preface to *Miss Julie*, he outlined how he hoped to make the play even more lifelike than Ibsen's plays. He wanted no intermission, so that the audience would remain absorbed in the action; he made his characters multidimensional, giving them complex, contradictory features; he wanted the scenery to be real, with genuine pots and pans sitting on the kitchen shelves instead of being painted on backdrops as they had been before; and he wanted the dialogue to be interrupted and fragmentary—again, as it is in real life.

Anton Chekhov. The third significant playwright in the birth of modern realism is the Russian Anton Chekhov (1860–1904), whose play *The Sea Gull* (1896) was at first a failure but was later successfully revived by the Moscow Art Theater. He wrote three other major plays: *Uncle Vanya* (1899), *The Three Sisters* (1900), and *The Cherry Orchard* (1904).

Chekhov introduced important variations to the realism of Ibsen and Strindberg. He moved away from melodramatic elements such as the suicides in Ibsen's *Hedda Gabler* and Strindberg's *Miss Julie*. He also dealt with a full gallery of characters—often 12 or 14 rather than five or six—and he orchestrated his characters in such a way that their stories overlapped and echoed one another. Chekhov also developed a blend of tragedy and comedy, creating a genre—often referred to as *tragicomedy*—that has characterized much of modern drama; tragicomedy is discussed in Chapter 7.

Naturalism

Naturalism is a form of theater that developed alongside the realism of Ibsen, Strindberg, and Chekhov; it can be seen as a subdivision of realism or an extreme form of realism. The naturalistic movement began in France in the nineteenth century and spread to other European countries. In naturalism, everything onstage—

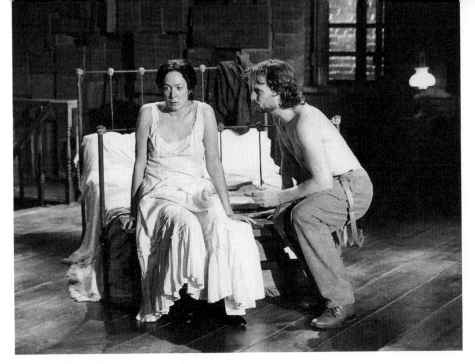

NATURALISM

An extreme form of realism is naturalism, which attempts to put onstage an unflinching, almost documentary version of people and events as they are encountered in real life. An early example is Thérèse Raquin *(1873), a drama by Émile Zola. In the preface to this play, Zola stated the tenets of naturalism. Here we see Elizabeth Marvel and Sean Haberle in a version of the play produced by the Classic Stage Company. (© T. Charles Erickson)*

characters, language, properties, settings, costumes—should seem to have been lifted directly from everyday life. Dramatic action should never seem contrived but rather should look like a "slice of life."

Many of the naturalists believed that the most appropriate subject matter for drama was the lower class, and they frequently focused on the sordid and seamy aspects of society in order to confront audiences with social problems and instigate reforms. The most famous naturalistic theorist and playwright was the French author Émile Zola (1840–1902).

Naturalism is a more stringent form than realism. One reason is its insistence on showing the stark side of life; the other is that its action cannot be shaped by the same kind of artistic techniques used in realism. Realism can use symbols and can structure events in a way that is often more aesthetically satisfying. In fact, the naturalists' extreme position ultimately prevented their movement from being more influential; realism was seen as a more viable theatrical form. In its original form, then, naturalism did not last long, though some of its ideas have shown up often in later drama as well as in films and on television, including recent reality-based TV series such as *Survivor* and *The Amazing Race*.

Producers of Realism: Independent Theaters

At the time when they were first written, realistic and naturalistic works were seen by the mainstream as too controversial for production; in England, for example, the lord chamberlain refused licenses to many of these works. Also, such plays were not considered commercially viable. In order to overcome this problem,

THE CHERRY ORCHARD BY CHEKHOV

The Russian dramatist Anton Chekhov created a type of modern realistic drama that has had a profound influence in the past century. Subtle, low-key, it avoided melodramatic elements but probed deeply and movingly into the hearts and souls of the characters. Chekhov's final masterpiece was The Cherry Orchard, *in which the main character, Madame Ranevskaya, unable to adjust to modern times, loses the family home and her precious cherry orchard. In this scene we see Ruben Garfias as Lopakhin, Lisa Harrow as Lyubov Ranevskaya, and Patrick Garner as Leonid in a production directed by Bill Rauch at the Yale Repertory Theatre.* (© Joan Marcus)

a number of independent theaters were established throughout Europe. They were exempted from government censorship because they were organized as subscription companies, with theatergoers being treated like members of a private club. These independent theaters were not striving for commercial success; they presented their plays to small audiences interested in new dramatic forms.

The best-known of these independent theaters were the Théâtre Libre (Free Theater), founded in Paris in 1887 by André Antoine (1858–1943); the Freie Bühne (Free Stage), founded in Germany in 1889 by Otto Brahm (1856–1912); and the Independent Theater, founded in London in 1891 by J. T. Grein (1862–1935). In 1892, the year after its founding, the Independent Theater introduced the Irish-born George Bernard Shaw (1856–1950) to the London public by producing his first play, *Widower's Houses*. (As a theater critic, Shaw defended the realists and naturalists; he believed that drama should inspire social reform. Unlike the works of other realists, however, many of his own socially conscious dramas are comedies.)

The Sea Gull

1898, Moscow It is the evening of December 17, 1898, and the Moscow Art Theater is about to give its first performance of *The Sea Gull* by the Russian playwright Anton Chekhov. Backstage, the actors and actresses are nervous—so nervous that just before the curtain is to rise, most of them have taken valerian drops, a tranquilizer. Konstantin Stanislavski, the director of the play, who is also playing the role of Trigorin—a bored commercial writer—finds it difficult to control a twitch in his leg.

The reason for their anxiety is easy to understand. The author, Anton Chekhov, who trained to be a doctor, is one of the best-known short-story writers in Russia. So far, however, his dramatic work has not met with the same approval as his stories. In fact, when *The Sea Gull* was first produced two years ago in Saint Petersburg, the performance was a fiasco, not because of the play but because the company presenting it had not rehearsed and had produced it very badly. So devastated was Chekhov by the experience that after the performance he left the theater in despair and swore never again to write plays or even to let *The Sea Gull* be performed.

One reason why the company in Saint Petersburg failed to give a decent performance of *The Sea Gull* is that the play was quite different from anything they were accustomed to. It takes place on a Russian country estate and is about two generations of actresses and writers. The leading female character, Madame Akardina, is a vain, self-absorbed actress. Her son Treplev, an idealistic young writer, is in love with Nina, a young woman who aspires to be an actress. Akardina's lover, Trigorin, with whom Nina falls in love, is a successful writer but dissatisfied with his life. (This is the character Stanislavski is now playing in Moscow.) A number of other people are also involved with these four main characters, and one of the unusual aspects of the play is that the characters' lives are all closely intertwined. This orchestration of a group of characters is unlike previous nineteenth-century dramas. Another unusual aspect is an absence of melodramatic confrontations and developments, such as the murders, suicides, and sudden plot twists that had been staples of most nineteenth-century theater. Rather, the action is subtle, modulated, and true to life.

Interestingly, the same lifelike qualities that have confused so many people have attracted a playwright and producer named Vladimir Nemirovich-Danchenko—a cofounder, with Stanislavski, of the Moscow Art Theater. Nemirovich-Danchenko and Stanislavski want their theater to be different from any other, and Nemirovich-Danchenko feels that *The Sea Gull* is just the kind of play that will set it apart. However, when he first asked Chekhov to let the Moscow Art Theater present this play, Chekhov adamantly refused, because of the debacle in Saint Petersburg. It has taken all of Nemirovich-Danchenko's powers of persuasion to win Chekhov's consent.

All this explains why there is so much at stake tonight in Moscow, as Act I of *The Sea Gull* begins. Chekhov himself is so worried about the outcome that he is not even here; he is far away, in Yalta—partly because of ill health, it is true, but also because of his nervousness.

Now the performers are halfway through Act I, but they cannot tell how the audience is responding. When the act ends, they are greeted by a monumental silence. Fearing failure, the actress Olga Knipper (who will later become Chekhov's wife) fights desperately to keep from breaking into hysterical sobs. Then, all of a sudden, the silence is broken; the audience breaks into thunderous, tumultuous applause. In the words of an eyewitness: "Like the bursting of a dam, like an exploding bomb, a sudden deafening eruption of applause broke out." The applause goes on and on, and Stanislavski dances a jig. The same reaction will greet the next three acts.

Both Chekhov and the Moscow Art Theater have triumphed, and a new chapter in modern theater has begun. So significant is this event that a century later the symbol on the curtain of the Moscow Art Theater will still be a sea gull.

Possibly the most influential of the late-nineteenth-century theaters dedicated to realism was the Moscow Art Theater, which mounted a landmark production of *The Sea Gull* as well as Chekhov's other major plays. Founded in 1898 by Konstantin Stanislavski (1863–1938) and Vladimir Nemirovich-Danchenko (1858–1943), it continues to produce drama today and celebrated its centennial in 1998.

In addition to giving the world an important theater, the Moscow Art Theater provided the first systematic approach to realistic acting: that of Stanislavski. The *Stanislavski system*, discussed in detail in Chapter 5, formed the basis for most realistic acting in the twentieth century. Naturally, there have been variations, additions, and challenges to Stanislavski's approach, but his emphasis on the performer's immersing himself or herself in a role, preparing mentally and physically for a role, and maintaining both relaxation and concentration onstage have remained cornerstones of realistic acting.

Realistic Theater between 1915 and 1945

Producing Organizations in the United States.   During the early decades of the twentieth century—after the initial objections and censorship had eased—realistic plays began to be presented commercially in both Europe and the United States. In the United States, however, for a long time small, independent groups like those that developed in France, Germany, and England produced these plays.

These small American theaters were part of what was called the *little theater* movement, which flourished between the two world wars. The Provincetown Playhouse, the Neighborhood Playhouse, and the Washington Square Players, all founded in 1915 as alternatives to commercial theater, often presented experimental, nonrealistic work; they also offered a haven for controversial or unknown realistic drama. The Provincetown Playhouse, in particular, supported the early work of the playwright Eugene O'Neill (1888–1953).

In terms of realism, the most important producing group between World War I and World War II was the Group Theater, a noncommercial company in New York's Broadway district. The Group Theater was dedicated to presenting socially relevant drama and to introducing Stanislavski's system in the United States. Its founding members were Lee Strasberg (1901–1982), Cheryl Crawford (1902–1986), and Harold Clurman (1901–1980); and its acting company included a number of performers who became well known in movies as well as on the stage. Its resident playwright was Clifford Odets (1906–1963), a leading realist in the 1930s; Odets's plays include *Awake and Sing* (1935) and *Golden Boy* (1937). The Group Theater disbanded in 1941, but its influence on realistic acting, directing, and playwriting continued for many years.

One additional experiment in American theater between the wars should be noted. During the Depression, President Franklin Delano Roosevelt established the Works Progress Administration (WPA), which organized governmentally subsidized agencies to put the unemployed back to work. The Federal Theater Project, headed by Hallie Flanagan Davis (1890–1969), a college professor, was one of these agencies. For four years the Federal Theater Project supported theatrical

THE GROUP THEATER'S *AWAKE AND SING*
Clifford Odets's play, produced in 1935, is an example of a realistic social drama dealing with American concerns of the 1930s. It is an intense family drama set in an apartment in the Bronx during the depression, and it required the realistic acting for which the Group Theater was noted. (Vandamm Collection/The Museum of the City of New York)

ventures throughout the United States and helped revitalize interest in theater outside New York City. The Federal Theater also assisted aspiring African American theaters and artists, supporting, for example, an all-black production of *Macbeth* directed by Orson Welles (1915–1985). The government, for political reasons, discontinued funding the project in 1939 (many members of Congress had claimed that the project was sympathetic to communism).

After World War II, small theaters in New York (off-Broadway and off-off-Broadway) and elsewhere continued to produce difficult, controversial realistic plays, as well as experimental avant-garde works.

Realistic Playwrights between the Wars. Playwrights in many countries throughout the twentieth century continued the realistic drama initiated by Ibsen, Strindberg, and Chekhov. In Europe, for example, two Irish playwrights who had a strong impact on realism were John Millington Synge (1871–1909), in plays like *Riders to the Sea* (1904); and Sean O'Casey (1884–1964), in such works as *Juno and the Paycock* (1924) and *The Plough and the Stars* (1926).

In the United States, Eugene O'Neill wrote a number of realistic plays early in his career, including *Anna Christie* (1921) and *Desire Under the Elms* (1924). After writing experimental plays through much of the 1920s and 1930s, O'Neill later returned to realism and wrote what many consider his finest plays: *The Iceman Cometh* (1939), *A Moon for the Misbegotten* (1947), and *Long Day's Journey into Night* (produced in 1957). Another well-known realistic playwright of the 1930s and 1940s was Lillian Hellman (1905–1984).

1915 TO 1945
Year

Theater

Culture and Politics

	1915	

Major futurist productions at Piccolo Teatro in Rome (1918)

Soviet renaissance: Meyerhold, Vakhtangov, Tairov, Erveinov

Toller's *Man and the Masses* Pirandello's *Six Characters* (1921)

O'Neill's *The Hairy Ape* (1922) Dullin's *Atelier* (1922)

Jouvet in *Doctor Knock* (1923)

Stanislavski's *My Life in Art;* Breton's *First Manifesto;* O'Neill's *Desire Under the Elms* (1924)

Meyerhold's *Inspector General* (1926)

Brecht's *Threepenny Opera* (1928)

O'Neill's *Mourning Becomes Electra* (1931)

Group Theater, United States (1931)

Socialist realism declared proper style in Soviet Union; Brecht and other German artists emigrate (c. 1934); Gielgud's *Hamlet* (1934)

Lorca's *House of Bernarda Alba,* Giraudoux's *The Trojan War Will Not Take Place;* Federal Theater Project in United States (1935)

Tyrone Guthrie appointed administrator at the Old Vic (1937)

Artaud's *Theater and Its Double* (1938)

Thornton Wilder's *Skin of Our Teeth* (1942)

Othello with Paul Robeson (1943)

Sartre's *No Exit* (1944)

Easter Rebellion in Ireland (1916)

Bolshevik revolution (1917)

Prohibition in United States; Peace of Versailles (1919)

Women's suffrage in United States (1920)

Joyce's *Ulysses;* Mussolini's march on Rome (1922)

Hitler's beer hall putsch in Munich (1923)

Ortega y Gassett's *The Dehumanization of Art;* Kafka's *The Trial;* Thomas Mann's *The Magic Mountain* (1924)

Schoenberg's twelve-tone music (1926)

Depression begins; Wolfe's *Look Homeward, Angel;* Faulkner's *The Sound and the Fury* (1929)

Spain's monarchy collapses (1931)

Hitler takes power in Germany; New Deal in United States (1933)

Italy attacks Ethiopia; purges in Soviet Union; Nuremberg laws against Jews in Nazi Germany (1935)

Spanish Civil War; first television broadcast (1936)

World War II (1939–1945)

Hemingway's *For Whom the Bell Tolls* (1940)

Camus's *Myth of Sisyphus* (1943)

United States drops atomic bomb on Japan; United Nations formed (1945)

1915 · 1920 · 1925 · 1930 · 1935 · 1940 · 1945

REALISTIC IRISH PLAYWRIGHTS

Among the important realistic playwrights who emerged between the two world wars in Ireland was Sean O'Casey. O'Casey carefully reconstructs Irish life and concerns in such plays as The Plough and the Stars *and* Juno and the Paycock. *Shown here is a scene from the latter play, staged at the Donmar Warehouse in London. Colm Meaney (right) is Jack Boyle (the Paycock) a ne'er-do-well braggart who neglects his family; and Ron Cook (left) is Joxer Daly, his sidekick and drinking companion. (© Robbie Jack/Corbis)*

DEPARTURES FROM REALISM

In spite of its substantial impact on our contemporary theater, as well as on film and television, theatrical realism is often seen as having serious limitations. Since the time when realism became pervasive, there have been playwrights and theorists who considered it too confining, including some of the early realists themselves. One impetus for experimenting with departures from realism is that realistic drama excludes a number of effective, long-standing theatrical devices, such as music, dance, symbolism, poetry, fantasy, and the supernatural. Some authors argue that theater can never truly be realistic, that the conventions of the art are always apparent.

From the outset of realism, then, there has been a strong countermovement of *departures from realism* or *antirealism*. Let us, therefore, turn our attention to the many artists who between 1875 and 1945 departed from the realistic traditions.

Antirealist Playwrights: Ibsen, Strindberg, and Wedekind

As we noted earlier in this chapter, Ibsen and Strindberg are remembered most for their realistic plays, but late in their careers they moved away from realism. In

DEPARTURES FROM REALISM

Toward the end of his career, August Strindberg wrote plays that departed from the realistic style. These dramas were forerunners of many avant-garde texts of the later twentieth century. Strindberg's A Dream Play *uses the structure of a dream to break many of the conventions of realistic drama. Seen here are Angus Wright, Mark Arends, and Anastasia Hille, in a new version of the play by Caryl Churchill, directed by Katie Mitchell and staged at the Royal National Theatre in London.* (© Geraint Lewis)

plays like *The Master Builder* (1892) and *When We Dead Awaken* (1899), Ibsen adopted many of the tenets of symbolism, discussed below; and August Strindberg's later antirealistic dramas, such as *A Dream Play* (1902) and *The Ghost Sonata* (1907), have been especially influential. As its title indicates, *A Dream Play* evokes the world of dreams. It deals with many of the same concerns as Strindberg's realistic drama—the destructiveness of marriage, materialism, and the class struggle. But as Strindberg says in his explanatory note to *A Dream Play*, these are dramatized in "the disconnected but apparently logical form of a dream. Everything can happen; everything is possible and likely."[1]

The German dramatist Frank Benjamin Wedekind (1864–1918), in such plays as *Spring's Awakening* (1891), combined symbolist and grotesque elements with realistic—sometimes controversial—subject matter.

Symbolism

The leading antirealistic movement between 1880 and 1910 was *symbolism*. Its major proponents were French, but it influenced playwrights and practitioners in many other countries. The symbolists believed that drama should present not mundane, day-to-day activities but the mystery of being and the infinite qualities

---

[1]August Strindberg, *A Dream Play*, Trans. Walter Johnson. In *Anthology of Living Theater*, edited by Edwin Wilson and Alvin Goldfarb, McGraw-Hill, New York, 1998, p. 225.

of the human spirit. They called for poetic theater in which symbolic images rather than concrete actions would be the basic means of communicating with the audience. Probably the most renowned symbolist authors were Maurice Maeterlinck (1862–1949) in Belgium and Paul Claudel (1868–1955) in France.

Symbolist plays often seem to take place in a dreamworld, and their most important dramatic goal is not to tell a story but rather to evoke atmosphere and mood. The symbolists, unlike the realists, did not try to create individual characters; instead, symbolist characters are figures representative of the human condition. The symbolists also argued against realistic scenic detail, believing that a stage picture should have only the bare essentials necessary to evoke a dramatic universe.

In one way, at least, the symbolists were like the realists: both needed independently organized theater companies to produce their plays. In France, two independent theater companies were dedicated to antirealistic drama and production style. The Théâtre d'Art was organized by Paul Fort (1872–1960) in 1890; when it closed three years later, the Théâtre de l'Oeuvre was established by Aurélien-Marie Lugné-Poë (1869–1940), who had acted for Fort and for André Antoine at the Théâtre Libre. Possibly the most notorious of Lugné-Poë's presentations was not a symbolist work but a play by Alfred Jarry (1873–1907) called *Ubu the King* (1896), a takeoff in comic-book style on Shakespeare—in particular, on *Julius Caesar, Macbeth,* and the history plays. The farcical plot details how the bungling and gluttonous Ubu conspires to take over as ruler of Poland and is later dethroned by the assassinated king's only surviving son. The play's opening word, "Merdre," a takeoff on the French slang term for feces, created an immediate furor, as did many of its other scatological references.

In Ireland, the Abbey Theatre and the poet William Butler Yeats (1865–1939), who was also a playwright, were associated with early symbolist drama.

ALFRED JARRY'S *UBU ROI*
Jarry's play, written in 1896, is often cited as a forerunner of many antirealist movements of the twentieth century. It is an insane takeoff of King Oedipus *and of several Shakespearean histories and tragedies. Shown here, with Denis Lavant as the King, is a production at the Théâtre de Gennevilliers in France. (© Jean-Paul Lozouet)*

Antirealist Designers: Appia and Craig

Scene designers also contributed to the departure from realistically based representations of life. Adolphe Appia (1862–1928) and Edward Gordon Craig (1872–1966), in particular, were able to present many of the symbolists' theories

ADOLPHE APPIA'S DESIGN FOR *IPHIGENIA IN AULIS*

Appia's ideas of lighting and scenery were revolutionary. He moved from realistic settings to the use of shapes and levels that would serve as acting areas. He was also among the first to realize the vast possibilities of modern lighting techniques. (Billy Rose Theatre Collection, New York Public Library for the Performing Arts, Astor, Lenox, and Tilden Foundations)

visually. Most of Appia's and Craig's ideas remained only in the form of sketches or drawings, but these ideas had great significance for twentieth-century scene design.

Appia (who was born in Switzerland) and Craig (who was English) both argued against photographic reproduction as a basic goal of scene design; they believed that a setting should suggest a locale but should not reproduce it. Both used levels and platforms to design spaces that would be functional for the performer. Moreover, both took full advantage of the introduction of electricity and used light as an integral visual element. Most of their designs are extremely atmospheric, stressing contrasts between light and dark.

Appia and Craig influenced many of the leading twentieth-century American designers; for example, devices such as Craig's ***unit set***—a single setting that can represent various locales—have been especially important.

Russian Theatricalism: Meyerhold

The reaction against realism also influenced a number of Russian artists who rejected the principles of Konstantin Stanislavski and the Moscow Art Theater. Possibly the most influential was the director Vsevolod Meyerhold (1874–1940), who was the leading Russian antirealist between 1905 and 1939 and frequently experimented with ***theatricalism***. Theatricalists liked to expose the devices of theater, such as the way stage machinery works, to make the audience conscious of watching a performance; they also borrowed techniques from the circus, the music hall, and similar entertainments.

The list of Meyerhold's innovations and experiments is astounding, and much of what was called avant-garde in the second half of the twentieth century can be traced back to his experiments early in the century. Meyerhold's theater was a director's theater: he was literally the author of his productions, and he frequently restructured or rewrote classics. He searched for suitable environments for his presentations, arguing for the use of *found spaces*—that is, spaces (such as streets, factories, and schools) not originally meant for theater. He experimented with, and theorized about, multimedia in stage productions.

Meyerhold also attempted to train his performers physically by using techniques of commedia dell'arte, the circus, and vaudeville. He devised an acting system known as **biomechanics**, which emphasized external, physical training; the implication of biomechanics was that the performer's body could be trained to operate like a machine. Meyerhold argued that through physical actions performers can evoke the necessary internal responses in themselves and audiences. Meyerhold's sets, known as **constructivist** settings, provided machines for his performers to work on; these settings consisted of skeletal frames, ramps, stairways, and platforms and often looked like huge Tinkertoys.

Early Eclectics

Some theater artists in the early twentieth century tried to bridge the gap between realism and antirealism. These practitioners—known as *eclectics*—were not doctrinaire; instead, they argued that each play should define its own form. Eclectic directors included the Austrian Max Reinhardt (1873–1943) and the Russian Yevgeny Vakhtangov (1883–1922).

Departures from Realism: 1915 to 1945

The period from 1915 to 1945—from World War I to the end of World War II—was, as we noted earlier, turbulent, and these were also turbulent years for theater, which reflected the chaotic world scene. Many theatrical innovators continued the reaction against realism, which by then had become the most popular form of theater. A number of new antirealistic movements developed in continental Europe, including expressionism, futurism, dada, and surrealism; and these movements, though they were most influential in the visual arts, also had an important impact on avant-garde theater. Some artistic movements were associated with political ideologies. Expressionism and epic theater, for example, supported socialism; others, such as futurism, supported fascism.

Before we turn to such movements, we should briefly mention influential playwrights whose works do not fit into any of the usual categories. First, there is the Italian dramatist Luigi Pirandello (1867–1936) who in *Six Characters in Search of an Author* (1921) has six characters from an unfinished play existing in a playwright's mind enter a theater and interrupt a rehearsal, in the hope that the troupe will act out their unfinished story. In the course of the action—as in several of his other plays—Pirandello deals very theatrically with questions of appearance versus reality and art versus life.

PAUL ROBESON IN EUGENE O'NEILL'S
THE EMPEROR JONES

This play, like many of O'Neill's dramas of the early 1920s, uses expressionistic techniques. The audience sees the drama through the eyes of the protagonist, a black dictatorial ruler of a Caribbean island who is fleeing his people in the jungle. (Billy Rose Theatre Collection, New York Public Library for the Performing Arts, Astor, Lenox, and Tilden Foundations)

Two significant playwrights of the period between World War I and World War II were Jean Giraudoux (1882–1944) and Jean Anouilh (1910–1987). Giraudoux, whose plays were frequently directed by Louis Jouvet (1887–1951), believed in the primacy of the word, and his language was usually eloquent as well as witty. He also stressed contradictions, ironies, and antithesis in working out the themes of his plays. Among his better-known works are *Amphitryon 38* (1929), *Judith* (1931), *The Trojan War Will Not Take Place* (1935), and *Ondine* (1939). As can be seen from their titles, many of his plays were based on classic themes or plots. Jean Anouilh also used a classic source for his best-known play, *Antigone* (1943), a reworking of the Greek classic that spoke to the situation in Nazi-occupied France.

Expressionism. *Expressionism*, which flourished in Germany at the time of World War I, was a movement in art and literature in which the representation of reality was distorted in order to communicate inner feelings. In a painting of a man, for example, the lines in his face would be twisted to indicate the turmoil he feels inside.

Expressionism in drama has well-defined characteristics. Expressionist plays are often highly subjective; the dramatic action is seen through the eyes of the protagonist and therefore frequently seems distorted or dreamlike. Many of these plays have common themes, such as the dehumanization of the individual by society and the deterioration of the family. The protagonist in a typical expressionist play is a Christlike figure who journeys through a series of incidents that may be causally unrelated. Characters are representative types, often given titles—such as Man, Woman, or Clerk—rather than names. The language of the plays is telegraphic, with most speeches consisting of one or two lines; but these speeches alternate with long lyrical passages. Many expressionist playwrights were politically motivated, supporting socialist and pacifist causes, though some were apolitical.

The major German expressionist playwrights were Georg Kaiser (1878–1945) and Ernst Toller (1893–1939). Shortly after expressionism flourished in Europe, its influence was felt in the United States—for example, in some of Eugene O'Neill's plays, including *The Emperor Jones* (1922), as well as in *The Adding Machine* (1923), by Elmer Rice (1892–1967).

In its pure form, the expressionist movement was short-lived, lasting only about 15 years, but many expressionistic techniques found their way into the mainstream of modern theater.

Futurism, Dada, and Surrealism.   Although futurism and dada—two other nonrealistic movements that emerged around the time of World War I—had less impact than expressionism on theater, the aesthetic principles of both movements have influenced avant-garde theater artists from the 1960s to the present.

Futurism originated in Italy around 1909. Unlike the expressionists, the futurists idealized war and the machine age. They attacked artistic ideals of the past, ridiculing them as "museum art" and arguing that new forms had to be created for new eras. They sought a "synthetic" theater of short, seemingly illogical dramatic pieces and argued against the separation of performers and audience. They also believed that audiences should be confronted and antagonized.

Dada, which originated in Switzerland in 1916, was a short-lived movement that never really caught on. Reacting against World War I, the dadaists argued that art should mirror the madness of the world. Like the futurists, they railed against museum art and wanted to confuse and antagonize their audiences. Unlike the futurists, however, they were not concerned with glorifying war or machines.

Surrealism, an outgrowth of dada, began in 1924. One of its major exponents was André Breton (1896–1966), and its center was France. Surrealists argued that the subconscious is the highest plane of reality and attempted to re-create its workings dramatically. Many of their plays seem to be set in a dream-world, mixing recognizable and fantastic events.

Artaud and Brecht.   The two most influential theatrical theorists in Europe between the world wars were Bertolt Brecht and Antonin Artaud. Both reacted vehemently against the principles of Stanislavski and the aesthetics of realistic theater.

Antonin Artaud (1896–1948), who was French and who had originally been associated with the surrealists, proposed a *theater of cruelty* in the 1930s. He argued that western theater needed to be totally transformed because its literary tradition, which emphasized language, was antithetical to its ritualistic origins. Artaud believed that western theater artists should study the stylized Asian theaters. He also asserted that there were "no more masterpieces," by which he meant that the classics should be produced not for their historical significance but only if they were still relevant to contemporary audiences. For Artaud, a text was not sacred but could be reworked in order to point up its relevance.

Artaud's theater of cruelty is characterized by its emphasis on the sensory. He did not literally mean that theater artists should be cruel to their audiences or physically brutalize them—although some avant-garde theater artists in the 1960s interpreted cruelty as actual physical confrontation with spectators. He felt, instead, that the viewers' senses should be bombarded. (A contemporary example of such sensory involvement would be a multimedia presentation or a sound and light show at a rock concert.) Artaud, like many of the antirealists

BERTOLT BRECHT

Brecht's epic theories and plays continue to be part of contemporary theater; his concepts, including alienation and historification, continue to be debated and are still influential. Brecht's personal life has been no less controversial than his work: recent scholarship suggests that some of his work was plagiarized and that his political stance was perhaps hypocritical. Shown here is a scene from one of his best-known plays, Mother Courage and Her Children, *with Robyn Hunt as Mother Courage, along with her two sons—J. P. Quicquaro as Eilif and Nathan Caron as Swiss Cheese. The production was by the Connecticut Repertory Theatre. (© Gerry Goodstein)*

who preceded him, wanted to reorganize the theater space to make the audience the center of attention.

Bertolt Brecht (1898–1956), who was German, developed what he called *epic theater*, though he was not the first to use that term or the first to use epic techniques. Brecht's major plays—including *Mother Courage* (1937–1941), *The Good Person of Setzuan* (1938–1940), and *The Caucasian Chalk Circle* (1944–1945)—were written between 1933 and 1945, while he was in exile from Hitler's Germany. As a director, Brecht worked with the Berliner Ensemble in East Berlin from 1949 until his death in 1956, making an international impact. His theories, most of which were formulated in the 1930s but frequently revised, have influenced many contemporary playwrights and directors.

As the term *epic theater* implies, Brecht's plays are epic in scope. They are, accordingly, episodic in structure: they cover a great deal of time, shift locale frequently, and have intricate plots and many characters. Brecht, an ardent socialist, believed that theater could create an intellectual climate for social change, and the goal of his epic theater is to instruct. He felt that for theater to teach successfully, the audience should not be emotionally hypnotized but should be involved intellectually. He believed that a production should force the audience to remain emotionally detached—or *alienated*—from the dramatic action. To prevent emotional involvement, Brecht's works are highly theatrical; the audience is always made aware of being in a theater. A narrator is frequently used to comment on the dramatic action, for example. To alienate the audience, Brecht also used a technique he referred to as *historification*. Many of his plays, such as *Mother Courage*, are set in the past, but it is apparent that he is really concerned with contemporary events paralleling the historic occurrences.

POPULAR THEATER TRADITIONS

We should remember that the popular forms, such as melodramas, comedies, and musical plays, as well as vaudeville and variety, continued to flourish during this period in the United States as well as throughout Europe.

Popular playwrights, such as Clyde Fitch (1865–1909), emphasized melodramatic plotlines and devices. There were also notable comedies by Phillip Barry (1896–1949), George S. Kaufman (1889–1961), and Moss Hart (1904–1961). We will discuss the development of musical theater in Chapter 18.

TOTALITARIANISM, THE SECOND WORLD WAR, AND THEATER

As might be expected, the rise of totalitarianism and the outbreak of World War II in 1939 curtailed the development of European theater and drama. Theatrical activity did not cease altogether, but in totalitarian societies—particularly the Soviet Union under Stalin and Germany under Hitler—government-supported theaters became instruments of propaganda. Courageous artists attempted to attack these regimes; for the most part, though, experimentation and freedom of expression were suppressed. The totalitarian rulers saw realistic art as easier to manipulate and to use for propaganda. Furthermore, they saw individual experimentation as dangerous because it implied freedom. Therefore, the fascists and communists vigorously attacked many of the artists who experimented with forms that departed from realism.

In Spain, for example, the playwright Federico García Lorca (1898–1936)—author of *Blood Wedding* (1933), *Yerma* (1934), and *The House of Bernarda Alba* (1936)—was killed by Franco's forces during the civil war. Productions of García Lorca's works, which poetically dramatized the oppression of Spanish women, were not allowed in Spain until after Franco's death in 1975.

Numerous German theater artists, because of their religion or politics, had to flee Germany after Adolf Hitler's takeover in 1933. They included the directors Max Reinhardt and Erwin Piscator (1893–1966) as well as the playwrights Bertolt Brecht and Ernst Toller. Many artists who opposed the Third Reich but did not leave were interned in the Nazi concentration camps.

Still, theatrical artists did resist totalitarianism; the most vivid example of such resistance was the theater organized by inmates of the Nazi concentration camps. In camps in conquered territories during World War II, such as Auschwitz, there were surreptitious entertainments in the barracks: these improvised presentations consisted of literature and drama recited from memory, satirical skits, and traditional songs. In the camp at Theresienstadt, in Czechoslovakia, satirical plays, operas, and cabaret entertainments were written and openly staged; this was allowed because the Nazis were using Theresienstadt as a "model" camp—they brought the Red Cross and foreign officials there in order to discredit rumors of atrocities. Most of the artists who passed through Theresienstadt were later sent to extermination centers.

In Chapter 18, we will see how the strands of our modern theater developed during the period immediately following World War II until about 2000.

SUMMARY

Modern theater began in the late nineteenth century with the realistic plays of Henrik Ibsen, August Strindberg, and Anton Chekhov. In realism, events onstage mirror observable reality in the outside world. The characters speak, move, dress, and behave as people do in real life; they are seen in familiar places such as living rooms, bedrooms, and kitchens.

One appeal of realism is that audiences can identify with and verify people and events onstage. One disadvantage of realism is that it excludes a number of traditional theatrical devices, such as poetry, music, ghosts, and special effects. Despite this drawback, however, realism is so effective that it has been a dominant theatrical form of the past hundred years.

Because of its uncompromising presentation of life, realism was initially produced not commercially but by small independent theaters. As it became more widely accepted, it entered the mainstream of theater.

In the twentieth century, Synge and O'Casey in Ireland, O'Neill and Hellman in the United States, and many other playwrights worldwide wrote powerful realistic drama.

From 1875 until 1945, there were also significant movements that departed from realism: these included symbolism, expressionism, futurism, dada, surrealism, and epic theater. Among practitioners who attempted to transform theater were the designers Appia and Craig as well as the director Meyerhold. Key theories arguing against realism are Artaud's theater of cruelty and Brecht's epic theater.

These movements have made audiences reevaluate realism, particularly since many "antirealistic" techniques were eventually fused into more traditional dramas and commercial productions.

KEY TERMS

Alienation Bertolt Brecht's theory that, in his epic theater, audiences' emotional involvement should be minimized to increase their intellectual involvement with the political message.

Biomechanics Meyerhold's theory that a performer's body should be machinelike and that emotion could be represented externally.

Constructivism Post–World War I scene-design movement in which sets—frequently composed of ramps, platforms, and levels—were nonrealistic and were intended to provide greater opportunities for physical action.

Dada Movement in art between the world wars, based on presenting the irrational and attacking traditional artistic values.

Epic theater Form of episodic drama associated with Bertolt Brecht and aimed at the intellect rather than the emotions.

Expressionism Movement in Germany at about the time of World War I, characterized by an attempt to dramatize subjective states through distortion; striking, often grotesque images; and lyric, unrealistic dialogue.

Futurism Art movement, begun in Italy about 1909, which idealized mechanization and machinery.

Naturalism Special form of realism developed in Europe in the late nineteenth century; it was not carefully plotted or constructed but was meant to present a "slice of life."

Stanislavski system Konstantin Stanislavski's techniques and theories about acting, which promote a naturalistic style stressing (among other things) "inner truth" as opposed to conventional theatricality.

Surrealism Departure from realism that attempted to present dramatically the working of the subconscious.

Symbolism Movement of the late nineteenth century and early twentieth century that sought to express inner truth rather than represent life realisically.

Theater of cruelty Antonin Artaud's visionary concept of a theater based on magic and ritual, which would liberate deep, violent, and erotic impulses.

Theatricalism Exposing the elements of theater to make the audience members aware that they are watching theater.

Unit set Single setting that can represent a variety of locales with the simple addition of properties or scenic elements.

THEATER ON THE WEB

For more research and to learn more about the topics in this chapter, please visit the Online Learning Center at **www.mhhe.com/livelyart6.**

18

Twentieth-Century Theatrical Diversity

◀ **TENNESSEE WILLIAMS'S A STREETCAR NAMED DESIRE**

After World War II, there were many new movements in dramatic literature. During this time, playwrights also mixed various styles to create their own unique dramas. The American playwright Tennessee Williams mixed realistic technique with a haunting poetic style. The scene shown here is from A Streetcar Named Desire, *with Natasha Richardson as Blanche DuBois, the fragile, doomed heroine who is challenged by her brother-in-law, Stanley Kowalski. (Sara Krulwich/The New York Times)*

Theater has experienced a turbulent period from 1945 to the present. There has been an explosion of experimentation, with new, nonrealistic avant-garde trends developing one after another. Because these movements are so close to our own lifetime, we are unable to evaluate their historical significance conclusively. It is clear, however, that established theatrical and dramatic forms have been questioned and reworked, and that movements such as absurdism and environmental theater have forced us to redefine our concept of drama and theater. While we review many international developments during this time period, we will also highlight the turbulent American theater scene.

POSTWAR REALISTIC THEATER
Background: The Postwar Era

After World War II, which ended in 1945 with the defeat of Germany and Italy in Europe and Japan in Asia, there was again hope for peace. The period after World War II was different from the period after World War I. For one thing, the atom bomb—which had been dropped on two cities in Japan at the close of World War II—and later the hydrogen bomb had been developed. These weapons were potentially so deadly that a stalemate developed between the superpowers controlling them, the United States and the Soviet Union.

At the end of World War II, the Soviet Union had annexed many nations in eastern and central Europe into an association known as the Warsaw Pact. There was also an association among western nations known as the North Atlantic Treaty Organization (NATO). Between these two blocs there developed what came to be called a *cold war.* The cold war was to last for decades, not ending until the countries of eastern Europe moved away from communist and Soviet domination in 1989 and 1990 and the Soviet Union was dissolved at the end of 1991.

The end of World War II did not mean the end of military conflicts. From 1945 to the present, there have been numerous other wars, including the Korean War, the Israeli-Arab conflicts in the Middle East, the Vietnam War, a Soviet-led war in Afghanistan, the Persian Gulf War, the Bosnian-Serb War in the former Yugoslavia, the Rwandan civil war in Africa, and the Iraq war.

There was also a great deal of social unrest, including civil rights movements by underrepresented groups such as African Americans, women, and homosexuals. This was a violent era, marked by assassinations, revolutions, and attempts by dictatorial regimes to put down revolutions—as in the Soviet bloc and in China.

Another development of the postwar period was a striking increase in the industrial power of two of the defeated nations: Germany and Japan. Economically and politically, the world became more interdependent, with developments in one part of the world—such as environmental pollution or the price of oil—directly affecting other areas around the globe: Central and South America, for instance, as well as Europe, Asia, and the United States.

Meanwhile, inventions continued at a rapid pace: nuclear power, for example, and computer technology, which revolutionized many aspects of life. Earlier,

1945 TO PRESENT
Year

Theater

Jean-Louis Barrault's theater company established (1946)

Genet's *The Maids*; Williams's *A Streetcar Named Desire* (1947)

Ionesco's *The Bald Soprano*; Berliner Ensemble; Miller's *Death of a Salesman*; Arena Stage in Washington (1949)

Vilar at Théâtre Nationale Populaire in France (1951)

Beckett's *Waiting for Godot* (1953)

Thornton Wilder's *The Matchmaker* (1954)

Osborne's *Look Back in Anger* Dürrenmatt's *The Visit* (1956)

Pinter's *Birthday Party*; Laterna Magika (1958)

Hansberry's *A Raisin in the Sun* Grotowski founds Polish Laboratory Theater (1959)

Café La Mama founded; Albee's *Who's Afraid of Virginia Woolf?* (1962)

National Theatre under Laurence Olivier (1963)

Lonne Elder's *Ceremonies in Dark Old Men* (1969)

Sam Shepard's *Buried Child* wins Pulitzer Prize (1979)

August Wilson's *Fences* wins Pulitzer Prize (1987)

Neil Simon's *Lost in Yonkers* wins Pulitzer Prize (1991)

Tony Kushner's *Angels in America* wins Pulitzer Prize (1993)

Eugène Ionesco dies (1994)

Heiner Müller dies (1996)

Wit by Margaret Edson wins Pulitzer Prize (1999)

Peter Stein directs *Faust*, Berlin, Germany (2000)

Topdog/Underdog by Suzan-Lori Parks wins Pulitzer Prize (2002)

Anna in the Tropics by Nilo Cruz wins Pulitzer Prize (2003)

Doubt by John Patrick Shanley wins Pulitzer Prize (2005)

Year markers
1945
1950
1955
1960
1965
1975
1985
1990
1995
2000
2005

Culture and Politics

Nuremberg trials (1946)

Orwell's *1984*; Germany divided (1949)

Korean War (1950–1953)

Stalin dies (1953)

McCarthy-Army hearings; hydrogen bomb tested (1954)

Russia crushes Hungarian revolt; Suez crisis (1956)

Sputnik I and II (1957)

Belgian Congo granted independence (1960)

Berlin Wall (1961)

Cuban missile crisis (1962)

Warfare escalates between North and South Vietnam; Martin Luther King arrested in Birmingham; John F. Kennedy, president of the United States, assassinated (1963)

Krushchev resigns (1964)

American astronauts walk on moon (1969)

Camp David accord reached between Israel and Egypt (1977)

Muslim revolution in Iran (1979)

Ronald Reagan elected president (1980)

Chinese government crushes pro-democracy demonstration (1989)

Berlin Wall taken down; eastern Europe democratized (1990)

Soviet Union dissolves (1991)

Bill Clinton elected president of the United States (1992)

Bill Clinton reelected president (1996)

George W. Bush elected president of United States (2000)

Terrorist attack on World Trade Center in New York City (9/11/2001)

War in Iraq (2003)

George W. Bush reelected president of United States (2004)

***ALL MY SONS* BY ARTHUR MILLER**

An American dramatist who carried forward the realistic tradition of Ibsen, Arthur Miller, also used selective realism (in Death of a Salesman*) and historical drama. But* All My Sons, *shown here, is one of his strictly realistic plays. In this drama, a man who made faulty airplane parts in World War II has lost a son killed in a plane. The man, played by Richard Dreyfuss (center), tries to deny his responsibility to his other son (Sam Trammel, right). At the left, as his wife, is Jill Clayburgh. (© T. Charles Erickson)*

this period saw the development of jet airplanes, television, and many advances in medical science.

At the same time, tremendous problems remained: economic inequality and conflicts between rich and poor in many nations, assaults on the environment, persistent racial prejudice, and starvation and homelessness in many parts of the world.

Clearly, then, western society after World War II was left with many haunting questions. How could the civilized world have engaged in a war that resulted in over 35 million deaths? How could rational societies undertake genocide? Would the atom bomb lead to annihilation of the human race? How could wealthy societies continue to have large numbers of poverty-stricken people? How could racism continue to survive? Questions like these have forced western society to reevaluate its most cherished beliefs.

THE SELECTIVE REALISM OF ALBEE

Among the American playwrights who have effectively combined realism with other forms such as symbolism, expressionism, and theater of the absurd is Edward Albee. His drama Seascape *features sea creatures (lizards) who come on land. They have decidedly human characteristics and interact with a couple who are clearly human. Seen here are George Grizzard and Frances Sternhagen as the humans and Frederick Weller and Elizabeth Marvel as the humanlike lizards who confront them. (© Joan Marcus)*

American Selective Realism

Between 1945 and 2000, there were many playwrights who continued to refine the realistic form and who created new types of dramas based on the earlier innovations of Ibsen, Chekhov, and Strindberg. One such trend was selective realism.

After World War II, two important American writers were Tennessee Williams (1911–1983) and Arthur Miller (1915–2005). Williams's important realistic plays include *A Streetcar Named Desire* (1947) and *Cat on a Hot Tin Roof* (1954)—both of which won the Pulitzer Prize—and *The Night of the Iguana* (1961). Miller's realistic works include *All My Sons* (1947) and *A View from the Bridge* (1955).

Some critics suggest that Miller and Williams write in a form known as *selective realism*—a type of realism that heightens certain details of action, scenery, and dialogue while omitting others. For example, in Miller's *Death of a Salesman*

(1949), the playwright highlights selected elements of the world of the main character, Willy Loman—elements that symbolize his downfall. Moreover, scenes in Willy's mind and scenes from the past are interspersed with scenes in the present. *Death of Salesman* is set in a recognizable, realistic world, but the elements have been carefully chosen to underline thematic concerns. Tennessee Williams combines the theatrical device of a narrator with realistic scenes in his play *The Glass Menagerie* (1945).

Throughout the twentieth century, the end of realism was pronounced periodically, but the form has continued with great vigor to the present day. In 1962, another American writer, Edward Albee (1928–   ), joined the list of important realists with his play *Who's Afraid of Virginia Woolf?* (1962). Albee's style is highly enigmatic, however, and some of his plays—such as *Three Tall Women* (1991); *The Play about the Baby* (1998); and *The Goat, or Who Is Sylvia?*, which won the Tony Award in 2002—combine realistic and nonrealistic techniques. Several outstanding American playwrights of the 1970s and 1980s wrote powerful plays using realistic techniques.

The "Angry Young Men" in England and Documentary Drama in Germany

In England in the 1950s, a group of antiestablishment playwrights known collectively as the *angry young men* dealt with the dissolving British Empire, class conflict, and political disillusionment. Most of the dramas by the "angry young men" are in the traditional realistic form, slightly modified. The most famous of these plays was *Look Back in Anger* (1956) by John Osborne (1929–1994).

A German movement of the 1960s called *documentary drama* has also been influential. Documentary dramas are based on historical documents, which give an air of authenticity and historical reality. The goal of documentary drama was to convince audiences that they were watching history unfold, even when these dramatists had modified the documents for dramatic or political effect. One of the most famous documentary dramas was *The Investigation* (1965) by Peter Weiss (1916–1982), which dramatizes the war crimes trials of people who had been guards at a Nazi extermination camp. Documentary dramas continued to be written into the twenty-first century. Today, docudramas—as they are sometimes referred to—are also popular as made-for-television movies. Docudrama for the stage also continues to be written. A good example is *Exonerated,* a documentary of 2002 about former death-row inmates who turned out to be innocent.

EXPERIMENTATION AND DEPARTURES FROM REALISM: 1945 TO 1980

The period from 1945 to 1980 saw a great deal of experimentation with theatrical forms and techniques. Much of this experimentation was inspired by political unrest and by a desire to question political authority through the questioning of traditional theatrical practices, styles, and techniques. One of the first of the

Waiting for Godot

1957, California The setting is San Quentin prison in California on November 19, 1957. In the prison's North Dining Hall, a stage is set up where a group from the Actors' Workshop will perform Samuel Beckett's *Waiting for Godot*. It will be the first performance at the prison in over forty years.

The Actors' Workshop is a theater group dedicated to performing provocative, experimental, avant-garde works by both national and international playwrights. Its members have made a name for themselves not only in the San Francisco area but throughout the United States. When performing, they work closely together as an ensemble.

The performers today are nervous, not only because they are performing in a penitentiary, but also because of the play itself. *Waiting for Godot* is a drama without much action, and it is filled with literary and religious references. It has already baffled intellectuals in Europe and the United States; how, the actors wonder, will a group of restless prisoners react to it?

The setting is described simply as "A country road. A tree." In actuality, it is a barren plain. The two central characters, Vladimir and Estragon, who are also known as Didi and Gogo, are tramplike clowns who are waiting for the Godot figure. They have the vague expectation that somehow, if and when he comes, Godot will be able to help them. It is never stated who Godot is: he may be

God, he may be someone else, or he may not even exist. While they wait, they try to break the painful monotony of their boring lives with bickering and occasional vaudeville routines.

The difficulty of the play is compounded by the fact that the second act seems to be almost the same as the first act. In both acts, Vladimir and Estragon try to entertain themselves; they move between hope and despair; they engage in vaudeville routines and philosophical speculation.

Meanwhile, two other characters, Pozzo and Lucky, appear. Pozzo is an overbearing creature who treats Lucky as his slave. Lucky, who has been mute, toward the end of the first act suddenly makes a long speech filled with legal terms. In the second act, the roles of Pozzo and Lucky are somewhat reversed, as Pozzo has become blind.

There is not the usual progress or story line expected in a traditional play. There is no building of suspense, no careful development of characters, no sudden plot twist, no big payoff at the end. In short, the play defies most of the conventional notions of both the content and the structure of drama.

At the end of the play, Godot's identity still has not been revealed, nor has he ever appeared. Instead, a young messenger arrives at the close of the first and second acts and announces that while Godot will not come that day, he will no doubt come the next.

The members of the Actors' Workshop have been acting together for a long time; and when they approach a play, they take their time, exploring the text, becoming familiar with the characters, and engaging in improvisation as they develop a performance. Even with this background they are apprehensive as they approach the performance at San Quentin. These, after all, are prisoners, not a sophisticated, intellectual audience, and this material is difficult for even the most scholarly spectators.

With these difficulties in mind, the performers from the Actors' Workshop begin their presentation. Shortly after the performance is under way, they have an indication that the production will go over better and be more readily understood than they had anticipated. Within the first few minutes, the audience grows quiet. A group of men sitting on some steps who had planned to leave early become engrossed and stay.

To the surprise of the performers, the audience sits in rapt attention. The prisoners follow the play closely from beginning to end and seem to understand what is happening. After the performance is over, it is clear that the prisoners have understood much of what they have seen—perhaps more than other audiences might understand. These prisoners, waiting out their sentences in boredom and frustration, have intuitively connected with the men onstage who wait for the unknown Godot, who never comes.

THEATER OF THE ABSURD: BECKETT'S *WAITING FOR GODOT*
One play typifying the spirit of alienation and loneliness of drama after World War II is Waiting for Godot, *about two men waiting to be saved by someone who never comes. Shown here are the tragicomic protagonists Alan Dobie (Estragon) and Julian Glover (Vladimir), and their two visitors, Terence Rigby (Pozzo) and Struan Rodger (Lucky), in a production at the Piccadilly Theatre, London. (© Robbie Jack/Corbis)*

nontraditional forms to develop immediately after World War II, theater of the absurd, was born out of the unanswerable questions this horrific conflict had left in the minds of the survivors.

Existentialism and Theater of the Absurd

Existentialism is a philosophy most clearly articulated by two Frenchmen, Jean-Paul Sartre (1905–1980) and Albert Camus (1913–1960), who were reacting, among other things, to World War II. Existentialists believe that existence has little meaning; that God does not exist; that humanity is alone in an irrational universe; and that the only significant thing an individual can do is accept responsibility for his or her own actions. Both Camus and Sartre wrote plays illustrating these beliefs. The best-known are Sartre's *The Flies* (1943), an adaptation of the Greek *Oresteia*; and *No Exit* (1944), in which hell is equated with other people.

In the early 1950s, a theatrical approach emerged that combined existentialist philosophy with revolutionary, avant-garde dramatic form. Their viewpoint was also highly influenced by the Holocaust of World War II and the development of nuclear weapons. Although not an organized movement, it was called *theater of the absurd* by the critic Martin Esslin (1918–2002). Esslin pointed out that the playwrights in this group have certain qualities in common: one is the notion that much of what happens in life is ridiculous or absurd and cannot be explained logically; another is the belief that this ridiculousness or absurdity should be reflected in dramatic action. Among the writers taking this approach are Samuel Beckett (1906–1989), Jean Genet (1910–1986), Eugène Ionesco (1912–1994), Edward Albee, and Harold Pinter (1930–   ).

Absurdist playwrights present our existence, including human relationships and human language, as futile or nonsensical. To reinforce this theme, they use seemingly illogical dramatic techniques. Their plots do not have either traditional climactic structure or episodic structure. Frequently, nothing seems to happen: the plot moves in a circle, concluding in the same way it began. The characters are not realistic, and the settings are sometimes strange and unrecognizable. The language is often telegraphic and sparse; the characters fail to communicate.

Waiting for Godot (1953) by Samuel Beckett is probably the most famous of these enigmatic, nontraditional dramas. As in many absurdist dramas, the plot is cyclical: the action in Act II appears to start over, with nothing having changed since Act I. The two main characters, Vladimir and Estragon, spend their time waiting; they accomplish nothing and are unable to take control of their lives. The other two men, Lucky and Pozzo, also have no control over their destiny; fate reverses their roles, transforming one from master into servant and the other from servant into master.

Beckett referred to *Waiting for Godot* as a "tragicomedy in two acts," a description that reveals his tragicomic view of the human condition. Human inaction is comical but has tragic consequences.

Experimental Theater

After absurdism, there were further attempts to supersede traditional theater practices. These experiments, carried out in Europe and the United States in the 1960s and 1970s, went in many directions—a reflection, no doubt, of the fragmentation of modern life. The experiments included happenings, multimedia, and environmental theater.

Happenings, Multimedia, and New Technology. Two significant developments of the 1960s and 1970s were happenings and experiments with multimedia.

Happenings were what the name suggests: unstructured events that occurred with a minimum of planning and organization. The idea—especially popular in the 1960s—was that art should not be restricted to museums, galleries, or concert halls but can and should happen anywhere: on a street corner, in a grocery store, at a bus stop.

Multimedia is a joining of theater with other arts—particularly dance, film, and television. In work of this sort, which is still being produced, live performers interact with sequences on film or television. The idea here is to fuse the art forms or to incorporate new technology into a theatrical event. A current form that combines theater, dance, and media is called *performance art*.

Any discussion of departures from realism after World War II must also take into account new technology in scene and lighting design (see Chapters 10 and 11). The Czechoslovakian designer Josef Svoboda (1920–2002), for example, experimented with such elements as projections, multimedia, movable platforms, and new materials, including plastics. Computer technology as well has been incorporated into many modern theater buildings and lighting systems.

Environmental Theater. The term *environmental theater* was coined in the 1960s by the American director and teacher Richard Schechner (1934–); many characteristics of environmental theater, however, had developed out of the work and theories of earlier avant-garde artists, including Vsevolod Meyerhold and Antonin Artaud. Proponents of environmental theater treat the entire theater space as a performance area, suggesting that any division between performers and viewers is artificial. For every production, spatial arrangements are transformed. (See the discussion of created and found spaces in Chapter 9.)

To Schechner, we should note, not only the theater space but also the dramatic text is subject to such transformation: a text is not sacred or even essential, and both improvisation and reworking of an existing drama are permissible.

The major influence on Schechner's theories is the Polish director Jerzy Grotowski (1933–1999). Works staged by Grotowski with the Polish Laboratory Theater from its founding in 1959 until 1970 had many characteristics of environmental theater. For each production, the theater space and the performer-audience relationship were arranged to conform to the play being presented. According to Grotowski, the essence of theater is interaction between live performers and audiences—hence his emphasis on reorganizing spatial arrangements. In his production of *Kordian* (1962), for instance, the space resembled a mental institution, with spectators scattered among the beds and patients (the performers). In his version of *Doctor Faustus,* the theater space was filled with two large dining tables at which audience members sat as if attending a banquet given by Faustus. As is true of Schechner, for most of Grotowski's productions existing scripts were radically modified by the performers and director. The acting style was externally based, emphasizing body and voice rather than emotions.

Grotowski called his theater *poor theater,* meaning poor in scenery and special effects. It relied on the performers for its impact. (Grotowski's stress on the importance of the environment and nonverbal aspects of performance has a strong affinity with the ideas of Antonin Artaud.)

Postwar Eclectics

It would be impossible to list every postwar European theatrical innovator. We can, however, note that there are numerous directors who borrow from various kinds of theatrical experiments—*eclectics* whose work incorporates a range of avant-garde techniques.

The English director Peter Brook (1925–) is a well-known contemporary eclectic. In staging Peter Weiss's *Marat/Sade* (1964), Brook applied concepts borrowed from Artaud's theater of cruelty. His production of Shakespeare's *Midsummer Night's Dream* (1970) was clearly influenced by Meyerhold's experiments with biomechanics and circus arts; for example, the fairy gods appeared on trapezes. Since 1971, when he became director of the International Center for Theater Research in Paris, Brook has tried to avoid what he calls "deadly" commercial theater, which does not allow for experimentation. Among his productions are a stripped-down version of the opera *Carmen;* a production of *The Cherry Orchard,* without intermission; and *The Man Who,* based on a popular book of case studies by a neurologist. Brook has explained his theories about theater in his book *The Empty Space* (1968). He has also published his autobiography, *The Shifting Point* (1988); and a memoir, *Threads of Time* (1998).

The work of Peter Brook and other postwar eclectics is indicative of the incorporation of nonrealistic techniques into more traditional, commercial theater.

DEVELOPMENTS IN POSTWAR AMERICAN THEATER

We will now look at two important forms of theater that came to prominence in the United States in the years following World War II: African American theater and musical theater. After that, we will consider "alternative" forms of theater in the United States.

African American Theater

As we noted in Chapter 3, there are many theaters that appeal to diverse audiences with specific political viewpoints, concerns about gender, and sexual orientations. The diversity of American theater is also reflected in dramatic art created for and by the many ethnic and racial groups in our complex society; in the twentieth century, for example, there were significant Italian, Jewish, German, Asian, and Hispanic theaters. Many historians note that the development of the realistic tradition in American theater at the beginning of the twentieth century was clearly aided by immigrants from eastern Europe, many of whom were Jewish. In addition, German immigrants who fled the Nazis during the 1930s and 1940s undertook experiments with departures from realism in American theater.

African American theater—also referred to as *black theater*—is a prime example of a theater that reflects the diversity of American culture and the contributions of a particular group to this culture. African American theater is theater written by and for black Americans or performed by black Americans. It partakes of two important traditions. One is the western theater tradition, in which actors like Paul Robeson (1898–1976) and writers like Lorraine Hansberry (1930–1965) have been significant. The other is a tradition that traces its origin to theater in Africa and the Caribbean.

Since African American theater has a long history, it will be helpful to trace its development from its beginnings so that we can better understand its significance and impact on our contemporary theater.

African American Theater in the Nineteenth Century. In American drama of the eighteenth and nineteenth centuries, comic black servants—who spoke a thick dialect, shuffled slowly, and wore ill-fitting costumes—were popular characters.

IRA ALDRIDGE AS OTHELLO

Ira Aldridge was an African American artist of the early nineteenth century who, because of racial segregation in the United States, was compelled to work abroad. Aldridge became a renowned Shakespearean actor in Europe, in such countries as England, Poland, and Russia. This illustration shows him in his most famous role, the Moor in Shakespeare's Othello. *(Billy Rose Theatre Collection, New York Public Library for the Performing Arts, Astor, Lenox, and Tilden Foundations)*

These roles, however, were usually enacted by white performers; it was rare to see black performers on the American stage in the nineteenth century.

An exception was the African Grove Theater—a black company founded in New York during the 1820–1821 season by William Brown (an African American) and the West Indian actor James Hewlett. The company was particularly noted for Shakespearean plays. Hewlett was the first black to play Othello, and the renowned actor Ira Aldridge (c. 1806–1867) made his stage debut with the company. Here, too, the drama *King Shotaway* (1823)—believed to be the first play written and performed by African Americans—was presented. The African Grove closed in 1827, however, after attacks by white audience members.

Short of abandoning their profession, African American performers in the nineteenth century were faced with two choices: accepting roles as stupid servants or going to Europe, where racism against blacks was not so virulent. Ira Aldridge, for one, performed in England, Russia, and Poland in the plays of Shakespeare, receiving great acclaim.

The *minstrel show* was a popular nineteenth-century form that caricatured blacks. The performers were usually white entertainers dressed in colorful costumes, with their faces blackened and eyes and mouth enlarged by white and red lines. The minstrel show comprised comic and sentimental songs, skits, jigs, and shuffle dances. While the vast majority of nineteenth-century minstrel performers were white, there were a few black minstrel companies, some of which, ironically, also performed in blackface.

African American Theater from 1900 to 1950. At the turn of the twentieth century, the popular syncopated rhythms of ragtime had a strong influence on the emerging musical theater and served as a bridge for a number of talented African Americans. Bob Cole (1864–1912) and William Johnson (1873–1954) conceived, wrote, produced, and directed the first black musical comedy, *A Trip to Coontown* (1898). The comedians Bert Williams (c. 1876–1922) and George Walker (1873–1911) and their wives joined composers and writers to produce musicals and operettas such as *In Dahomey* (1902) and *Abyssinia* (1906), in which Americans for the first time saw blacks on the Broadway stage without burnt-cork makeup, speaking without dialect, and costumed in high fashion.

The early twentieth century also saw the formation of African American stock companies. The most significant was the Lafayette Players, founded in

1914 by Anita Bush (1883–1974), originally as the Anita Bush Players. By the time it closed in 1932, this company had presented over 250 productions and employed a number of black stars.

Black performers and writers were also making inroads into commercial theater in the 1920s. Twenty plays with black themes were presented on Broadway in this decade, five of them written by African Americans, including *Shuffle Along* (1921), with lyrics and music by Noble Sissle (1889–1975) and Eubie Blake (1883–1983). The decade also saw some black performers achieve recognition in serious drama, among them Charles Gilpin (1878–1930), Paul Robeson, and Ethel Waters (1896–1977).

The depression forced black performers to find other ways of earning a living or to invent ingenious ways to create their own theater. There were a few Broadway productions of plays by blacks, such as the folk musical *Run Little Chillun* (1933) and *Mulatto* (1935) by Langston Hughes (1902–1967).

Possibly the most significant development for black theater during the 1930s was the Federal Theater Project, discussed in Chapter 17. This project, which was meant to help theater artists through the depression, formed separate black units in twenty-two cities which mounted plays by black and white authors and employed thousands of African American writers, performers, and technicians. The Federal Theater Project created a new generation of African American theater artists who would develop the theater of the 1940s and 1950s.

The 1940s saw a stage adaptation, in 1941, of the controversial novel *Native Son* by Richard Wright (1908–1960), directed by Orson Welles for his Mercury Theater. Other important Broadway ventures included Paul Robeson's record run of 296 performances in *Othello* in 1943, and *Anna Lucasta* (1944), adapted by Abram Hill (1911–1986).

African American Theater since 1950. The 1950s saw an explosion of black theater that would continue over the next five decades. *Take a Giant Step* by Louis Patterson (1922–), a play about growing up in an integrated neighborhood, premiered in 1953. In 1954, the playwright-director Owen Dodson (1914–1983)—a significant figure in black theater since the 1930s—staged *Amen Corner* by James Baldwin (1924–1987) at Howard University.

Off-Broadway, the Greenwich Mews Theater began casting plays without regard to race and also produced *Trouble in Mind* (1956) by Alice Childress (1920–1994)—the first play by an African American woman to receive a commercial production. Possibly the most important production of the postwar era was *Raisin in the Sun* (1959) by Lorraine Hansberry. It is about a black family in Chicago, held together by a God-fearing mother, who is planning to move into a predominantly white neighborhood where the family will be unwelcome. The son loses money in a get-rich-quick scheme but later assumes responsibility for the family. Hansberry's play was directed by Lloyd Richards (1922–2006), the first black director on Broadway. Richards later became head of the Yale School of Drama, where in the 1980s he nurtured the talents of the black playwright August Wilson (1945–2005), author of *Jitney* (1982), *Ma Rainey's Black Bottom* (1984), *Fences*

(1985), *Joe Turner's Come and Gone* (1986), *The Piano Lesson* (1990), *Seven Guitars* (1995), *King Hedley II* (2000), *Gem of the Ocean* (2003), and *Radio Golf* (2005).

From 1960 to the 1990s, there was an outpouring of African American theater, much of it reflecting the struggle for civil rights. Amiri Baraka (1934–) came to theatergoers' attention in 1964 with *Dutchman*, a verbal and sexual showdown between an assimilated black male and a white temptress, set in a New York subway. His plays *The Slave* (1965), *The Toilet* (1965), and *Slave Ship* (1970) also deal with the political, sociological, and psychological dilemmas confronting blacks. Among other significant plays of these two decades were Lonne Elder's *Ceremonies in Dark Old Men* (1969); Charles Gordone's *No Place to Be Somebody* (1969); Douglas Turner Ward's *Day of Absence* (1970); and Charles Fuller's *A Soldier's Play* (1981), which won a Pulitzer Prize for drama.

In 1970 the Black Theater Alliance listed over 125 producing groups in the United States. While only a few of these survived the decade, many had a significant impact. The Negro Ensemble Company, founded in 1967, holds the contemporary record for continuous production by a professional black theater company. The New Lafayette Theater, which operated from 1966 until 1972, introduced the playwright Ed Bullins (1935–), experimented with black ritual, and published the journal *Black Theater*.

In addition to the emergence of these producing organizations, another major change in the 1970s was the presence of a larger black audience at Broadway theaters, which accounted for a significant number of commercial African American productions, such as *Don't Bother Me, I Can't Cope* (1972); *The Wiz* (1975); and *Bubbling Brown Sugar* (1976). This trend continued in the 1980s and 1990s with such hits as *Black and Blue* (1989), *Jelly's Last Jam* (1992), and *Bring in da' Noise, Bring in da' Funk* (1996).

African American artists continued to make an impact on commercial and noncommercial theater. For example, George C. Wolfe (1955–), author-director of *The Colored Museum* (1986), *Spunk* (1990), *Jelly's Last Jam,* and *Bring in da' Noise, Bring in da' Funk,* also directed both parts of the award-winning *Angels in America*. Wolfe was artistic director of the Public Theater, a renowned off-Broadway theater facility founded by the New York producer Joseph Papp (1921–1991) from 1993 to 2004. Wolfe also directed *Caroline, or Change* in

A LANDMARK AFRICAN AMERICAN PLAY

A significant event in the history of black theater was the presentation in 1959 of A Raisin in the Sun, by Lorraine Hansberry, the first African American female playwright to have a major dramatic success on Broadway. The play was also directed by an African American: Lloyd Richards. It is a sensitive drama about a family in Chicago trying to buy a home in a white neighborhood. In this production, directed by Seret Scott at the Hartford Stage, the actors are, left to right, standing: April Yvette Thompson (as Ruth), Lynda Gravátt (Lena, the mother), and Crystal Noelle (Beneatha). Billy Eugene Thomas (Walter Lee) is on the floor. (© T. Charles Erickson)

HARLEM SONG
A production celebrating the African American contribution to American music, as well as the black experience in American theater, was a revue arranged and directed by George C. Wolfe at the famous Apollo Theater in New York's Harlem. The joy as well as the sadness, the exuberance as well as the difficulties of African Americans, reflected in music, made for a lively and poignant musical work. (© Michal Daniel)

2003, with a book by Tony Kushner. Another African American director, Kenny Leon (1955–), in 2002 founded the True Colors Theatre in Atlanta; and in 2004 he directed a production of *A Raisin in the Sun* on Broadway.

Suzan-Lori Parks (1964–), Pearl Cleage (1948–), and Cheryl West (1956–) are three contemporary African American female playwrights whose works deal with issues of racism and feminism and have been produced in regional and alternative theaters. Parks's *Venus* (1966), for example, depicts the life of a nineteenth-century black woman who was exhibited in England as the Venus Hottentot, a sideshow freak. Parks's other critically acclaimed plays include *The American Play* (1993), *The Death of the Last Black Man in the Whole Entire World* (1990), and *Topdog/Underdog*, which won a Pulitzer Prize in 2002 and was directed by George C. Wolfe. Pearl Cleage's best-known plays are the one-act *Chain* (1992) and *Flyin' West* (1992), which was produced by Atlanta's Alliance Theatre Company; she has also created a number of performance pieces, a form that will be discussed later in this chapter. Cheryl West, trained as a social worker, deals with domestic crises in such works as *Before It Hits Home* (1989) and *Holiday Heart* (1994).

Another female African American dramatist whose work is politically charged is Kia Corthron (1961–). Corthron's works, which include *Seeking the Genesis* (1996), *Force Continuum* (2000), and *Breath, Boom* (2001), have been commissioned by leading regional and off-Broadway companies.

Musical Theater

American theater has long been dominated by a popular commercial theater that appeals to the masses. The rich history of this popular theater is often ignored because of a bias toward what some critics refer to as "high art" theater. Many contemporary historians and critics have pointed out that popular theater, which appeals to the general public, is worthy of study and has influenced many authors and theater artists who work outside the commercial mainstream. Possibly the most popular and distinctive theatrical form developed in America is the *musical*.

Antecedents. In the nineteenth century, melodrama used music to accompany the action of plays. Singing and dancing also played a key role in other forms of nineteenth-century theatrical entertainment, such as *vaudeville* and *burlesque*. In its later phases, burlesque became synonymous with vulgar sketches and "girlie shows," including striptease; but for most of the nineteenth century, burlesque featured dramatic sketches and songs that satirized or made fun of other theatrical forms. Vaudeville was a series of variety acts—music, sketches, juggling, animal acts—that made up an evening's entertainment. Another type of musical production that flourished in the nineteenth century was the minstrel show, a variety show featuring white performers wearing blackface.

The Black Crook, produced in 1866, is considered a significant forerunner of the modern musical. This was a melodrama whose plot was so far-fetched that the producer had little faith in it. However, just at this time a nearby theater in which a French ballet troupe was to perform burned down, and the producer of *The Black Crook* quickly hired the French dancers as part of his own production. The combination of drama and dance, much to everyone's surprise, proved to be immensely successful.

Another form that developed in the late nineteenth century was *operetta*. An operetta is a romantic musical piece featuring melodic solos, duets, and choruses interspersed with spoken dialogue. Examples of operetta include the works of W. S. Gilbert (1836–1911) and Arthur Sullivan (1842–1900), such as *The Pirates of Penzance* (1879) and *The Mikado* (1885). The American composer Victor Herbert (1859–1924) also composed operettas, such as *Naughty Marietta* (1910).

American Musicals from 1900 to 1940. In the early twentieth century, the musical shows of George M. Cohan (1878–1942), such as *Little Johnny Jones* (1904) and *Forty-Five Minutes from Broadway* (1906), had songs with an American flavor and more realistic dialogue and better plot development than earlier musicals. Cohan's shows moved a step closer to to-day's "book" musicals—musicals that tell a story. (The dialogue and action of a musical are sometimes called the *book,* though the term *libretto* is also used.)

Around the time of World War I and in the period following, a truly native American musical began to emerge. It featured a story that was typically frivolous and silly, and very popular songs with hypnotic lyrics and melodies; these successful songs were played over and over and became known as *standards.* Among the famous composers of this period were Irving Berlin (1888–1989), Jerome Kern (1885–1945), George Gershwin (1898–1937), Cole Porter (1891–1964), and Richard Rodgers (1902–1979). Matching the inventiveness of the composers were the lyricists, including Ira Gershwin (1896–1983), who wrote lyrics for many of his brother's tunes; and Lorenz Hart (1895–1943), who teamed up with Richard Rodgers. Berlin and Porter wrote their own lyrics.

In 1927, Oscar Hammerstein II (1895–1960), who wrote the lyrics and libretto, and Jerome Kern, who composed the music, combined some of the best aspects of operetta and musical comedy to create *Show Boat.* The story was thoroughly American, rather than an exotic romantic fable, and it dealt with serious material—including the love story of a black woman and a white man. It was also innovative in that the songs were carefully integrated into the plot, and the chorus line was eliminated. There have been several versions of *Show Boat* and numerous revivals, underscoring its historical significance; a spectacular revival in 1993 was staged by the director Harold Prince (1928–).

GEORGE M. COHAN'S *FORTY-FIVE MINUTES FROM BROADWAY*
Cohan was a leading figure in the development of the American musical at the beginning of the twentieth century. He wrote book, music, and lyrics for his musicals and also performed in them. In Cohan's work, music and plotlines were better integrated than they had been in earlier musicals. Cohan was one of the first writers to focus on American subjects, and his characters and stories were also more down-to-earth. (White Studio Photo, Billy Rose Theatre Collection, New York Public Library for the Performing Arts, Astor, Lenox, and Tilden Foundations)

Another milestone of musical theater was Gershwin's *Porgy and Bess* (1935), with a book by DuBose Heyward (1885–1940). Set in the African American community of Charleston, South Carolina, it is even more realistic than *Show Boat;* and its score is so powerful that some people consider it an opera rather than a musical. (In fact, *Porgy and Bess* has been performed in a number of opera houses.)

The High Point of American Musicals. *Oklahoma!*—which was produced in 1943 and brought the team of Rodgers and Hammerstein together for the first time—heralded a significant era of the American book musical. *Oklahoma!* has been praised for seamlessly fitting together story, music, lyrics, and dances so that tone, mood, and intention became a unified whole. Its choreography, by Agnes deMille (1905–1993), included a famous ballet sequence and influenced many

SHOW BOAT

When Show Boat *opened in 1927, it began a new chapter in the history of the American musical. The chorus line was eliminated, miscegenation (a romance between a white man and a black woman) was treated for the first time, and other problems facing African Americans were touched on. Also, it has a glorious score by Jerome Kern and Oscar Hammerstein. Shown here is a revival, staged by Harold Prince in 1993—a Canadian production that later moved to London and also Broadway. (© Catherine Ashmore)*

later choreographers in musical theater, including Jerome Robbins (1918–1998) and Bob Fosse (1927–1987). Rodgers and Hammerstein went on to create other significant musicals such as *Carousel* (1945), *South Pacific* (1949), *The King and I* (1951), and *The Sound of Music* (1959).

Among other notable musicals during the 1940s and 1950s were Irving Berlin's *Annie Get Your Gun* (1946), based on the life of Annie Oakley; Cole Porter's musical version of *The Taming of the Shrew,* called *Kiss Me, Kate* (1948); *Guys and Dolls* (1950) by Frank Loesser (1910–1969); *My Fair Lady* (1956), by the librettist and lyricist Alan Jay Lerner (1918–1986) and the composer Frederick Loewe (1904–1988), based on George Bernard Shaw's *Pygmalion* (1913); and *West Side Story,* a modernization of *Romeo and Juliet* which was created by the composer Leonard Bernstein (1918–1990), the lyricist Stephen Sondheim (1930–), and the librettist Arthur Laurents (1918–). Many of these have recently had successful Broadway revivals, including *Annie Get Your Gun,* starring Bernadette Peters (1948–   ) in 1999; and *Kiss Me, Kate* later in that same year.

Some commentators believe that *Fiddler on the Roof* (1964)—with music by Jerry Bock (1928–   ), lyrics by Sheldon Harnick (1924–   ), and book by Joseph Stein (1912–   )—marks the end of this era of book musicals. *Fiddler on the Roof,* about a Jewish family whose father attempts to uphold tradition in a Russian village where the Jewish community faces persecution, was directed and choreographed by Jerome Robbins.

American Musicals since 1965. One example of changes in the musical following *Fiddler on the Roof* was the rock musical *Hair* (1967), by Galt McDermot (1928–   ) and Gerome Ragni (1942–   ), which had no actual story line and was a celebration of the antiestablishment lifestyle of the 1960s.

After *Hair,* the musical scene became increasingly fragmented, with fewer and fewer book musicals being written. In place of book musicals, there were other approaches, one being the *concept musical,* in which a production is built around an idea rather than a story. Two examples, both composed by Stephen Sondheim and directed by Harold Prince, are *Company* (1970) and *Follies* (1971). Two of Sondheim's more recent works, *Sunday in the Park with George* (1985) and *Into the Woods* (1988), can also be considered concept musicals, though in *Passion* (1994), Sondheim returned to the traditional book musical.

Another significant trend in musicals of the 1970s and 1980s is the ascendancy of the choreographer as director, providing the vision for a musical. *A Chorus Line* was developed by the director-choreographer Michael Bennett (1943–1987). Jerome Robbins, director of *West Side Story* and *Fiddler on the Roof,* was generally recognized as the leading director-choreographer in the United States. Other significant director-choreographers were Gower Champion (1920–1980), who was responsible for *Hello Dolly!* (1964) and *42nd Street* (1980); Bob Fosse, who directed *Sweet Charity* (1966) and *Pippin* (1972); and Tommy Tune (1939–   ), who directed *Nine* (1982), *Grand Hotel* (1989), and *The Will Rogers Follies* (1991). A recent example of the director-choreographer is Susan Stroman, responsible for *The Producers* (2001).

Still another trend of the decades since 1965 has been the emergence of British composers and lyricists. The leading figure in this movement is the composer Andrew Lloyd Webber (1948–   ), who, with the lyricist Tim Rice (1944–   ), wrote *Jesus Christ Superstar* (1971) and *Evita* (1979). Webber has also written *Cats* (1982), *The Phantom of the Opera* (1987), and *Sunset Blvd.* (1993). Two

THE GOLDEN AGE OF AMERICAN MUSICALS
The two decades beginning in 1943—with the production of Oklahoma!*—were an illustrious period for new American musicals. Works created then by Irving Berlin, Cole Porter, Lerner and Loewe, and Rodgers and Hammerstein are still produced frequently today. A good example is* Kiss Me, Kate, *revived on Broadway in 1999. In the scene shown here, Marin Mazzie is Kate and Brian Stokes-Mitchell is Petruchio.* (© Joan Marcus)

MUSICAL REVIVALS

The American musicals of the period from the 1940s through the 1960s were so entertaining and so successful that a half a century later they are frequently revived. A good example was a revival in 2006 of the musical Pajama Game, *originally written and directed by George Abbott, with music and lyrics by Richard Adler and Jerry Ross. The revival featured Harry Connick, Jr., seen here with his costar, Kelli O'Hara.* (Sara Krulwich/The New York Times)

other lavish musicals that originated in Britain are *Les Misérables* (1987) and *Miss Saigon* (1989).

Along with British imports, there has also been a movement toward revivals of earlier musicals. However, in the late 1990s there was a sense that the American musical was rebounding. The popularity of George C. Wolfe's *Bring in da' Noise, Bring in da' Funk* and the huge success of *Rent* by Jonathan Larson (1960–1996), first off-Broadway in 1995 and then on Broadway in 1996, seemed to reawaken interest in the American form. *Rent,* an adaptation of the opera *La Bohème,* uses many musical forms (rock, jazz, Latin, opera) to tell a story about starving artists in the East Village of New York. Disney's musicals have also been highly successful, including *The Lion King* (1997) and *Aida* (1999).

There are several noticeable trends in recent musicals in the United States. One that continues is the flow of revivals of established musicals from the past. Another is the adaptation of films into stage musicals such as *The Producers* (2001), *Hairspray* (2003), *Monty Python's Spamalot* (2005), and *Dirty Rotten Scoundrels* (2005), among others. Still another trend has been the "jukebox" or "songbook," musical in which the well-known songs of composers or singers are the basis for the show. Two examples are *Mamma Mia* (2001), featuring the music of the Swedish group ABBA; and *Jersey Boys* (2005), based on music made popular by the singer Frankie Valli. Scattered among these kinds are original musicals: some more traditional, like *Wicked* (2003) and *Light in the Piazza* (2005); and others unconventional and somewhat irreverent, such as *Urinetown* (2001), *Avenue Q* (2003), and *The Drowsy Chaperone* (2005).

Alternatives to Commercial Theater

A crucial development in American theater in the second half of the twentieth century was the creation of important alternatives to traditional Broadway commercial theater. These alternative theaters tended to be able to offer theater for special audiences, as well as theater that was often more daring, bold, fresh, and experimental. Three manifestations were regional theater, off-Broadway, and off-off-Broadway. In the case of the latter two, it should be noted that this movement occurred all over the country, not just in New York City.

Regional Theater. An important development in the United States in the past half century has been the growth of major established regional theaters. (The phenomenon of important theaters established outside of major cities is, again, a worldwide trend.) A number of significant regional theaters were founded in the 1940s and 1950s, including the Alley Theatre in Houston, Texas; and the Arena Stage in Washington, D.C. Also, resident professional theaters began to flourish in the 1960s and 1970s in large cities around the country—cities such as Boston, New Haven, Louisville, Milwaukee, Minneapolis, Seattle, San Francisco, Los Angeles, and San Diego. These are nonprofit rather than commercial theaters, but they employ professional performers, directors, and designers. They present the best dramas from the past as well as interesting new plays. In fact, in recent years nonprofit theaters have been the chief source of new works in the United States.

These established nonprofit theaters have produced the work of many significant playwrights and directors. Among the better-known playwrights are John Guare (1938–), Lanford Wilson (1937–), Marsha Norman (1947–), and Wendy Wasserstein (1950–2006). Directors emerging from these theaters include Mark Lamos (1946–), at the Hartford Stage Company in Connecticut; Arvin Brown (1940–) of the Long Wharf Theater in New Haven; Jon Jory (1938–) of the Actors Theater of Louisville; and Des McAnuff (1952–), who has directed at many regional theaters, including La Jolla Playhouse in California, which he has headed for several years.

It is noteworthy that in New York City, a comparable group of permanent theaters have become an important force; among the best-known are the Manhattan Theater Club and Playwrights Horizons.

Off-Broadway, Off-Off-Broadway, and Alternative Regional Theaters. In New York City, *off-Broadway* theater began in the 1950s as an alternative to commercial Broadway, which was becoming increasingly costly. Off-Broadway theaters were smaller than Broadway theaters—most of them had fewer than 200 seats—and were located outside the Times Square neighborhood where the Broadway houses are situated. Because off-Broadway was less expensive than Broadway, it offered more opportunity for producing serious classics and experimental works.

In the 1960s and 1970s, however, off-Broadway itself became expensive and institutionalized. As a result, small independent producing groups had to develop another forum. The result was *off-off Broadway*. Off-off-Broadway shows are produced wherever inexpensive space is available—in churches, lofts, warehouses, garages—and are characterized by low prices and a wide variety of offerings. It is in these theaters, too, that much experimental work takes place: for example, productions in which performers create their own work and in which theater is combined with painting, dance, or television.

One important off-off-Broadway theater is Café LaMama; among the significant groups that have worked off-off-Broadway are the Living Theater, the Open Theater, the Performance Group, Mabou Mines, and the Wooster Group. All have experimented with physical performance techniques, improvisation, texts created by performers and directors, and environmental presentations.

Two experimental directors whose works were first seen off-off-Broadway are Robert Wilson (1944–) and Richard Foreman (1937–). Their work is typically unified by a theme or point of view determined by the director, and their

CONTEMPORARY THEATER: ECLECTICISM AND DIVERSITY

Theater today is eclectic and widely diversified. An excellent example of a mixture of styles and material was a revival of The Emperor Jones *by the Wooster Group, known for its experimental work. The play was written in the early twentieth century by the American playwright Eugene O'Neill, but in this production it was deconstructed and commented on at the same time that the original script was incorporated into the whole. Shown here are Scott Shepherd, Kate Valk (in the title role), and Ari Fliakos. (© Paula Court)*

material is often organized into units analogous to frames in television or film. Stunning theatrical images containing the essence of the ideas that interest these directors are often the key to their work.

Counterparts of the off- and off-off-Broadway movements have also sprung up in other major cities across the United States—Washington, Atlanta, Chicago, Minneapolis, Los Angeles, San Francisco, Seattle, and others—where small groups perform as alternatives to the larger, established regional theaters. In Chicago, for example, there was an explosion of off-Loop theaters in the 1970s. (*Off-Loop* refers to theaters located outside the Loop—commercial downtown Chicago.) One, Steppenwolf Theater, founded in 1976, whose original company included many actors who became well-known stars, including John Malkovich (1953–), Gary Sinise (1955–), and Laurie Metcalf (1955–), evolved into a leading established regional theater. Other major off-Loop Chicago theaters include Wisdom Bridge (where Robert Falls, currently artistic director of the Goodman, began his directing career), the Organic, the Body Politic, St. Nicholas, and Victory Gardens. These theaters also introduced successful actors, including Joe Mantegna (1947–), and many significant playwrights.

Lookingglass Theatre was founded in Chicago in 1988 and has received praise for its productions of literary adaptations that use intriguing staging devices. (The star of the television series *Friends,* David Schwimmer, is a founding member of the company.) In 2002, Lookingglass's artistic director, Mary Zimmerman, won the Tony Award for best direction, after her production of *Metamorphoses* (1998) moved to New York City.

Presentations by these alternative theaters include classics, new plays, and experimental works. One particular virtue of such theaters and artists is that they can present productions of interest to specific groups—for example, feminist theater, labor theater, Hispanic theater, gay and lesbian theater, and African American theater.

Again, this trend of creating out-of-the-way alternative theaters outside the commercial centers of major cities is taking place worldwide. In London, for example, there is a long history of "fringe" theaters: theaters outside London's commercial West End, which were originally established to circumvent the English censorship laws and which present more experimental works.

SAM SHEPARD'S *FOOL FOR LOVE*
Sam Shepard is a playwright who came out from the off-off Broadway movement of the late 1960s and the alternative regional theater scene of the 1970s. Shepard is best known for the plays he wrote in the late 1970s and early 1980s, which combine traditional family drama with explosive theatricality. One such play is Fool for Love, *shown here in a recent revival starring (left to right) Glenn Fleshler, Laila Robins, James Morrison, and Mark Hammer. (© T. Charles Erickson/The McCarter Theatre Center for the Performing Arts)*

Two Contemporary American Playwrights with Roots in Alternative Theater. Two American playwrights whose work was first presented in small alternative, nonprofit theaters and who then became prominent in regional and off-Broadway theaters are Sam Shepard (1943–) and David Mamet (1947–). Like many of our contemporary playwrights, Shepard and Mamet mix concerns of high art—such as the plight of the American family and the demise of the American dream—with techniques borrowed from mass entertainments such as film, popular music, and melodrama. Also, they often blur the distinction between realism and abstraction.

Sam Shepard first developed his playwriting skills off-off-Broadway with works that fused surreal and absurdist styles and abandoned traditional plot structure and development. His later dramas include *Buried Child* (for which he won a Pulitzer Prize in 1979), *True West* (1980), *Fool for Love* (1982), *A Lie of the Mind* (1985), *Simpatico* (1994), *The Late Henry Moss* (2000), and *The God of Hell* (2004). These plays deal with American mythology, the violence of American society, and the degeneration of the American family. Shepard has also acted in many well-known films. David Mamet came out of the Chicago theater scene. His plays have naturalistic language and settings and down-and-out characters whose struggles are clearly recognizable, but they do not provide the clear-cut exposition or dramatic resolutions of traditional realism. Like Shepard's, they attack many accepted ideals of American life. Among Mamet's best-known works are *American Buffalo* (1977), *Glengarry Glen Ross* (1983), *Oleanna* (1992), *The Cryptogram* (1994), *The Old Neighborhood* (1997), and *Boston Marriage* (1999). Mamet has also written and directed a number of films.

In Chapter 19, our final chapter, we will examine some of the contemporary trends that developed in recent years of theater history. Many of these trends set the stage for the theater of the twenty-first century.

SUMMARY

A number of theatrical movements were in evidence between 1945 and 1980. The absurdist dramas of Beckett, Ionesco, and Pinter have had a profound influence on contemporary playwriting. Other movements included the "angry young men" in England and documentary drama in Germany. The two leading American dramatists—Arthur Miller and Tennessee Williams—worked in a style that can be described as selective realism.

Happenings, multimedia, environmental theater, and poor theater forced theatergoers to reevaluate their traditional expectations about the performer-audience relationship and other aspects of drama.

African American theater artists wrote plays and organized production companies that focused on racial issues confronting American society. In the United States, the musical reached a golden age in the 1940s. At the same time, artists began to break away from commercialism, working off-Broadway, off-off-Broadway, and in regional and alternative theaters.

KEY TERMS

Book Spoken (as opposed to sung) portion of the text of a musical play.

Burlesque Satire of a serious form of literature.

Environmental theater Branch of avant-garde theater stressing the environment in which a performance takes place.

Existentialism Term applied to plays illustrating a philosophy whose modern advocate was Jean-Paul Sartre and which holds that there are no longer any fixed standards or values.

Happening Nonliterary or unscripted theatrical event using a scenario that allows for chance occurrences.

Multimedia Use of electronic media, such as slides, film, and videotape, in live theatrical presentations.

Musical theater Broad category that includes opera, operetta, musical comedy, and other musical plays (sometimes called lyric theater).

Poor theater Term coined by Jerzy Grotowski to describe his theater, which was stripped to the bare essentials.

THEATER ON THE WEB

For more research and to learn more about the topics in this chapter, please visit the Online Learning Center at **www.mhhe.com/livelyart6**.

CHAPTER 19

Contemporary Trends

◀ **THEATRICAL DIVERSITY**

Today's theater is open to all theatrical styles and subjects. One of the best-known practitioners of diversity and eclecticism is the French director Ariane Mnouchkine. At her Théâtre du Soleil in Paris, she has undertaken a number of innovative and daring theatrical experiments and created many memorable productions, a number of them based on the classics. The scene here is from her production Le Dernier Caravanserail; *the title refers to the inns that once were resting stops for caravans. This particular production, based on visits to refugee camps and detention centers in many parts of the world, was developed over a long time by the thirty-six members of her troupe, and lasts six hours.* (© Martine Franck/Magnum Photos)

In this chapter we will examine important trends in contemporary theater. Our focus will be mainly on American theater, but much of what we discover will be representative of theatrical conditions in other parts of the world. We will focus most closely on theatrical movements and forms that reflect the great diversity of contemporary society, such as feminist theater, and those that embody continuing experimentation, such as postmodernism and performance art. Our ultimate goal in this chapter, however, will be to consider whether theater as we know it will survive in the twenty-first century.

THE DAWNING OF A NEW CENTURY

As we noted in Chapter 18, social unrest and violence marked the second half of the twentieth century. Worldwide political, economic, and cultural turmoil continued as the century ended—and, as always, the arts have continued to reflect the world in which they are being created.

To take just two examples, theater has been affected by the rise of political, religious, and social conservatism and, deeply, by AIDS. AIDS, a disease that destroys the body's immune system, began to reach alarming proportions in the 1980s, and it has been one reason for the growing activism of homosexual groups. A significant number of theater figures have died of AIDS, including the Broadway musical director Michael Bennett and the founder of the Ridiculous Theatrical Company, Charles Ludlam (1943–1987). Also, AIDS has been the subject of many plays, perhaps most notably the epic *Angels in America* by Tony Kushner (1965–   ).

Meanwhile, various conservative movements have attempted to question the advances made by gays, feminists, and other minorities, and conservative politicians worldwide have questioned government support of the arts.

Contemporary society has again been confronted by genocide in Bosnia and Rwanda, and by reports of torture of prisoners by American military or CIA personnel in the aftermath of the Iraq war, forcing us to question whether there have been any real changes in moral outlook since World War II. While the fall of totalitarian communism was celebrated in eastern Europe, the world has also been troubled by continued poverty, crime, and intolerance toward racial minorities, even with a vibrant economy. At the same time, the American presidency, under Bill Clinton, was rocked by a number of scandals and impeachment hearings. In 2000, George W. Bush, while losing the popular vote, was elected president in a highly contested election.

There has also been increased violence in the Middle East. The culmination of this instability was the terrorist attack on the United States on September 11, 2001. The United States proclaimed a war on terror and toppled the fundamentalist Islamic regime in Afghanistan. The United States and Great Britain also deposed the regime of Saddam Hussein in Iraq in 2003. Still, there were some signs of peace in the region when the United States and many European nations restarted negotiations between Israelis and Palestinians that same year. However, these negotiations continued to falter as violence escalated, and George W. Bush's presidency divided the American electorate more deeply than any other administration in modern history.

TODAY'S THEATER: DIVERSITY AND ECLECTICISM

It is against the background of this complex, unsettled, often confusing political and social turmoil that contemporary theater must be viewed. Two words that can characterize today's theater are *diversity* and *eclecticism*: diversity because the types of theater available to audiences are so wide-ranging and, as we noted in Chapter 1, because the audiences themselves are so diverse; and eclecticism because contemporary theater embraces such a wide variety of events.

Audiences today can see revivals of the best theater from the past: Greek, Elizabethan, French, and Spanish. They can see theater from Asia, Africa, and Latin America; new plays; and avant-garde and experimental works. There are productions in translation of the best new plays from other countries. What's more, these productions can be seen in a wide variety of theater environments: in outdoor as well as indoor theaters; in proscenium theaters and on thrust stages; in huge theaters seating 3,000 or 4,000 people; and in small theaters seating only 50 or 75.

One hallmark of contemporary theater is that all these strands exist simultaneously. This is an expression of its eclecticism. Forms of both realistic theater and departures from realism continue to flourish today. Alongside them are such diverse forms as musical theater, ethnic theater, political theater, feminist theater, and gay and lesbian theater.

As all this suggests, our contemporary theater is complex. If theater mirrors the society in which it is produced, then it is not surprising that ours is fragmented, reflecting the complexity of today's life. We have already surveyed African American theater in Chapter 18; we now turn our attention to other examples of diversity in contemporary theater.

Asian American Theater

For most of the nineteenth century and the first half of the twentieth century, Asians appeared in dramatic offerings strictly as stereotypes. With the coming of cultural and ethnic awareness in the 1960s and 1970s, things began to change. In 1965 several Asian American performers and directors founded the East West Players in Los Angeles. In 1973, two more groups were formed—the Asian Exclusion Act in Seattle and the Asian-American Theatre Workshop in San Francisco—and in 1977 the director-actor Tisa Chang (1945–) founded the Pan Asian Repertory Theatre in New York. These groups employed Asian American performers, produced dramas from the Asian cultural heritage, and emphasized new plays written by and for Asian Americans.

A number of plays by Asian American writers were produced in the 1970s and 1980s, including a memory play by Philip Kan Gotanda (1950–) called *Song for a Nisea Fisherman* (1980). A playwright who came to prominence in the

PING CHONG: ASIAN AMERICAN THEATER ARTIST

Ping Chong, often referred to as a performance artist, works in a variety of performance styles. His work mixes eastern and western theatrical elements to call into question the representation of Asians and Asian Americans in theater. His production Obon Tales of Rain and Moonlight, *shown here, is a puppet piece that weaves together three Japanese ghost stories, merging poetry, shadows, music, and bunraku puppets. The musical score was by Guy Klucevsek. (© Chris Bennion/Seattle Repertory Theatre)*

1980s was David Henry Hwang (1957–), son of first-generation Americans who immigrated from China to California. Hwang wrote several plays that won wide recognition, beginning with *FOB*, produced in 1980; and *The Dance and the Railroad*, produced in 1981. Later in the decade, in 1988, Hwang's *M. Butterfly* opened successfully on Broadway. Based on a true story, the play deals with a French diplomat who meets and falls in love with a Chinese opera singer who he thinks is a woman but turns out to be a man and a spy. A new play by Hwang, *Golden Child*, opened in the 1996–1997 theater season. In 2003, Hwang collaborated with the composer Philip Glass on *The Sound of a Voice*. Hwang also cowrote the revised book for the musical *Flower Drum Song* for a revival in 2001.

There has also been a movement to have more Asian Americans employed as performers in appropriate roles. Hwang and the actor B. D. Wong, who played the Chinese opera singer in the original production of *M. Butterfly*, led a vigorous protest against the hiring of an English actor to play the leading role in the musical *Miss Saigon*. That battle was lost; but by 1996, when a revival of *The King and I* opened on Broadway, it had a large proportion of Asian American performers.

Latino-Latina Theater

Contemporary Latino-Latina or Hispanic theater in the United States can be divided into at least three groups: Chicano theater, Cuban American theater, and

Puerto Rican or Nuyorican theater. All three address the experiences of Hispanics living in the United States, and the plays are sometimes written in Spanish but are usually in English.

Chicano theater, which originated primarily in the west and southwest, came to prominence during the time of the civil rights movements of the 1960s. The theater troupe known as El Teatro Campesino ("farmworkers' theater") grew out of the work of Luis Valdéz (1940–), who joined César Chavez in organizing farmworkers in California. Valdéz wrote *actos*, short agitprop pieces dramatizing the lives of workers. (The term *agitprop* means "agitation propaganda"; it was applied in the 1930s to plays with a strong political or social agenda.)

El Teatro Campesino became the prototype for other groups such as Teatro de la Gente ("people's theater"), founded in 1967; and Teatro de la Esperanza ("theater of hope"), begun in 1971 in Santa Barbara, California. Also in 1971, a network of these theaters across the country was established. In the 1990s a well-known theater, Teatro Vista, performed for Mexican and Hispanic communities in Chicago.

Valdéz's play *Zoot Suit* (1978), about racial violence in Los Angeles in 1943, opened in Los Angeles to considerable acclaim; it later moved to Broadway. Other plays about the Chicano experience followed, one of the most notable being *Roosters* (1987) by Milcha Sanchez-Scott (1955–), in which cockfighting is a metaphor used to explore Chicano concerns and family conflicts. Among other writers who have dealt with Chicano as well as wider themes is Arthur Giron (1937–), an American writer from Guatemala.

Cuban American theater developed chiefly in Florida. The Federal Theater Project of the 1930s resulted in fourteen Cuban American productions in 1936 and 1937. A highly regarded Cuban American dramatist who began to be produced in the 1970s was Maria Irene Fornes (1930–). Among the current generation of Cuban American writers who have emerged in the past quarter century are Manuel Martin, Mario Peña, Dolores Prida, Iván Acosta, and Omar Torres. (Torres's work is centered in Miami and New York.) Another Cuban American playwright, Nilo Cruz, won the Pulitzer Prize in 2003 for *Anna in the Tropics*. A new play by Cruz, *Beauty of the Father,* opened in 2006.

Nuyorican is a term that refers to Puerto Rican culture, mostly in New York, but elsewhere as well. Works by playwrights with a Puerto Rican orientation began to be produced in the 1960s and 1970s by groups such as the Teatro Repertorio Español, the Puerto Rican Traveling Theatre, and the New York Public

HISPANIC THEATER

Among the important representatives of theatrical diversity in the United States is Hispanic theater. Luis Valdéz's Zoot Suit *was the first play on Broadway to be written and directed by a Chicano. The production shown here was staged by Chicago's Goodman Theatre, with Marco Rodriguez as Pachuco. (© Liz Lauren)*

Theatre founded by Joseph Papp (1922–1991). The Nuyorican Poets' Café presented plays by a number of Hispanic writers, including an ex-convict, Miguel Piñero (1947–1988), whose *Short Eyes*, a harshly realistic portrait of prison life, proved to be very successful and won a number of awards in the 1973–1974 season. Today new Puerto Rican playwrights have come to prominence, including Yvette Ramírez, Cándido Tirado, Edward Gallardo, and Juan Shamsul Alam.

Native American Theater

Strictly speaking, there was not a Native American theater tradition; rather, there were spiritual and social traditions that had theatrical elements. These were found primarily in ancient rituals and communal celebrations, which were often infused with cosmic significance. Also, in these traditions, unlike traditional western theater, there was no audience as such: those observing were considered participants just as much as the principal performers. Many of these ceremonies and the like were outlawed by the American government in the nineteenth century. Thus, the legacy of rituals and ceremonies, which had strong theatrical components—not to mention significant spiritual and cultural value—was forced to go "underground" if it continued at all.

The American Indian Religious Freedom Act of 1972 made it legal once again for certain ceremonies, such as the sun dance, to resume. This increased awareness of these rituals and celebrations contributed to the emergence of a Native American theater. Two groups that led the way in the past three decades were the Native American Theatre Ensemble and Spiderwoman.

The Native American Theatre Ensemble, which was originally called the American Indian Theatre Ensemble, was founded by Hanay Geiogamah. (It is important to note that those familiar with Native American theater invariably identify theater companies and theater artists not with the generic term Native American theater, but in terms of their nations. Thus, Geiogamah is identified as Kiowa/Delaware.) Geiogamah's organization gave its premiere performance at La Mama in New York City in 1972, and later toured widely, not only in North America but also in Europe and elsewhere.

Spiderwoman Theatre comes under the headings of both Native American theater and feminist theater. Founded in 1975, it is the longest continually run-

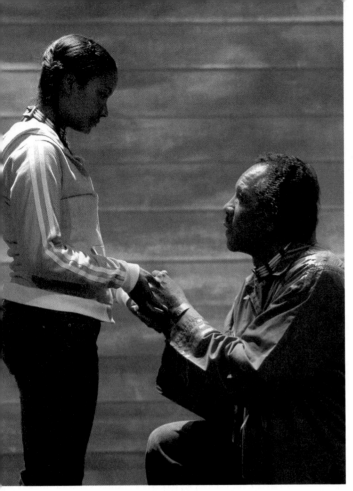

NATIVE AMERICAN THEATER

Native American theater, also known as indigenous theater, is written by and for Native Americans. The participants frequently attempt to recapture not only themes and subjects appropriate to Native American culture but also the production styles and approaches of the original theatrical presentations. The scene here is from a play by William S. Yellow Robe, Jr., Grandchildren of the Buffalo Soldiers; *it dramatizes the visit of a man, Craig Robe (James Craven), who returns to his tribe after having lived elsewhere. In this scene he is with August Jackson (Maya Washington) as part of his confrontation with his past and with the present circumstances of his people. The drama was coproduced by Penumbra Theatre Company and Trinity Repertory Company and was directed by Lou Bellamy. (Photo credit: Ann Marsden, 2005, Penumbra Theatre Company.)*

ning women's theater in North America, as well as a Native American theater. Three of its founding members, Lisa Mayo, Gloria Miguel, and Muriel Miguel, draw on storytelling and other theatrical traditions to celebrate their identities as American Indian women and to comment on stereotypes of women in general.

What is important to note about Native American theater today is that it is not primarily historical or ceremonial. Though elements of tribal traditions may be incorporated, the emphasis among playwrights and producers is really on contemporary work, fusing the problems and aspirations of today's Native Americans with their heritage. The challenges and preoccupations of young Native American playwrights are similar to those addressed by their Euro-American counterparts.

Several Native American playwrights have recently published single-author anthologies of their works. These include William F. Yellow Robe, Jr. (Assiniboine), Diane Glancy (Cherokee), and E. Donald Two-Rivers (Anishinabe). Another important contemporary playwright is Bruce King (Turgle Clan, Hodenausaunee-Oneida). King and Yellow Robe are also directors who have founded their own companies in the recent past and have taught playwriting and performance at the Institute of American Indian Arts in Santa Fe, New Mexico, an organization that nurtures the next generation of Native American theater artists.

Feminist Theater

In the United States, many female playwrights have questioned traditional gender roles and the place of women in American society. In the 1970s and 1980s, there were a number of successful female American playwrights. Representative works include *Fefu and Her Friends* (1977) by Maria Irene Fornes; *'Night, Mother* (1983) by Marsha Norman (1947–   ); *Crimes of the Heart* (1977) by Beth Henley (1952–   ); *The Heidi Chronicles* (1988), *The Sisters Rosensweig* (1992), and *An American Daughter* (1997) by Wendy Wasserstein; and *How I Learned to Drive* (1988) by Paula Vogel (1951–   ). In Chapter 18, we discussed three significant African American female playwrights: Suzan-Lori Parks, Pearl Cleage, and Kia Corthron. To this list we can add Lynn Nottage, and there are others as well.

Feminist theater companies have forced audiences to reexamine their own gender biases and those of their society. Some scholars estimate that more than 100 feminist companies have been founded in the United States; these companies include At the Foot of the Mountain, Women's Experimental Theatre, and Omaha Magic Theater. One company, Split Britches, became well-known for its production of *Belle Reprieve* (1991), which made satiric references to Tennessee Williams's *A Streetcar Named Desire* and was created collaboratively with an English gay company, Bloolips.

Feminist theater has roots in the past. One significant forerunner, for example, was the American playwright Rachel Crothers (1878–1958). Crothers wrote and directed many successful plays from 1906 to 1937; all of them dealt with women's moral and social concerns, and most of them were set in urban high society. In the summer of 1995, the Looking Glass Theater in New York revived Crothers's *A Man's World* (1909), which attacks the double standard. Its heroine,

a writer named Frank Ware, is raising the illegitimate son of a woman who died in childbirth. Frank has developed strong feelings against the code that allows fathers of such children to avoid responsibility; she then discovers that in this case the father is actually one of her own suitors—and she must choose between her love for him and her detestation of what he represents. Rachel Crothers's plays are skillful, entertaining comedies, but she always focused on the issue of sexual equality.

Feminist theater is, of course, also a worldwide phenomenon. There are many feminist playwrights and theater companies throughout the world. In England, for example, there are a number of significant female playwrights, including Caryl Churchill (discussed later), Timberlake Wertenbaker (1946–   ), and Pam Gems (1925–   ).

Gay and Lesbian Theater

Lesbian theater groups can be part of feminist theater, but gay and lesbian theater is also a distinct movement.

A number of plays and performers, introduced homosexual and lesbian themes into theater before the 1960s. For example, in the nineteenth century and the early twentieth century there was a considerable amount of cross-dressing in performances: men often appeared in "drag" and women in men's clothing, raising questions about sexual and gender roles. Also, plays included material on this subject; one example is Lillian Hellman's *The Children's Hour* (1934), in which a presumed lesbian relationship between two schoolteachers was presented.

However, the play that first brought gay life to the forefront was *The Boys in the Band* (1968), by Mart Crowley (1935–). Crowley depicted a group of men living an openly gay life. Ironically, in 1969, the year after it opened, gay patrons of the Stonewall Inn in New York's Greenwich Village fought against police officers attempting to close the bar. This uprising, considered the beginning of the modern gay rights movement, changed attitudes of gay activists, who now rejected what they considered a stereotype of homosexuals depicted in *The Boys in the Band*. However, a significant New York revival for its thirtieth anniversary led to a reevaluation of the play's significance in the history of gay and lesbian theater in the United States.

In the years that followed, complex gay characters were presented unapologetically. Plays in the 1970s and 1980s included *The Ritz* (1975) by Terrence McNally (1939–) and *Torch Song Trilogy* (1983) by Harvey Fierstein (1954–). Since then, more and more plays have dealt expressly with gay issues. In these dramas, not only is the lifestyle of gays and lesbians presented forthrightly, but frequently a gay or lesbian agenda is also put forward. In addition to a general concern for gay and lesbian issues, there is a sense of urgency engendered by the AIDS crisis and gay rights issues. This has led to a number of significant dramas, including *The Normal Heart* (1985) by Larry Kramer (1935–), *As Is* (1985) by William M. Hoffman (1939–), Tony Kushner's two-part play *Angels in America* (1993–1994), Terrence McNally's *Love! Valour! Compassion!* (1995), and Richard Greenberg's *Take Me Out*, which won a Tony Award in 2003.

GAY AND LESBIAN THEATER

Among the many alternative theaters that emerged in the late twentieth century was theater centering on the gay and lesbian experience. One important group calls itself the Five Lesbian Brothers. Shown here is its play Oedipus at Palm Springs, *with Peg Healey (left) as Terri and Dominique Dibbel as Prin. The play, written by four members of the troupe, is a modern transgender view of the Greek myth of Oedipus. (© Joan Marcus)*

"Gender-bender" groups such as the Cockettes and the Angels of Light in San Francisco and Centola and Hot Peaches in New York are an offshoot of gay and lesbian theater. An important company in New York was the Theater of the Ridiculous, founded by John Vaccaro, which developed an extraordinary writer and performer—Charles Ludlam (1943–1987). Ludlam rewrote the classics to include a good deal of wild parody and frequent cross-dressing; he also created the long-lived Ridiculous Theatrical Company.

Though a number of groups have not survived, individual performers and playwrights in gay and lesbian theater remain very much in the spotlight.

Performance Art

In the past three decades, a number of artists have experimented with forms that force audiences to confront certain issues: What is performance? What is theater? What is the subject of theatrical representation? Some of these artists are also political-minded; some are not. ***Performance art*** is one recent form that poses these questions and then some.

PERFORMANCE ART

A well-known performance artist is Margaret Cho, seen here in her one-woman show, Cho Revolution. Cho *deals with controversial social and personal problems, including a frank presentation of sexual issues, in a performance that in part resembles a nightclub act. She has been described as a "compulsively confessional comedian." The performance here is at the Wiltern Theater in Los Angeles.* (© Phil Nee)

Performance art has two important antecedents: first, earlier avant-garde experiments of the twentieth century—such as dada, surrealism, and happenings, which stressed the irrational and attacked traditional artistic values and forms—and second, the theories of Antonin Artaud and Jerzy Grotowski.

During the past three decades, the term *performance art* has stood for various things. In its earliest manifestations, performance art was related on one hand to painting and on the other hand to dance. In the 1970s, one branch of performance art emphasized the body as an art object: some artists suffered self-inflicted pain, and some went through daily routines (such as preparing a meal) in a museum or in a theater setting. Another branch focused on *site-specific* or environmental pieces in which the setting or context was crucial: performances were created for specific locations such as a subway station, a city park, or a waterfront pier.

In some of the earliest forms of performance art, story, character, and text were minimized or even eliminated. The emphasis was not on narrating a story or exploring recognizable characters but rather on the visual and ritualistic aspects of performing. This type of theater was often the work of an individual artist who incorporated highly personal messages, and sometimes political and social messages, in the event. The overall effect was often like a continually transforming collage. As might be expected, there was, as mentioned earlier, an affinity between this kind of theater—with its emphasis of the visual picture formed onstage—and painting. Often, stage movement in performance art was also closely related to dance.

In an article in *Artsweek* in 1990, Jacki Apple explained how the emphasis in performance art shifted in the 1970s and 1980s:

> In the 1970s performance art was primarily a time-based visual art form in which text was at the service of image; by the early 80s performance art had shifted to movement-based work, with the performance artist as choreographer. Interdisciplinary collaboration and "spectacle," influenced by TV and other popular modes . . . set the tone for the new decade.[1]

In recent years the connotation of the term *performance art* has changed yet again. It is now often associated with individual artists who present autobiographical material onstage. Several such artists—Karen Finley (1956–) is one of the most visible—became a center of controversy when their work was seized on by ultraconservative religious groups and members of Congress as a reason to op-

---

[1]Jacki Apple, "Art at the Barricades," *Artsweek,* Vol. 21, May 3, 1990, p. 21.

pose funding the National Endowment for the Arts. These artists often espouse such causes as feminism and civil liberties for lesbians and homosexuals. Often nudity and other controversial representations of sexuality or sexual orientation are used to confront audiences. Such was the case in *Alice's Rape* (1989), in which Robbie McCauley performed nude as her great-great grandmother, a slave on the auction block. These performance artists are continuing a trend begun by early realistic and antirealistic dramatists, whose works challenged the social status quo and were often banned.

Off-off-Broadway has been the initial home of many performance artists. Two artists who began performing solo pieces in alternative spaces but later received commercial productions are Spalding Gray (1941–2004) and Bill Irwin (1950–). Gray, a monologuist who discussed issues that ranged from his own personal concerns to politics, was reminiscent of ancient storytellers who created a theatrical environment single-handedly. Irwin's performances are mime-like, and he uses popular slapstick techniques to reflect on the contemporary human condition.

Anna Deavere Smith (1952–), an African American performance artist, won considerable acclaim in the early 1990s for pieces dealing with racial unrest. In her works, she portrays numerous real people she has met and interviewed. Her *Twilight: Los Angeles 1992* presented people affected by the uprising that followed the acquittals in the first trial of police officers charged with brutalizing Rodney King. In 1997, Smith premiered a new work, *House Arrest: First Edition,* that was based on interviews recorded during the presidential campaign of 1996; in this work, however, Smith did not initially appear, but instead directed 14 performers in her performance style. She revised this work as a solo piece in 1999.

Other well-known performance artists are Eric Bogosian (1953–), Danny Hoch (1970–), John Leguizamo (1965–), and Ping Chong (1946–), an Asian American who mixes multimedia into his works.

A number of spaces have become recognized for their presentation of performance artists. These include two in New York City: PS 122, a converted public school in the east Village in Manhattan; and the Kitchen, also located downtown. In addition, many museums throughout the United States are known for presenting series of performance artists, including the Walker Museum in Minneapolis and the Museum of Contemporary Art in Chicago. The fact that performance art is most often presented in converted, found spaces or museums again reflects the diversity of the form and its relationship to earlier avant-garde movements and the visual arts.

Along with those in the United States, there are also significant performance artists in most major cities around the world, such as Issei Ogata (1952–) in Japan and the French-Canadian Robert Lepage (1957–), who founded Ex Machina, a multimedia center in Quebec City.

Postmodernism

Contemporary theater, as can be seen from the examples of performance art above, is highly eclectic. Some works focus on political concerns; others focus on formal concerns. Many works mix techniques and styles. In contemporary theater many diverse and complex works are often described by critics as *postmodernist*. A. O. Scott, film critic for the New York Times, in a recent article noted that postmodernism is characterized by the following attributes: "a cool, ironic affect; the overt pastiche of work from the past; the insouciant mixture of high and low styles." Postmodernism, which is difficult to define specifically, has several facets.

For one thing, postmodernism reflects issues of power in art. Postmodernists question the idea of an accepted "canon" of classics; they also ask why certain artists (such as playwrights) and certain groups (such as white males) should have held positions of power or "privilege" throughout theater history.

Accordingly, postmodernists rebel against traditional readings of texts, arguing that theater productions may have a variety of "authors," including directors and even individual audience members: they argue that each audience member creates his or her own unique reading. Postmodernist directors are noted for *deconstructing* classic dramas—that is, taking the original play apart, developing a new individual conceptualization, and trying to represent onstage the issues of power embedded in the text. When a classic is deconstructed in this way, it may serve simply as the scenario for a production.

One of the most famous groups known for deconstuction of texts is the Wooster Group, under the artistic direction of Elizabeth LeCompte (1944–). The Wooster Group's best-known productions are *Routes I & 9* (1981), which used sections of Thornton Wilder's classic *Our Town*; *L.S.D.* (1983); and *Brace Up* (1991), a performance adaptation of Chekhov's *The Three Sisters*. In 1997, the Wooster Group presented a highly theatricalized and physical version of Eu-

POSTMODERNISM:
BLUE MAN GROUP
*Blue Man Group is an
improvisational troupe that
uses a variety of theatrical
techniques to engage the
audience. The group,
which has played all over
the world, features
acrobatics, percussion, and
unusual visual effects, such
as the one seen here.*
(© Geraint Lewis)

gene O'Neill's *The Hairy Ape,* in a rundown theater in the Times Square area. The group usually performs in a transformed space in downtown Manhattan known as the Performing Garage. As with many of the Wooster Group's works, *The Hairy Ape* had been workshopped before this presentation, the performers adopted a highly presentational style, microphones and amplification were used to create unsettling vocal sounds, and video was also used. The production starred a film actor, Willem Dafoe (1955–), who began his acting career with this company and who has frequently returned to work with it.

The term *postmodernism* also suggests that the "modernist" interest in realism, antirealism, and form is no longer central to theater, that artists have now moved beyond being concerned with representing either reality or abstraction. Instead, postmodernists mix abstraction and realism, so that their works cannot be easily classified. Furthermore, the distinction between "high" art and popular art can no longer be clearly defined: postmodernists mix popular concerns and techniques with those of high art.

An intriguing example is the musical *The Lion King* (1997). Produced by Disney, a company whose presence has spurred on the economic revitalization of the Broadway theater district in New York City, this musical is based on a popular Disney animated film and has music by the rock composer Elton John. The director of *The Lion King,* as well as the designer of the masks and puppets, is Julie Taymor (1952–). Taymor, who is a designer, director, and adapter of literature for the stage, is known for her avant-garde use of puppet techniques borrowed

AFRICAN PLAYWRIGHTS: JOHN KANI

The playwright John Kani (center) is also a performer, and here we see him in his drama Nothing but the Truth. *Africa is a large continent, and no one label or trend can characterize it. Still, from a theatrical standpoint one of the most provocative and productive sections has been South Africa, and* Nothing but the Truth *is an excellent example of important South African drama. Shown here is a production at Lincoln Center. The play is a gripping investigation into the complex relationship between the blacks who remained in South Africa during apartheid and those who fought apartheid from abroad.* (© Paul Kolnik)

from Asian theaters. For example, she used puppets in staging Shakespeare's *The Tempest* (1986) at New York's Theatre for a New Audience, in her frequently revived adaptation of a short story *Juan Darien* (1988), in a production in Tokyo of Igor Stravinsky's opera *Oedipus Rex* (1992), and in a production of *The Green Bird* (1996), an eighteenth-century comedy by Carlo Gozzi. The huge commercial success of *The Lion King,* however, clearly reflects the merging of popular and experimental theaters.

Disney continued this tradition when it produced the musical *Aida,* with music by Elton John (1947–), and directed by Robert Falls (1954–), a well-known director in Chicago who had won critical acclaim in 1999 for his revival of *Death of a Salesman. Aida* opened on Broadway in 2000, after being repeatedly reworked out of town. In 2006, Disney opened *Tarzan,* with a book by the Asian American author David Henry Hwang and music and lyrics by the rock composer Phil Collins.

Many alternative theaters, playwrights, and performance artists can be categorized as postmodernist.

International Trends

Although Chapters 18 and 19 have focused on contemporary theater in the United States, the theatrical fragmentation found here can also be seen throughout the world. A number of theater artists worldwide have experimented with similar issues and concerns in the past four decades.

African Theater and Drama. It is not possible for us to review the complete history of world theater in this survey. However, it is important to note the significant theatrical contributions of African civilizations and their influence on western traditions. As we noted in Chapter 1, early African societies had many traditional performances that were connected to ceremonies and rituals and used music, song, and dance. African theater artists in the twentieth century used these traditional forms and subverted forms of popular western theater in order to create work that reflects anticolonial struggles as well as attacks against totalitarian regimes in the newly independent African nations. Contemporary African theater and society are divided into English-speaking Africa, French-speaking Africa, and Portuguese-speaking Africa. In all these regions, which were originally defined by nineteenth-century colonial powers, there are also attempts to experiment with the indigenous languages of the peoples of Africa.

The concern for political and social equality in many African American dramas, which was noted in Chapter 18, is also at the heart of the work of the South African playwright Athol Fugard (1932–), who began writing in the 1960s and achieved international acclaim in the 1980s as apartheid, the separation of races in South Africa, came under increasing attack. Fugard, a white author who sometimes stages and acts in his own works, attacked apartheid in such plays as *The Blood Knot* (1964), *Sizwe Banzi Is Dead* (1973), *Master Harold . . . and the Boys* (1982), *Lesson from Aloes* (1987), and *Playland* (1992).

Another significant African playwright is the Nigerian Wole Soyinka (1934–), who is also a poet, essayist, and novelist. Soyinka began his career with the Royal Court Theatre in London in the late 1950s. His politically charged works led to his arrest in Nigeria in 1967, and to two years' imprisonment. In 1973, he adapted Euripides's *The Bacchae* for the National Theatre in England. Soyinka gained international recognition in 1986, when he received the Nobel Prize in literature. Among his best-known dramas are *The Swamp Dwellers* (1957), *The Road* (1965), *Death and the King's Horsemen* (1975), and *Play of Giants* (1985).

Latin American Theater.   Contemporary Latin American theater defies generalizations, given the complexity of the various countries making up the geographical region. In this brief survey, we cannot do justice to its complexity or variety. Still, we will try to note some similarities in theatrical practice among the many countries.

Latin American theater is heavily indebted to the cultures of the indigenous peoples who populated the region before the European conquests. These indigenous peoples did take part in performances, often associated with religious rituals.

Colonial Latin American theaters were greatly influenced by the practices of Spain during its golden age. The secular comedias and the religious autos sacramentales of Lope de Vega and Calderón de la Barca had an impact on the earlier Spanish-language dramatists who were born in the colonies—for example, in Mexico in the seventeenth century. In Brazil, early theater was influenced by the Portuguese.

During the early nineteenth century, known as the age of independence, neoclassical and romantic forms of drama, again reflecting the European influence, dominated the theaters of the newly independent countries. However, there were also attempts to establish cultural independence during this time. In Argentina, for example, there were works that dealt with the issues of immigration and the plight of *criollos* (persons of Spanish heritage born in the Americas.)

In the twentieth century, there was a development of realistic drama, experimental theater, radical sociopolitical drama, and popular forms, all existing side by side. While there have been economic, political, and social problems, including periods of censorship and governmental repression (for example, in Chile during the dictatorship of Pinochet from 1973 to 1989), all the countries in Latin America have significant theaters and playwrights. Frequently these artists have responded to the political and social turmoil in their societies.

One of the most renowned is the Brazilian playwright, director, and theorist Augusto Boal. Boal has written many plays, including *Lean Wife, Mean Husband*

THEATER IN THE MIDDLE EAST

Here, an audience watches a performance of Shakespeare's Love's Labours Lost *in the Babur Garden of Kabul, Afghanistan, in September 2005. Afghan people and visitors gathered to view this version of the Shakespearean comedy, which had been adapted for the local culture to help revive what was once a thriving theater scene and to promote peace in this war-torn country. (Tomas Munita/AP Images)*

(1957); *Revolution in South America* (1961); and *Joe, from the Womb to the Tomb* (1962). In the 1960s, Boal created works about historical figures, theatrical and revolutionary. Because of his Marxist point of view, this Brazilian theater artist was forced into exile, traveling throughout South America and other parts of the world.

In exile, Boal experimented with different types of theater. He created a documentary-like drama that focused on current political issues and an environmental style of theater that presented performances in public spaces to surprised audiences. Boal became internationally known for his theoretical work *Theatre of the Oppressed* (1975), which became a manifesto for revolutionary and socially conscious theater. Boal continues to teach, give workshops, and lecture throughout the world.

Theater in the Middle East. Contemporary theater in the Arab world is greatly affected by the politics of the region. While the Islamic religion has strong prohibitions against theater, there have always been storytelling, folkloric, and popular comic traditions throughout the Middle East, before Islamic times and since. As in Africa and Latin America, the close of the nineteenth century and the beginning of the twentieth century saw a rise in western colonial influence on the theaters of the Arab Middle East.

Another tradition in Arab dramaturgy at the close of the nineteenth century and the beginning of the twentieth century was the adaptation of historic events into plays.

After World War II and through the 1970s, there was significant development of professional theatrical activity throughout the Middle Eastern region, including Egypt, Iran, Syria, Lebanon, and Iraq. The theaters of these countries continued to be influenced by western practices and artists, but there also developed a good deal of theatrical cross-fertilization. Iran, for example, was host to a significant international festival of avant-garde artists in the early 1970s. The festival featured works by such notable western artists as Peter Brook, Jerzy Grotowski, and Robert Wilson, and many of these works clearly reflected the influence of Middle Eastern theater and literature. However, many Arab theater artists' works were highly nationalistic during this era and returned to traditional folk materials.

With the rise of Islamic fundamentalism and totalitarianism in many of these countries, theatrical activities have been halted, significantly curtailed, or rigidly controlled by the state. For example, the theatrical infrastructure in Iraq was severely damaged by Iraq's war with Iran in the 1980s, by economic hardships after the Persian Gulf War in the early 1990s, and then again with the invasion and occupation of Iraq by the United States and Britain in 2003. In Saudi Arabia, for example, there is great controversy over the support of theatrical art.

There are currently a number of significant theater artists who deal with the contemporary political turmoil of the Middle East, including the ongoing battles with Israel, particularly in Egypt and in the Palestinian territories.

A Palestinian company that is gaining international recognition from its visits to the Royal Court Theatre in London is Al-Kasaba Theatre, originally founded in Jerusalem in 1970 but now located in Ramallah in the occupied West Bank. In 2001, Al-Kasaba staged *Alive from Palestine: Stories behind the Headlines*, which consists of a series of monologues dealing with the intifada, the Palestinian uprising against Israel. The company's artistic director is George Ibrahim.

Israeli theater has also developed since the founding of the stage of Israel in 1948. Israeli drama has been influenced by the eastern European origins of many of its founders as well as the Middle Eastern traditions of those Jews who left Arab nations to settle in the Jewish state.

One national theater of Israel is the Habimah, which was established in Russia in the early twentieth century and settled in what was then British-controlled Palestine in 1931. The other large national theater in Israel is the Tel Aviv Municipal Theater, referred to as the Cameri, founded in 1944. There are many other active Israeli theaters throughout the country—in Tel Aviv, Jerusalem, Haifa, and elsewhere. As in Europe and the United States, there are also smaller fringe theatrical groups, which experiment with avant-garde techniques, and performance artists. Most of the theaters in Israel receive some governmental subsidy.

Israeli drama also reflects the tumultuous history of the nation. Early drama dealt with the establishment of the state and nationalism. More recent dramatic works explore the complexities of Middle Eastern politics, including Israel's relationship with the Palestinians.

Asian Theater. In Chapter 14, we examined early Asian theater: the development and the maturing of theater in a variety of Asian countries, particularly India, China, and Japan.

During the nineteenth century, the western world came into closer contact with Asia. As western nations began to establish "spheres of influence," or imperialistic control, over Asian countries, there was a great deal of cross-cultural influence. Late in the 1800s and then in the twentieth century, western theater would adopt many practices of traditional Asian theaters, and Asian theater would be influenced by western practices.

The period at the end of the nineteenth century and the beginning of the twentieth saw increasing interchange between Asian and western theaters. Particularly, western theater had a growing influence on the modern theaters of India, China, and Japan. In all three countries, traditional theater continued: kathakali in India, Peking opera in China, and nō and kabuki in Japan. But awareness of western theater was widening.

As in Latin America, Asian countries were influenced in the early twentieth century by western dramatic forms, particularly the modernist traditions of realism and the departures from realism. The colonial influence also led to a weakening of the traditional forms of theatrical practice, both popular and classical.

Following World War I, there was a politicization of Asian theaters. There were theater artists who opposed western influences and the colonial mentality. In the past four decades, there has been a unique return of traditional forms blended into the sociopolitical sensibilities of the Asian theater artists. This return to traditional forms, in itself, is a rejection of colonial and postcolonial western intrusions into the continent.

Japanese theater since the end of World War II reflects the various trends in contemporary Asian theater. A number of truly gifted playwrights have emerged, chief among them Kinoshita Junji (1914–   ), whose work combines social concerns with humor and, when appropriate, elements from Japanese folk tradition.

In the second half of the twentieth century there were three main branches of theater in Japan. One was traditional theater—nō, bunraku, and kabuki, of which the most active was kabuki.

A second branch consisted of various manifestations of *shingeki,* a word that means "new theater." Shingeki began in the late nineteenth century and in one form or another continued throughout the twentieth century. Broadly speaking, it was a modern theater, in contrast to the traditional classic theaters. For one thing, it was more realistic than the traditional theaters. In addition, at the beginning it was influenced by such western playwrights as Ibsen and Chekhov. In the early part of the twentieth century, shingeki banished the gods and the fantastic from theater, partly because they had played such a large role in classic theater. Later, after World War II, nonrealistic elements were admitted to shingeki dramas. Overall, shingeki has undergone changes of its own and has at times been influenced by western theater. In general, it remains a theater in which the playwright is a central figure; in recent years it has included female playwrights, who were almost nonexistent in earlier times.

The third strain of modern Japanese theater has been avant-garde or experimental theater. A good example of this movement is the work of Tadashi Suzuki, who began his work at Waseda University in Tokyo and then developed a theater community in the mountains at Toga. Following the models of men such as Jerzy Grotowski and Peter Brook, Suzuki led a director-centered theater that was international in its ideas and its reach. Theater pieces were developed by the company under the guidance of the director, and there was an emphasis on ensemble playing, on physical movement, and on combining the old and the new, the traditional and the experimental. Other theater figures created their own brand of avant-garde work, some of it paralleling that being done in the west, but some distinctly Japanese.

Alternative European Theater. Alternative theaters exist in most major cities worldwide. In London, there is an alternative to commercial theater known as *fringe theater,* and it is in fringe theater that many contemporary political playwrights began their careers. These British playwrights are in the postmodernist tradition, mixing reality with theatrical techniques and fusing concerns of high art with techniques of popular art. A good example is Caryl Churchill (1938–), in plays like *Cloud Nine* (1979), *Top Girls* (1982), *Mad Forest* (1990), *Blue Heart* (1997), and *Far Away* (2002).

Of course, there are many other significant playwrights in England. Tom Stoppard (1937–) continues to write dramas emphasizing wordplay and intellectual concerns. A significant number of "angry" playwrights continue to attack traditional political, social, and economic institutions; among the best-known are David Hare (1947–) and Howard Brenton (1942–). More contemporary sociopolitically oriented British playwrights include Patrick Marber (1964–), author of *Dealer's Choice* (1995) and *Closer* (1997); Jez Butterworth (1969–), author of *Mojo* (1995); and Sarah Kane (1971–1999), author of *Blasted* (1995), *Cleansed* (1998), and *Crave* (1998).

CONTEMPORARY WOMEN PLAYWRIGHTS

In the past quarter century, women playwrights have emerged throughout the English-speaking world. An award for the best new play in the English language, the Susan Smith Blackburn Prize, has coincided with this development. Shown here is a scene from a play by one of the most innovative and creative voices among women dramatists, the British writer Caryl Churchill. The play is her inventive piece about role playing, Top Girls. *The characters seen here are in costumes from different time periods because part of the plot has to do with women from various ages meeting at a dinner table.* (© Geraint Lewis)

There is also a new generation of young Irish playwrights who dramatize social, political, and historical issues. One of the best-known is Martin McDonagh (1970–   ), whose works include *The Beauty Queen of Leenane* (1996), *The Cripple of Inishmaan* (1996), *A Skull in Connemara* (1997), and *The Lonesome West* (1997). Conor McPherson (1971–   ) has gained international attention for *St. Nicholas* (1996), *The Weir* (1997), *Dublin Carol* (2000), and *Shining City* (2004).

There have also been many directors on the European continent who have experimented with avant-garde theater techniques. Some of these directors have worked only in alternative environments, but others have brought their more experimental style of production into leading government-subsidized national theaters. Among the most renowned are Peter Stein (German, 1937–   ); Yuri Lyubimov (Russian, 1917–   ); Tadeusz Kantor (Polish, 1915–1990); and Ariane Mnouchkine (French, 1940–   ).

An English director who has used a more experimental style of production, along with reinterpretations of texts that focus on feminist, gender, and other sociopolitical issues, is Deborah Warner (1959–   ). Warner began her career with an alternative London troupe, the Kick Theatre Company, which she founded in 1980, when she was 21. She has since directed unique interpretations of the classics for the Royal Shakespeare Company and the National Theatre in London. She is best-known for the many productions she has directed that star the actress Fiona Shaw (1959–   ), including Shakespeare's *Richard II*, with Shaw in the title role; Beckett's *Footfalls*, in which Beckett's precise stage directions were ignored and lines were transposed, leading to a lawsuit by the Beckett estate; and a site-specific staging of T. S. Eliot's *The Waste Land*, which used a variety of spaces, including a disco in Brussels, a fort in Dublin, an old movie theater in Montreal, a lecture hall in a Parisian medical school, and a dilapidated theater in New York's Times Square. In the summer of 2000 and again in the winter of 2001, Warner directed Shaw in an adaptation of *Medea*. In 2005, Warner directed an all-star cast with Shaw in Shakespeare's *Julius Caesar*.

TODAY AND TOMORROW: A LOOK AHEAD

In the twentieth century, theater faced a series of unprecedented challenges. First came silent films, then radio, then sound films, then television. With each new challenge, it was assumed that theater would suffer an irreversible setback. After all, each of these new media offered drama in a form that was less expensive and much more accessible than the traditional theater setting. When sound film appeared, for example, it was argued that anyone who went out for entertainment would go to the movies rather than theater: film would be cheaper and would offer more glamorous stars. When television appeared, it was argued that people did not even need to leave their homes to see drama.

BRITISH WOMEN COLLABORATE
The director Deborah Warner and the actress Fiona Shaw have worked together to create several unusual and memorable theater pieces. A good example is their production of Medea *by Euripides. Shaw is shown here, covered with the blood of her sons, whom she murdered in order to get revenge on their father, Jason.* (© Donald Cooper/Photostage, England)

Inevitably, some changes in audiences' habits have resulted from new customs and from competition by films and television. For most of the eighteenth and nineteenth centuries, theater was the main source of escapist dramatic entertainment—both comedies and suspense melodramas. Today, television, with its situation comedies, provides much of the light entertainment formerly offered by theater, and film also provides much escapist entertainment. In addition, there is now concern that even newer technologies—such as interactive video and television as well as new multimedia computer technologies—will further erode interest in theater.

But despite these shifts, theater has not suffered as predicted. Much to the surprise of the prophets of doom, there is probably more theatrical activity in the United States today—as the discussions in this chapter and Chapters 17 and 18 suggest—than at any time since the advent of movies.

Why is this so? First, in spite of their similarities, there is a basic difference between theater on the one hand and films and television on the other. As we pointed out in Chapter 4, the difference is the presence in theater of the live performer. Both film and television provide images or pictures of people, not the real thing. Human contact between audience and performers meets a profound, fundamental need that neither the large screens in movie theaters nor the small screens in our living rooms can ever satisfy. The human electricity that flows back and forth between performers and audience—the laughter at comic moments and the hushed silence at serious moments—cannot be created in these other media.

Second, there is the human impulse to create theater. Earlier, we said that this universal impulse leads every society to create its own theatrical activity, unless such activity is expressly forbidden. The need and desire for theater will continue into the future, throughout Europe and the Americas as well as other parts of the world.

Regional and alternative theaters are excellent examples of the powerful pull of live theater. The major American regional theaters have all been established during the very time when television was becoming firmly rooted in American life. And—as noted earlier—there are now many alternative theater companies that reflect specific concerns of ethnic and minority groups and that have helped shape American theater.

Influential playwrights and performers as well as important issues have been brought to the attention of the theatergoing public by African American theater companies and artists; by Hispanic groups such as INTAR, the Puerto Rican Traveling Company, and El Teatro Campesino; and by Asian American groups, including the Pan Asian Repertory Theatre. Similarly, gay and lesbian theater companies, such as the Ridiculous Theatrical Company, and feminist groups have forced audiences to reexamine sexual and gender biases.

When we turn from the theater of today to the future, a question arises: Where will theater go from here? It is impossible, of course, to answer with any certainty. We can assume, though, that the trends described in this chapter and Chapters 17 and 18 will continue. Theater of the future will no doubt continue to present new works alongside a rich mixture of plays from the past. In both writing and production, theater will draw on many sources. We cannot know whether or not new plays will attain the greatness of the past, but playwrights show no sign of abandoning theater, despite the larger financial rewards offered by film and television.

We can be sure that theater will survive in a vigorous form, no matter what challenges it faces from electronic media. At the same time, modern technology will play an important role in theater: in lighting effects, with the use of computerized lighting boards; in the shifting of scenery; and in other ways. There will also, no doubt, continue to be multimedia experiments, fusing theater with film, video, dance, and computer-generated media.

With all its innovations, however, theater of the future will no doubt be an extension of theater of the past. Theater will continue to be enacted by women and men in person before an audience, and the plays they perform will deal primarily with the hopes, fears, agonies, and joys of the human race.

It is clear that the complexity of the modern world will result in a heterogeneous theater. Ongoing exploration of the diversity of contemporary society means that diverse theaters will continue to spring up. There is no question that in the twenty-first century, theater will be as complex and fragmented as the world in which it exists. Yet from the start theater has always focused on human concerns, and they will remain the source of its appeal as far ahead as we can see.

SUMMARY

Contemporary theater is eclectic, combining styles and techniques from earlier periods as well as from other art forms. Today's playwrights and directors draw from a wide range of sources. The types of theater available include realism and departures from realism (similar to the movements covered in Chapters 17 and 18), and additional forms such as musical theater and many forms of ethnic and political theater: African American theater, Latino-Latina theater, Native American theater, feminist theater, gay and lesbian theater, and so forth. All these exist side by side in numerous production settings: the rich storehouse of theater available today includes regional, commercial, and noncommercial theater.

The vitality of today's theater in the face of challenges by film and television demonstrates the continuing appeal of live theater and the performer-audience relationship. If the present age is not one of great drama, it is a period of tremendous activity in writing and producing, in avant-garde experimental work, and in the revival of classics.

KEY TERMS

Performance art Experimental theater that initially incorporated elements of dance and the visual arts. Since performance art often is based on the vision of an individual performer or director rather than a playwright, the autobiographical monologue has become a popular performance art form.

Postmodernism A contemporary concept suggesting that artists and audiences have gone beyond the modernist movements of realism and the various departures from realism.

THEATER ON THE WEB

For more research and to learn more about the topics in this chapter, please visit the Online Learning Center at **www.mhhe.com/livelyart6**.

APPENDIX A

Play Synopses

King Oedipus, Sophocles

Sotoba Komachi, Kan'ami

Tartuffe, Molière

The Way of the World, William Congreve

A Doll's House, Henrik Ibsen

The Cherry Orchard, Anton Chekhov

Mother Courage and Her Children, Bertolt Brecht

A Streetcar Named Desire, Tennessee Williams

Death of a Salesman, Arthur Miller

Waiting for Godot, Samuel Beckett

A Raisin in the Sun, Lorraine Hansberry

Fefu and Her Friends, Maria Irene Fornes

Fences, August Wilson

Play Synopsis

KING OEDIPUS (c. 430 B.C.E.)

Sophocles (496–406 B.C.E.)

Sophocles. (Réunion des Musées Nationaux)

Chief Characters

Oedipus—*King of Thebes*
Jocasta—*wife of Oedipus*
Creon—*brother-in-law of Oedipus*
Teiresias—*a blind seer*
Shepherd, Priest, Chorus

Setting

The entire play takes place in front of the palace at Thebes in Greece.

Background

When Oedipus was born, an oracle told his parents, the king and queen of Thebes, that their son would kill his father and marry his mother. Fearing this prophecy, the king and queen gave Oedipus to a shepherd to be killed. But the shepherd pitied the child and instead of killing him sent him to Corinth, where he was adopted by the Corinthian king and queen. Oedipus grew up, learned of the oracle's prediction, and thinking that the king and queen of Corinth were his real parents, fled from Corinth. On the journey toward Thebes, at a place where three roads met, Oedipus argued with a man and killed him—not knowing that the man was his natural father, Laius. When Oedipus arrived in Thebes, the city was plagued by a sphinx who killed anyone who could not answer her riddle. Oedipus answered the riddle correctly and the sphinx died. Oedipus then became king and married Jocasta, not realizing she was his mother. Years later, the city was struck by another plague; this is the point at which the play begins.

Prologue

Oedipus learns about the plague that has struck the land and learns from his brother-in-law, Creon, that an or-acle says the plague will not end until the murderer of the former king is found and punished.

Parados: The chorus of elderly men prays that the plague will end.

First Episode

Oedipus says that he will find and punish whoever is guilty. The blind prophet Teiresias arrives and says he knows nothing of past events; but when Oedipus accuses Teiresias of conspiring with Creon against him, Teiresias hints that Oedipus himself may be the guilty one. Oedipus becomes angry.

Choral Ode: The chorus asks who the murderer can be and expresses doubt that it can be Oedipus.

Second Episode

Creon defends himself against an angry Oedipus, who accuses him of conspiring with Teiresias. Jocasta, the wife of Oedipus, enters to tell her husband to ignore the oracle; it had predicted that her first husband, the former king referred to in the oracle, would be killed by his son, she says, but according to all reports he was killed by thieves at a cross-roads. Oedipus remembers that he had killed a man at a crossroads and begins to fear that he is the murderer, but Jocasta urges him to ignore such fears. Oedipus sends for a witness to the murder at the crossroads.

Choral Ode: The chorus begins to have doubts about the innocence of Oedipus and says that reverence for the gods is best: prosperity leads to pride and will be punished.

Third Episode

A messenger arrives from Corinth stating that the king there is dead. Queen Jocasta is jubilant at first because this means that the oracle cannot be trusted: it had said that Oedipus would kill his father, the king of Corinth; this news means that the father died of natural causes. The messenger then reveals that Oedipus is not the real son of the king of Corinth. Fearing the worst, Jocasta tries to persuade Oedipus to call off his search for the murderer. When he will not, she rushes into the palace.

Choral Ode: The chorus prays to the gods to help Oedipus find out the truth about his birth.

Fourth Episode

Oedipus sends for a shepherd who knows the full story of his origins. He forces the shepherd to reveal the truth. When he learns it, Oedipus himself rushes into the palace.

Choral Ode: The chorus recounts the story that has just happened concerning the fall of the great king, Oedipus, and expresses sorrow over the tragedy.

Exodus

A messenger from the palace describes how Jocasta has killed herself and Oedipus has put out his own eyes. The blind Oedipus reappears to recite his sad story. He courageously accepts his fate of self-imposed exile and leaves. The chorus warns that man should take nothing for granted and then exits.

Play Synopsis
SOTOBA KOMACHI (14TH CENTURY)
Kan'ami (1333–1384)

Characters

First priest
Second priest
Ono-no-Komachi
Chorus

Background

Sotoba Komachi is based on a fable. Ono-no-Komachi is a woman who was once a famous courtesan. At the time when she is young and at the apex of her beauty—and also extremely haughty and proud—a man named Shii-no-Shōshō falls deeply in love with her; he ardently pursues and courts her, hoping to win her favor and her love. Komachi, however, mocks and rejects Shōshō. She will not even let him enter her house, though she tells him that if he will come to her doorstep for 100 consecutive nights, she will admit him on the hundredth. For 99 nights, Shōshō comes faithfully to the entrance to her house. Each night, he cuts a new notch on the "shaft-bench" of his chariot. On the hundredth night, a terrible snowstorm is raging; he fights his way through it, but by the time he reaches her doorstep, he is so exhausted that he dies there.

The text of a nō drama is usually about the length of a western one-act play. It is important to note that in a nō drama like *Sotoba Komachi*, there is very little action or conflict of the kind found in the west. Most of the text is recited or sung to musical accompaniment; most of the stage movements are formal and ritualistic, as in stylized dance such as ballet.

The Play

The play seems to take place in autumn—a gloomy season when the days are growing shorter. Komachi is now distraught, unhappy, and very old: in fact, she is approaching her hundredth year—a symbolic echo of her suitor's last, fatal visit to her doorstep on the hundredth night. In her final years, she has become destitute, her friends have deserted her, and her mind has begun to fail.

An early section of the play presents a theological debate between Komachi and a priest. Moving unsteadily across the stage, Komachi appears to sit on a fallen stone that the priest says is a Buddhist stupa (monument). The priest accuses Komachi of profanation—of desecrating the stupa. She argues that there can be no sacrilege in her act because all things in life and nature are holy, including even a wrecked life such as hers. She insists that the ruined monument and the ruined old woman have a great deal in common. This notion will be a recurrent theme.

Although Komachi appears to win this religious argument, she is then quickly struck by madness. She imagines that she is once more in the storm that raged on the hundredth night of her lover's visits, and that he is once again lying dead at her feet.

At this point the character of Komachi mimes the release of her emotions in a wild, mad dance which is one of the high points of the drama, theatrically fusing words, music, and movement. The priest narrates the past occurrence while the performer playing Komachi physicalizes it, using highly symbolic gestures and movements. For a brief time during this dance, she relives the glorious days of her youth, becoming young again.

Komachi's agony as she gives release to her emotions is an expiation of her sins. At the conclusion of the play, there is an indication that she will receive a form of salvation. This idea is embraced in an overall theme: that ultimately—in the cosmic vision of life—evil and good, self-gratification and purity become one.

Molière. (Bibliothèque nationale de France)

Play Synopsis
TARTUFFE (1664)
Molière (1622–1673)

Chief Characters

Tartuffe, *a hypocrite*
Mme. Pernelle, *Orgon's mother*
Orgon, *Elmire's husband*
Elmire, *Orgon's wife*
Damis, *Orgon's son*
Mariane, *Orgon's daughter, in love with Valère*
Valère, *in love with Mariane*
Cléante, *Orgon's brother-in-law*
Dorine, *Mariane's maid*

Setting

Orgon's house in Paris in the 1600s.

Background

Tartuffe, a hypocrite who pretends to be a holy man and dresses in a religious habit, is staying at Orgon's home. He has completely fooled Orgon by feigning a virtuous lifestyle.

Act I: When Orgon's mother, Mme. Pernelle, tells the family that they should be virtuous like Tartuffe, they try to persuade her that he is a fraud. The maid, Dorine, tells Orgon's brother-in-law Cléante that Tartuffe has bewitched Orgon, who shows more affection toward Tartuffe than toward his own family. Orgon opposes the wedding of his daughter Mariane to Valère, the young man she loves. This is distressing to her brother Damis, because he wants to marry Valère's sister. When the maid Dorine tells Orgon that his wife was sick while he was away, Orgon, instead of pitying his wife, commiserates with Tartuffe, who is perfectly healthy. Cléante tells Orgon that he is being deceived by Tartuffe, but Orgon continues to believe in Tartuffe's virtue.

Act II: Orgon tells his daughter Mariane that she should marry Tartuffe. Mariane is outraged. When Dorine tries to persuade Orgon that Tartuffe and Mariane are ill-suited, Orgon defends the hypocrite. After Orgon leaves, Dorine tries to persuade Mariane to stand up to her father, but Mariane is weak-willed. Mariane's fiancé Valère confronts her with a rumor that she is planning to marry Tartuffe. The two quarrel until Dorine gets them to make up.

Act III: Dorine tells Damis that his stepmother Elmire—Orgon's wife—might persuade Tartuffe not to marry Mariane. As Damis hides in a closet, Tartuffe, alone with Elmire, tries to seduce her. Elmire says she will not tell Orgon of Tartuffe's advances if he agrees not to marry Mariane. Damis appears and tells Tartuffe that he will reveal all. When Damis tells Orgon of Tartuffe's adulterous offer, Tartuffe begs Orgon to drive him out. Orgon, however, disbelieves Damis. When Tartuffe says that he should leave the house, Orgon insists that he stay and, furthermore, he disinherits his children and makes Tartuffe his sole heir.

Act IV: Damis has left. Cléante accuses Tartuffe of exerting influence on Orgon in order to get Damis's inheritance. Dorine tries to enlist Cléante's aid in helping Mariane get out of marrying Tartuffe, but Orgon enters with a marriage contract. Elmire develops a plan to expose Tartuffe. She decides that Orgon should hide in the room while she is alone with Tartuffe. When Tartuffe enters, Elmire expresses her passion for him. Tartuffe wants "palpable assurance" of her favor, meaning that she must let him make love to her. Elmire expresses concern that her husband might be around, but Tartuffe says, "Why worry about that man?" Upon hearing this, Orgon jumps out from under the table and confronts Tartuffe, who boldly replies that he now owns everything in the house. In desperation Orgon goes to find his strongbox.

Act V: Orgon tells Cléante that he had libelous papers in the strongbox and he fears they are now in Tartuffe's possession. M. Loyal, a bailiff, enters with an eviction notice ordering the family to leave. Orgon expects to be arrested because of the libelous papers, but when an officer and Tartuffe enter, Tartuffe is arrested instead. The prince of the realm has realized the sham, invalidated the deed, and pardoned Orgon. All ends happily as Orgon gives his blessing to the marriage of Valère and Mariane.

Play Synopsis
THE WAY OF THE WORLD (1700)

William Congreve (1670–1729)

William Congreve.
(V&A Images)

Chief Characters

Mirabell, *in love with Millamant*
Millamant, *niece of Lady Wishfort*
Lady Wishfort, *enemy of Mirabell*
Fainall, *in love with Mrs. Marwood*
Mrs. Fainall, *Fainall's wife and
    daughter of Lady Wishfort*
Mrs. Marwood, *friend to Fainall*
Sir Wilfull Witwoud, *Lady
    Wishfort's nephew*
Another Witwoud, *follower of
    Millamant*
Waitwell, *Mirabell's servant*
Foible, *Lady Wishfort's maid*

Background

The play takes place among members of the upper class in London in the late seventeenth century. The society it depicts is highly artificial and values gossip, intrigue, deception, seduction, and sparkling conversation above everything else.

Act 1: A chocolate shop. Mirabell complains to Fainall that his attempt to win the love of Millamant is not succeeding because Millamant's aunt and guardian, Lady Wishfort, has turned against him. Lady Wishfort is infatuated with Mirabell but she feels he has not been attentive enough. Witwoud and Petulant, followers of Millamant, join the conversation.

Act II: In St. James Park, Mrs. Fainall and Mrs. Marwood are talking when Fainall and Mirabell join them. (Mrs. Fainall is Mirabell's mistress, though he really loves Millamant.) When Mirabell and Mrs. Fainall are alone, Mrs. Fainall complains that she detests Fainall, whom Mirabell compelled her to marry. Though

Mrs. Fainall is disappointed in Mirabell, her passion for him leads her to help him in his next scheme, even though it involves her mother, Lady Wishfort. Mirabell wants to marry the beautiful and wealthy Millamant, but her aunt is jealously withholding her consent. With Mrs. Fainall's collaboration, Mirabell arranges to have his servant, Waitwell, in the guise of an imaginary uncle called Sir Rowland, pay court to Lady Wishfort. Then, since Mirabell already has accomplished a secret marriage between Waitwell and Lady Wishfort's maid, Foible, he declares his intention to expose the scandal. He will remain silent only if he can have Millamant and her fortune.

Act III: With the scheme perfected, the scene shifts to Lady Wishfort's house: Foible tells Lady Wishfort that a man known as Sir Rowland has seen her picture and is infatuated with her. A meeting is arranged but their plot is overheard by Mrs. Marwood, another of Mirabell's conquests and herself a crafty schemer. Mrs. Marwood promptly persuades Lady Wishfort that Millamant should be married to Sir Wilfull Witwoud, a rich and amiable dunce. Fainall agrees to Mrs. Marwood's plan: she will write a letter exposing "Sir Rowland" as a fraud.

Act IV: Lady Wishfort is unnerved as she awaits the bogus Sir Rowland. Meanwhile, Mirabell and Millamant discuss a commonsense "contract" they believe a husband and wife should agree to, for their marriage to succeed. The action

then returns to Lady Wishfort and the arrival of "Sir Rowland." He begs for an early marriage, declaring that his nephew, Mirabell, will poison him for his money if he learns of the romance. The jealous Lady Wishfort promptly agrees. Then Mrs. Marwood's letter arrives, but Sir Rowland declares it to be the work of Mirabell.

Act V: Lady Wishfort learns that she is being deceived and turns on her maid Foible. The frightened Foible confesses that Mirabell conceived the whole plot, and Lady Wishfort is planning a dire revenge when more trouble comes: Fainall, her son-in-law, demands that his wife turn over her fortune to him, or else he and Mrs. Marwood will reveal to the world that Mrs. Fainall was Mirabell's mistress before her marriage and that she continues to be. Lady Wishfort is reflecting on this new humiliation when Mirabell comes asking for forgiveness.

Mirabell offers a compromise: if Lady Wishfort will permit her niece to marry him, he will contrive to save Mrs. Fainall's reputation and fortune. Lady Wishfort agrees. Mirabell then tells her, "As regards your daughter's reputation, she has nothing to fear from Fainall. . . . He and Mrs. Marwood . . . have been and still are lovers. . . . And as regards your daughter's fortune, she need have no fear on that score, either: acting upon my advice, . . . she has made me the trustee of her entire estate." Cries Fainall: "'Tis outrageous!" Says Mirabell: "'Tis *The Way of the World*."

Play Synopsis
A DOLL'S HOUSE (1879)
Henrik Ibsen (1828–1906)

Henrik Ibsen. (Norwegian Information Service)

Chief Characters
Torvald Helmer, *a lawyer*
Nora, *his wife*
Dr. Rank
Mrs. Linde
Nils Krogstad, *a bank clerk*
the Helmers' three small children
Anne-Marie, *the Helmer children's nurse*
Helene, *a maid*
Delivery boy

Setting and Time
The Helmers' home; Christmastime, 1879.

Background
Before the play opens, Nora Helmer, having been brought up as a carefree innocent in a sheltered household, forged a check, not knowing this was illegal. She did this to help her sick husband but did not want him to know about it. Meanwhile, she worked hard in order to pay back the debt. But Krogstad, a man working in her husband's bank, knows about the forgery. Also in the past, Krogstad had been involved with Mrs. Linde, a woman who has since left the small town in Norway where the play takes place. The scene is the living room of the Helmer home.

Act I: Nora returns home from shopping for Christmas. She has bought a tree, toys for the children, and macaroons for herself. Torvald enters and banters with her, asking if his "sweet tooth" has visited a confectioner. Nora insists that she would never go against Torvald. The conversation is interrupted by the arrival of Torvald's acquaintance Dr. Rank. Mrs. Linde, an old friend of Nora's whom she hasn't seen for 10 years, also appears. Nora tells Mrs.

Linde about Torvald's recent promotion to bank manager. Nora also confides to Mrs. Linde that seven years ago, Torvald was very ill and his doctors said that unless he went to a warmer climate he would die. Nora felt trapped because they could not afford the trip. Nora explains that she did the only thing possible and forged the signature of her father (now dead) to borrow the money from a man named Krogstad. To meet the payments on the loan, Nora took small jobs that she kept secret. During this conversation, Nora promises that she will persuade Torvald to give Mrs. Linde a position at the bank he now manages.

Torvald had planned to fire Krogstad, and the position he offers Mrs. Linde is that of Nora's moneylender. When Krogstad finds out that Torvald means to fire him, he visits Nora and threatens to ruin both her and her husband unless she persuades Torvald to allow him to stay on at the bank. Before he leaves, Krogstad reminds Nora of her forgery. After Krogstad leaves, Nora begs Torvald to let him keep his position at the bank, but Torvald adamantly refuses.

Act II: Receiving an official notice from Torvald that he has been relieved of his position at the bank, Krogstad writes a letter to Torvald, exposing all the details of Nora's forgery. Meanwhile, Torvald and Nora prepare for a costume ball for the following night. Realizing that Krogstad has delivered the letter, Nora begs Torvald and Dr. Rank to help her practice a dance for the ball, as a way to keep Torvald from going to the mailbox. Nora again confides in Mrs. Linde, who at one

time was in love with Krogstad. Mrs. Linde promises to try to avert Krogstad's intentions. Nora also considers disclosing her situation to Dr. Rank. However, when Nora speaks with Dr. Rank, he makes it clear that he is in love with her, and this dissuades her.

Act III: Mrs. Linde promises to marry Krogstad, and so he rescinds his threat to ruin the Helmers. Mrs. Linde, however, tells him not to retrieve the letter, as she is convinced that Nora's secret must be aired. Krogstad and Mrs. Linde rediscover their affection for one another. Krogstad leaves. Meanwhile, Nora and Torvald return from the dance and Nora, wearing a brightly colored Italian costume, is brought reluctantly into the room. Nora tries to delay Torvald's seeing the letter from Krogstad, but eventually Torvald goes to the letter box. Torvald reads the letter and berates Nora, calling her a hypocrite, a liar, and a criminal. Nora pleads with Torvald to listen to her, saying that she acted only to save his life, but her appeals fall on deaf ears. Another letter from Krogstad arrives, saying that he will not ruin either of the Helmers. With that, Torvald's attitude changes and he claims that he is saved. Nora, however, cannot forget Torvald's transformation and his failure to understand her. She informs Torvald that she is leaving him, explaining that she needs to find out what the world is like beyond the dollhouse in which she has been living. After her speech, Nora leaves the house, slamming the door behind her.

Play Synopsis

THE CHERRY ORCHARD (1904)

Anton Chekhov (1860–1904)

Anton Chekhov.
(Bettmann/Corbis)

Chief Characters

Lyubov Andreyevna, *owner of the estate*
Anya, *her daughter, age 17*
Varya, *her adopted daughter, age 24*
Gaev, *her brother*
Lopahin, *a merchant*
Trofimov, *a student*
Charlotta, *a governess*
Firs, *an old servant*
Yasha, *a young servant*

Act I

The nursery in the country estate of Lyubov Andreyevna, who has returned to Russia from a self-imposed exile in Paris to seek peace in her girlhood home. With her are her brother Gaev, an ineffectual aristocrat; and her daughter, Anya, age 17, who had gone to Paris to make the return trip with her. Lyubov's estate, with its famous cherry orchard, is heavily mortgaged and about to be foreclosed, leaving the family virtually penniless. Lyubov, absent since the death of her husband seven years before, laments her past. Among those who have come to greet her is Lopahin, a merchant who recalls her as a splendid, kindhearted woman. Lopahin's father had been a serf on the estate.

Varya, Lyubov's adopted daughter, is the housekeeper of the estate. Anya tells Varya that her mother cannot comprehend the change in their fortunes. Although they had only enough money for the trip from Paris, Lyubov brought her young valet Yasha with her, as well as Anya's governess Charlotta. The merchant, Lopahin, is supposed to marry Varya, but Varya tells Anya that Lopahin has still failed to propose to her.

Act II

A meadow near an old chapel near the house. Lopahin tells Madam Lyubov that he will always be grateful to her for her kindness to him when he was a boy. He tells her that she can avert the forced sale of the estate, if she will tear down the house and cherry orchard and develop the land for summer villas. He offers a loan to help, but Lyubov and Gaev cannot bear the thought of destroying the beautiful old orchard. Trofimov, a student, makes a speech, saying that the lazy intelligentsia of Russia should work; he himself, however, does not work.

Later, Lopahin persists in his attempts to get Lyubov to act to save the estate, but she talks of summoning an orchestra for a dance and laments the drabness of the peasants' lives. She discourages Gaev's plan to work in a bank. In other words, she does nothing to save the estate. Although the servants and family have only soup to eat, she gives a beggar a gold piece and asks for another loan from Lopahin.

Act III

The drawing room of the house on an evening in August. Lyubov has engaged an orchestra for a dance, although it is the evening of the sale of the estate. Her daughter Varya comforts her with the assurance that Gaev has probably bought the estate with money to be sent by a wealthy great-aunt, but Lyubov knows that the sum is not enough. She tells Trofimov, the penniless student who has won Anya's heart, that he should experience more of life, perhaps even have a mistress. He stamps angrily out of the room. Gaev and Lopahin, the latter giddy with joy, return. Lyubov demands to know if the home is lost. Lopahin cries, "I have bought it! . . . Now the cherry orchard's mine! Mine! . . . I have bought the estate where my father and grandfather were slaves." Lyubov sits down, crushed and weeping.

Act IV

The same scene as Act I. The nursery is now stripped bare, and the time for leave-taking has come. Lyubov is going to Paris to live as long as possible on the money sent by the great-aunt. Gaev is to work in a bank; Varya is to be a house-keeper in a distant town; Anya is to remain in school while Trofimov, her betrothed, completes his studies in Moscow. An ax is heard in the distance, and Anya pleads for the workers chopping down the cherry trees to wait until Lyubov has gone. Lyubov speaks of two cares: the health of the old butler Firs and Varya's future. She is assured that Firs has been sent to the hospital; and Lopahin promises to marry Varya, but left alone with Varya, he again fails to propose.

Lyubov and Gaev, the last to go, fall into each others arms. Lyubov weeps: "Oh, my sweet, beautiful orchard! My life, my youth, my happiness, good-bye!" They leave, and Firs, who is quite ill, totters in; he has not been sent to the hospital but left behind. We hear an ax cutting down the cherry orchard—and the symbolic sound of a broken string.

Play Synopsis

MOTHER COURAGE AND HER CHILDREN (1937–1941)

Bertolt Brecht (1898–1956)

Bertolt Brecht. (Courtesy German Information Center/IN Press)

Chief Characters

Mother Courage
Kattrin, *her mute daughter*
Elif, *her elder son*
Swiss Cheese, *her younger son*
Cook
Chaplain
Yvette Pottier, *a prostitute*

Setting

Various army camps in Sweden, Poland, Bavaria, and Germany

Background

Mother Courage follows army camps with her wagon and sells wares to soldiers. She has two sons and a daughter—each from a different father—who help pull the wagon.

Scene 1: Spring 1624, on a highway. Courage and her children enter, pulling the wagon. A Swedish officer persuades Elif, the son of Courage, to join the army.

Scene 2: The years 1625 and 1626; the kitchen of the Swedish commander, where the cook is arguing with Courage. The commander enters and praises Elif's bravery. When Courage hears Elif singing "The Song of the Wise Woman and the Soldier," she recognizes his voice and joins in.

Scene 3: Three years later. Courage, her two children, and soldiers from a Finnish regiment are prisoners. Courage's friend Yvette, a prostitute, sings about loving a soldier. When cannons are heard, Courage lends the Protestant Chaplain a cloak as a disguise. Swiss Cheese hides the cash box in the wagon, while Courage rubs ashes on Kattrin's face to make her less attractive to the soldiers. While Courage and the Chaplain are gone, Swiss Cheese hides the cash box, but two soldiers capture him. When the soldiers return with Swiss Cheese, Courage denies knowing him. Courage finds that she can free her son if she will bribe the sergeant—but she haggles too long, and Swiss Cheese is executed.

Scene 4: Outside an officer's tent. A young soldier enters, raging against the captain who took his reward money. Mother Courage sings "The Song of the Great Capitulation," which persuades them both that there is no use complaining.

Scene 5: Two weeks later. The Chaplain tells Courage that he needs some linen to help the peasants bind up their wounds; when she refuses, he takes the linen by force. After Kattrin rescues a child, Courage tells her to give it back to the mother.

Scene 6: Bavaria, 1632—the funeral of the fallen commander. The men are getting drunk instead of going to the funeral. When Kattrin is wounded, Courage thinks it is lucky because it will make her less appealing to the soldiers.

Scene 7: A highway, with the Chaplain, Mother Courage, and Kattrin pulling the supply wagon. Courage sings a song about war as business.

Scene 8: A camp, 1632. Voices announce that peace is at hand. Courage is distraught because no one will buy the supplies she just bought. Elif is arrested for killing peasants. Courage rushes back in with the news that the war is on again. The Cook and Kattrin pull the wagon while Courage sings.

Scene 9: In front of a half-ruined parsonage; 1634. The Cook tells Courage that he wants to run away with her, but without Kattrin. Kattrin overhears and is about to leave when Courage stops her; Courage turns the Cook down.

Scene 10: 1635. Courage and Kattrin pull the wagon up to a farmhouse and hear someone singing about warmth, comfort, and safety—a sharp contrast with their situation.

Scene 11: January 1636. Soldiers gather up the peasants and pull Kattrin out of the wagon, asking the way to town. An old man climbs onto the roof and sees the soldiers preparing to attack the town. Kattrin gets a drum, climbs up on the roof and beats a warning to the town. Kattrin is killed, but her warning is successful.

Scene 12: Courage sits in front of the wagon by Kattrin's body, singing a lullaby. The peasants tell Courage that she must leave and that they will bury Kattrin. Courage harnesses up and alone pulls the wagon.

Play Synopsis

A STREETCAR NAMED DESIRE (1947)

Tennessee Williams (1911–1983)

Tennessee Williams. (Theatre Collection/ Museum of the City of New York)

Chief Characters

Blanche DuBois, *30 years old*
Stella Kowalski, *her sister, 25 years old*
Stanley Kowalski, *Stella's husband, 28 years old*
Harold Mitchell (Mitch), *Stanley's friend*
Eunice Hubbell, *upstairs neighbor*

Setting

A two-story apartment building in New Orleans. The section is poor but has a raffish charm.

Scene 1: Blanche DuBois arrives from Laurel, Mississippi, at the apartment of her sister Stella and Stella's husband Stanley. Blanche is destitute and has lost her home. Despite this, she expresses disapproval of Stella's "earthy" living conditions.

Scene 2: The next evening. Before Stanley's friends arrive for a poker game, Stella has taken Blanche out for dinner because Blanche's "sensibilities" would be upset by the men's crudeness. Stanley accuses Blanche of swindling them by selling the family estate, without giving Stella her share.

Scene 3: The poker night. The women come home late; Blanche flirts with Mitch, one of the men, while Stella dances to music on the radio. Stanley, now drunk, gets angry, throws the radio out the window, and attacks Stella. The men subdue him while Blanche takes Stella, who is pregnant, to Eunice's apartment upstairs. Stanley yells for Stella to come home, and she

obeys; Mitch sits with the distraught Blanche on the front steps.

Scene 4: The next morning. Blanche is upset, but Stella is happy. Blanche tells Stella she should leave Stanley, whom she calls an "ape," but Stella tells her that she loves him. Stanley, who had overheard Blanche, sneaks out and reenters loudly, pretending that he hasn't heard.

Scene 5: Blanche, highly nervous, begins drinking. Stanley asks her if she ever knew a man from a disreputable hotel in Laurel. She denies it, somewhat unconvincingly. She finds relief in the idea of a forthcoming date with Mitch and admits to Stella that she is attracted to him.

Scene 6: Two a.m. that night. Mitch and Blanche come home from their date, go inside, have a drink, and seem to get along well. Blanche confides to him that her first husband was a homosexual who killed himself.

Scene 7: A late afternoon in mid-September. Stella is preparing for Blanche's birthday party while Blanche is taking a prolonged bath. Stanley tells Stella that he has heard bad stories about Blanche's former life. Stanley has told Mitch these stories and Mitch won't be coming to the party. When Blanche comes out of the bathroom, she realizes that something is wrong.

Scene 8: Forty-five minutes later. Mitch has not appeared and Blanche is miserable. Stanley belligerently

presents Blanche with his "present"— a one-way bus ticket back to Laurel. Blanche becomes hysterical and runs into the bathroom; Stella confronts Stanley, becoming so agitated that she goes into labor and is rushed to the hospital.

Scene 9: Later that evening. Blanche is home alone when Mitch arrives, drunk. Mitch rips the paper lantern off the lightbulb and turns it on. When he looks closely at her, she cries out and covers her face. He makes a play for Blanche, but she breaks away and he runs out.

Scene 10: A few hours later. Blanche, who has been drinking, is alone. Stanley returns from the hospital; he has been drinking too. She tells him that a millionaire has invited her to go away. She also makes up a story about Mitch's coming to beg her forgiveness. Stanley knows it is a lie. He puts on the silk pajamas that he "wore on his wedding night." He brutally carries Blanche offstage, where he rapes her.

Scene 11: Several weeks later. Stella is packing Blanche's clothes while the men again play poker: she and Stanley are sending Blanche to a mental hospital. Blanche has told Stella what Stanley did to her, but Stella won't believe it. When a doctor arrives, Blanche thinks it is her millionaire; when she sees it is not, she runs into the bedroom. The doctor comes in and gently leads Blanche out. Eunice hands the baby to Stella, as she stands crying, and Stanley comforts her.

Arthur Miller.
(AP Images)

Play Synopsis
DEATH OF A SALESMAN (1949)
Arthur Miller (1915–2005)

Chief Characters

Willy Loman
Linda, *his wife*
Biff, *his older son*
Happy, *his younger son*
Bernard, *Biff's friend*
the Woman, *Willy's mistress*
Charley, *a neighbor, Bernard's father*
Uncle Ben, *Willy's brother*

Setting and Time

Willy Loman's house in New York, and various other locations in New York and Boston. The present and flashbacks to the past.

Background

Willy is an aging traveling salesman who doesn't produce much business anymore. Many of his friends and business contacts are dead; his sons are not the successes he expected them to be—Biff, for example, was a football star but did not graduate from high school. Willy has a tendency to daydream. Linda is a devoted wife and mother, trying desperately to keep her husband and family from falling apart.

Act I: Willy arrives home unexpectedly, having cut short a sales trip. He tells Linda that he kept driving off the road. Linda tells Willy that he should persuade the company to let him work in New York rather than travel. Willy expresses disappointment about his son Biff, who has just returned home after living as a drifter in the west. Meanwhile, in their bedroom upstairs, Biff and Happy discuss their concern about their father and an old dream of starting their own business.

Downstairs, Willy moves into a scene from the past in which he brags to young Biff about what a great salesman he is. Bernard, a neighbor who is the same age as Biff, is a good student. Because he idolizes the athletic Biff, Bernard wants to help Biff study so that he can pass his exams. Willy puts Bernard down as the "studious type" and tells Biff that personality will get him farther than studying. Willy, in a different flashback, is shown in Boston with the Woman, with whom he is having an affair. Back in the present, Willy and his neighbor Charley have a minor confrontation during which Willy speaks out loud to his brother Ben's ghost. In Willy's fantasy, Ben is a successful self-made man who once, years ago, offered Willy a chance to go with him, a chance Willy refused.

Linda defends Willy and asks Biff to try to get along better with him. She confesses that she thinks Willy is trying to kill himself. Willy confronts Biff about his career and is rude to Linda while Biff stands up for her. Later, Biff finds rubber tubing attached to a gas line in the basement—a suicide device that Willy is evidently planning to use.

Act II: The next morning. Willy seems optimistic about the future: Biff represents Willy's final chance to prove that he himself has not been a total failure. He believes that Biff's former boss will give Biff a job. Also, Linda thinks that Willy has taken the rubber hose away and is no longer contemplating suicide, but later she finds out that Biff removed it.

The scene shifts to Willy's office, where he meets with his boss, Howard Wagner, and asks to be assigned to the New York office. Willy is aggressive but becomes desperate when Howard refuses his request and then fires him. Willy leaves in despair and vents his frustration on Ben's ghost.

The scene shifts to Charley's office, where Willy and Charley's son, Bernard, now a successful lawyer, discuss the time when Biff failed mathematics. Willy blames Biff's failures on that one incident. Bernard says that he always wondered why Biff didn't go to summer school after he failed. Willy is evasive and asks Charley for a loan; but when Charley offers him a job, Willy turns it down, out of pride. Meanwhile, Biff and Happy are in a restaurant waiting for Willy. Biff tells Happy that he had an unsuccessful meeting with his ex-boss; but Willy, when he arrives, won't let Biff tell the real story—Willy wants to hear an upbeat version, though he admits to the boys that he himself has been fired. The scene shifts to the past and Willy's hotel room in Boston; because he has failed in school, the young Biff shows up unannounced and finds Willy with the Woman. He decides that everything Willy stands for is false, and returns home beaten. Back in the present, Happy and Biff leave Willy alone in the restaurant, distraught and fantasizing.

At home, Linda accuses her sons of deserting Willy. Willy, still caught up in his fantasies, has returned home to plant a garden at night. He tells Ben about his insurance policy—the $20,000 would help Biff get on his feet.

Back in the present, Biff tells Willy that he has finally come to realize the truth about himself and tries to make Willy see the truth also. Alone, Willy gets into his car, drives off, and kills himself in an automobile accident. At his funeral, Linda expresses her sorrow and confusion.

Samuel Beckett.
(AP Images)

Play Synopsis
WAITING FOR GODOT (1953)
Samuel Beckett (1906–1989)

Chief Characters

Estragon, Vladimir, Lucky, Pozzo, Boy

Setting and Time

A country road with a tree. The present.

Background

Estragon and Vladimir have been coming to the same bleak spot every day for some time to wait for an unknown person called Godot. It is a crossroads, bare except for a small leafless tree in the background. While the men wait, they pass the time discussing the nature of humankind, religion, what they did yesterday, or anything else on their minds.

Act I: Estragon is trying to pull off his boot when Vladimir enters. The two men discuss where Estragon spent the night and that he was beaten again. Vladimir relates the tale of the two thieves crucified with Christ and explains that current religious scholars cannot agree on what happened to the thieves. As Estragon paces, the scene is punctuated by pauses, which enhance the feeling of waiting. Occasionally the men talk of leaving and then decide that they cannot leave, because they are waiting for Godot. They consider leaving each other; they argue; they make up. They discuss hanging themselves from the tree but decide that they can't do it, because the limbs are slender and might break.

At the point when they have decided not to do anything, two other men, Pozzo and Lucky, enter. Lucky is carrying heavy baggage and wears around his neck a rope held by Pozzo. Pozzo jerks occasionally on the rope and barks commands to Lucky, who responds mechanically. Pozzo sits, eats, and smokes his pipe. Estragon asks why Lucky doesn't put down the bags, and Pozzo explains that Lucky wants to impress Pozzo so that Pozzo will keep him. Pozzo says that it would be best to kill Lucky; this makes Lucky cry.

Estragon tries to comfort Lucky, and Lucky kicks him. As the sky changes from day to night, Pozzo tells Lucky to dance, which he does. Pozzo tells Lucky to think, and Lucky, who has been silent until this moment, goes into a long, incoherent tirade which agitates the others. When they take Lucky's "talking hat" off, he stops talking and collapses in a heap. The men say goodbye, but no one is able to leave. Pozzo finally gets up and exits—with Lucky in the lead, wearing the rope around his neck. A boy enters, telling Vladimir and Estragon that Godot will not come today but will surely come tomorrow. After he exits, the moon suddenly rises. Estragon says he will bring some rope the next day so that they can hang themselves. They talk about parting but don't part. The curtain falls.

Act II: The next day at the same time, in the same place. The scene opens with Estragon's boots and Lucky's hat onstage. The small tree, which was bare, now has four or five leaves. Vladimir enters in an agitated state, paces back and forth, and begins to sing. Estragon enters, apparently in a foul mood. He and Vladimir embrace, and Estragon says that he was beaten again the night before—but he can't remember what happened the day before.

They discover Estragon's boots, which seem to be the wrong color. They discuss leaving but can't leave, because they are waiting for Godot. Estragon takes a nap, and Vladimir sings a lullaby. They discover the hat and do a comic hat-switching routine. They hear a noise and think that finally Godot is coming. They are frightened and rush around excitedly. Nothing happens; no one comes. Pozzo, now blind, enters with Lucky. Lucky stops short, falls, and brings Pozzo down with him. Pozzo calls for help, but Vladimir and Estragon think Godot has arrived. They discover that it is Pozzo and Lucky. Vladimir and Estragon try to help Pozzo up, but they fall also. Finally, everyone gets up. Estragon goes to Lucky and, kicking him, hurts his own foot. Lucky gets up and gathers his things together; he and Pozzo exit.

Estragon tries to take off his boots and then falls asleep as Vladimir philosophizes. The boy enters, tells Vladimir that Godot will not come that night but will come the next night, and exits. The sun sets, and the moon rises quickly. Vladimir and Estragon talk again of hanging themselves on the tree, but they have no rope. They test the strength of Estragon's belt, but it breaks and his pants fall to the ground. Vladimir says, "Well? Shall we go?" Estragon says, "Yes, let's go"—but they do not move.

Lorraine Hansberry.
(Bettmann-UPI/Corbis)

Play Synopsis
A RAISIN IN THE SUN (1959)
Lorraine Hansberry (1930–1965)

Chief Characters

Lena Younger, *Mama*
Walter Lee Younger, *her son*
Ruth Younger, *Walter's wife*
Travis Younger, *Ruth and Walter's son*
Beneatha Younger, *Walter's sister*

Setting

The Youngers' apartment in a poor section of Chicago, sometime after World War II.

Background

The Youngers are a black family with dreams of improving their lives. The father has died, and his only legacy is a $10,000 life insurance policy.

Act I, Scene 1: Friday morning; the family is looking forward to the arrival of the insurance check. Walter tells Ruth that he has a chance to buy a liquor store with some friends. Walter's sister Beneatha, an aspiring doctor, tells him that the insurance money is Mama's, not theirs. After Walter goes to work, Mama enters. Ruth talks to Mama about Walter's liquor store. Mama, a God-fearing woman, doesn't like the idea of selling liquor. Mama wants money for Beneatha's education and to buy a house in a nice neighborhood. Ruth suddenly becomes ill.

Scene 2: The following morning, Saturday, is cleaning day. Walter goes out to talk with his friend Willy about buying the liquor store. Ruth comes back from seeing the doctor

and tells Mama that she is pregnant. Beneatha's friend Asagai arrives with an African outfit for her to wear. Beneatha is pursuing her African roots. Asagai is from Africa, an intellectual who is attracted to Beneatha, but she wants to find her own identity. The insurance check arrives, and it reminds Mama that instead of a warm, loving husband, all she now has is a piece of paper. Walter enters, excitedly talking about buying the liquor store, and Ruth storms out. Mama tries to tell Walter that she understands his frustration, but she explains to him that Ruth is pregnant and wants an abortion.

Act II, Scene 1: Later the same day. Beneatha enters, ready for a date with George, a wealthy, successful black man. Walter is jealous of George's success. Mama enters and tells everyone that she has made a down payment on a house with part of the insurance money. Ruth and Travis are happy to hear the news, but Walter is depressed—this is another setback to his dream of owning the liquor store. When the young people discover that the house Mama plans to buy is in an all-white section, they wonder whether they will be accepted.

Scene 2: Friday night, a few weeks later. The apartment is strewn with packing crates in anticipation of the move to the new house. Walter has not gone to work for three days, spending his time in a bar. Mama

fears that she may be destroying her son. She decides to give Walter $6,500—the remainder of the insurance money—to invest as he chooses. She tells Walter that he should become the head of the family. He excitedly begins to talk to his son about his dreams.

Scene 3: Saturday, a week later—moving day. Walter enters, followed by Mr. Lindner, a middle-aged white man who has come to discourage the Youngers from moving into their new house. Walter throws him out. Mama is greatly moved when the others give her some presents for the new house. In the midst of the celebration, Walter's friend Bobo enters with bad news: Willy has run off with all their money. Walter breaks down and tells the family that he had invested the whole $6,500 with Willy. Mama is distraught.

Act III: An hour later. The mood is despairing. Beneatha attacks Walter and he exits. Mama starts unpacking because now they must stay in the old house. Walter returns and tells them that he has called Lindner to make a deal. Mama is against it: "We ain't never been that poor." Walter is about to sell out to "the Man" when his pride stops him; he tells Lindner that they have decided to move into the new house because his father earned it. The family members bustle into activity. After everyone else has left, Mama stands alone, and then exits into the future.

Play Synopsis
FEFU AND HER FRIENDS (1977)
Maria Irene Fornes (1930–   )

Maria Irene Fornes.
(© Susan Johann)

Characters
Fefu, Cindy, Christina, Julia, Emma, Paula, Sue, Cecilia

Setting
A house belonging to Fefu and her husband in the New England countryside. Spring 1935.

Background
Eight women who went to college together gather for a day to visit and plan a collaborative presentation urging educational reform.

Part I
The living room: Midday. Fefu tells Cindy and Christina, "My husband married me to have a constant reminder of how loathsome women are." As they discuss this provocative idea, Fefu picks up a shotgun, aims out the door, and fires at her husband. Fefu explains to her shocked friends that she plays a game with her husband—she shoots blanks at him and he falls down. He has told her that he may load the gun with real bullets someday.

Julia arrives in a wheelchair, then goes off to wash up. Cindy explains to Christina the bizarre accident that led to Julia's paralysis. Julia fell down at the moment a hunter had shot and killed a deer. Julia became delirious, talking about torturers who would kill her if she did not recant. The bullet had grazed her forehead, but the doctors found no spinal cord injury that would adequately explain her inability to walk. Fefu remembers that Julia used to be afraid of nothing.

Emma arrives wearing a theatrical Turkish dress. Paula and Sue are with her. The women decide that they will eat lunch and then rehearse their presentation. Emma concentrates on the theatrical elements, suggesting which colors the other women should wear. Emma, Fefu, Paula, and Sue exit.

Part II
For this section of the play, the audience is divided into four groups. Each group is taken to one of four different locations in Fefu's house and lawn, to observe one of four separate scenes, which are enacted simultaneously: "on the lawn," "in the study," "in the bedroom," and "in the kitchen." When these four scenes have been played once, each audience group rotates to the next location and the scenes are repeated. All the audience members see every scene, but not in the same order.

On the lawn: Fefu and Emma play croquet and agree that admission to heaven is probably determined by sexual performance on earth. Fefu leaves to fetch lemonade, while Emma recites a sonnet. Returning, Fefu is followed by Paula and Cecilia.

In the study: Christina and Cindy engage in idle conversation while reading. Christina says she is frightened by Fefu's unconventional behavior. Sue comes in, looking for Julia, and then goes off to look in the bedroom. Cindy describes a strange dream in which a doctor attacks her. Fefu comes through the room and invites them to play croquet.

In the bedroom: Wearing a white hospital gown, Julia rests on the floor. She hallucinates, talking about the judges who have crippled her and have the power to kill her. She says Fefu is in danger. Sue comes with a bowl of soup for Julia.

In the kitchen: Sue heats soup. Paula explains her theory of how long an affair lasts. Sue puts a bowl of soup on a tray and exits. Cecilia enters, and she and Paula awkwardly discuss their past relationship. Fefu comes in for lemonade, and all three go out to play croquet.

Part III
For Part III, the entire audience reassembles and watches together.

The living room: Evening. All eight women are present. The women decide on the order of their presentation. Emma delivers her speech, on the importance of environment in education. Then all the women except Julia and Cindy go into the kitchen, but they run into and out of the living room having a water fight. When they return to the kitchen, Fefu is alone in the living room. Julia enters, walking, picks up the sugar bowl, and exits. Then, in her wheelchair, she reenters with the other women, who reminisce about their school days. After the other women go outside, Fefu confronts Julia about having seen her walk, but Julia denies this. Christina and Cecilia enter, and Fefu gets her gun. She exits and fires the gun. Julia puts her hand to her forehead, which is bloody. Fefu reenters with a rabbit she has killed, as Julia slumps in her chair—apparently dead.

Play Synopsis

FENCES (1987)

August Wilson (1945–2005)

August Wilson.
(AP Images)

Characters

Troy Maxon—53, *a sanitation worker*
Jim Bono—*a fellow worker*
Rose—43, *Troy's wife of 18 years*
Cory—17, *their son*
Lyons—*Troy's son by his first wife*
Gabriel—*Troy's younger brother*
Raynell—*Troy's daughter by another woman*

Setting

The backyard of Troy Maxon's house in a northern industrial city.

Act I, Scene 1: A Friday evening, fall 1957. Troy, a large, self-confident man; and Bono, his sidekick, enter. Rose tells Troy that their son Cory is being recruited by a college football team. Troy objects because he himself was a talented baseball player, but African Americans could not play in the major leagues at that time. Troy describes a past encounter with Death, whom he "wrassled" and beat.

Lyons, Troy's older son, who wants to be a jazz musician, comes to borrow money, which Troy refuses to give him.

Scene 2: The next morning. Troy's younger brother Gabriel enters. Gabriel has a metal plate in his head—a result of a wound in World War II. He carries a trumpet because he thinks he is the angel Gabriel. Soon, Troy disappears, claiming that he is going to listen to a ball game on the radio.

Scene 3: A few hours later. Cory enters and then Troy arrives. Troy is building a fence around the backyard and wants Cory to help him. Troy again expresses strong disapproval of Cory's taking a football scholarship. Cory asks why Troy doesn't like him. Troy says that he puts food on the table for Cory and a roof over his head. That's enough: "What law is there say I got to like you?"

Scene 4: The following Friday. Troy and Bono enter. Troy tells about his past: his family in the south lived in poverty; he left home at 14 and had to steal to live; he was thrown in jail for 15 years. When he got out of jail, it was too late for him to star in baseball. Then he met Rose and settled down. Cory arrives, and there is another confrontation between him and Troy.

Act II, Scene 1: Saturday. Bono warns Troy that he shouldn't mess around with Alberta, another woman—Rose is a good woman and doesn't deserve such treatment. Troy starts to work on his fence as Rose arrives. Troy, with great difficulty, tells Rose that he has made another woman pregnant. Rose denounces him, explaining all that she has sacrificed for him.

Scene 2: Friday, spring 1958. Troy, who has stayed away from the house, returns to get his clothes. Rose accuses him of committing Gabriel to an institution, so that he

himself can take part of the money that will come as a result. Troy angrily denies this, but it becomes clear that it is true. The phone rings, and Rose learns that Alberta has had a baby girl but has died in childbirth. Left alone, Troy once more challenges Death to come get him.

Scene 3: Three days later. Troy shows up at the house with Alberta's baby daughter, Raynell. He wants Rose to raise her. Rose says no, but later she agrees.

Scene 4: Two months later. Cory has graduated from high school, and he and Troy have another confrontation. Troy orders Cory out of the house; Cory says that the house was built partly with money that Troy took from Gabriel's disability payments. The two fight with a baseball bat. Troy finally gets the bat but does not hit Cory.

Scene 5: Summer 1965. Troy has died, and it is the morning of his funeral. Cory, now a Marine, is home, but he refuses to go to the funeral. Rose says that staying away is not the way to become his own man. Rose explains how much she sacrificed to be Troy's wife, but life has given her as compensation little Raynell, whom she loves like her own daughter. Cory decides that he will go to the funeral. Gabriel attempts to blow his trumpet, unsuccessfully, but instead does a dance that announces Troy's arrival at heaven's gate.

Index